Interdisciplinary Public Finance, Business and Economics Studies – Volume I

Adil Akinci (ed.)

Interdisciplinary Public Finance, Business and Economics Studies – Volume I

PETER LANG

Bibliographic Information published by the Deutsche Nationalbibliothek
The Deutsche Nationalbibliothek lists this publication in the Deutsche Nationalbibliografie; detailed bibliographic data is available online at http://dnb.d-nb.de.

Library of Congress Cataloging-in-Publication Data
A CIP catalog record for this book has been applied for at the Library of Congress.

Cover image: fotolia, archerix
Cover Design: © Olaf Glöckler, Atelier Platen, Friedberg

ISBN 978-3-631-77173-0 (Print)
E-ISBN 978-3-631-78224-8 (E-PDF)
E-ISBN 978-3-631-78225-5 (EPUB)
E-ISBN 978-3-631-78226-2 (MOBI)
DOI 10.3726/b15307

Peter Lang – Berlin · Bern · Bruxelles · New York · Oxford · Warszawa · Wien

This publication has been peer reviewed.

www.peterlang.com

Foreword

The book "Interdisciplinary Public Finance, Business and Economics Studies – Volume I" is a collection of research papers on a wide range of social science issues written by researchers from several different universities.

The study of Aral and Bayram Arlı examine the classification of cities' employment rates with cluster and exploratory spatial data analysis methods. Yıldız reviews tax competition and tax havens. Tuncer and Ozcelik examine the issue of ethnic economies in context of Syrian refugees in Turkey. Yıldız makes an assessment on the development of the TR90 region. The study of Tıraşoğlu examines relationship between inflation and economic growth in Mexico, Indonesia, South Korea and Turkey. Odabaşı analyses the effects of exchange rate volatility on exports.

In their study, Gezer ve Gezer examine the relationship between consumer confidence and real exchange rate changes in Turkey. Hepsağ researches into the asymmetric stochastic volatility in stock market in northern European countries and Çimen and Sağlam tested the life cycle hypothesis for developing countries. Kilci examines the relationship between the interest rates and the following loan rate in context of inverse election problem, Ballı studies the macroeconomic performance of Russia in transition period. Kurnaz ve Kestane examine the effects of culture on internal control of the participation banks. Gülerci reviews the protection of financial consumer; and Durmuş and Canbay Çiğdem assess the status of fruit gardens within TMS 41 in their study.

Çetinoğlu reviews the independent auditing profession in Turkey, Aktaş examines mortgage-backed securities as an innovative financial instrument. Saldanlı and Bektaş measure the performance of Bist 50 companies by Moora method. Kaya examines risk management and the changing frame of risk management in his study, Karahan studies the reactions of soccer investors. The study of Konak examines electronic commerce and its types. Dülgeroğlu views for green consumption in Kırklareli scale. Öztürk studies the effect of success factors of new product development on product development performance. Gök Kısa and Cindiloğlu examine the role of multi-criteria decision-making in knowledge management strategies, while Çetindere Filiz, Duran and Behdioğlu examine the Just In Time production system. In his study, Acar examines total quality management in public administration, Erdoğan analyses socio-political base of the constitutional movements in Turkey.

Views and ideas present in parts of the published book have been expressing the personal thoughts of the authors, and merely possible to be used as a reference.

Contents

List of Contributors

Neşe Aral
Department of Econometrics, Faculty of Economics and Administrative Sciences, Uludağ University, Bursa. nesearal@uludag.edu.tr

Nuran Bayram Arli
Department of Econometrics, Faculty of Economics and Administrative Sciences, Uludağ University, Bursa. nuranb@uludag.edu.tr

Barış Yildiz
Asst. Prof., Gümüşhane University, Faculty of Economics And Administrative Sciences, Department Of Public Finance, barisyildiz61@gmail.com.

Guner Tuncer
Asst.Prof.Dr., Dumlupınar University, Department of Public Finance, guner.tuncer@dpu.edu.tr

Ozer Ozcelik
Asst.Prof.Dr., Dumlupınar University, Department of Economics, ozer.ozcelik@dpu.edu.tr

Gizem Yildiz
Asst. Prof., Gümüşhane University, Faculty of Economics And Administrative Sciences, Department Of Economics, gizem-akbulut@hotmail.com

Muhammed Tıraşoğlu
Faculty of Economics and Administrative Sciences, Department of Econometrics, Kırklareli University, muhammedtirasoglu@klu.edu.tr

Yavuz Odabaşi
Asst. Prof. Dr., Dumlupınar University, Faculty of Economics and Administrative Sciences, Department of Economics, yavuz.odabasi@dpu.edu.tr

Mesut Alper Gezer
Research Fellow Mesut Alper Gezer, Kütahya Dumlupınar University, Department of Economics, e-mail: alper.gezer@dpu.edu.tr

Tuba Gezer
Research Fellow Tuba Gezer, Kütahya Dumlupınar University, Department of Public Finance, e-mail: tuba.yildirim@dpu.edu.tr

Aycan Hepsag
Istanbul University, Faculty of Economics, Department of Econometrics, Beyazit, 34452, Istanbul, Tel.: +90 212 440 01 60, E-mail: hepsag@istanbul.edu.tr

Ayşegül Çimen
Dokuz Eylül University, Faculty of Economics and Administrative Sciences, aysegul.cimen@deu.edu.tr

Yağmur Sağlam
Sinop University, Faculty of Economics and Administrative Sciences, yagmur.saglam@sinop.edu.tr

Esra N. Kilci
Asst. Prof. Dr., Istanbul Arel University, International Trade and Finance Department, esrakilci@arel.edu.tr

Esra Balli
Asst.Prof.Dr., Erzincan Binali Yıldırım University, Faculty of Economics and Administrative Sciences, esra.balli@erzincan.edu.trNiyazi Kurnaz
Assoc.Prof.Dr., Kütahya Dumlupınar University, Faculty of Economics and Administrative Sciences, niyazi.kurnaz@dpu.edu.tr

Ali Kestane
Research Assistanat, Kilis 7 Aralık University, , Faculty of Economics and Administrative Sciences, alikestane@kilis.edu.tr

Altan Fahri Gülerci
PhD. Afyon Kocatepe University Faculty of Law, Commercial Law Department, afgulerci@aku.edu.tr

Ahmet Fethi Durmuş
PhD. Inönü University Department of Business administration ahmet.durmus@inonu.edu.tr

Figen Canbay Çiğdem
PhD. The Central Union of the Agricultural Credit Cooperativesi Malatya Regional Union, figencanbay@tarimkredi.org.tr

Tansel Çetinoğlu
Asst.Prof., Kütahya Dumlupinar University, School of Applied Sciences, tansel.cetinoglu@dpu.edu.tr

M. Murat, Aktaş
Full-time Faculty staff of the T.R. Kütahya Dumlupınar University Faculty Of Economics and Administrative Sciences; LL. M. in Commercial Law and Ph. D. in Commercial Law candidate at Ankara University. Mmurat.aktas@dpu.edu.tr

Arif Saldanlı
Asst. Prof., Istanbul University, Faculty of Economics, Department of Business Administration, saldanli@istanbul.edu.tr

Hakan Bektaş
Asst. Prof., Istanbul University, Faculty of Economics, Department of Econometrics, hbektas@istanbul.edu.tr

Yusuf Kaya
Asst. Prof., Pamukkale University, Buldan Vocational High School, ykaya@pau.edu.tr

Ferit Karahan
Kütahya Dumlupinar University, Faculty of Economics and Administrative Sciences, ferit.karahan@dpu.edu.tr

Ali Konak
Karabuk University, Faculty of Economics and Administrative Sciences, Economics Department, alikonak@karabuk.edu.tr

İsmail Dülgeroğlu
PhD, Kırklareli University, Faculty of Economics and Administrative Sciences, Business Administration Department, email: ismail.dulgeroglu@klu.edu.tr

Derya Öztürk
PhD. Faculty Member, Ordu University, Ünye Faculty of Economics and Administrative Sciences, Department of Business, Ordu, Turkey.
E-mail: deryaozturk@odu.edu.tr

A.Cansu Gök-Kisa
Asst. Prof. Hitit University, Faculty Of Economics And Administrative Sciences, Department of International Trade And Logistics Management, cansugok@hitit.edu.tr

Mihriban Cindiloğlu Demirer
Asst. Prof. Hitit University, Faculty Of Economics And Administrative Sciences, Department of International Trade And Logistics Management, mihribancindiloglu@hitit.edu.tr

Aysel Çetindere Filiz
Asst.Prof., Ondokuz Mayıs University, Faculty of Economics and Administrative Sciences, aysel.cetindere@omu.edu.tr

Cengiz Duran
Assoc.Prof., Dumlupınar University, Faculty of Economics and Administrative Sciences, cengiz.duran@dpu.edu.tr

Sema Behdioğlu
Professor, Dumlupınar University, Faculty of Economics and Administrative Sciences, sema.behdioglu@dpu.edu.tr

Aykut Acar
Asst Prof., Ph.D., Kütahya Dumlupınar University, Faculty of Economics And Administrative Sciences, Public Administration Department, aykacar@yahoo.com

Selami Erdoğan
Asst.Prof., Kütahya Dumlupinar University, Faculty of Economics and Administrative Sciences, e-mail: selami.erdogan@dpu.edu.tr.

Neşe Aral and Nuran Bayram Arli

The Classification of Cities' Employment Rate with Cluster and Exploratory Spatial Data Analysis

1 Introduction

An approach where economic development and regional development, essential dynamics of economic growth, are addressed individually and not in connection would lead to losses in the economy, let alone ensuring its growth. As advocated by experimental studies reported in the fields of economy, there must be emphasis placed on regional development policies if it is to ensure the development of a nation. Another important reason behind this need is the difficulties brought in by the varying regional development elements many developing countries have on their plate (Gül, 2014). There are significant interregional disparities in Turkey, especially with respect to population density, income distribution, distribution of workforce and employment, education level, etc. Such disparities, in turn, lead to important differences between the development level of regions and even between urban areas in a region. Although there are several measures in place to eliminate such disparities, it has not been possible to reduce interregional disparities to an acceptable level (Özdemir et al., 2006). In this context, the purpose of this study was to explore the regional differences in employment rate in Turkish cities using spatial analysis and cluster analysis.

2 Method

2.1 Cluster Analysis

There are many statistical analysis techniques that allow finding similarities or differences among datas. The reason behind the selection of cluster analysis, a multivariate analysis technique, was that this technique allows for grouping of highly similar data or variables. Cluster analysis allows for the identification of similarities and differences between the variables of a dataset and it helps unfold the structure of complex datasets. It is expected that each variable in a cluster to have high degree of "natural association" among themselves while clusters are "relatively distinct" from one another. To do so, many criteria have been described. (Sala ve Bragulat, 2004). In defining the groups in cluster analysis, two methods, namely, hierarchical cluster analysis and non-hierarchical cluster analysis, are used (Özdamar, 2002). If there is a predefined number of clusters to be formed in a study or if the researcher has defined the number of clusters needed, then, non-hierarchical agglomeration methods would be preferred over hierarchical ones, i.e. non-progressive grouping methods are used. Another reason behind the selection of the methods used in this study was the high theoretical validity they offer. Among these methods, K-means clustering developed by MacQueen and maximum likelihood estimation were used in a great extent (Tatlıdil, 1996).

2.2 Exploratory Spatial Data Analysis

Spatial statistics and spatial econometrics have received interest of the academic community as the need for measuring the spatial effects related to the data becomes even more pressing (Zeren, 2010). The First Law of Geography, according to Waldo Tobler (1970), is "*everything is related to everything else, but near things are more related than distant things*." Accordingly, similar results are observed in close proximity to each other which is called spatial cluster. For example, it is likely to find higher crime rates from neighboring cities of a city with a high crime rate. The assumption of independence does not apply in the presence of such spatial clusters (Anselin, 1992). Classical analyses methods are not preferred to process these data due to spatial dependence or spatial autocorrelation observed in the data (Eryılmaz, 2010). The use of classical statistics theory with these data proves problematic (Haining, 2003; Başar, 2009).

Spatial autocorrelation measurements are about the covariance or correlation between nearby observations. In this context, autocorrelation compares two types of information, i.e. similarity of observations (value similarity) and similarity among locations. If nearby observation values are similar, then they show a positive spatial autocorrelation pattern as a whole (Fischer & Wang, 2011; Griffith, 2003). The lack of spatial autocorrelation, on the other hand, shows that there is no spatial relationship between observed values (Schabenberger & Gotway, 2005). Today, many methods are proposed to measure spatial autocorrelation. Moran's (Spatial Statistics) I is one of the commonly used methods to measure spatial autocorrelation (Fischer & Wang, 2011). Possible values of Moran's I are constrained to lie in the (-1, 1) range. The weight of positive spatial autocorrelation increases as the value approaches 1 (Çetin, 2012).

Exploratory Spatial Data Analysis (ESDA) is a useful tool for interregional spatial analysis. ESDA consists of techniques used to visualize and explain spatial distribution, to explore the pattern of spatial clustering and to identify the locations with contradictory values (Anselin, 1988, Dall'erba, 2005). In spatial data analysis, spatial weight matrix files are generated in order to show the interactions between regions. The reason behind the use of such matrix is to show that the event in question is in closer interaction in locations closer to each other when compared to distant regions (Başar, 2009). Spatial data analysis may be generated using two methods, distance-based spatial weights and contiguity-based spatial weights. Distance-based spatial weight matrix involves the measuring of the distance between locations, while contiguity-based spatial weight matrix considers similarities or shared borders between locations (Zeren, 2011).

3 Findings

This study explored the employment rate data collected from the cities in Turkey for the period between 2008 and 2013 using spatial analysis and cluster analysis in a comparative perspective. The data used in this study were obtained from the official website of Turkish Statistical Institute.

The maps used to visualize the spatial distribution pattern play an important role in explanatory spatial data analysis. A quartile map was used in the applications dividing the dataset into four equal parts (Fischer & Wang, 2011). In this context, these quartile maps were evaluated first with respect to employment rates. Fig. 1 shows the maps generated for the spatial distribution of the data.

The darkest color on the map represents the cities with the highest employment rates. Employment rate drops as the color becomes lighter. It can be observed that similar cities form a cluster and they are represented with the same color. Moreover, it can be observed that the cities located especially in the Southeastern Anatolia Region have a negative impact on each other and agglomerated in the low employment rate cluster.

The Moran scatter plot was used to explore the spatial interaction between the employment rates after defining the regional differences in a quartile map. Developed by Anselin (1995, 1996), this plot allows for the analysis of observations, y, made for a location and the means of neighboring observations, Wy (Anselin et al., 2007; LeSage & Pace, 2009). The Moran scatter plot generated for the employment rates in the period between 2008 and 2013 is illustrated below.

The Moran scatterplot is divided into four quadrants corresponding to the four types of local spatial association between a region and its neighbors (Dall'erba, 2005):

- Quadrant I (This quadrant is usually noted HH) displays the regions with a high employment rate (above the average) surrounded by regions with high employment rate (above the average).
- Quadrant II (This quadrant is usually noted LH) shows the regions with low value surrounded by regions with high values.
- Quadrant III (This quadrant is usually noted LL) displays the regions with low value surrounded by regions with low values.
- Quadrant IV (This quadrant is usually noted HL) shows the regions with high value surrounded by regions with low values.

Regions located in quadrants I and III represent the spatial clustering of similar values (positive spatial autocorrelation), whereas quadrants II and IV refer to the spatial clustering of dissimilar values (negative spatial autocorrelation). A closer look into Fig. 2 showed that the values are not distributed randomly, that there was

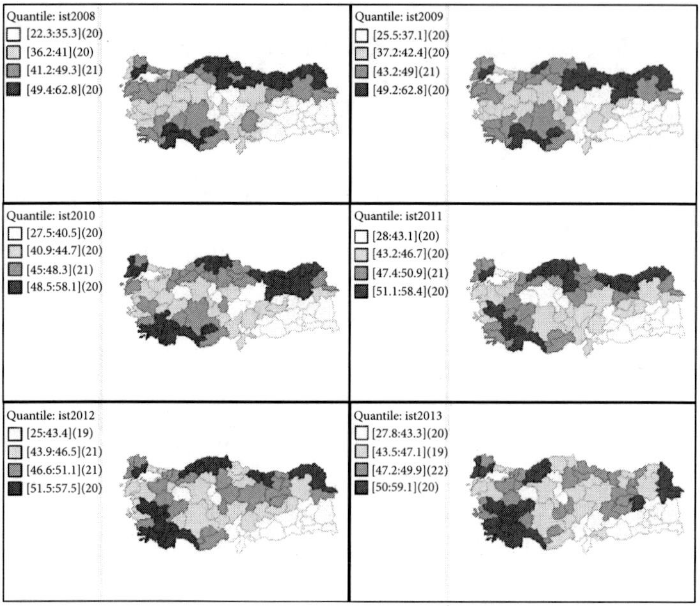

Fig. 1: Mapping the Distributions

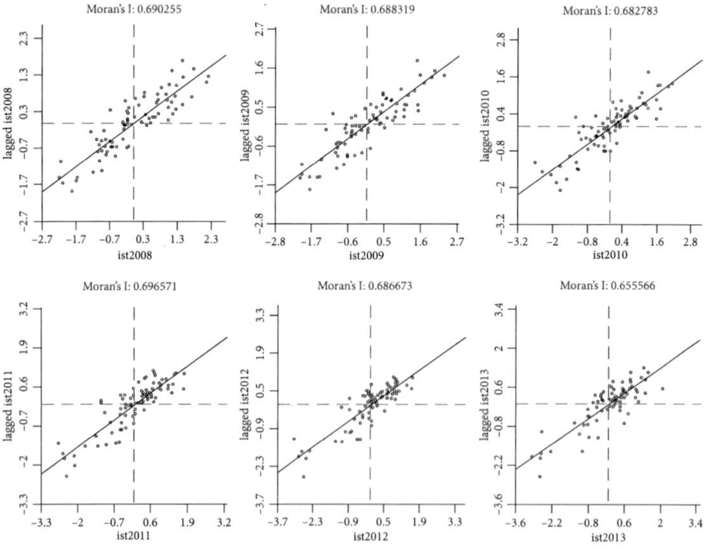

Fig. 2: Moran's Scatter Plot for Employment Rates

a positive autocorrelation and that it was clustered in QI and QIII. Tab. 1 shows the names of the cities located in these regions.

After defining the regional differentiations on the Moran scatter plot, employment ratios were explored using non-hierarchical cluster analysis. Tab. 2 shows the finding of 4 clusters as a result of the analysis.

A comparison of both analyses (Tab. 1 & Tab. 2) showed that located in the HH region of the Moran scatter plot based on the employment rates for the period between 2008 and 2013, the cities were placed in cluster 1 in the cluster analysis; while located in the LL region of the Moran scatter plot, the cities were placed in cluster 3 in the cluster analysis. Tab. 3 shows clusters similar to those explained above.

A closer look into Tab. 3 showed that located in the HH region of the Moran scatter plot based on the employment rates of 2008, the cities of Çanakkale, Düzce, Erzurum, Denizli, Tekirdağ, Samsun, Iğdır, Bursa, Zonguldak, Kars, Çankırı, Sakarya, Kastamonu, Muğla, Çorum, Tokat, Antalya, Bayburt, Sinop, Giresun, Amasya, Bartın, Konya, Isparta, Karaman, Erzincan, Kırklareli, Bilecik. were placed in cluster 1 in the cluster analysis; while located in the LL region of the Moran scatter plot, the cities of Kütahya, Ankara, Elazığ, Kayseri, Tunceli, Yozgat, Bingöl, Malatya, Gaziantep, Şanlıurfa, Niğde, İzmir, Aksaray, Kırşehir, Eskişehir, Kilis, Manisa, Nevşehir, Muş, Uşak, Balıkesir, Adıyaman, Adana, Kahramanmaraş, Hatay, Van, Osmaniye, Mardin, Bitlis were placed in cluster 3 in the cluster analysis.

4 Conclusion

This study explored the employment rates for the period between 2008 and 2013 using spatial analysis methods and cluster analysis with a comparative perspective. Spatial clusters of the cities were defined using the Moran scatter plot and statistically significant effects of being neighbors were underlined. In the cluster analysis, the cities were grouped in similar clusters based on the employment rates over the years. These clusters were then compared with each other and it was found that the analyses results were in agreement. In other words, it was found that the cities grouped in the HH and LL regions in the Moran scatter plot were grouped in cluster 1 and 3 in cluster analysis, respectively. A comparison of both analyses showed that located in the HH region of the Moran scatter plot based on the employment rates of 2013, the cities of Edirne, Kütahya, Yalova, Gümüşhane, Tunceli, Ordu, Samsun, Bursa, İzmir, Bolu, Bilecik, İstanbul, Sakarya, Artvin, Tokat, Bayburt, Kocaeli, Trabzon, Amasya, Konya, Giresun, Rize, Isparta, Karaman, Erzincan, Kırklareli were placed in cluster 1 in the cluster analysis; while located in the LL region of the Moran scatter plot, the cities of Hakkari, Ankara, Gaziantep, Kırşehir, Kilis, Muş, Adıyaman, Kırıkkale, Adana, Kahramanmaraş, Hatay, Van, Osmaniye, Bitlis were placed in cluster 3 in the cluster analysis. Thus, it was found that the findings of spatial analysis and cluster analysis were in agreement.

Tab. 1: Moran Scatterplot

Employment Rate 2008	
HH	Çanakkale, Gümüşhane, Ordu, Düzce, Erzurum, Denizli, Tekirdağ, Samsun, Iğdır, Bursa, Burdur, Zonguldak, Kars, Çankırı, Sakarya, Artvin, Kastamonu, Muğla, Çorum, Tokat, Antalya, Bayburt, Ardahan, Karabük, Trabzon, Sinop, Giresun, Amasya, Bartın, Konya, Mersin, Rize, Isparta, Karaman, Erzincan, Kırklareli, Bilecik.
LH	Edirne, Yalova, Bolu, İstanbul, Afyonkarahisar, Aydın, Kocaeli, Sivas.
LL	Kütahya, Hakkari, Ankara, Elazığ, Kayseri, Tunceli, Şırnak, Siirt, Yozgat, Bingöl, Diyarbakır, Malatya, Gaziantep, Şanlıurfa, Niğde, İzmir, Aksaray, Batman, Kırşehir, Eskişehir, Kilis, Manisa, Nevşehir, Muş, Uşak, Balıkesir, Adıyaman, Kırıkkale, Adana, Kahramanmaraş, Hatay, Van, Osmaniye, Mardin, Bitlis.
HL	Ağrı.
Employment Rate 2009	
HH	Edirne, Gümüşhane, Çanakkale, Ordu, Düzce, Erzurum, Denizli, Tekirdağ, Samsun, Burdur, Bolu, Zonguldak, Kars, Çankırı, Sakarya, Artvin, Kastamonu, Muğla, Çorum, Tokat, Aydın, Antalya, Bayburt, Ardahan, Karabük, Trabzon, Sinop, Giresun, Amasya, Bartın, Konya, Mersin, Rize, Isparta, Karaman, Erzincan, Kırklareli.
LH	Iğdır, İstanbul, Eskişehir, Afyonkarahisar, Sivas.
LL	Kütahya, Hakkari, Ankara, Yalova, Elazığ, Kayseri, Tunceli, Şırnak, Siirt, Yozgat, Bingöl, Diyarbakır, Malatya, Bursa, Gaziantep, Şanlıurfa, Niğde, İzmir, Aksaray, Batman, Kırşehir, Eskişehir, Kilis, Manisa, Kocaeli, Muş, Uşak, Adıyaman, Kırıkkale, Adana, Kahramanmaraş, Hatay, Van, Osmaniye, Mardin, Bitlis.
HL	Bilecik, Ağrı, Nevşehir, Balıkesir.
Employment Rate 2010	
HH	Edirne, Gümüşhane, Çanakkale, Ordu, Düzce, Erzurum, Denizli, Tekirdağ, Samsun, Iğdır, Burdur, Bolu, Zonguldak, Kars, Çankırı, Sakarya, Artvin, Kastamonu, Muğla, Çorum, Tokat, Aydın, Antalya, Bayburt, Ardahan, Uşak, Karabük, Trabzon, Sinop, Amasya, Bartın, Konya, Giresun, Mersin, Rize, Isparta, Karaman, Erzincan, Kırklareli.
LH	İzmir, İstanbul, Afyonkarahisaar, Sivas.
LL	Kütahya, Hakkari, Ankara, Yalova, Elazığ, Kayseri, Tunceli, Şırnak, Siirt, Yozgat, Bingöl, Diyarbakır, Malatya, Bursa, Gaziantep, Şanlıurfa, Niğde, İzmir, Aksaray, Batman, Kırşehir, Kilis, Ağrı, Kocaeli, Muş, Adıyaman, Kırıkkale, Adana, Kahramanmaraş, Hatay, Van, Osmaniye, Mardin, Bitlis.
HL	Bilecik, Sakarya, Nevşehir.

Tab. 1: Continued

Employment Rate 2011	
HH	Edirne, Kütahya, Gümüşhane, Ordu, Düzce, Denizli, Tekirdağ, Samsun, Iğdır, Bursa, Burdur, Bolu, Zonguldak, Bilecik, Kars, Çankırı, Sakarya, Artvin, Afyonkarahisar, Manisa, Kastamonu, Muğla, Çorum, Tokat, Aydın, Antalya, Bayburt, Ardahan, Uşak, Karabük, Trabzon, Sinop, Amasya, Bartın, Giresun, Mersin, Rize, Isparta, Karaman, Erzincan, Kırklareli.
LH	Çanakkale, Tunceli, Erzurum, İzmir, İstanbul, Eskişehir, Balıkesir, Kırıkkale, Sivas, Konya.
LL	Hakkari, Ankara, Yalova, Elazığ, Kayseri, Tunceli, Şırnak, Siirt, Yozgat, Bingöl, Diyarbakır, Malatya, Bursa, Gaziantep, Şanlıurfa, Niğde, İzmir, Aksaray, Batman, Kırşehir, Eskişehir, Kilis, Manisa, Kocaeli, Muş, Uşak, Adıyaman, Kırıkkale, Adana, Kahramanmaraş, Hatay, Van, Osmaniye, Mardin, Bitlis.
HL	Yozgat, Nevşehir, Ağrı.
Employment Rate 2012	
HH	Edirne, Kütahya, Yalova, Gümüşhane, Çanakkale, Ordu, Düzce, Denizli, Tekirdağ, Iğdır, Bursa, Burdur, Bolu, Zonguldak, Bilecik, Kars, Çankırı, Sakarya, Artvin, Afyonkarahisar, Manisa, Kastamonu, Muğla, Çorum, Aydın, Antalya, Bayburt, Ardahan, Kocaeli, Uşak, Karabük, Sivas, Trabzon, Sinop, Bartın, Giresun, Mersin, Rize, Isparta, Karaman, Erzincan, Kırklareli.
LH	Yalova, Erzurum, Samsun İzmir, İstanbul, Çankırı, Eskişehir, Tokat, Balıkesir, Amasya, Konya.
LL	Hakkari, Ankara, Elazığ, Şırnak, Siirt, Diyarbakır, Gaziantep, Şanlıurfa, Niğde, Aksaray, Batman, Kırşehir, Kilis, Muş, Adıyaman, Kırıkkale, Adana, Kahramanmaraş, Hatay, Van, Osmaniye, Mardin, Bitlis.
HL	Yozgat, Bingöl, Malatya, Nevşehir, Ağrı.
Employment Rate 2013	
HH	Edirne, Kütahya, Yalova, Gümüşhane, Tunceli, Ordu, Düzce, Tekirdağ, Samsun, Iğdır, Bursa, Burdur, İzmir, Bolu, Zonguldak, Bilecik, İstanbul, Kars, Sakarya, Artvin, Afyonkarahisar, Manisa, Muğla, Tokat, Ağrı, Aydın, Antalya, Bayburt, Ardahan, Kocaeli, Uşak, Karabük, Trabzon, Amasya, Bartın, Konya, Giresun, Rize, Isparta, Karaman, Erzincan, Kırklareli.
LH	Çanakkale, Çankırı, Eskişehir, Kastamonu, Balıkesir, Sivas, Sinop, Konya, Mersin.
LL	Hakkari, Ankara, Kayseri, Şırnak, Siirt, Diyarbakır, Gaziantep, Şanlıurfa, Batman, Kırşehir, Kilis, Muş, Adıyaman, Kırıkkale, Adana, Kahramanmaraş, Hatay, Van, Osmaniye, Mardin, Bitlis.
HL	Elazığ, Yozgat, Bingöl, Malatya, Niğde, Aksaray, Çorum, Nevşehir.

Tab. 2: Cluster Analysis

Employment Rate 2008	
1	Çanakkale, Düzce, Erzurum, Denizli, Tekirdağ, Samsun, Iğdır, Bursa, Zonguldak, Kars, Çankırı, Sakarya, Kastamonu, Muğla, Çorum, Tokat, Antalya, Bayburt, Sinop, Giresun, Amasya, Bartın, Konya, Isparta, Karaman, Erzincan, Kırklareli, Bilecik, Ağrı.
2	Gümüşhane, Ordu, Burdur, Artvin, Ardahan, Trabzon, Rize.
3	Kütahya, Ankara, Elazığ, Kayseri, Tunceli, Yozgat, Bingöl, Malatya, Gaziantep, Şanlıurfa, Niğde, İzmir, Aksaray, Kırşehir, Eskişehir, Kilis, Manisa, Nevşehir, Muş, Uşak, Balıkesir, Adıyaman, Adana, Kahramanmaraş, Hatay, Van, Osmaniye, Bitlis, Edirne, Yalova, Bolu, Karabük, İstanbul, Afyonkarahisar, Aydın, Kocaeli, Sivas, Mersin.
4	Hakkari, Şırnak, Siirt, Diyarbakır, Batman, Kırıkkale, Mardin.
Employment Rate 2009	
1	Edirne, Çanakkale, Düzce, Erzurum, Denizli, Tekirdağ, Iğdır, Bolu, Bilecik, Kars, Çankırı, Sakarya, Kastamonu, Muğla, Tokat, Nevşehir, Ağrı, Aydın, Antalya, Balıkesir, Karabük, Sinop, Giresun, Amasya, Bartın, Konya, Mersin, Isparta, Erzincan, Kırklareli.
2	Gümüşhane, Ordu, Samsun, Burdur, Zonguldak, Artvin, Çorum, Bayburt, Ardahan, Trabzon, Amasya, Bartın, Giresun, Rize, Karaman.
3	Kütahya, Ankara, Yalova, Elazığ, Kayseri, Tunceli, Yozgat, Bingöl, Malatya, Bursa, Gaziantep, Niğde, İzmir, Aksaray, Kırşehir, İstanbul, Eskişehir, Afyonkarahisar, Kilis, Manisa, Kocaeli, Muş, Uşak, Adana, Kahramanmaraş, Sivas, Hatay, Van, Osmaniye, Bitlis.
4	Hakkari, Şırnak, Siirt, Diyarbakır, Urfa, Batman, Adıyaman, Kırıkkale, Mardin.
Employment Rate 2010	
1	Kütahya, Çanakkale, Düzce, Erzurum, Denizli, Samsın, Iğdır, Malatya, Bursa, Niğde, Aksaray, Bolu, Zonguldak, Bilecik, Kars, Çankırı, Sakarya, Afyonkarahisar, Kilis, Manisa, Çorum, Tokat, Nevşehir, Ağrı, Aydın, Uşak, Balıkesir, Karabük, Kahramanmaraş, Amasya, Hatay, Bartın, Konya, Mersin, Isparta, Karaman, Kırklareli.
2	Edirne, Gümüşhane, Ordu, Tekirdağ, Burdur, Artvin, Kastamonu, Muğla, Antalya, Bayburt, Ardahan, Trabzon, Sinop, Giresun, Rize, Erzincan.
3	Ankara, Yalova, Elazığ, Kayseri, Tunceli, Yozgat, Bingöl, Gaziantep, İzmir, Kırşehir, İstanbul, Eskişehir, Kocaeli, Adıyaman, Kırıkkale, Adana, Sivas, Van, Osmaniye, Bitlis.
4	Hakkari, Şırnak, Siirt, Diyarbakır, Urfa, Batman, Muş, Mardin.

Tab. 2: Continued

Employment Rate 2011	
1	Edirne, Kütahya, Yalova, Çanakkale, Erzurum, Yozgat, Bingöl, Samsun, Iğdır, Bursa, İzmir, Aksaray, Bolu, Bilecik, Kars, Çankırı, Sakarya, Afyonkarahisar, Muğla, Tokat, Nevşehir, Ağrı, Aydın, Kocaeli, Amasya, Konya, Mersin, Isparta, Karaman, Erzincan, Kırklareli.
2	Gümüşhane, Ordu, Düzce, Denizli, Tekirdağ, Burdur, Zonguldak, Artvin, Manisa, Kastamonu, Çorum, Antalya, Bayburt, Ardahan, Trabzon, Sinop, Bartın, Giresun, Rize.
3	Hakkari, Ankara, Elazığ, Kayseri, Tunceli, Malatya, Gaziantep, Niğde, Kırşehir, İstanbul, Eskişehir, Kilis, Muş, Balıkesir, Kırıkkale, Adana, Kahramanmaraş, Sivas, Hatay, Van, Osmaniye, Bitlis.
4	Şırnak, Siirt, Diyarbakır, Urfa, Batman, Adıyaman, Mardin.
Employment Rate 2012	
1	Edirne, Kütahya, Gümüşhane, Ordu, Düzce, Denizli, Yozgat, Çanakkale, Erzurum, Yozgat, Tekirdağ, Iğdır, Burdur, Zonguldak, Kars, Artvin, Afyonkarahisar, Manisa, Kastamonu, Muğla, Aydın, Antalya, Bayburt, Ardahan, Uşak, Karabük, Trabzon, Sinop, Bartın, Giresun, Rize.
2	Ankara, Yalova, Çanakkale, Elazığ, Kayseri, Tunceli, Erzurum, Bingöl, Samsun, Malatya, Bursa, Niğde, İzmir, Aksaray, Bolu, Bilecik, İstanbul, Çankırı, Sakarya, Çorum, Tokat, Nevşehir, Ağrı, Kocaeli, Balıkesir, Adana, Kahramanmaraş, Sivas, Amasya, Hatay, Van, Isparta, Karaman, Erzincan, Kırklareli, Konya, Mersin.
3	Hakkari, Gaziantep, Kırşehir, Eskişehir, Kilis, Muş, Adıyaman, Kırıkkale, Osmaniye, Bitlis.
4	Şırnak, Siirt, Diyarbakır, Urfa, Batman, Mardin.
Employment Rate 2013	
1	Edirne, Kütahya, Yalova, Gümüşhane, Elazığ, Kayseri, Tunceli, Ordu, Erzurum, Yozgat, Samsun, Malatya, Bursa, Niğde, İzmir, Aksaray, Bolu, Bilecik, İstanbul, Sakarya, Artvin, Çorum, Tokat, Nevşehir, Bayburt, Kocaeli, Trabzon, Amasya, Konya, Giresun, Rize, Isparta, Karaman, Erzincan, Kırklareli.
2	Düzce, Denizli, Bingöl, Tekirdağ, Iğdır, Burdur, Zonguldak, Kars, Afyonkarahisar, Manisa, Muğla, Ağrı, Aydın, Antalya, Ardahan, Uşak, Karabük, Bartın.
3	Hakkari, Ankara, Çanakkale, Gaziantep, Kırşehir, Çankırı, Eskişehir, Kilis, Kastamonu, Muş, Balıkesir, Adıyaman, Kırıkkale, Adana, Kahramanmaraş, Sivas, Sinop, Hatay, Mersin, Van, Osmaniye, Bitlis.
4	Şırnak, Siirt, Diyarbakır, Urfa, Batman, Mardin.

Tab. 3: Similar Clusters of Moran Scatter Plot & Cluster Analysis

Employment Rate 2008				
Moran Diyagramı	HH	Çanakkale, Düzce, Erzurum, Denizli, Tekirdağ, Samsun, Iğdır, Bursa, Zonguldak, Kars, Çankırı, Sakarya, Kastamonu, Muğla, Çorum, Tokat, Antalya, Bayburt, Sinop, Giresun, Amasya, Bartın, Konya, Isparta, Karaman, Erzincan, Kırklareli, Bilecik.	1	Kümeleme Analizi
	LL	Kütahya, Ankara, Elazığ, Kayseri, Tunceli, Yozgat, Bingöl, Malatya, Gaziantep, Şanlıurfa, Niğde, İzmir, Aksaray, Kırşehir, Eskişehir, Kilis, Manisa, Nevşehir, Muş, Uşak, Balıkesir, Adıyaman, Adana, Kahramanmaraş, Hatay, Van, Osmaniye, Mardin, Bitlis.	3	
Employment Rate 2009				
Moran Diyagramı	HH	Edirne, Çanakkale, Düzce, Erzurum, Denizli, Tekirdağ, Bolu, Kars, Çankırı, Sakarya, Kastamonu, Muğla, Tokat, Aydın, Antalya, Karabük, Sinop, Giresun, Amasya, Bartın, Konya, Mersin, Isparta, Erzincan, Kırklareli.	1	Kümeleme Analizi
	LL	Kütahya, Ankara, Yalova, Elazığ, Kayseri, Tunceli, Yozgat, Bingöl, Malatya, Bursa, Gaziantep, Niğde, İzmir, Aksaray, Kırşehir, Eskişehir, Kilis, Manisa, Kocaeli, Muş, Uşak, Adana, Kahramanmaraş, Hatay, Van, Osmaniye, Bitlis.	3	
Employment Rate 2010				
Moran Diyagramı	HH	Çanakkale, Düzce, Erzurum, Denizli, Samsun, Iğdır, Bolu, Zonguldak, Kars, Çankırı, Sakarya, Çorum, Tokat, Aydın, Uşak, Karabük, Amasya, Bartın, Konya, Mersin, Isparta, Karaman, Kırklareli.	1	Kümeleme Analizi
	LL	Ankara, Yalova, Elazığ, Kayseri, Tunceli, Yozgat, Bingöl, Gaziantep, İzmir, Kırşehir, Kocaeli, Adıyaman, Kırıkkale, Adana, Van, Osmaniye, Bitlis.	3	

Employment Rate 2011				
Moran Diyagramı	HH	Edirne, Kütahya, Samsun, Iğdır, Bursa, Bolu, Bilecik, Kars, Çankırı, Sakarya, Afyonkarahisar, Muğla, Tokat, Aydın, Amasya, Mersin, Isparta, Karaman, Erzincan, Kırklareli.	1	Kümeleme Analizi
	LL	Hakkari, Ankara, Elazığ, Kayseri, Tunceli, Malatya, Gaziantep, Niğde, Kırşehir, Eskişehir, Kilis, Muş, Kırıkkale, Adana, Kahramanmaraş, Hatay, Van, Osmaniye, Bitlis.	3	
Employment Rate 2012				
Moran Diyagramı	HH	Edirne, Kütahya, Gümüşhane, Ordu, Düzce, Denizli, Tekirdağ, Iğdır, Burdur, Zonguldak, Kars, Artvin, Afyonkarahisar, Manisa, Kastamonu, Muğla, Aydın, Antalya, Bayburt, Ardahan, Uşak, Karabük, Trabzon, Sinop, Bartın, Giresun, Rize.	1	Kümeleme Analizi
	LH	Yalova, Erzurum, Samsun İzmir, İstanbul, Çankırı, Tokat, Balıkesir, Amasya, Konya.	2	
	LL	Hakkari, Gaziantep, Kırşehir, Kilis, Muş, Adıyaman, Kırıkkale, Osmaniye, Bitlis.	3	
Employment Rate 2013				
Moran Diyagramı	HH	Edirne, Kütahya, Yalova, Gümüşhane, Tunceli, Ordu, Samsun, Bursa, İzmir, Bolu, Bilecik, İstanbul, Sakarya, Artvin, Tokat, Bayburt, Kocaeli, Trabzon, Amasya, Konya, Giresun, Rize, Isparta, Karaman, Erzincan, Kırklareli.	1	Kümeleme Analizi
	LL	Hakkari, Ankara, Gaziantep, Kırşehir, Kilis, Muş, Adıyaman, Kırıkkale, Adana, Kahramanmaraş, Hatay, Van, Osmaniye, Bitlis.	3	

Bibliography

Anselin, L. (1988). *Spatial Econometrics: Methods and Models.* Kluwer Academic Publishers, Dordrecht.

Anselin, L. (1992). *Spatial Data Analysis with GIS: An Introduction to Application in the Social Sciences.* National Center for Geographic Information and Analysis, University of California, Santa Barbara, Technical Report 92/10.

Anselin, L. (1995). Local Indicators of Spatial Association - LISA. *Geographical Analysis*, 27(2), 93–115.

Anselin, L. (1996). The Moran Scatterplot as an ESDA Tool to Assess Local Instability in Spatial Association. Fisher M., Scholten H.J., Unwin D. (Eds.), *Spatial Analytical Perspectives on GIS in Environmental and Socio-Economic Sciences.* (pp. 111–125). London: Taylor and Francis.

Anselin, L., Sridharan, S., & Gholston, S. (2007). Using Exploratory Spatial Data Analysis to Leverage Social İndicator Databases: The Discovery of İnteresting Patterns. *Social Indicators Research*, 82(2), 287–309.

Başar, Ö. D. (2009). *Uzamsal regresyon analizi* (Yayımlanmamış Doktora Tezi). Mimar Sinan Güzel Sanatlar Üniversitesi Fen Bilimleri Enstitüsü, İstanbul.

Çetin, D. (2012). *Exports and Clusters: A Spatial Econometric Analysis on Ankara and Istanbul Oizs (Ph.D.).* Middle East Technical University, Ankara.

Dall'Erba, S. (2005). Distribution of Regional İncome and Regional Funds in Europe 1989–1999: An Exploratory Spatial Data Analysis. *The Annals of Regional Science*, 39(1), 121–148.

Eryılmaz, H. (2010). *Mekansal İstatistikte Nokta Örüntü Teknikleri ve Bir Uygulama* (Yayımlanmamış Doktora Tezi). Anadolu Üniversitesi Fen Bilimleri Enstitüsü, Eskişehir.

Fischer, M. M., & Wang J. (2011). *Spatial Data Analysis: Models, Methods and Techniques.* Springer Science & Business Media. Berlin.

Griffith, D. A. (2003). *Spatial Autocorrelation and Spatial Filtering.* Springer, Berlin.

Gül, T. G. (2014). Türkiye İçin İstihdamın Belirleyicileri: İbbs-2 Bölge Düzeyi, Mekansal Analiz Uygulaması, *Dokuz Eylül Üniversitesi İktisadi ve İdari Bilimler Fakültesi Dergisi*, 29(1), 105–135.

Haining, R. P. (2003). *Spatial Data Analysis: Theory and Practice.* Cambridge University Press, New York.

Lesage, J. P. & Pace, R. K. (2009). *Introduction to Spatial Econometrics.* Boca Raton: Chapman &Hall/CRC.

Özdamar, K. (2002). *Paket Programlar İle İstatistiksel Veri* er*Analizi–2 (Çok Değişkenli Analizler).* Kaan Kitabevi, Eskişehir.

Özdemir S., Ersöz, H. Y. & Sarıoğlu, İ. (2006). İşsizlik Sorununun Çözümünde KOBİ'lerin Desteklenmesi, *İstanbul Ticaret Odası Yayınları.* Yayın No: 2006:45, İstanbul.

Sala, C. H. & Bragulat, E. J. (2004). A Program to Perform Ward's Clustering Method on Several Regionalized Variables. *Computers & Geosciences*, 30, 881–886.

Schabenberger, O. & Gotway, C. A. (2005). *Statistical Methods for Spatial Data Analysis.* Chapman & Hall/CRC, Boca Raton.

Tatlıdil, H. (1996). *Uygulamalı Çok Değişkenli İstatistiksel Analiz.* Cem Web Ofset, Ankara.

Tobler, W. R. (1970). A Computer Movie Simulating Urban Growth in the Detroit Region. *Economic Geography*, 46(sup1), 234–240.

Turkish Statistical Instute, https://biruni.tuik.gov.tr/bolgeselistatistik/

Zeren, F. (2010). Mekânsal Etkileşim Analizi. *Ekonometri ve İstatistik e-Dergisi*, (12), 18–39.

Zeren, F. (2011). *Mekânsal ekonometri ve mekânsal panel ekonometri yaklaşımları: AB üye ülkeleri için gelir yakınsama hipotezi üzerine bir uygulama* (Yayımlanmamış Doktora Tezi), İstanbul Üniversitesi Sosyal Bilimler Enstitüsü, İstanbul.

Barış Yildiz

Tax Competition: Evaluation in Terms of Tax Havens

1 Introduction

Taxes that have vital importance for the states to continue their existence have the biggest share within public revenues. Due to this vital importance of taxes, states put in efforts in order to ensure that tax revenues are increased and to provide that tax potential is transformed into tax revenues at the highest level. For this purpose, tax offices try to ensure simultaneously that taxable incomes are declared accurately, records are kept accurately, the elements necessary to be deducted from income to determine the net income to be deducted accurately, tax statements to be submitted on time and to tax debts are calculated accurately (Şentürk, 2014, p. 132 and 139). One of the most important problems that tax offices, which try to ensure these, encounter is tax competitions.

Increase of capital and labor mobility enabled different production factors to acquire new returns. Increased mobility enabled countries to react to different tax-related arrangements. Particularly capital resorted to incline to countries or regions, which provide tax-related advantages, and to seek suitable financial environment. Thus, countries or regions that are named as tax havens that leads to harmful tax competition emerged. A great number of countries, who see the contribution of foreign investments to employment, positively affecting national income and enabling access to advanced technology, removed the barriers against foreign investors. Most of the countries opened their borders to a large extent to foreign capital in order to abolish exchange controls (Aktan and Vural, 2004, 6–7; Clausing, 2015; Karakurt, 2016, 321) and started a critical tax competition on a global level.

Since open borders permit the transfer of international capital, the capital and income on these capital move to tax havens where taxes are relatively lower and confidentiality is high. Although these changes are legal to some degree, they are not to some degree. Illegal translocation of capital is a great concern for at least three reasons: i) they decrease tax revenues; ii) they decrease efficient taxation of the rich; iii) majority may lose their trust in tax system and in general in government agencies. (Miethe ve Menkhoff, 2017, s.2).

When we look at the economical dimensions of tax havens, it is possible to see that policy makers are right about their concerns. Although there are different figures regarding the economic size of the havens, in accordance with OECD this figure is between 5 trillion USA Dollars and 7 Trillion Dollars. In another study carried out by PriceWaterhouseCoopers (PwC) in 2012, a figure between 21 trillion USA Dollars and 32 trillion USA Dollars is mentioned (Bennedsen and Zeume,

2017, 1222). In accordance with Financial Secrecy Index (FSI) 2015 announced by International Tax Justice, financial assets amounting approximately to 21 and 32 trillion dollars in the whole world are kept in countries, where taxes are quite low or there are no taxes. It is estimated that each year from 1 up to 1.6 trillion dollars are laundered via tax havens (Akdiş, 25.04.2017). In accordance with Bloomberg Billionaires Index, more than 30 % of the world's 200 richest people, who have more than 2.9 trillion dollars of net collective value, are controlling a part of their personal wealth by way of an offshore holding company or another legal entity who held their wealth implicitly (Hodges, 03.05.2013).

2 Tax Competition and Its Features

The first person who theoretically mentioned tax competition was Charles Tiebout in the year of 1956. Explanations regarding tax competition emphasized the possibility that competition may cause low tax rates for capital and therefore lead to public expenditure levels. This view was articulated by Oates (1972) and was officially modelled by Zodrow and Mieszkowski (1986) and Wilson (1986). In case the regions differentiate to the extent that they compete for capital, then tax competition leads up to disruption of capital distribution. A large number of successive writers extended and discussed the view that tax competition (Wilson and Wildasin, 2004, p. 1065–1066).

The literature regarding tax competition, attached impressively small importance to definition of this phenomenon. Therefore, it is quite not possible to find a definition that have a single context regarding tax competition. Tax competition is defined as tax environment, where independent governments do not want to be in cooperation in any way (Wilson and Wildasin, 2004, p. 1066). This tax environment contains areas where effective tax rates are decreased in consequence of financial consolidation and economic integration increase. Apart from tax rates, other tax-related privileges may enable to decrease tax burden. From this point of view, a wider definition of tax competition is possible. Accordingly, tax burden may be defined as the effects of tax policies of the organizations who have taxation authority such as centralized administration, public administration, local administration and other administrative units on other states (Öz and Yaraşır, 2009, 3 and 5).

When related literature is viewed, it stands out that tax competition causes pressure on tax rates. For example, when a state increases (or decreases) corporate income tax, this condition has a mobile positive (or negative) effect on other states. Tax base reacts to changes of the tax rates. Moreover, tax competition also decreases the tax income of states who have high tax rates. It is observed that tax rates decrease as international integration process continues. When average corporate income tax rates of member states of Organization for Economic Cooperation and Development (OECD), it is observed that there is a decrease from 41 % in 1981 to 23 % in 2014. And when the decreases are analyzed, it is observed that smaller economies decrease their corporate income tax at a greater level when compared to bigger economies (Clausing, 2015).

The view arguing that tax competition caused by capital mobility creates a downward pressure on corporate income tax rates is more prevalent than the opposite view. Nevertheless, there is insignificant amount of consensus about whether this condition is either beneficial, harmful or irrelevant for economic welfare (Griffith and Klemm, 2004, p.3).

2.1 Tax Competition and OECD

Today, many national and international organization, particularly European Union (EU) and OECD, exert vigorous efforts to contend with the negativities caused by tax competition. The content of these efforts vary depending of the struggling organization. For example, with regards to EU, while precautions in the field of indirect tax are considered as tax adjustment, for direct taxes this situation appears as tax competition (Öz and Yaraşır, 2009, 3 and 5).

OECD's works regarding the struggle against the negativities that may arise due to tax competition contains; (i) strengthening the rules of corporate income tax at an international level, (ii) adjustment of taxation with principles of economic activities and (iii) increasing transparency (OECD, 2017: 1). One of the most important struggles against tax competition is Base Erosion and Profit Shifting (BEPS) Action Plan.

BEPS Action Plan was prepared by OECD upon the call of G20 countries, signed with joint venture of member states of G20 and OECD, announced on the date of July 19, 2013 and approved and put into effect at the G20 Leaders' Summit, which congregated on September 2013 in Saint Petersburg. United Nations (UN) and EU carry out some works in the field of BEPS and attract notice to this problem at an international level. The objective of BEPS Action Plan is to try and enable that income is taxed at the place where the economic activities that generate the income are and where the value is created. BEPS Action Plan comprises 15 actions that are prepared in order to prevent tax losses. These actions are (OECD, 2015: 13);

1 Determining the problems caused by digital economy, actions aimed at these problems and particularly solve the tax problems that arise.
2 Neutralizing the effects of Hybrid dissonance (such as double taxation, double erosion, long-term deferment) adjustments.
3 Strengthening the rules of the controlled foreign companies.
4 Limiting the base erosion by means of interest discounts and other financial payments.
5 Taking more efficient precautions against harmful tax applications by taking transparency and substance into consideration.
6 Preventing misuse of agreements.
7 Preventing forgery of avoiding permanent establishment status.
8-9-10 Adjustment of Transfer Pricing results by creating value.
11 Generating suggestions in order to improve harmful tax competition environment by gathering existing data about BEPS, analyzing the results and better benefiting from existing tax data. Developing methodologies for related actions.

12 Mandatory Information Rules: It requires tax payers to explain aggressive tax planning regulations.
13 Counselling regarding Transfer Pricing documents and country-based reporting: Reviewing Transfer Pricing documents. Determining minimum standards in country reporting. Identifying common templates in reporting.
14 Making dissonance solution mechanisms more efficient: Countries state that the changes that BEPS project bring about may cause some uncertainties, may lead to double taxation in short-term before getting into action and may increase the disputes regarding mutual agreement procedures. Double taxation is accepted as an obstacle to cross-border trade and investment. Therefore, the importance of removing double taxation was accepted and the countries decided on a minimum standard for solution of disputes regarding the agreements. This standard contains a strong political commitment with regards to solving the disputes efficiently and on time by way of this mutual agreement procedure. Aforementioned commitment also contains setting of a monitoring mechanism that enables minimum standard to be fulfilled and countries to make more progress for solving disputes rapidly. Moreover, a big group of countries made a commitment to rapidly adopt mandatory and binding arbitration in bilateral tax agreements.
15 Developing multilateral agreements to regulate bilateral tax agreements: Applying precautions related with BEPS and searching technical feasibility of a multilateral tool to change bilateral tax agreements. It is stated that in order to develop such a tool, it is necessary to carry out projects that are open to participation of all countries.

2.2 Harmful Tax Competition

Tax competition divide into two branches as horizontal (global) and vertical (national) depending on the position of the competitors. Horizontal tax competition may be clarified as countries or states, who are at the same taxation level, levying tax over mobile source of taxation and therefore the administration receiving the tax affecting the tax income of the other administration. In case tax competition is not occurring between different countries but between administrative unit, which are at different levels, then it is vertical tax competition. The competition between the federal government and state governments in United States of America may be cited as an example (Yordadoğ and Albayrak, 2017, p. 126: Akmaz, 2007, p. 1).

Tax competition may be classified as beneficial tax competition or harmful tax competition depending on the results the competitor countries obtain. In case the decision made in taxation authority usage has positive effects on the country, while at the same time encourages and invigorates other countries, then it is a desirable situation and this situation is beneficial tax competition. Beneficial tax competition enables lower taxation and therefore reinforces capital accumulation. Therefore, more investment, employment and high level of welfare would be provided.

Hence, tax competition leads to decrease of tax rates and causes positive results on countries' growth and development. Moreover, it is argued that tax incomes will increase with low tax rates (Peker and Kılıçer, 2014, p. 167).

OECD indicated on the report it published in the year of 1998 preferential tax regimes and tax havens as harmful tax applications. On the report it is stated that the tax havens or harmful preferential tax regimes, which reduce effective tax rates obtained from mobile activities much lower than the rates in other countries, are potentially harmful by; i) contorting real investment flow financially and indirectly; ii) sabotaging the integrity and equity of tax structures; iii) disturbing the concord of all the tax payers; iv) reshaping the desired structure and level of taxes and public expenditures; v) causing undesired shifts of part of the tax burden to less mobile tax bases, such as labor, property and consumption; vi) increasing administrative expenses and compliance burden on tax administrations and tax payers (OECD, 1998, p. 16).

3 Tax Havens

It is never possible to understand economical history of the modern world implicitly without understanding tax havens. Although tax havens have a history that continues for a long time, they are most probably as old as the taxes themselves. However, it is needless to say that their forms were dependent on the prevalent taxation type and current technology. Although it is indicated that the first tax haven example in the modern sense was in 1815 and in Switzerland (Hodges, 03.05.2013) it is possible to state that the origins of this practice goes well back to Ancient Greece or Vatican. It is known that the merchants in Ancient Greece stock their goods in islands close to Athens in order to avoid 2 % import duty, which was applied to imported goods (Öztürk and Ülger, 2016, p.239).

Tax havens are places, which enable non-residents (real or legal entities) to minimize the amount of tax they pay in where they perform economic activities. They are countries or regions that have exceptionally low (or zero) tax rates, that have high confidentiality level regarding information sharing, that have tax application lacking transparency and whose financial and legal frameworks are internationally accepted. Tax havens create grey areas for the companies to carry out their business strategies and financial planning. Although it is legitimate to save money from different countries, to protect business secrets or even to use offshore companies in order to provide savings from unstable economies, these postbox-like companies may also use tax havens to conceal illegal behaviors such as tax fraud or bribery (OECD, 2009: 11: Berkhout, 2016, p.1; Su and Tan, 2018).

3.1 Countries in Tax Havens

Tax havens is the undermost expression pf global corporate income tax competition and they may be found in every region of the world. While preparing the lists regarding tax havens, some countries, which have the characteristics of tax havens, are not included in these lists and this situation causes the countries preparing the lists to be criticized. EU wishing to keep countries like Switzerland out of the black list only because these countries cooperate with EU on topics related with financial information exchange (Berkhout, 2016, p.5) is only one of the examples that justify the critiques.

The number of tax havens vary depending on the organization identifying the tax havens and criteria that are taken into consideration. In OECD 1998 report, the number of tax havens was stated to be 41, however this figure dropped to 5 after these countries reply affirmatively to cooperation calls. In accordance with other organizations such as Tax Justice Network (TJN), The International Monetary Fund (IMF), Oxford Committee for Famine Relief (OXFAM), the number of tax havens is much more. In some sources, Ireland and Luxemburg in Europe, Hong Kong and Singapore in Asia and some Caribbean islands in America are considered tax havens. There are some people defending that zones that apply low tax rates within the country (preferential tax regime), special exclusive economic zones that apply low tax rates (China) and enterprise zones (America) and sub-zones that provide tax concession (East Germany, South Italy, East Canada) shall be considered as tax havens (Karakurt, 2016, p.323).

While countries were evaluated on the list generated by Oxfam, three criteria were used to measure the harmful tax use of these countries. These three harmful tax policy are; i) corporate income tax rates, ii) offered incentives and iii) lack of cooperation with international efforts against tax fraud. Oxfam's first 15 corporate income tax havens are as follow: Bermuda, Cayman Islands, Holland, Switzerland, Singapore, Ireland, Luxemburg, Curacao, Hong Kong, Cyrus, Bahamas, Jersey, Barbados, Mauritius and British Virgin Islands. These countries fall within Oxfam's "world's worst" list. Because these countries generate the most extreme forms of tax fraud. Many Oxfam analysis, 90 % of the world's largest companies are within at least one tax haven (Berkhout, 2016, p.4–5).

EU published a list regarding tax havens on December 2017 in order to stop harmful tax applications arising from controversies. While preparing this list; i) low or zero taxation, ii) unreal place of residence and iii) tax confidentiality aspects were taken into consideration as distinguishing features of tax havens (Remeur, 2018, p.9). 47 countries, who made a commitment to make amendments on tax applications fall within the grey list. Turkey is one of these countries. The black list prepared by EU contains 17 countries, who do not agree to fill the tax loopholes and do not cooperate for tax issues. These countries are; American Samoa, Bahrain, Barbados, Grenada, Guam, South Korea, Korea, Macau, Marshall Islands, Mongolia, Namibia, Palau, Panama, Saint Lucia, Trinidad and Tobago, Tunisia and The United Arab Emirates. However, no sanction is projected for these countries and regions (Deutsche Welle Türkçe, 05.12.2017). Moreover, it is attention-grabbing that many of these countries are close to developed countries and some of them are subject to existing kingdoms.

OECD determined on June 2000 that there are more than 40 countries, which meet tax haven criteria. However, OECD revised this approach in 2001 dated Progress

Report. In accordance with this report, low or zero rated tax applications or activities that do not have economic importance are not enough to determine tax havens. This situation lead transparency to be considered as a functional tool in fight against tax havens. In consequence, in year 2007 many tax havens made commitments to apply transparency and efficient information exchange (OECD, 2009: 11).

4 Legal Regulations Concerning Tax Havens in Turkey

İstanbul Offshore Banking and Free Zone Regimes took place in OECD's year 2000 report as two regimes from Turkey. İstanbul Offshore Banking Regime was abolished in year 2002. And for Free Zone Practices, legislative amendment was made in year 2004 and it was provided that Turkish tax acts are valid and applied. Unrestricted and indefinite tax exemption provided for the users in these zones were abolished. In consequence of the extensive evaluations that OECD performed later, it was concluded that these zones do not affect tax competition negatively (Armağan and İçmen, 2012, p. 152).

Turkey granted Ministry of Finance authority regarding the tax subjects started within the body of OECD for international information exchange. In accordance with the 9th article of Law no 6487 (Date of Ratification: 24/5/2013) article 152/A was added to TPL (Tax Procedure Law), and in compliance with international agreements subject of information exchange was regulated for the first time in the legislation and following provision entered into force: "Ministry of Finance Revenue Administration or entities that are entitled to perform tax audit may gather information not limited to the extent determined in the first article of the Law, within the framework of information exchange provisions partaking in duly executed international agreements and in accordance with procedures established by Ministry of Finance."

Avoidance of double-taxation agreements are one of the most important legal foundations of Turkey for the fights against harmful tax competition and tax fraud. As of March of year 2016, Turkey has avoidance of double-taxation agreement with 80 countries. Turkey started to sign information exchange agreements with island states such as Jersey, Bermuda, Guernsey and Man Island in order to increase her capacity to obtain international information on tax-related subjects. Agreements signed with Jersey and Bermuda entered into force (Çakmak, 2016, p. 145)

It was determined that Turkey focused on indirect taxes during EU harmonization process and therefore, direct taxes remained in the background. Transfer pricing and tax havens concepts were added to Corporate Income Tax. Direct taxes were last included in the year 2014 progress report, and it is stated that Corporate Income Tax Draft Law is continued to be reviewed in Grand National Assembly of Turkey (Keşmir, 2016, p.41).

Recently, methods that states employ unilaterally against tax haven countries started to take place in legislative regulations in Turkey. In this respect, particularly the regulations within Corporate Income Tax Law no 5220 attract attention. Aforementioned regulations are as follows;

- ***Taxation of Controlled Foreign Organizations' Income:*** In accordance with 7th article of Corporate Income Tax Law no 5520, it is projected that corporation profits of foreign affiliates of fully responsible real or legal entities shall be subject to corporate income tax in Turkey under certain conditions. With this regulation it is aimed to tax income of foreign entities that are controlled in order to tax the income of the tax payers, who direct their enterprises by means of their affiliates to foreign countries with low tax rates, under certain conditions without waiting them to transfer the income they gained to Turkey.
- ***Implementing Concealed Gain Provisions by Way of Transfer Pricing:*** "Concealed Gain" concept of abolished Corporate Income Tax Law no 5422 was reorganized under the title of "Distribution of Concealed Gain by way of Transfer Pricing" on the 13th article of Corporate Income Tax Law no 5520 by taking the developments in the international arena and particularly regulations of Organization for Economic Cooperation and Development's (OECD)into consideration (GIB, 2010, p.1). OECD frequently updates transfer pricing principles in order to prevent tax loss and evasion of particularly multinational companies by transfer pricing. 13th article of Corporate Income Tax Law no 5520 mentions "Distribution of Concealed Gain by way of Transfer Pricing" implementation. In accordance with this implementation, in case corporate taxpayers "purchase or sale of goods or services from or to related parties, over the cost or price that is determined in defiance of arm's length principle", the gain is deemed to be distributed in full or partially in a concealed manner by way of transfer pricing. Persons or organizations, who are located at countries or zones that are announced tax haven by Council of Ministers are regarded as related party in any case.
- ***Withholding Tax Application on Payments Made to Tax Havens:*** In 7th paragraph of 30th article of Corporate Income Tax Law no 5520, it is projected to apply 30 % withholding tax on any payments made to the organization established in countries that implement harmful tax competition. In this regulation, the payments that fully responsible organization made to the establishments located at the countries that take place on the list, which will be published by Council of Ministers, are included in the scope of withholding tax. However, Council of Ministers has not published which countries shall be considered tax havens and therefore this provision has not entered into application yet.
- ***Determination of Countries and Zones that Employ Harmful Tax Competition:*** Although the regulation in question entered into force on the date of June 21, 2006, it took effect as of January 1, 2006. Accordingly, the list of countries implementing harmful tax competition will be published by Council of Ministers. It is expected for this list to comprise of the countries called tax havens.

5 Result

Tax competition is one of the prominent examples of mutually dependent policy making. Decision makers of a single area of jurisdiction are affected by the tax rates determined by others. Because, tax rates affect countries to attract and maintain valuable sources of income such as companies necessary for investment or taxpayers. The consensus in the literature is that this is a real case. Many studies convincingly document this situation both at national and also international level (Gilardi and Wasserfallen, 2016, 46). The focal point of the definitions regarding tax competition is the competition between independent governments over a mobile tax base (Wilson and Wildasin, 2004, p.1067).

Tax competition creates pressure on countries. Countries are not affected by tax competition pressure equally. Studies display that economies, which are smaller and more integrated to international area, have a greater chance in determining lower tax rates. Multinational companies may shift their income between locations by various methods. For example, they may employ transfer pricing method in order to make affiliates in countries with low tax rates to seem more profitable than the affiliates in countries with high tax rates. Thus, multinational companies created a complicated property chains in order transform the incomes, which may not be taxed under any tax-related area of jurisdiction, into "stateless income". There is a large number of evidence that multinational companies are "taxational" in their economic decision. Even basic figures demonstrate that financial decisions are made depending more on tax-related decision rather than economic decisions (Clausing, 2015). This situation frequently leads to harmful tax competition and results in favor of countries expressed as tax havens.

With ring-fenced (protecting tax haven funds) tax systems (low tax – zero tax) taxation costs of other countries are increasing and these systems harm the efficiency of financial markets by organizing their regulations only in favor of foreign investments. The companies in such countries are free from control and audit and a great majority of these companies carry on a business only in a postbox-like manner. These international companies do not keep records. Tax havens have a well-functioning banking system, high quality mail, telephone and telex services. Their close geographical position to developed countries and direct means of transport attract notice (Eriksson, 2009, p.5 and 9).

In order to preclude the international companies' actions regarding the transfer of their profits, BEPS Action plan, which is one of the greatest reforms in international taxation system, was prepared by OECD. Partic ularly the problems that digital economy is taxed insufficiently deficiently and that it is not clear from where, whom and at what stage the tax will be collected are planned to be solved with the regulations BEPS will carry into effect. With BEPS, substance over form concept gains importance and "Permanent establishment" definition is planned to be enlarged. It is expected that with BEPS there will be some changes on the subject of transfer pricing. It is anticipated that BEPS Action Plan will abolish international companies' base erosion and profit shifting mechanisms and will ensure that they pay their share of tax fairly. At the same time BEPS Action Plan also aims at minimizing the tax frauds (Saraçoğlu, 2015, p.83–84). In accordance with OECD/G20's explanatory notification, 2015 final report; the findings of the studies conducted since 2013 demonstrate that corporate income tax revenues are decreasing and the loss may be between 4 % and 10 % of the global corporate income tax revenues. These predictions confirm the potential size of the issue. Aforementioned size is predicted to be approximately between 100 and 240 billion USA Dollars per year. In accordance with the report, losses are caused by various reasons including aggressive tax planning (OECD, 2015: 4).

EU is determining minimum tax rates for different tax types and trying to enable tax adjustment by coordination on tax base in order to decrease tax competition (Aktan and Vural, 2004, 16). EU is particularly struggling against harmful tax competition regarding corporate taxes. However, although some detections and solution recommendations are elaborated, it is quite difficult to mention that the desired steps are taken (Bağdınlı, 2016, p.126).

Turkey signed BEPS agreement together with 71 companies as of October, 2017. Today, this agreement became the source of international law as an incarnational version of wishes that the negativities regarding tax competition will be fixed in Turkey (Özdiler Küçük and Küçük, 2017, p.44). In Turkey, there are structural problems in respect of taxes and awareness level of public opinion with regards to the issue is low (Biçer and Erginay, 2015, p.68). Particularly the provisions of Corporate Tax Law stand out regarding tax competition in Turkey. However, in spite of everything, the fact that the list about tax havens is not published yet slows down the reforms that shall be made in this area and makes it difficult to implement the provisions of the law.

Tax havens and policies encouraging harmful tax competition create some winners and a great numbers of losers. Global companies and their shareholders are the net beneficiaries. And the losers are the ones who experience the result of the gap between state's tax revenues and state expenditures. Eventually, it is the community who suffers the most. Particularly, the tax revenues that underdeveloped and developing countries lose due to informality and eroded tax system, make the already existing resource shortage problem even more visible in these countries. Thus, many tax havens are forced to implement strict regulations such as adjusting their tax laws and changing their banking confidentiality applications. Governments need to call for a new international tax reform aiming to stop corporate tax rates to hit the bottom. Tax administration and tax laws, which are built upon a solid tax culture, of the countries making the call will make a contribution for this reform invitation to be reciprocated. This reform shall comprise the developing countries equally. Lists, which are based upon objective standards but not on political intervention, displaying the worst tax havens shall be formed. Then, forcible precautions such as sanctions and incentives aiming at restricting base erosion and profit shifting shall be taken. Public tax transparency shall be improved by setting the condition that all multinational companies have to publish country reports including different data for each country they operate in including the developing countries (Berkhout, 2016, p.11 and 33: Günaydın and Yıldız, 2016). These precautions will contribute to decrease the costs of the tax system. It is not sufficient for the countries to control only their sovereignty areas in order to prevent their tax losses. Therefore, it is necessary for the countries to develop their skill of being able to trace tax payers all over the world.

Bibliography

Akdiş, M. (25.04.2017). "Off-Shore ve Vergi Cennetindeki Ülke Gelirlerinin Vergilendirilmesi", *MuhasebeTr*, http://www.muhasebetr.com/yazarlarimiz/muhammetakdis/003/ (Erişim Tarihi:23.06.2018).

Akmaz., K. (2007). "Uluslararası Vergi Rekabeti", *E-Yaklaşım*, 51(Ekim). http://frekansdenetim.com.tr/wp-content/uploads/ULUSLARARASI-VERGİ-REKABETİ.pdf (Erişim Tarihi: 14.06.2018)

Aktan, C.C. ve Vural, İ. Y. (2004). "Vergi Rekabeti", *Erciyes Üniversitesi İktisadi ve İdari Bilimler Fakültesi Dergisi*, (22), 1–18.

Armağan, R., ve İçmen, Ö. G. M. (2012). "Vergi Rekabeti ve Türkiye'ye Yansıması", *Süleyman Demirel Üniversitesi İktisadi ve İdari Bilimler Fakültesi Dergisi*, 17(2), 145–172.

Bağdınlı, İ.H. (2016). "Vergi Yükü ve Vergi Rekabeti", *KPMG Sorumlu Vergicilik* (Ed. Dr. Burak Koçer), 119–128, Günce Reklam Yayıncılık Matbaa San. ve Tic. Ltd. Şti., İstanbul.

Bennedsen, M., ve Zeume, S. (2017). "Corporate Tax Havens and Transparency". *The Review of Financial Studies*, 31(4), 1221–1264.

Berkhout, E. (2016). *Tax Battles: The Dangerous Global Race to the Bottom on Corporate Tax*, Oxfam Polıcy Paper. Published by Oxfam GB for Oxfam International under

Biçer, R., ve Erginay, M. (2015). "OECD Matrahın Aşındırılması ve Kârın Aktarılması Eylem Planı ve Türkiye'ye Etkileri". *Vergi Sorunları Dergisi*, 326(2015), 54–68.

Clausing, K. A. (2015). *The Nature and Practice of Capital Tax Competition*, https://papers.ssrn.com/sol3/papers.cfm?abstract_id=2489224 (Erişim Tarihi: 13.06.2018).

Çakmak, T., (2016). "Otomatik Bilgi Değişim Anlaşmalarının Ulusal Vergi Hukukuna Yansımaları", *KPMG Sorumlu Vergicilik* (Ed. Dr. Burak Koçer), 143–151. Günce Reklam Yayıncılık Matbaa San. ve Tic. Ltd. Şti., İstanbul.

Deutsche Welle Türkçe. (05.12.2017). "AB 17 vergi cennetini kara listeye aldı", https://www.dw.com/tr/ab-17-vergi-cennetini-kara-listeye-aldı/a-41665647 (Erişim Tarihi:08.06.2018).

Eriksson, F. (2009). *Tax Havens and Development*, NORAD. Retrieved November, 19, 2013.

GİB (2010). *Transfer Fiyatlandırması Yoluyla Örtülü Kazanç Dağıtımı Hakkında Rehber*, Gelir İdaresi Başkanlığı. Yayın No: 114.

Gilardi, F., ve Wasserfallen, F. (2016). "How Socialization Attenuates Tax, Competition". *British Journal of Political Science*, 46(1), 45–65.

Griffith, R., ve Klemm, A. (2004). *What has been the Tax Competition Experience of the Past 20 Years?*, THE Institute For Fiscal Studies, WP04/05. http://discovery.ucl.ac.uk/2900/1/2900.pdf (Erişim Tarihi: 20.05.2018).

Günaydın, İ. ve Yıldız, B. (2016). "Vergi politikası ile yoksulluk azaltılabilir mi?", *Global Journal of Economics and Business Studies*, 5(9), 90–104.

Hodges, J., (03.05.2013). *Offshore Tax Havens in Spotlight After 200-Year History*, Bloomberg https://www.bloomberg.com/news/articles/2013-05-03/offshore-tax-havens-in-spotlightafter-200-year-history (Erişim Tarihi: 04.07.2018)

Karakurt, B. (2016). "Vergi Cennetleri ve Posta Kutusu Şirketlerin Kamu Maliyesine Etkileri", *Atatürk Üniversitesi İktisadi ve İdari Bilimler Dergisi*, 30(2). 319–341

Keşmir, D. (2016). "Avrupa Birliği Yolunda Türk Vergi Mevzuatının Uyumlaştırılması", *KPMG Sorumlu Vergicilik* (Ed. Dr. Burak Koçer), 36–45. Günce Reklam Yayıncılık Matbaa San. ve Tic. Ltd. Şti., İstanbul.

Miethe, J., ve Menkhoff, L. (2017). *Dirty Money Coming Home: Capital Flows Into and Out of Tax Havens*, DIW Berlin 1711, German Institute for Economic Research, Discussion Papers. https://ideas.repec.org/p/zbw/vfsc17/168082.html (Erişim Tarihi: 12.06.2018).

OECD (1998). *Harmful Tax Competition. An Emerging Global Issue*, Organisation For Economic Co-Operation And Development.

OECD (2009), *Countering Offshore Tax Evasion Some Questions and Answers on the Project*, OECD Centre for Tax Policy and Administration. http://www.oecd.org/ctp/exchange-of-tax-information/42469606.pdf (Erişim Tarihi: 12.06.2018)

OECD (2015), *OECD/G20 Base Erosion and Profit Shifting Project Explanatory Statement*, 2015 Final Reports.

OECD (2017), *Inclusive Framework on BEPS Progress report*, July 2016–June 2017.

Öz, E., ve Yaraşır, S. (2009). "Global Bir Kavram: Vergi Rekabeti", *Maliye Araştırma Merkezi Konferansları*, Prof. Dr. Şerafettin Aksoy'a Armağan, (52.Seri), 1–39.

Özdiler Küçük, E., ve Küçük, E. (2017). "Küresel Vergi Yönetimi: Yeni Ortak Hukuka Doğru", *Research Journal of Politics, Economics & Management/Siyaset, Ekonomi ve Yönetim Arastirmalari Dergisi*, Spesial Isue of ICPESS, 5(5).39–46.

Öztürk, S., ve Ülger, Ö. (2016). "Vergi Cennetlerinin Küresel Finansal Kriz Üzerine Ekonomik Etkileri: Vergi Kaçırma, Vergiden Kaçınma Ve Kara Para Aklamadaki Rolü", *Ömer Halisdemir Üniversitesi İktisadi ve İdari Bilimler Fakültesi Dergisi*, 9(1), 237–254.

Peker, İ., ve Kılıçer, E. (2014). "Türkiye Boyutu İle Vergi Rekabeti". Vergi Sorunları Dergisi, Nisan (307), 165–186.

PwC (2018), *History and Milestones*, https://www.pwc.com/us/en/about-us/pwc-corporate-history.html (Erişim tarihi; 01.07.2018).

Remeur, C.(2018). *Listing of Tax Havens by the EU-Think Tank*, EPRS,European Parliamentary Research Service. http://www.europarl.europa.eu/RegData/etudes/BRIE/2018/621872/EPRS_BRI(2018)621872_EN.pdf (Erişim Tarihi:10.07.2018)

Saraçoğlu, F. (2015). "G20 Antalya Liderler Bildirgesi Ve Matrah Aşındırma ve Kâr Aktarımı (Beps) Eylem Planı". *Mali Çözüm Dergisi/Financial Analysis*, 25(131), 73–88.

Su, W., & Tan, D. (2018). "Business Groups and Tax Havens". *Journal of Business Ethics*, 1–15.

Şentürk, S. H. (2014). "Vergiye Gönüllü Uyum Sağlanmasında Fayda İlkesinin Rolü", *Eskişehir Osmangazi Üniversitesi İİBF Dergisi*, 9(3), 129–143.

TJN (2018), *Our Goals and Methods, Tax Justice Network*, https://www.taxjustice.net/about/who-we-are/goals/ (Erişim Tarihi: 24.06.2018).

Türkçe, D. W. (05.12.2017). "AB 17 vergi cennetini kara listeye aldı", https://www.dw.com/tr/ab-17-vergi-cennetini-kara-listeye-aldı/a-41665647 (Erişim Tarihi:08.06.2018).

Wilson, J. D., ve Wildasin, D. E. (2004). "Capital Tax Competition: Bane or Boon", *Journal Of Public Economics*, 88(6), 1065–1091.

Yordadoğ, V. & M. Albayrak (2017), "OECD Ülkelerinde Vergi Rekabeti", *Sosyoekonomi*, 25(32), 121–148.

Guner Tuncer and Ozer Ozcelik

Ethnic Economies and the Case of Syrian Refugees in Turkey[1]

1 Introduction

Ethnicity plays an important role in the social and economic structure of many countries, in particular with intensive migration. Different groups of immigrants cause ethnic commercial areas where they locate. There are also foreign born in a country and the people develop various economic activities. Ethnic economies are created by ethnic commercial areas where different groups of immigrants locate and various economic activities of foreign born in a country. Immigrants and various ethnic groups can make a difference in the geographies of economic life and create notable economic landscapes. The aim of this paper is to present ethnic economies and evaluate Syrian refugees in Turkey in the context of ethnic economies.

2 Framework of Ethnic Economies

Ethnic economies are created by ethnic commercial areas where different groups of immigrants locate and various economic activities of foreign born in a country. Ethnic economies can be classified by ethnic-controlled economy and ethnic ownership economy. Ethnic ownership economy is classified by ethnic enclave economy, ethnic (non-clave) economy and mixed economy as well. The following diagram shows the definitions of these basic classifications.

3 Syrian Refugees in Turkey and Ethnic Economies

Along with the beginning of the civil war in Syria, many Syrians began to migrate to different countries. Syria's neighbor Turkey has become one of the major migration regions.

Numbers of Syrian refugees living in Turkey during the period 2011–2018 is shown in the table above. The number of immigrants has been reached 3.562.523 in 2018 from 14.237 in 2012.

By the date of 28.06.2018, 214.618 sheltered and 3.347.905 unsheltered Syrian refugees live in Turkey. According to the distribution of Syrian refugees in the

1 This study is developed from the report presented as an abstract at the "International Congress on Afro-Eurasian Research III" congress with the title " Ethnic Economies: A Descriptive Study".

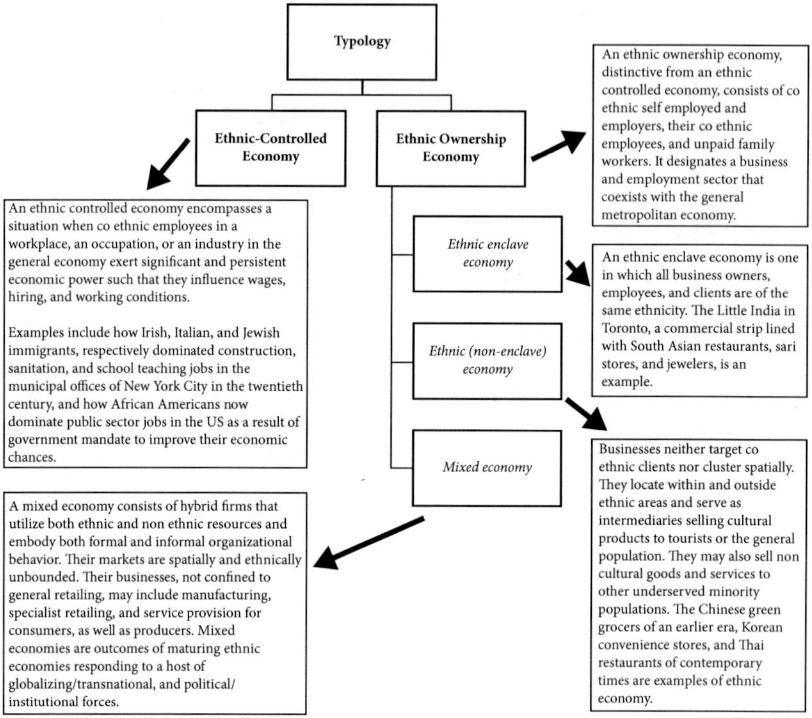

Fig. 1: Typology of Ethnic Economies. Source: (Lo, 2009)

scope of temporary protection by top ten provinces, İstanbul is the first place with 563.133 refugees.

About 3.5 million Syrian refugees play an important ethnicity in Turkey. By the end of 2017, 6.589 Syrian joint venture companies were established in Turkey and total Syrian share capital of companies is 179 million Turkish liras (TEPAV, 2018).

According to the Syria joint capital companies of the most active 15 sectors in 2017, wholesale trade is the first sector with 427 companies. Real estate activities is the second sector with 148 companies. Manufacture of leather and related products is the 15th sector with 10 companies.

Recent literature of impact of Syrian refugees on the Turkish economy is as follows:

Akgunduz, Berg & Hassink (2015) analyze how the Syrian refugee influx in Turkey has affected food and housing prices, employment rates and internal migration patterns in regions of Turkey where refugees are being accommodated. They find that housing and to a lesser degree food prices increased, but

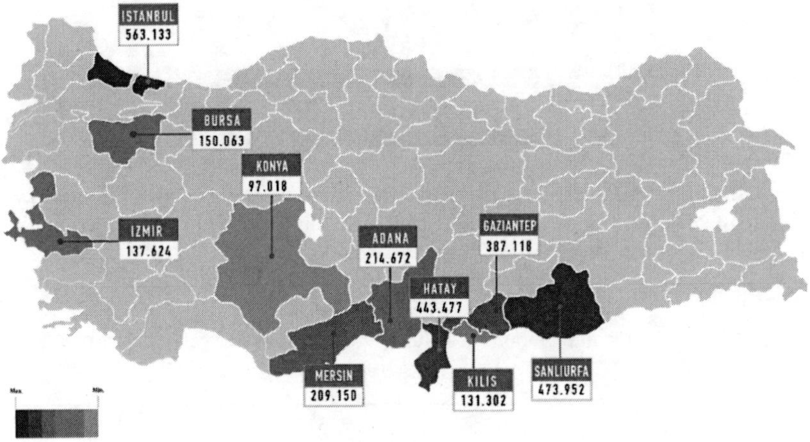

Fig. 2: Distribution of Syrian Refugees in the Scope of Temporary Protection by Top Ten Province by the date of 28.06.2018. Source: (Republic of Turkey Ministry of Interior Directorate General of Migration Management, 2018)

Tab. 1: Distribution of Syrian Refugees in the Scope of Temporary Protection. Source: (Republic of Turkey Ministry of Interior Directorate General of Migration Management, 2018)

Years	Distribution of Syrian Refugees in the Scope of Temporary Protection
2011	0
2012	14.237
2013	224.655
2014	1.519.286
2015	2.503.549
2016	2.834.441
2017	3.426.789
2018	3.562.523
by the date of 28.06.2018	

employment rates of natives in various skill groups are largely unaffected. Incumbent natives appear to be staying put considering the limited migration out of the region, but there is a significant decline in internal migration into regions hosting refugees. Nevertheless, the decline in internal in-migration is less than

Fig. 3: Sheltered and Unsheltered Syrian Refugees by Temporary Shelter Centers by the Date of 28.06.2018. Source: (Republic of Turkey Ministry of Interior Directorate General of Migration Management, 2018)

Tab. 2: Syria Joint Capital Companies Number (The Most Active 15 Sectors in 2017). Source: (TEPAV, 2018)

Sectors (Nace Rev. 2)	**number of companies**
wholesale trade	427
real estate activities	148
construction of buildings	124
retail trade	120
travel agency, tour operator reservation service and related activities	41
food and beverage services	34
manufacture of food commodities	31
wholesale and retail trade of motor land vehicles and motorcycles and repairing	31
activities of head offices; management consultancy activities	22
manufacture of wearing apparel	17
land transport and transport via pipelines	14
other services	14
Education	12
computer programming, consultancy and related activities	11
manufacture of leather and related products	10

a tenth of the refugee influx, implying that there is little evidence of refugees crowding out natives in local labor markets. Bahcekapili and Cetin (2015) examine economic impacts of the Syrian immigrant crisis since 2011 on Southeastern Anatolia region and the effects of migration on unemployment, prices, internal migration and regional foreign trade is evaluated. Esen and Binatlı (2017) investigate the impact of Syrian refugees on regional labor markets for Turkey. They use panel data 2004–2016 periods for 26 regions in Turkey and find Syrian refugees are found to increase unemployment and decrease informal and formal employment. Turkcan (2017) finds Syrian refugee population does not affect well-being of regions where refugee camps exist in Turkey and there are statistically significant relationships between Syrian refugee population, unemployment rate, inflation rate and residential prices. Salur and Erdogdu (2017) focus on the effects of Syrian migrants on the Turkish economy and they examine the impacts of Syrian immigrants on employment, investment and export activities. Ceritoglu, Yunculer, Torun & Tumen (2017) estimate the impact of Syrian refugees on the labor market outcomes of natives in Turkey. Their study is most closely related to the strand of the literature focusing on exogenous refugee inflows rather than voluntary immigration. Ozguler (2018) uses a literature review to examine the effects of mass migration by Syrian refugees on labor markets in Turkey and evaluates mass migrations have negative consequences for laborers in countries with structural problems such as high unemployment and poverty.

4 Conclusion

Not only social, political, economic, geographical etc. but also global developments cause people to migrate. Migrant ethnic groups carry out various economic activities and these activities are concentrated where they are located together for example Chinatowns and Greektowns in USA.

At this point, ethnic economies are emerging and can reveal social, political and economic events in a country's economy. Syrian refugees living in Turkey can cause also social, political, cultural and economic events via ethnic economies.

About 3.5 million Syrians in Turkey can cause social, political and cultural reflections based on social acceptability, social cohesion, cultural conflicts and diaspora. In addition, economic reflections such as capital inflows, development of commercial ties, housing problems, tax loss and unfair competition caused by shadow economic, negative perception caused by social aid for Syrian refugees can also bring out threats, opportunities, strengths and weaknesses for Turkey. If Policy makers in Turkey develop policies to achieve economic and fiscal advantages of ethnic economies, can be also solved social, political and cultural problems of Syrian refugees.

Bibliography

Akgunduz, Y. E., Berg, M. v., & Hassink, W. (2015). The Impact of Refugee Crises on Host Labor Markets: The Case of the Syrian Refugee Crisis in Turkey. Discussion Paper No. 8841. Bonn: IZA – Institute of Labor Economics.

Bahcekapili, C., & Cetin, B. (2015). The Impacts of Forced Migration on Regional Economies: The Case of Syrian Refugees in Turkey. International Business Research, 8(9), 1–15.

Ceritoglu, E., Yunculer, H. B., Torun, H., & Tumen, S. (2017). The Impact of Syrian Refugees on Natives' Labor Market Outcomes in Turkey: Evidence from a Quasi-Experimental Design. IZA Journal of Labor Policy, 6(5), 1–28.

Esen, O., & Binatli, A. O. (2017). The Impact of Syrian Refugees on the Turkish Economy: Regional Labour Market Effects. Social Sciences, 6(4), 1–12.

Lo, L. (2009). Ethnic Economies. R. Kitchin, & N. Thrift içinde, International Encyclopedia of Human Geography (s. 608–614). Elsevier.

Ozguler, V. C. (2018). Kitlesel Göçlerin Emek Piyasalarına Etkisi: Türkiye'deki Suriyeliler. Sosyal Siyaset Konferansları Dergisi(74), 77–102.

Republic of Turkey Ministry of Interior Directorate General of Migration Management. (2018, July 28). Migration Statistics Temporary Protection. 2018 tarihinde http://www.goc.gov.tr/icerik6/temporary-protection_915_1024_4748_icerik adresinden alındı

Salur, S., & Erdogdu, M. M. (2017). The Effects of the Syrian Refugees on the Turkish Economy. S. A. Ismail Siriner içinde, Current Debatres in Economics & Econometrics (Cilt 2, s. 305–332). IJOPEC Publication Limited.

TEPAV. (2018, January 24). The Economic Policy Research Foundation of Turkey. TEPAV Suriye Sermayeli Şirketler Bülteni: http://www.tepav.org.tr/tr/haberler/s/4295 adresinden alınmıştır

Turkcan, B. (2017). Suriye Krizi Sonrası Göçün Türkiye'de Bölge Ekonomilerine Etkisi. Adıyaman Üniversitesi Sosyal Bilimler Enstitüsü Dergisi, 9(26), 769–795.

Gizem Yildiz

Situation Assessment on Development Performance of TR90 Region

1 Introduction

Regional economy is a branch of economy that includes "area" dimension in order to analyze market forces. The branch performs this by including area concept to logic diagrams, codes and models that interpret price formation, demand, production capacity, output level, development, growth rates and income distribution based on unequal regional sources (Capello, 2009, p.10).

Globalization movements, which are rapidly taking place starting from 1960's, affect both national and regional dynamics. There have been some discussions regarding the definition, scope and importance of regional development in recent years. Concept of regional development is expressed both as a process and also as a product. Regional development is a product of an economic development that represents working conditions, life standards, wealth level and investments in the regions. Generally, improvements and developments in these factors are considered equivalent to economic development. Regional development as a process is expressed by industrial support, infrastructure, labor and labor markets (Stimson, Stough and Roberts, 2006, p.4). Regional development policies are implemented in countries in order to decrease the inequalities between regions.

Regional development policies continue to maintain their importance and validity since 1950's. While the countries are trying to adopt to the World and create opportunities along with the globalization movements, they also attach importance to the developments in regional level. Essentially, regional development policies necessitate state assistance that will maximize social benefits in the long-term. In case the investments planned within the framework of social benefit principle are not made, it is not possible to mention regional development (Takım, 2010, p.261).

Regional development policies are implemented not only in developing countries but also are one of the top priority policies implemented in developed countries. However, differences arise in implementation of these policies. Regional development policies in developed countries are rather implemented in regions deserving the priority. Thus, while convergence is provided between regions, the differences in income distribution within a region is also decreased. Whereas in developing countries, since income distribution injustice is quite high, preparation and implementation of regional development policies remain rather restricted (TUSIAD – Turkish Industrialists' and Businessmen's Association -, 2008, p.93).

Although Turkish economy made significant progress in many fields, interregional development level differences still continue to exist. In the long term,

Turkish economy's great growth performance remains incapable in decreasing interregional development differences. When the subject is evaluated with regards to socio-economic perspective (education, healthcare, environment, employment etc.) apart from income, inequalities continue to be experienced between regions. In spite of the fact that policies aimed at interregional imbalances are implemented in Turkey, desired objectives are not attained yet (DPT, 2003a, p.122).

"Nomenclature of Territorial Units for Statistics (NUTS)" was identified country-wide in order to gather statistical data on regional level in accordance with European Union Regional Statistics System, make socio-economic analysis of the regions with different criteria and determination of the framework of the regional policies.

In this classification, cities are defined as 3rd Level and neighboring cities, which show economic, social and geographical similarities were grouped as 1st Level and 2nd Level by taking regional development plans and population size into consideration and NUTS was generated in this manner with a hierarchical structure. Accordingly, there are 12 1st Level Statistical Territorial Units, there are 26 2nd Level Statistical Territorial Units and there are 81 3rd Level Statistical Territorial Units (Turkish Statistical Unit, 2014). A classification formed in this manner is quite important in terms of Turkey's European Union (EU) accession process. One of the regions fall within Level 2 is TR90 region. TR90 region contains 6 cities in total and these cities are Trabzon, Rize, Artvin, Giresun, Ordu and Gümüşhane.

When the cities fall within TR90 are considered, it may be observed that although they are located in the same geographical region, their social, demographical and economic standards differ from each other. Therefore, evaluation of social and economic condition of TR 90 both on the basis of region and on the basis of cities separately and determination of the areas that make progress and/or lose their superiorities reveal the objective of the study. In the study, primarily the social conditions will be presented with various indicators. Then, the situation will be assessed in consideration of economic indicators.

2 Social Case Analysis

2.1 Demographic Structure

Population and migration information with regards to TR90 region is presented on Tab. 1. The city that has the highest population among the cities in TR90 region is Trabzon. The city that has the lowest population is Artvin with 166.143. When gender is examined, whereas male population in Turkey is higher, it may be observed that female population is more in TR90 region. Net migration and net migration speed data is also presented on relevant Table. In accordance with this, Trabzon is a migration-receiving city. The city with the highest immigration rate is Ordu.

Tab. 1: Population and Migration Data, 2017. **Source:** Turkish Statistical Institute (2018a)

Cities	Total	Male	Female	Net Migration	Net Migration Speed (per thousand)
Trabzon	786.326	388.713	397.613	511	0.65
Rize	331.041	164.978	166.063	−1.749	−5.27
Artvin	166.143	83.524	82.619	−2.358	−14.09
Giresun	437.393	217.251	220.142	−9.146	−20.69
Ordu	742.341	371.061	371.280	−12.194	−16.20
Gümüşhane	170.173	86.097	84.076	−8.553	−49.03
TR90	2.633.417	1.311.624	1.321.793	−33.489	−12.64
TR	80.810.525	40.535.135	40.275.390	–	–

Tab. 2: Unemployment and Unemployment Ratio with Reference to Educational Status (%). **Source:** Turkish Statistical Institute (2018a)

Years	Unemployment Ratio		Higher Education Unemployment Rate	
	TR90	**TR**	**TR90**	**TR**
2005	5.5	10.6	9.7	10.0
2010	6.1	11.9	12.2	11.0
2016	4.5	10.9	6.6	12.0
2017	3.6	10.9	7.3	12.7

2.2 Labor and Employment

Regional results with reference to labor statistics are published by Turkish Statistical Institute annually. Unemployment data of TR90 and Turkey by years with reference to unemployment and educational status is presented on Tab. 2. The unemployment rate in TR90 region, which was 5.5 % in year 2005, this figure increased by years reached to 6.8 % in year 2013. Whereas unemployment rate in Turkey decreases as of year 2010, it is quite remarkable that regional unemployment rate showed a tendency to increase. It is also important to examine what kind of alteration unemployment showed with regards to educational status along with general unemployment rate. As an indicator of high quality education, unemployment rate of higher education in Turkey was 10 %. However, when TR90 region is examined, it may be observed that the higher education unemployment rate was above the average of Turkey since the year 2013. In years 2016-2017 higher education unemployment rate showed an increase both in Turkey and TR90 region.

Tab. 3: Employment and Labor Force Participation (%). **Source:** Turkish Statistical Institute (2018a)

Years	Employment Rate		Labor Force Participation Rate	
	TR90	TR	TR90	TR
2005	60.2	41.5	63.7	46.4
2010	54.6	43	58.2	48.8
2016	52	46.3	54.4	52
2017	52.2	47.1	54.1	52.8

Employment and level of participation to labor data both of Turkey and TR90 region is presented on Tab. 3. Whereas employment rate increased generally in Turkey, it may be observed that there is a decrease in TR90 region. The employment rates of Turkey and TR90 region were 60.2 % and 41.5 % respectively in year 2005, these rates were 52.2 % and 47.1 % in year 2017. In parallel with this, labor force participation rate that is expressed as the ratio of labor force to active population decreased in TR90 region in comparison with Turkey.

2.3 Healthcare

Information with regards to number of hospital beds that was used as an indicator of the healthcare infrastructure regarding TR90 region is presented on Tab. 4. In accordance with data of year 2016, Trabzon is the city with the highest total number of beds. Ordu, Giresun and Rize follow Trabzon. On the contrary, the city with the highest number of private beds is Ordu. There are no private hospitals in Artvin and Gümüşhane.

2.4 Education

It is possible to state that TR90 does not differ much from Turkey generally on the subject of education. As it may be observed on Tab. 5, schooling rate in elementary schools is below Turkey's average both for TR90 region and the related cities. With regards to schooling rate in junior high school education, TR90 region being above Turkey average demonstrates that the region is making progress in terms of education.

The rates of high school or equivalents and college or faculty graduate rates, which reflects more qualified education level, are presented on Tab. 6. When data regarding year 2016 is considered, it may be observed that the rate of graduates of high school and equivalents are higher than Turkey average. When it is considered on the basis of cities, this ratio is higher than TR90 in the cities excluding Rize and Artvin. Only Trabzon higher than Turkey average as of college and

Tab. 4: TR90 Number of Hospital Beds, 2016. **Source:** Turkish Statistical Institute (2018a)

City/Region/ Country	Number of Total Beds	Number Public of Beds	Number of University Beds	Number of Private Beds	Total Hospital Number of Beds Per Person
Trabzon	3.193	2.053	780	360	410
Rize	1.100	1.052	–	48	332
Artvin	346	346	–	–	206
Giresun	1.552	1.255	36	261	349
Ordu	2.053	1.548	–	505	274
Gümüşhane	311	311	–	–	181
TR90	8.555	6.565	816	1.174	323
TR	217.771	132.921	37.707	47.143	273

Tab. 5: Schooling Rates of Primary Education, Secondary High School and Secondary Education (%), 2016. **Source:** Turkish Statistical Institute (2018a)

City/Region/ Country	Schooling Rate in Elementary School	Schooling Rate in Junior High School	Schooling Rate in Secondary Education
Trabzon	90.76	97.5	95.46
Rize	90.05	98.02	87.66
Artvin	90.97	98.24	89.06
Giresun	86.19	91.26	100
Ordu	88.59	94.76	96.58
Gümüşhane	58.96	61.19	58.21
TR90	87.23	93.34	90.59
TR	91.16	95.68	82.54

faculty graduates. The city with the lowest rate of graduates of high school or equivalents is Rize.

2.5 Income Distribution

Gini Coefficient, which is the most common and best measurement of income distribution inequality, represents the inequality in a community and was derived from Lorenz curve that is a graphical tool (Morgan, 1961; Gaswirth, 1972; Clarke, 1995). Gini coefficient is a value between 0 and 1 and as it gets closer to 0 income

Tab. 6: Educational Status of Cities lerin (%), 2016. **Source:** Turkish Statistical Institute (2018a)

City/Region/Country	Ratio of High School Graduates or Equivalents	Ratio of College Graduates or Equivalents 1
Trabzon	26.85	15.57
Rize	20.7	11.23
Artvin	22.83	12.73
Giresun	25.18	13.72
Ordu	26.45	14.31
Gümüşhane	26.96	13.26
TR90	24.9	13.4
TR	22.97	14.94

distribution inequality decreases and as it gets closer to 1 income distribution inequality increases. Gini coefficient values of TR90 region and Turkey with regards to years 2014-2016 are presented on Graph 1. While Gini coefficient of Turkey in year 2014 was 0.391, it increased and was 0.404 in year 2016. Therefore, income distribution inequality in Turkey increased in Tukey. Likewise, Gini coefficient showed an increase from year 2014 to 2016 in TR90 region. It may also be observed that income distribution inequality increased in TR90 region.

3 Economic Conditions

3.1 Income (GDP)

TR90 region ranks among the regions that differ both on the basis of region and also on the basis of cities regarding development level. GDP per capita data with regards to year 2005 and year 2014 is presented on Tab. 7. As it may be observed on the Table, the cities with highest GDP per capita do not change by years. These cities are Trabzon, Rize and Artvin and they have a growth performance above TR90 region's average.

Along with the GDP per capita indicator, it is quite important how the income generated was distributed in accordance with ISIC Rev.2[1]. GDP data with current

1 International Standard Industrial Classification of All Economic Activities (ISIC) - It is the international reference classification of the economic activities. It provides a series of categories for production statistics based on these kind of activities. As of the admission of Rev 1, which is the original version of ISIC, in year 1948, ISIC was used by majority of the countries of the world or the national classifications derived from ISIC were improved. Thus, ISIC became an important tool in comparison of statistical data with regards to economic activities at an international level (UN, 2012).

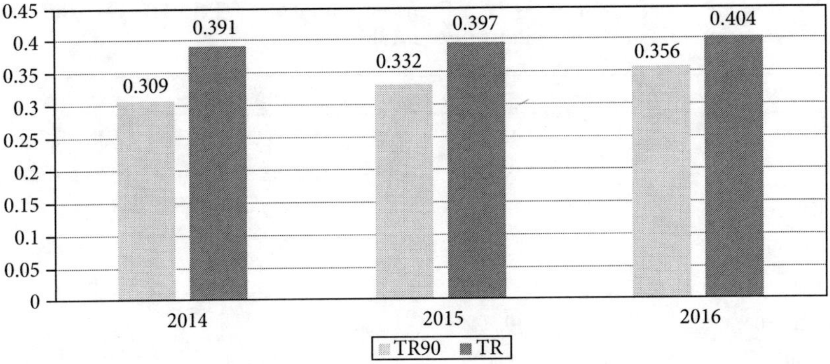

Graph 1: Gini Coefficient (2014–1016). **Source:** Turkish Statistical Institute (2018a)

Tab. 7: Per Capita GDP (2005–2014), (Dollars). **Source:** Turkish Statistical Institute (2018b)

City/Region/Country	2005	2014
Trabzon	5.678	10.093
Rize	5.547	10.210
Artvin	5.740	10.059
Giresun	4.484	6.844
Ordu	4.198	6.665
Gümüşhane	4.825	8.394
TR90	4.994	8.493
TR	7.304	12.112

prices with regards to economic activity branches of year 2014 is presented on Tab. 8. The sector that the highest GDP is obtained among the sectors is service sector. The city that has the highest income among service sector s Trabzon. It may be observed that there is an increase in TR90 region in GDP on the basis of sectors in parallel with Turkey.

3.2 Export

Generally, exportation on the basis of region is as important as exportation on the basis of Turkey. Whereas Russia was the country that TR90 region exported most in year 2010, Germany took her place in years 2015 and 2017. Italy's rank has not changed by years. When generally evaluated, although there is an increase from

Tab. 8: GDP with Regards to Activity Branches with Current Prices (2014), (Thousand TL). **Source:** Turkish Statistical Institute (2018b)

City/Region/Country	Agriculture	Industry	Services
Trabzon	1.130.703	3.874.534	9.880.539
Rize	1.063.882	2.061.728	3.371.512
Artvin	482.566	882.099	1.933.277
Giresun	523.574	1.216.284	3.919.148
Ordu	1.174.183	2.244.133	5.964.334
Gümüşhane	310.153	635.007	1.390.775
TR90	4.685.062	10.913.784	26.459.585
TR	134.724.745	576.440.635	1.097.024.575

Tab. 9: Five Countries with Most Exportation (Thousand Dollars). **Source:** Turkish Statistical Institute (2018b)

Country	2010	Rank	2015	Rank	2017	Rank
Germany	288.458	2	338.190	1	256.668	1
Fed. Russia	412.155	1	311.720	2	208.956	2
Italy	134.077	3	240.734	3	192.427	3
Georgia	126.608	4	139.234	5	128.645	4
France	125.859	5	180.817	4	122.988	5
Total	1.915.458		2.216.419		1.841.049	

year 2010 to year 2015, it may be observed that there is a decrease in exportation of TR90 region in year 2017 (Tab. 9).

Information with regards to 5 sectors with most exportation of TR90 region in year 2017 is presented on Tab. 10. Sectoral exportation data of Turkey regarding 2017 period and the shares of the region among Turkey's exportation are also presented on the relevant table. In accordance with ISIC Rev. 3, the sector that TR90 period has most exportation in year 2017 was agriculture and stockbreeding. Food products and beverage and metal ores follow this sector. Motor land vehicles and trailers is the sector that Turkey has most exportation among these sectors. Although the sector that the regions has the greatest share within Turkey's total exportation is manufacturing industry, exportation of TR90 regions in this sector remains low.

Alongside of total exportation data, exportation per capita is also quite important. Exportation per capita data of TR90 region and Turkey is presented

Tab. 10: Five Sectors with Most Exportation (Thousand Dollars). **Source:** Turkish Statistical Institute (2018b).

Sectors	TR90	Turkey	*TR90/ Turkey*[*]
Agriculture and Stockbreeding	917.972	5.260.798	17.5
Food products and beverages	541.920	10.678.292	5.1
Metal ores	151.331	1.379.738	10.9
Machines and equipment not classified elsewhere	35.015	12.883.393	0.3
Motor land vehicles and trailers	27.618	25.531.065	0.1
Total	1.841.049	156.994.293	1.2

Note: *[*] Calculated by the writer in accordance with Turkish Statistical Institute*

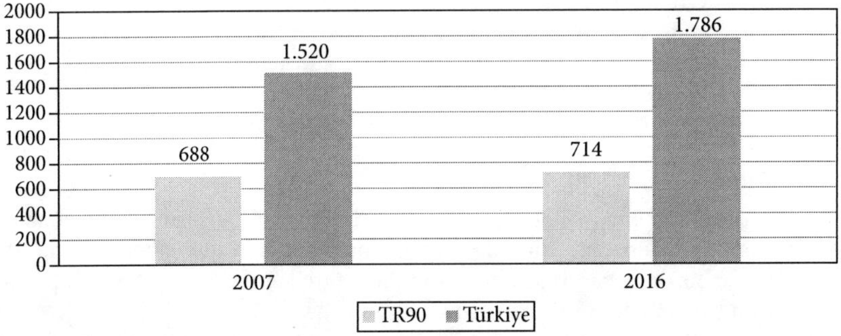

Graph 2: *TR90 and Turkey's Export Per Capita (2007-2016), (Dollars).* **Source:** Turkish Statistical Institute (2018b)

on Graph 2. Turkey's exportation per capita increased from 1.520 $ to 1.786 $ from year 2007 to year 2016. In parallel with this exportation per capita of TR90 region increased from 688$ to 714$ by years. However, TR90 region having lower increase rate than Turkey, demonstrates that the region has not made a qualified progress.

3.3 Importation

5 countries that TR90 region imports from the most are presented on Tab. 11. 5 countries that TR90 region has most importation are presented on Tab. 11. Russia is ranked as 1st and Germany is ranked as 2nd in the ranking regarding the countries with most importation by years. Whereas China was ranked as 3rd in year 2010,

Georgia took her place in year 2015. However, it may be observed that there is once more an increase in importation from China. While importation from Ukraine was 13 million Dollars in year 2010, in years 2015 and 2017 China and Georgia took her place as rank number 4. 5th country with most importation is USA in year 2017. When generally evaluated, it may be observed that there has been an increase in total importation of the region from year 2010 to years 2015 and 2017.

Five sectors with most exportation of TR90 region in years 2017 is presented on Tab. 12. When the share of the region's importation within Turkey's importation is examined, the sectors that have the greatest rates is pit coal, lignite and turbary sector. As for total importation, it may be observed that TR90 region's importation remains at a quite low level.

Development rankings of the cities in TR90 region with regards to years 2003 and 2011 are presented on Tab. 13. While Rize was ranked as 37th in year 2003, the city rose to rank 34th in year 2011. Although Gümüşhane made a significant progress by years, she still continued to remain behind other cities in the region. Nevertheless, Trabzon made an important progress and rose to 31st rank in year 2011 while she ranked as 38th in year 2003. Artvin and Giresun displayed a weak performance and were on the decline in the ranking from year 2003 to year 2011. While TR90 region was ranked as 19th among 26 sub-regions in year 2003, she rose to 17th place in year 2011.

4. Result

Regional development differences are one of the leading issues that concerns developing countries more than developed countries in a globalizing world. It is quite significant that economic policies implemented at the macro level to be integrated with the policies implemented at regional level.

Regional inequality problem was first discussed by western countries after the World War I for the first time. Although many economic policies were implemented in Turkey since Republic period until today, regional inequality problem still continue to be experienced. At this point, it is necessary to determine of strengths and weaknesses of each region and to implement policies regarding these problems.

When economic, social and spatial developments of the cities located within TR90 Region are evaluated, Trabzon is at the position of a most attention-grabbing city. Therefore, regional central position of Trabzon, which is one of the 12 regional growth centers (attraction centers) of Turkey within the scope of Ninth Development Plan (2007-2013) and related programs, shall be concentrated on. Within this context, it is quite important to take steps to contribute regional development particularly for Trabzon city. Thus, the projects that will be carried out at other cities will be supported and therefore an integrative effect will emerge (DOKAP, 2015: 20). Consequently:

When TR90 region is evaluated by taking all the existing social data into consideration;

- The city with highest total and female population is Trabzon. As a strong indicator of this, it may be claimed that her migration-receiving potential is high.

Tab. 11: Five Countries 5 Most Import (Thousand Dollars). **Source**: Turkish Statistical Institute (2018b)

Country	2010	Rank	Country	2015	Rank	Country	2017	Country
Fed. Russia	105.949	1	Fed. Russia	60.732	1	Fed. Russia	67.123	1
Germany	24.875	2	Germany	35.383	2	Germany	23.333	2
China	21.143	3	Georgia	32.061	3	China	19.275	3
Ukraine	12.970	4	China	13.354	4	Georgia	14.563	4
İtaly	10.435	5	India	8.548	5	USA	8.740	5
Total	249.409		**Total**	238.673		**Total**	199.352	

Tab. 12: 5 Sectors with Most Imports (2017), (Thousand Dollars). **Source:** Turkish Statistical Institute (2018b)

Sectors	TR90	Turkey	*TR90/ Turkey*[*]
Pit coal, lignite and turbary	54.678	3.923.819	1.4
Agriculture and stockbreeding	29.143	8.898.643	0.3
Machines and equipment not classified elsewhere	27.185	20.373.369	0.1
Food products and beverages	25.589	4.908.392	0.5
Non–metallic other minerals	7.359	1.817.014	0.4
Total	199.352	233.803.864	0.08

Not: *[*] Calculated by the writer in accordance with Turkish Statistical Institute.*

Tab. 13: Socio-Economic Development Level (2003–2011). **Source:** DPT (2003b), Study of Socio-Economic Development Ranking of Cities and Regions; Ministry of Development (2011), SEGE-2011

Cities	Development Ranking Among 81 Cities	
	2003	**2011**
Trabzon	38	31
Rize	37	34
Artvin	43	44
Giresun	50	52
Ordu	62	61
Gümüşhane	71	62
TR90	19	17

- Unemployment ratio in TR90 region decreases by years. On the other hand, employment rate and labor force participation rate decreases. In accordance with this data, it is possible express that old age population took place of the young population, whose ages are 15 and above.
- Education and healthcare are the most important indicators of human capital. It is observed that all the cities located within TR90 region have public hospitals, however they remain weak with regards to university hospitals. As for field of education, apart from 14-year compulsory education, number of higher education graduates may be considered as a distinguishing data. In this regard, the only city that has the highest number of higher education graduates and that is above Turkey's average is Trabzon and Rize is the city with the lowest number of higher education graduates. The points that attention shall be paid are mobile teaching system and therefore migration from rural to urban in the region (DOKAP, 2015).
- In accordance with Gini coefficient, which is an important indicator in providing the income equality within regional development, TR90 region has a value below Turkey average. However, as it is in Turkey, income distribution inequality also increases by years in TR90 region. In this case, it may be mentioned that the reflections of the effects of the policies that will be implemented at macro level will also be seen on the regional level.

When TR90 region is evaluated in consideration with existing economic data;

- Income per capita in TR90 region and in Turkey is doubled in the 10-year period. In accordance with economic activity branches, most income was generated in service sector.
- 5 countries that TR90 has the most exportation with have not changed by years. Nevertheless, exportation of TR90 is highly based on agriculture and stockbreeding. Eventually, it may be claimed that the exportation pattern of the region has not changed and has not showed an alteration in quality. Implementing product diversification instead of increasing exportation by means of increasing the amount of the same products may be implemented as a policy to increase competitive power of the region with other regions.
- Two countries with most importation has not changed by years. These countries are Federal Russia and Germany respective. Having counter trade relationships with these countries is quite a significant point. The sector that has the highest share in total importation is pit coal, ignite and turbary. A significant reason for the region's importation to be low is that the region has a pattern mainly based on agriculture and therefore, industry sector remains weak.

Bibliography

Capello, R. (2009). "Regional Growth and Local Development Theories: Conceptual Evolution over Fifty Years of Regional Science", Géographie, économie, société 2009/1 (Vol. 11), p. 9–21.

Clarke, G. R. (1995). More Evidence On Income Distribution And Growth, Journal of development Economics, 47(2), 403–427.

DOKAP (2015). TR90 Doğu Karadeniz Kalkınma Planı (2014-2023), İber Matbaası, Trabzon.

DPT (2003a). "Ön Ulusal Kalkınma Planı (2004-2006)", T.C. Başbakanlık Devlet Planlama Teşkilatı Müsteşarlığı, Bölgesel Gelişme ve Yapısal Uyum Genel Müdürlüğü, 2003, Ankara, (http://ekutup.dpt.gov.tr/plan/o-ukp.pdf).

DPT (2003b). İllerin ve Bölgelerin Sosyo-ekonomik Gelişmişlik Sıralaması Araştırması, Yayın No DPT 2671.

Gastwirth, J. L. (1972). The Estimation of the Lorenz Curve and Gini Index, The Review of Economics and Statistics, 54(3), 306–316.

Kalkınma Bakanlığı (2011). İllerin ve Bölgelerin Sosyo-Ekonomik Gelişmişlik Sıralaması Araştırması (SEGE-2011).

Morgan, J. (1962). The Anatomy of Income Distribution, The Review of Economics and Statistics, 44(3), 270–283.

Stimson, R. J., Stough, R. R., & Roberts, B. H. (2006). Regional Economic Development: Analysis and Planning Strategy. Second Edition, Springer Science & Business Media.

Takım, A. (2010). Türkiye'de Bölgesel Kalkınma Planlarının İktisat Politikalarının Performansına Etkisi: Zonguldak- Bartın ve Karabük Örneği, e-Journal of New World Sciences Academy, 5(3), pp.259–275.

TÜİK (2014). Gayri Safi Katma Değer Bölgesel Sonuçlar (2004-2011), https://biruni.tuik.gov.tr/yayin/views/visitorPages/index.zul, Erişim Tarihi (10.06.2018).

TÜİK (2018a). https://biruni.tuik.gov.tr/bolgeselistatistik., Erişim Tarihi (20.06.2018).

TÜİK (2018b). https://biruni.tuik.gov.tr/disticaretapp/disticaret.zul?param1=9&param2=2&sitcrev=0&isicrev=3&sayac=5811. Erişim Tarihi (18.06.2018).

TÜSİAD (2018). Türkiye'de Bölgesel Farklar ve Politikalar, Yayın No. TÜSİAD-T/2008-09/471.

UN (2012). International Standard Industrial Classification of All Economic Activities (ISIC) Revision 3.1, United Nations Publication, New York, ISBN 92-1-161456-2.

Muhammed Tıraşoğlu

Investigating the Relationship between Inflation and Economic Growth in the MIST Countries: Evidence from Combined Cointegration Tests

1 Introduction

One of the most important issues of economic life is undoubtedly economic growth. Economic growth can be defined as an increase in the capacity of goods and services produced in a country. The relationship between economic growth and macroeconomic variables has drawn the interest of many researchers and policy makers. One of the topics drawing attention is the relationship between economic growth and inflation. The investigation of this relationship has been continuing for about seven decades. Inflation is defined as a sustained increase of the general level of prices. Inflation is not desirable situation as it means that the price stability in a country is deteriorating and it has got numerous negative effects on the economy of the country. Especially the high inflation experienced at the end of World War II has increased the interest in examining the relationship between inflation and economic growth.

Various central banks have taken important steps to ensure price stability in the given global economic structure. Monetary policy whether expressed in terms of interest rates or growth of monetary aggregates has been increasingly geared toward the achievement of low and stable inflation. Monetary policy makers see price stability as an important goal as they think inflation is costly. Some of these costs are related to the average inflation rate while others are related to inflation variability and uncertainty. With respect to this issue, the general idea is that business and households are thought to perform poorly when inflation is high and unpredictable (Barro, 2013: 85). In a country where price stability is achieved, there will be no uncertainty linked to high inflation and significant success will be achieved in economic growth.

When the current economic literature is examined, it is widely accepted that inflation has a negative impact on economic growth. However, this negative impact was not detected in the data of 1950s and 1960s. The view accepted on the basis of the data pertaining to these years was that there was no significant relationship between inflation and economic growth. Many studies concluded that this impact was insignificant until 1970s. The view changed after severe and persistent periods of inflation were experienced in many countries especially in the 1970s and 1980s. It has been confirmed many times that inflation had a negative impact on economic growth, as more data was available after those years. Inflation, which has statistically significant impact on economic growth even if it is low, has been identified as one of the variables affecting growth rate (Sarel, 1996: 199-200).

While the relationship between inflation and economic growth is important for all countries, it is much more important for developing countries. In developed countries, price stability has been achieved to a significant extent and inflation has fallen below a certain level. However, this is often not the case in developing countries because inflation is one of the most important problems of many developing countries. Although high growth rates have been achieved in developing countries, inflation may still be at high levels.

The study will explore the relationship between inflation and economic growth for the MIST countries (Mexico, Indonesia, South Korea and Turkey). Coined by Jim O'Neill from the Goldman Sachs, MIST is an acronym which refers to the large and surprisingly growing economies. The MIST countries are a group of four countries with significant position among the developing countries. In addition, the MIST countries, which are also among the G20 countries, are an important group of countries in terms of crowded population density, large markets, high productivity and high economic growth.

The study first focuses on the relationship between inflation and economic growth. In the second part, the empirical studies between inflation and economic growth in the literature are explained. The data and econometric methods to be used in the empirical application are introduced in the third part of the study. The fourth part focuses on the application results of the relationship between inflation and economic growth for the MIST countries. The final part of the study focuses on the results obtained and their evaluation.

2 Literature

In the literature, there are important studies that show the relationship between inflation and economic growth. Some of these studies are given in chronological order: Logue and Sweeney (1981), Fischer (1983), Jung and Marshall (1986), De Gregorio (1992), Barro (1995), Sarel (1996), Mallik and Chowdhury (2001), Gylfason and Herbertsson (2001), Valdovinos (2003), Burdekin et al. (2004), Bick (2010), Barro (2013), Manamperi (2014) and Thanh (2015).

The empirical studies that examine the relationship between inflation and economic growth are important for policy makers and researchers. There is no study that examines the relationship between inflation and economic growth specifically in the MIST countries. Some of the important empirical studies exploring this relationship for different countries and/or country groups using various econometric methods will be discussed. Mallik and Chowdhury (2001) is one of the first empirical studies to examine the relationship between inflation and economic growth. Mallik and Chowdhury (2001) investigated this relationship for the South Asian countries (Bangladesh, India, Pakistan and Sri Lanka). As a result of the analyses made using the Johansen cointegration and error correction model, it was found that there was a long-term relationship between inflation and economic growth.

For these countries, continent inflation is helpful for growth, but faster economic growth feeds back into inflation. Valdovinos (2003) studied the long-term relationship between inflation and economic growth for eight Latin American countries. Valdovinos (2003) carried out the analyzes using the Baxter and King filter based on the data for the period 1970–2000. It was concluded that these two variables were found to be negatively related in the long term.

Pollin and Zhu (2005) examined the relationship between inflation and economic growth using the data for the period 1961-2000 for 80 countries. In the empirical study, the analysis was conducted in four groups: all countries, OECD countries, middle-income countries and low-income countries. The findings obtained using the panel regression method are as follows: (i) no clear pattern emerges at all with either the inflation coefficient or their estimated turning point in the OECD countries, (ii) there is no justification for inflation targeting policies as they are currently being practiced throughout the middle and low-income countries, namely maintaining inflation within a 3–5 percent band. In another study by Bick (2010), the relationship between inflation and economic growth for 40 developing countries was examined. The generalized panel threshold model was used in the analysis for the period 1960–2004. The panel data analysis showed that low inflation rates had a positive impact on economic growth.

Bittencourt (2012) investigated the relationship between inflation and economic growth for four Latin American countries. The panel data analysis was used to analyze the annual data for the period 19702007. The findings confirm the evidence that inflation has a detrimental impact on economic growth in these four countries. It was also found that high inflation leads to excessive costs. Manamperi (2014) studied the relationship between inflation and economic growth in the BRICS (Brazil, Russia, India, China, South Africa) countries for the period 1980–2012. The Johansen cointegration test, the ARDL bounds test and the Granger causality test were used in the analyzes. According to the findings, long and short-term relationship between inflation and economic growth was found in India. No significant relationship was identified in the other four countries. In a recent study, Thanh (2015) examined the relationship between inflation and economic growth for ASEAN-5 countries. The panel used the smooth transition regression model and the data for the period 1980-2011 were taken into account. Thanh (2015) reached the conclusion that the central banks in these countries could increase economic growth by lowering inflation when they are above or around the forecasted thresholds. The threshold inflation level could be considered, therefore, as an inflation targeting indicator.

3 Data and Econometric Methodology

In this study analyzing the relationship between inflation and economic growth in the MIST countries, GDP represents the Gross Domestic Product and CPI represents inflation. The data used for empirical analysis were obtained from the World Bank and cover the annual data for the period 1967–2016. The natural logarithm of the variables was used and was expressed as LGDP and LCPI.

In the study, the integration degrees of the variables will be determined by using unit root tests. Then the long-term relationship between the variables will be examined using the Bayer and Hanck (2013) test. In addition, the causality relation between the variables for the relevant countries will be investigated using the Granger Causality test.

In the time series literature, the first test to investigate the existence of unit root was developed by Dickey and Fuller (1979) (DF). The Dickey and Fuller (1979) test, applied to autoregressive processes from the first order, was developed for high-level autoregressive processes and was named as the Generalized Dickey and Fuller (ADF) (1981) test. Phillips and Perron (1988) developed a new nonparametric test by developing the DF and ADF unit root tests. The DF and ADF unit root tests assume that the error terms are independent of each other and have a constant variance. Phillips and Perron (PP) (1988) developed this hypothesis further in their study and stated that there could be autocorrelation between error terms.

Economic time series can exhibit non-stationary characteristics. As non-stationary time series contain unit root, spurious regression is a problem encountered in regression models established using these variables (Hepsağ, 2009: 176). In the time series analysis, difference is taken to ensure stationarity in the series that are not stationary. Taking the difference causes loss of long-term knowledge. The concept of cointegration was therefore introduced into the literature. Cointegration is defined as the stationary composition of the non-stationary series (Güriş, 2018: 362-363).

Cointegration testing is a standard tool in applied economics. Various cointegration tests have been suggested, most of which are implemented in econometric software packages. The most renowned and widely used one of these tests is of course the Engle and Granger (1987) and the Johansen (1987) cointegration tests. One of the most current tests of the time series analysis is the combined cointegration test introduced into the literature by Bayer and Hanck (2013). This test consists of a combination of commonly used cointegration tests in the time series literature.

Bayer and Hanck (2013) used the Fisher (1932) type test statistic in the study. This test statistic can be expressed as follows.

$$\tilde{\chi}_I^2 := -2\sum_{i \in I} \ln(p_i) \tag{1}$$

Bayer and Hanck (2013) proposed new tests combining four cointegration tests the consider Fisher's test statistic. These cointegration tests are expressed as EG = Engle and Granger (1987), JOH = Johansen (1988), BO = Boswijk (1994) and BDM = Banerjee et al. (1998). Bayer and Hanck (2013) proposed to combine the computed significance level (p-values) of the individual cointegration test with the following Fisher's (1932) formulas;

$$EG - JOH = -2\left[\ln(p_{EG}) + \ln(p_{JOH})\right] \tag{2}$$

$$EG - JOH - BO - BDM = -2\left[\ln(p_{EG}) + \ln(p_{JOH}) + \ln(p_{BO}) + \ln(p_{BDM})\right] \tag{3}$$

In these formulates, $p_{EG}, p_{JOH}, p_{BO}, p_{BDM}$ are the p-values of various individual cointegration tests. The null and alternative hypotheses of this test are as follows:

$$\begin{aligned} &H_0: \text{There is no cointegration relationship between variables.} \\ &H_1: \text{There is a cointegration relationship between variables.} \end{aligned} \tag{4}$$

An insight emerging from applying the Bayer and Hanck (2013) combined cointegration test is that it provides informed econometric knowledge to the researcher on the cointegrating relationship between the series by eliminating undue multiple testing procedures which is a common problem associated with other traditional cointegration techniques. Efficient and conclusive results are also guaranteed from employing the Bayer and Hanck (2013) combined cointegration technique which is not found in other traditional cointegration approaches available in the field of econometrics (Shahbaz et al., 2016; 58). Bayer and Hanck (2013) obtained the tabulated critical values determined according to the number of variables for these tests.

After investigating the long-term relationship between inflation and economic growth, the causality relationship between variables will be examined using the Granger (1969) causality test in this study. If the Granger causality explains the changes in the past values of an independent and dependent variable together with the changes in the dependent variable, it is explained as this independent variable is the Granger cause for the relevant dependent variable.

While specifying and estimating the Granger type models, it is necessary to first examine the stationary properties because Engel and Granger (1987) point out that though two variables are non-stationary and cointegrated, the standard Granger causality test results will be invalid. Additionally, the standard Granger causality test should be accepted if these two variables are not cointegrated (Kiran and Guris, 2009: 168). The study investigates the causality relationship between variables according to the cointegration test results.

4 Empirical Results

The relationship between inflation and economic growth for the MIST countries is investigated in the study. In this context, the integration degree of the series were determined first and then the relationship between variables was investigated with the cointegration and causality analyses. Tab. 1 shows the unit root test results for the logarithmic GDP and CPI variables. The ADF and PP unit root tests are given for intercept and intercept and trend structure.

According to the results in Tab. 1, the ADF unit root test results for inflation and economic growth variables in all of the countries that constitute the MIST countries show that the unit root null hypothesis cannot be rejected for both

Tab. 1: ADF and PP Unit Root Test Results

Countries	Variables	ADF				PP	
		k	Intercept	k	Int + Trend	Intercept	Int + Trend
Indonesia	LGDP	0	−2.2264	1	−2.0776	−2.0180	−2.2275
	LCPI	6	−1.2532	4	−2.2636	−2.4398	−1.3050
	ΔLGDP	0	−5.0646***	0	−5.1838***	−5.0647***	−5.2118***
	ΔLCPI	0	−5.1911***	0	−5.2034***	−6.0842***	−6.0099***
Mexico	LGDP	0	−2.1634	1	−2.1988	−1.6914	−2.4672
	LCPI	1	−1.7191	1	−1.3196	−1.2281	−0.5492
	ΔLGDP	0	−5.3030***	0	−5.6739***	−5.3030***	−5.6438***
	ΔLCPI	0	−6.7176***	0	−6.7722***	−6.7251***	−7.7587***
South Korea	LGDP	5	−0.5087	0	−0.0783	−1.9792	−0.1684
	LCPI	2	−1.7716	2	−1.5736	−1.9278	−1.7519
	ΔLGDP	0	−4.5023***	0	−6.6961***	−4.4741***	−6.8053***
	ΔLCPI	1	−3.7716***	1	−4.3968***	−2.6351*	−3.5504**
Turkey	LGDP	0	−0.1364	0	−2.7221	−0.0431	−2.8825
	LCPI	1	−1.4221	1	−1.8021	−0.4006	−1.5166
	ΔLGDP	0	−6.7238***	0	−6.6668***	−6.7211***	−6.6625***
	ΔLCPI	0	−7.6440***	0	−7.8636***	−7.6888***	−8.5130***

Note: Δ in the table shows the first difference, k means the appropriate lag length. *, ** and *** indicate that the unit root null hypothesis is rejected for 10 %, 5 % and 1 %, respectively.

Tab. 2: Bayer and Hanck (2013) Cointegration Test Results

Countries	Lag Order	EG-JOH	EG-JOH-BO-BDM	Cointegration
Indonesia	2	3.9883	8.3862	No
Mexico	2	13.5516**	28.5057**	Yes
South Korea	2	8.9772*	26.4312**	Yes
Turkey	2	2.0381	2.1901	No

Note: *, ** and *** denote statistical significance at the 10 %, 5 % and 1 %, respectively. Lag order is based on minimum value of AIC. The critical values for the EG-JOH test for 10 %, 5 % and 1 % are 8.678, 11.229 and 17.304, respectively. The critical values for the EG-JOH-BO-BDM test for 10 %, 5 % and 1 % are 16.964, 21.931 and 33.969, respectively.

intercept and intercept and trend structure. Similarly, it was concluded that these two variables are not stationary according to the PP unit root test. By taking the first differences of the variables of inflation and growth, it was found that these two variables are stationary according to the unit root test. Therefore, the results show that these two variables are stationarity at first degree.

The Bayer and Hanck (2013) cointegration test was used to investigate the long-term relationship between inflation and economic growth in the MIST countries. The Bayer and Hanck (2013) test suggests two test statistics which are EG-JOH and EG-JOH-BO-BDM. EG-JOH is the combination of two cointegration tests developed by Engle and Granger (1987) and Johansen (1988). EG-JOH-BO-BDM is the combination of four cointegration tests developed by Engle and Granger (1987), Johansen (1988), Boswijk (1994) and Banerjee et al. (1998).

According to the Bayer and Hanck (2013) cointegration test in Tab. 2, the null hypothesis in Indonesia and Turkey that there is no cointegration according to the EG-JOH and EG-JOH-BO-BDM test statistics cannot be rejected. Therefore, a long-term relationship between inflation and economic growth was not detected in these countries. However, it was concluded for Mexico and South Korea that there was a long-term relationship between inflation and economic growth according to both test statistics.

The direction of causality between inflation and economic growth in the MIST countries was investigated using the Granger causality test and the results are summarized in Tab. 3. According to the results obtained, there was no causality relationship between two variables in Indonesia. It was concluded for Mexico that there was a causality from economic growth to inflation. It was also found that there was a causality from inflation to economic growth in South Korea and Turkey.

5 Conclusion

Economic growth is one of the most important issues of economic life. The relationship between economic growth and macroeconomic variables has been the

Tab. 3: Granger Causality Test Results

Countries	Null Hypothesis	Test Stat.	Prob.
Indonesia	Inflation does not Granger cause Growth	0.2452	0.6204
	Growth does not Granger cause Inflation	0.0411	0.8394
Mexico	Inflation does not Granger cause Growth	0.0714	0.7892
	Growth does not Granger cause Inflation	4.1066**	0.0427
South Korea	Inflation does not Granger cause Growth	6.3632**	0.0117
	Growth does not Granger cause Inflation	0.6733	0.4119
Turkey	Inflation does not Granger cause Growth	5.8680**	0.0171
	Growth does not Granger cause Inflation	2.0226	0.1550

Note: *, ** and *** denote statistical significance at the 10 %, 5 % and 1 %, respectively.

subject of study of many researchers. One of these variables related to economic growth is inflation. Although it is widely accepted that inflation has an adverse impact on economic growth, findings from studies may differ. While the relationship between inflation and economic growth is important for all countries, it is crucial for developing countries.

This study investigates the relationship between inflation and economic growth for the MIST countries (Mexico, Indonesia, South Korea and Turkey), which have a significant place among developing countries. In the study, the series containing the unit root were first examined using the ADF and PP tests. The findings show that the variables are stationary at the first order. Then the long-term relationship between inflation and economic growth was explored using the cointegration test of Bayer and Hanck (2013), which is one of the current topics of the time series literature. Test results show that there is a long-term relationship between inflation and economic growth for Mexico and South Korea. No cointegration relationship was found for Indonesia and Turkey. Finally, the causality relationship between the variables is examined using the Granger (1969) causality analysis. While there was no causality relationship between the two variables in Indonesia, it was concluded that there was a causality from economic growth to inflation in Mexico. In South Korea and Turkey, the causality is from inflation to economic growth. According to these findings, it could be concluded that it is important to maintain price stability especially in Mexico and South Korea to attain the targets related to economic growth.

Bibliography

Banarjee, A., Dolado, J.J & Mestre, R. (1998). Error-correction mechanism tests for cointegration in a single-equation framework. *Journal of Time Series Analysis*, 19(3), 267-283..

Barro, R. J. (1995). Inflation and economic growth. *NBER Working Paper Series*, No: 5326, 1–34.

Barro. R. J. (2013). Inflation and economic growth. *Annals of Economics and Finance*, 14(1), 85–109.

Bayer, C. & Hanck, C. (2013). Combining non-cointegration tests. *Journal of Time Series Analysis*, 34, 83–95.

Bick, A. (2010). Threshold effects of inflation on economic growth in developing countries. *Economic Letters*, 108, 126–129.

Bittencourt, M. (2012). Inflation and economic growth in Latin America: Some panel time-series evidence. *Economic Modelling*, 29, 333–340.

Boswijk, H. P. (1994). Testing for an unstable root in conditional and unconditional error correction models. *Journal of Econometrics*, 63, 37–60.

Burdekin, R. C. K., et al. (2004). When does inflation hurt economic growth? Different nonlinearities for different economies. *Journal of Macroeconomics*, 26, 519–532.

De Gregorio, J. (1992). The effects of inflation on economic growth: lessons from Latin America. *European Economic Review*, 36(2–3), 417–425.

Dickey, D. & Fuller W. (1979). Distribution of the estimators for autoregressive time series with a unit root, *Journal of the American Statistical Association*, 74, 427–431.

Dickey, D. & Fuller W. (1981). Likelihood ratio statistics for autoregressive time series with a unit root, *Econometrica*, 49(4), 1057–1072.

Engle, R.F. & Granger, C.W. (1987). Co-integration and error correction: representation, estimation, and testing. *Econometrica*, 55(2), 251–276.

Fischer, S. (1983). Inflation and Growth. *NBER Working Paper Series*, No: 1235, 1–18.

Granger, C. W. J. (1969). Investigating causal relations by econometric models and cross-spectral methods. *Econometrica*, 37(3), 424–438.

Gylfason, T. & Herbertsson, T. T. (2001). Does inflation matter for growth? Japan and World Economy, 13(4), 405–428.

Güriş, B. (2018). Yapısal kırılmalı panel birim kök testleri ve eşbütünleşme. In S. Güriş (Ed.), Uygulamalı panel veri ekonometrisi (pp. 349–370). Der Yayınları, İstanbul.

Hepsağ, A. (2009). Türkiye'de enflasyon ile işsizlik arasındaki ilişkinin analizi: Sınır testi yaklaşımı. *İktisat Fakültesi Mecmuası*, 59(1), 169–190.

Johansen, S. (1988). Statistical analysis of cointegration vectors. *Journal of Economic Dynamics and Control*, 12, 231–254.

Jung, W. S., & Marshall, P. J. (1986). Inflation and economic growth: some international evidence on structuralist and distortionist positions: note. *Journal of Money, Credit and Banking*, 18(2), 227–232.

Kiran, B. & Guris, B. (2009). Relationship between electricity consumption and GDP in Turkey. *Problems and Perspectives in Management*, 7(1), 166–171.

Logue, D. E., & Sweeney, R. J. (1981). Inflation and real growth: Some empirical results: Note. *Journal of Money, Credit and Banking*, *13*(4), 497–501.

Mallik, G. & Chowdhury, A. (2001). Inflation and economic growth: evidence from four South Asian countries. *Asia-Pasific Development Journal*, 8(1), 123–135.

Manamperi, N. (2014). The short and long-run dynamics between inflation and economic growth in BRICS. *Applied Economics Letters*, 21(2), 140–145.

Phillips, P. C.B. & Perron, P. (1988). Testing for a unit root in the time series regression. *Biometrika*, 75(2), 335–346.

Pollin, R. & Zhu, A. (2005). Inflation and economic growth: A cross-country non-linear analysis. *Political Economy Research Institute, Working Paper Series*, No: 109, 1–21.

Sarel, M. (1996). Nonlinear effects of inflation on economic growth. IMF Staff Papers, 43(1), 199–215.

Shahbaz, M., Mallick, H., Mahalik, M. K. & Sadorsky, P. (2016). The role of globalization on the recent evoluation of energy demand in India: Implications for sustainable development. *Energy Economics*, 55, 52–68.

Thanh, S. D. (2015). Threshold effects of inflation on growth in the ASEAN-5 countries: A panel smooth transition regression approach. *Journal of Economics, Finance and Administrative Science*, 20, 41–48.

Valdovinos, C. G. F. (2003). Inflation and economic growth in the long run. *Economics Lettres*, 80, 167–173.

Yavuz Odabaşi

A Theoretical Approach to the Effect of Exchange Rate Volatility on Exports: Example of Turkey[1]

1 Introduction

Following the collapse of the Bretton Woods system, foreign trade between countries has increased significantly with the release of exchange rates. As a result, the interaction between exchange rates has increased. The changes that occur in exchange rates are of great importance both in terms of economic stability and their effects on economic activities, particularly trade.

The movements in exchange rates have also set the stage for uncertainty and risk environment to develop on many of the economic indicators, from financial markets, foreign direct investments, consumption-production to foreign trade. The uncertainty in exchange rates has led to a reduction especially in the foreign trade level of the countries. Because producers who do not favor the risk have started to avoid foreign trade because of the fluctuations in exchange rates. Accordingly, the foreign trade volume of the countries has started to decrease. Negative effects of uncertain and risky environment arising from foreign exchange rates are the primary problems that countries inevitably will face, especially in foreign trade.

The main source of exchange rate risk and uncertainty is the volatility in exchange rates. Therefore, measuring exchange rate volatility and examining its effects on the economy has taken an important place in the literature. Measurement of the volatility of exchange rate and its effects of on foreign trade in the study are addressed in the context of literature studies.

2 Exchange Rate Volatility

Volatility literally means; "frequent and wide-ranging tendency to change", "instability" and "sudden changes". In addition to these, volatility is used as synonyms for the words uncertainty, risk, fragility, sensitivity and volatility are used synonymously. Basically, volatility means variability and uncertainty. Variability refers to all movements, and uncertainty refers to unknown movements (Çiçek, 2010:2).

After the Bretton Woods system, the transition to a floating exchange rate system of the countries that have an important place in world trade has started a new era for the global economy. With the introduction of the floating

1 This study is derived from the author's PhD dissertation titled "Effect of Exchange Rate Volatility on Export: An Application to Turkey" which was completed in 2011.

exchange rate system, a new debate has emerged in the economic circles. While some economists accept this adaptation, some economists have thought that switching to a floating exchange rate system would have a negative effect on world trade. According to economists who do not want to switch to free floating exchange rate system, the increase in volatility due to fluctuating exchange rates will reduce the output of exporters who do not favor the risk. When considered in this context, the exchange rate volatility can be interpreted as the risk arising from unexpected fluctuations in the exchange rate (McKenzie, 1999:71).

2.1 Measuring the Exchange Rate Volatility

The uncertainty that exchange rate volatility brings to the market and the resulting risk environment are of great importance to almost all sectors. Measuring exchange rate volatility has become increasingly significant as it has a major impact on the economy. Sengupta (2002) emphasized that exchange rate volatility is important because of two main reasons. The first is that national governments are increasingly feeling the effects of volatility in their monetary policy. These effects are particularly vital for economies implementing export-based growth strategies. The second reason is that with the influence of globalization, investors are increasingly involved in international portfolios and the asset market approach has become the dominant model for such investors.

Sudden changes in the economy will increase volatility; therefore, uncertainty and risk environment. In order to be protected from this growing uncertainty and risk environment, studies for the prediction of the potential negativities in the market have gathered speed. This has been the foundation of measuring the volatility.

Studies of the up and down movements in the financial markets and the magnitude of these movements have led to the development of many techniques. Previous studies have assumed that variance, a measure of volatility, is constant over a certain period. However, recent empirical studies using high frequency data have shown that the variance in the exchange rate series is not constant. Therefore; traditional time series models based on the constant variance assumption have been insufficient to reveal the relationship between variables. Thus, new modeling techniques have been developed that use the changing variance structure (Güloğlu and Akman, 2007:45). This is due to certain characteristics of financial data. These characteristics are (Aydın, 2004: 15):

- Leptokurtosis: The distributions of the returns of the financial assets show a fat tail and high peak in the mean. In other words, as the number of observations do not diminish along to the sides, but are concentrated around a value.
- **Volatility Clustering**: Volatility in financial markets generally follow each other; in other words, they form in clusters. It is possible to see both high and low values within a period. In general, higher values follow higher values while lower values follow lower values.

- **Leverage Effect**: The volatility effect of a decline in value prices is stronger than the same amount of increase.

The following volatility models are used to overcome the shortcomings of mentioned characteristics (Brooks, 2008):

- The historical volatility model

Implied volatility models

- Exponentially weighted moving average models
- Autoregressive volatility models
- Autoregressive conditional heteroskedasticity variance models (ARCH)
- Generalized autoregressive conditional heteroskedasticity variance models (GARCH)

3 Exchange Rate Volatility and Foreign Trade Relationship

Along with the tendency to globalization that began in the mid-1980s and accelerated in the 1990s, a more fragile economic structure emerged, with countries being more mutually connected and more easily affected by developments in other countries. In this new economic structure, the effects of the exchange rate volatility due to floating exchange rates on the volume of international trade have begun to be considered as a new research topic both in the theoretical and empirical area. The factors such as the inflation rate, the interest rate and the balance of payments become more variable, the capital being more active in the international arena along with the globalization, technological developments, speculations and so on contributed to the exchange rate volatility (Öztürk and Acaravcı, 2002–2003: 197–198). The effect of exchange rate volatility on trade has been controversial in the literature as a result of both empirical and theoretical studies. Some studies have shown that exchange rate volatility affects trading positively, while others have provided evidences for negative effect. In some studies; it has also been argued that exchange rate volatility is not a significant influence on trade. In general, these differences in theoretical models arose from assumptions such as employment, capital strength, time preference of investors, competitiveness, etc. In empirical studies, the reasons for the differences are the criteria used to determine volatility.

Hooper and Kohlhagen (1978) analyzed the effect of exchange rate volatility on multilateral and bilateral trade flows for the periods of 1965–1975 in the USA and Germany. In their study, Hooper and Kohlhagen (1978) found that exchange rate volatility is the source of exchange rate risk and they argued that it does not have an important influence on foreign trade. They also argue that exchange rate volatility will cause higher costs to the firms that avoid the risk and this will lead to an increase in foreign trade. The increase in exchange rate volatility will cause uncertainty in future exchange rates and it will create risk. Reflecting these risks, which constitute a cost on companies, as high prices to consumers will lead to a decrease in the demand for tradables. Also, depending on the risk of the companies, they will be reluctant to make international trade. This situation will cause the export to be negatively affected. Cushman (1983), in the study covering the period 1964–1977, reached a significant negative effect on 6 of the bilateral trade flows among the 14 countries. In addition, the finding that there is a positive effect among some countries is also included in the study. Kenen and Rodrik (1986) reached the conclusion that fluctuations did not diminish despite the markets gain experience with fluctuating exchange rates, it differs according to the company whether it will experience fluctuations in short-term, and fluctuations made international trade volume stagnate.

De Grauwe (1988) stated that foreign exchange volatility has a positive effect on foreign trade and it depends on the degree of risk avoidance of exporting firms. It is suggested that as the exchange rate volatility increases, the income expected from exports may increase more rapidly than the cost, the trade volume may increase. The uncertainty that occur as a result of the exchange rate volatility, will lead to income and substitution effects according to the degree of risk avoidance. Depending on which of these effects will dominate, exports will either increase or decrease. Koray and Lastrapes (1989) examined bilateral trade flows of the US with Britain, France, Germany, Japan and Canada, with the help of the data from the US for the 1959–1985 period. In the study; it is concluded that the bilateral trade flows of US and exchange rate volatility have a weak relationship. Assery and Peel (1991) find that the influence of exchange rate volatility on exports is positive, rather than negative, in the majority of the countries they examined. Chowdhury (1993) found that exchange rate volatility has a significant negative effect on the trade flows of the G-7 countries. It is expressed that moving from the assumption that market participants do not favor the risk, the uncertainty that develops due to exchange rate volatility has caused market participants; to reduce their activities, to change prices, or to change demand and supply sources in order to minimize the effects of exchange rate volatility. Arize (1995) suggested that the exchange rate volatility has a statistically significant negative effect on the US export volume. Doroodian examined developing countries in the study conducted in 1999. The relationship between exchange rate volatility and foreign trade is analyzed by taking into account the multiple, bilateral and sectoral data of these countries. According to the analysis results it is emphasized that exchange rate volatility has a negative effect on foreign trade. In the study covering the 1973–1996 period, Arize, Osang and Slottje (2000) have reached the conclusion that exchange rate volatility affects exports negatively both in the long term and the short term. They argued that the exchange rate volatility will direct producers and exporters non-tradables from tradables and will affect the foreign trade negatively. Egert and Zumaquero (2005) found that exchange rate volatility had a negative effect on export flows and that the manufacturing sector among exports sectors in particular was seriously affected. Wang and Barrett (2007) tested the effect of the risk on exports developed by the real exchange rate volatility with the hypothesis that merchants will be affected by future contract behavior. As a result of the study, Wang and Barrett have found that the real exchange rate risk has no significant effect on many sectors, yet the agricultural trade volume is affected by the real exchange rate volatility. Empirical studies examining the effect of exchange rate volatility on trade volume give mixed results. Gotur (1985) and Bailey et al. (1986) found no significant relationship between exchange rate volatility and foreign trade. However, in general, studies show that trade is negatively affected by foreign exchange rates.

3.1 Exchange Rate Volatility and Turkey

Following the currency crisis in November 2000 and February 2001, Turkey was also obliged to implement a floating exchange rate policy instead of a fixed exchange rate policy in line with the recommendations of the IMF. Thus, the exchange rate volatility also started to change in Turkish economy. This led to the volatility that took place in the exchange rate to affect the trade. Turkey's exports in recent years are shown in Graph 1 below.

Examining the Graph 1, the highest export figures in Turkey was reached in 2011 and it increased to 115 billion dollars. Between 2010 and 2011 the export figures entered a rapid increase. However, starting from the second half of 2011, it is observed that the export figures entered into a decreasing trend until 2016. Between 2016 and 2017, exports, which generally realized around 90 billion dollars, rose to 100 billion dollars again in the second quarter of 2017. There are many domestic and foreign factors affecting the export figures between mentioned periods. Volatility in exchange rates is also one of these variables. Graph 2 below shows the change in exchange rates between 2010–2018 in US Dollar and Euro.

Examining the Graph 2, even though some monthly fluctuations in exchange rates are observed between 2010–2018, in general, exchange rates are in increase trend. This change in exchange rates can be considered as another issue. From the point of the study, fluctuations in the exchange rate set the ground for the uncertainty in the exchange rates and the development of the risk environment. Naturally, this has made it necessary to address the volatility that has occurred in exchange rates and its effects on exports. Below is a list of studies on the effects of exchange rate volatility on the exports of Turkey.

Özbay (1999) who examined the effect of real exchange rate volatility on foreign trade in Turkey, with the help of GARCH model, stated that real exchange rate volatility has a significant negative effect on exports, but there is no statistically significant relationship between the real exchange rate volatility and imports. Vergil (2002) examined the effects of the real exchange rate volatility on exports of Turkey to the USA and three major trading partners (Germany, France, Italy), which are members of the European Union. In the conclusion of the study, long-term relationship between real exports of Turkey and the exchange rate volatility has been found to be negative and significant for Germany, France and the United States. Doğanlar (2002), in the study investigating Turkey, South Korea, Indonesia and Pakistan, concluded that the exchange rate volatility reduces real exports. In

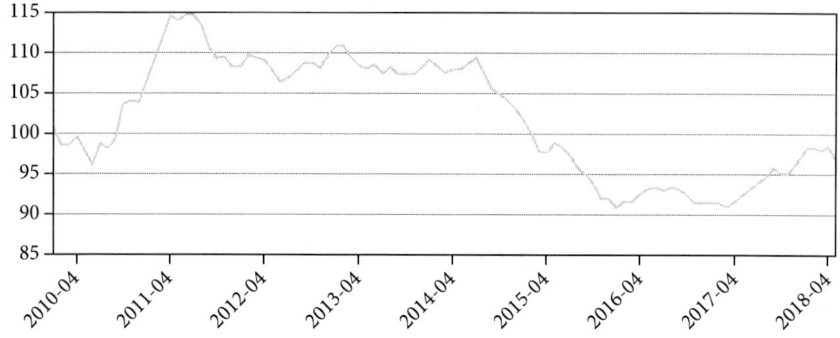

Graph 1: Turkey's Export Figures in 2010–2018 Period. **Source:** The graph was created by the author using the data from the official website of the Central Bank of the Republic of Turkey (TCMB).

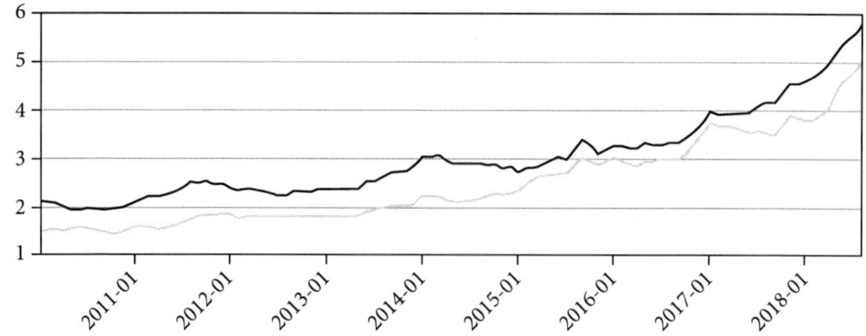

Graph 2: Exchange Rate Figures in Turkey between 2010–2018 Period. **Source:** The graph was created by the author using the data from the official website of the Central Bank of the Republic of Turkey (TCMB).

their study, Öztürk and Acaravcı (2002) found that the increase in exchange rate volatility affected the real exports negatively. Özturk and Acaravcı argued that even though the exchange rate volatility affects exports negatively in Turkey, it is not permanent but rather a short-term situation. In addition, it is stated that the imbalances are not permanent, but it should also be noted that practices aimed at reducing uncertainty in terms of economic policy will make exports less fluctuating.

Kasman (2003) predicted the exports model both at the sectoral and the aggregate level using cointegration test and the error-correction model. The findings show that the real effective exchange rate volatility is an important variable in determining the level of exports. Kasman expresses that the effect of exchange rate volatility on total exports is negative, both in long and short term. Saatçioğlu and Karaca (2004) concluded that the exchange rate volatility in Turkey not affects the exports negatively not only in short-term but also in long-term. In the light of the findings, Saatcioğlu and Karaca argued that stabilization in the currencies should be achieved in order to increase exports. In their study, Demirel and Erdem (2004) examined the effects of real exchange rate and real exchange rate volatility on the exports of Turkey to the United States, Germany, England, France and Italy in the period of 1990–2001. Demirel and Erdem (2004) concluded that real exchange rate volatility has a negative effect on exports in mining and agriculture sectors in some but not all of the countries included in the study.

Köse, Ay and Topallı (2008) examined the long and short-term effects of exchange rate volatility on real exports using the data of Turkey in the period of 1995 – 2008. As a result of the analysis, they emphasized that real exchange rate volatility has a negative impact on Turkey's exports both in the long and the short term. According to the study, the increases in real exchange rate volatility increase the uncertainty about the future trend of exchange rate. As a result, exporters tend to orient to the domestic market rather than the foreign market. Thus, volatility in the real exchange rate causes a negative effect on exports. Tarı and Yıldırım (2009) concluded that long term exchange rate uncertainty in Turkey has a negative effect on exports, but this is not applicable for short term uncertainty. Tarı and Yıldırım have argued that the negative effect of the exchange rate uncertainty in the long term on exports stemmed from the exporters' inability to protect themselves from uncertainty. On the other hand, they argued that short-term exchange rate uncertainty's not being effective on the volume of exports could be due to the reasons that exporters benefiting from prevention methods or ignoring exchange rate ambiguity. As a result, it has been stated that the long-term liberation of the exporters from the exchange rate uncertainty will increase the export volume. In order to realize this, exchange rate should be stabilized with the help of the government or exporters should use risk prevention methods. In his study, Odabaşı (2011) analyzed the impact of exchange rate volatility on the exports of Turkey, by using the variables determined from the model of traditional export demand model. As a result of the analyzes; it is found that exchange rate volatility has negative effects on Turkey's exports both in the short and long term.

In general, both national and foreign literature most of the studies have resulted that the effects of exchange rate volatility on exports are generally negative.

4 Conclusion

Exchange rates are one of the important indicators providing information about the economic structure of countries. In order to ensure stability in an economy, it is necessary to maintain stability in exchange rates. Providing stability in exchange rates will cause the exchange rate volatility to decrease. Thus, governments and firms will be protected from uncertainty and risk environment caused from the volatility.

The increase in exchange rate volatility will cause uncertainty in future exchange rates and it will create risk. Reflecting these risks, which constitute a cost on companies, as high prices to consumers will lead to a decrease in the demand for tradables. Also, depending on the risk of the companies, they will be reluctant to make international trade. This situation will cause the export to be negatively affected. Effects of real exchange rate volatility on export volume can differ according to the tendencies of firms avoiding risks. If foreign trade performing firms tend to avoid risk, an increase in exchange rate volatility will lead to unexpected costs and it may lead to a decrease in foreign trade. If foreign trade payments are made after delivery, changes that are not foreseeable in exchange rates between delivery and payment dates will increase uncertainty about the expected profits. For this reason, uncertainty in exchange rate will reduce profit expectation and therefore exports. At this point, if firms are not protected against exchange rate risk, then increases in exchange rate volatility will reduce exports.

Considering the economic effects of exchange rate volatility, it seems that determining the direction of influence is not enough. In order to avoid the risk and uncertainty in the new economic order, volatility should be calculated and predicted prospectively. The determination of exchange rate volatility and prospective prediction will have an impact on decisions taken by exporters, investors and governments. Thanks to the predictions, clarity of risk and uncertainty will help economic actors to make more rational preferences. Besides; taking the necessary precautions and applying the policies in accordance with the economic conditions will make it possible to protect from the risk and uncertainty arising from the exchange rate volatility. Considering that exports negatively affected by the volatility of the exchange rate in Turkey, Turkey is to put emphasis on policies that will stabilize the exchange rates. Ensuring stability in exchange rates will prevent risks and uncertainties arising from volatility and will provide protection for exporting companies that would prefer to avoid risk. Implementation of policies to stabilize the exchange rate will affect the export volume of Turkey in the long term in a positive way.

Bibliography

Arize, A., (1995), "Trade Flows and Real Exchange Rate Volatility: An Application of Cointegration and Error-Correction Modeling". North American Journal of Economics and Finance, Vol: 6, pp. 37–51.

Arize, A., Osang, T. ve D.J. Slottje, (2000), "Exchange-Rate Volatility and Foreign Trade: Evidence from Thirteen LDCs". Journal of Business and Economic Statistics, Vol: 18, Issue: 1, pp. 10–17.

Assery, A. ve D.A. Peel, (1991), "The Effects of Exchange Rate Volatility on Exports". Economics Letters, Vol: 37, pp. 173–177.

Aydin, S., (2004) "Faiz Oranları Oynaklığının Modellenmesinde Koşullu Değişen Varyansın Rolü", Türkiye Cumhuriyet Merkez Bankası Uzmanlık Tezleri, Haziran, ss. 15–20.

Bailey, M.J., Tavlas, G.S. ve M. Ulan, (1986), "Exchange Rate Variability and Trade Performance: Evidence For the Big Seven Industrial Countries". Weltwirtschaftliches Archiv, Vol: 122, pp. 466–477.

Brooks, C., (2008), Introductory Econometrics for Finance, Cambridge: Cambridge University, Second Edition.

Chowdhury, A.R., (1993), "Does Exchange Rate Volatility Depress Trade Flows? Evidence From Error- Correction Models". Review of Economics and Statistics, Vol: 75, pp. 700–706.

Cushman, D.O., (1983), "The Effects of Real Exchange Rate Risk on International Trade". Journal of International Economics, Vol: 15, pp. 45–63.

Çiçek, M., (2010), "Türkiye'de Faiz, Döviz ve Borsa: Fiyat ve Oynaklık Yayılma Etkileri". Ankara Üniversitesi SBF Dergisi, Cilt: 65, Sayı: 2, ss. 1–28.

De Grauwe P., de Bellefroid B. (1987), Long run exchange rate variability and international trade, in: S. Arndt, J.D. Richardson (eds.), Real Financial Linkages Among Open Economies, London: MIT Press.

Demirel, B. ve C. Erdem, (2004), "Döviz Kurlarındaki Dalgalanmaların İhracata Etkileri: Türkiye Örneği". İktisat, İşletme ve Finans Dergisi, Cilt: 19, Sayı: 223, ss. 116–127.

Doganlar, M., (2002), "Estimating the Impact of Exchange Rate Volatility on Exports: Evidence From Asian Countries". Applied Economics Letters, Vol: 9, pp. 859–863.

Doroodian, K., (1999), "Does Exchange Rate Volatility Deter International Trade in Developing Countries?". Journal of Asian Economics, Vol: 10, pp. 465–474.

Egert, B. ve A. M. Zumaquare, (2005), "Exchange Rate Regimes, Foreign Exchange Volatility and Export Perdormance in Central and Eastern Europe". Focus I/2005, pp. 76–97.

Gotur, P., (1985), "Effects of Exchange Rate Volatility on Trade: Some Further Evidence". IMF Staff Papers.

Güloğlu, B. ve A. Akman, (2007), "Türkiye'de Döviz Kuru Oynaklığının SWARCH Yöntemi ile Analizi". Finans Politik & Ekonomik Yorumlar, Cilt:44, Sayı:512, ss.43–51.

Hooper, P. ve S. Kohlhagen, (1978), "The Effect of Exchange Rate Uncertainty on The Price and Volume of International Trade". Journal of International Economics, Vol: 8, pp. 483–511.

Kasman, A. (2003), "Türkiye'de Reel Döviz Kuru Oynaklığı ve Bunun İhracat Üzerine Etkisi: Sektörel Bir Analiz". Uludağ Üniversitesi ve İktisadi ve İdari Bilimler Fakültesi Dergisi, Cilt: 22, Sayı: 2, ss. 169–186.

Kenen, P. ve D. Rodrik, (1986), "Measuring and Analyzing The Effects of Short-Term Volatility on Real Exchange Rates". Review of Economics and Statistics, Vol: LXIII, Issue: 2, pp.311–315.

Koray, F. ve W.D. Lastrapes, (1989), "Real Exchange Rate Volatility and U.S. Bilateral Trade: A VAR Approach". The Review of Economics and Statistics, Vol: 71, pp. 708–712.

Köse, N., Ay, A. ve N. Topalli, (2008), "Döviz Kuru Oynaklığının İhracata Etkisi: Türkiye Örneği (1995–2008)". Gazi Üniversitesi İktisadi ve İdari Bilimler Fakültesi Dergisi, Cilt: 10, Sayı: 2, ss. 25–45

Mckenzie, M.D., (1999), "The Impact of Exchange Rate Volatility on International Trade Flows". Journal of Economic Surveys, Vol: 13, No: 1, pp. 71–106.

Odabaşi, Y. (2011), Döviz Kuru Volatilitesinin İhracat Üzerindeki Etkisi ve İleriye Dönük Volatilite Tahmini: Türkiye İçin Bir Uygulama, Doktora Tezi, Dumlupınar Üniversitesi Sosyal Bilimler Enstitüsü, Kütahya.

Ozbay, P. 1999. "The Effect of Exchange Rate Uncertainty on Exports: A Case Study for Turkey", Central Bank of the Republic of Turkey Research, Department Working Papers.

Öztürk, İ. ve A. Acaravci, (2002), "Döviz Kurundaki Değişkenliğin Türkiye İhracatı Üzerine Etkisi: Ampirik Bir Çalışma". Review of Social, Economic and Business Studies, Vol: 2, Fall 2002–2003, pp. 197–206.

Saatcioğlu, C. ve O. Karaca, (2004) "Döviz Kuru Belirsizliğinin İhracata Etkisi: Türkiye Örneği", Doğuş Üniversitesi Dergisi, Cilt: 5, Sayı: 2, ss.183–195.

Sengupta, J. K., (2002),"Modelling Exchange Rate Volatility", Department of Economics, UCSB Departmental Working Papers, pp. 1–27.

Tari, R. ve Ç. Yildirim, (2009), "Döviz Kuru Belirsizliğinin İhracata Etkisi:Türkiye İçin Bir Uygulama", Yönetim ve Ekonomi Dergisi, Cilt: 16, Sayı: 2, ss. 95–105.

Vergil, H.(2002),"Exchange Rate Volatility in Turkey and Its Effect on Trade Flows", Journal of Economic and Social Research, Vol: 4, No: 1, pp. 83–99.

Wang, B. ve C. B. Barrett, (2007), "Estimating The Effect of Exchange Rate Volatility on Export Volumes", Journal of Agricultural and Resource Economics, Vol: 32, No: 2, ss. 225–255.

Mesut Alper Gezer and Tuba Gezer

The Relationship between Consumer Confidence and Real Exchange Rate: The Case of Turkey

1 Introduction

Expectations always create a powerful impact towards the future of economics, and this powerful impact is one of the points of interest of people who deal with economics science. The measurement of expectation is necessary in order to measure impact. Thus, consumer confidence index calculations are made for this purpose. The gauge of future expectations of economics is found considerable for researches with the mediations of factors inside economics.

One of the economic decision units of macroeconomics theory is the consumers. Consumer behaviours have an important place for both decision takers, and people who deal with the future predictions of economics. "The only irreplaceable capital is the confidence among economic agents in an economy" (Özsağır, 2007: pp.55). Consumer confidence is an indicator designed to measure change in economic activity, and used widespread in evaluations and predictions in macroeconomics. Consumer confidence index is a dimension and gauge of consumer attitude (Karagöz and Aktaş, 2015: pp.31). If attitudes change, consumption is going to change, even if consumer's willingness to purchase is stable (Roos, 2008: pp.388).

The consumer confidence is a discussion subject area of psychological economics discipline. This discipline states that household behaviours depend on both the purchasing power, and the willingness to purchase from the aspect of notion (Katona, 1968: pp.19). Purchasing power of consumers and their willingness to purchase are together important concepts giving clue for the future of the economy. Purchasing power depends on individual's income, fixed expenditures, and etc. objective conditions. As for willingness to purchase depends on individual's sudden psychologic situation and subjective conditions as like necessities (Roos, 2008: pp.388).

Consumer confidence index has emerged in two different types at the University of Michigan Consumer Sentiment Index and The Conference Board Consumer Confidence Index. These indices are frequently followed by policy makers, financial analysts, and journalists. Expectations and opinions of consumers are directly related with economics according to common understanding. Lots of researches state that there is a relationship between consumers' attitude and economics variables (Bram and Ludvigson, 1998: pp.59).

Consumer confidence index bases on surveys and consist of two indices in Turkey. One is created and published monthly by Turkey Statistical Institute and Central Bank of Turkey. Other is created and published monthly by CNBC-e.

Consumer confidence index takes value between 0 and 200. Values of indices over 100 reflect optimistic situation and values below 100 suggests pessimistic situation of consumer confidence (TurkStat, 2017).

2 Literature

Consumer confidence studies are divided into three groups. First group investigates the prediction and the explanatory power of consumption expenditures of consumer trend. Second group investigates the relationship between consumer confidence and macroeconomics variables. Third group examines the impact of consumer confidence over stocks and markets. Otoo (1999) emphasizes the relationship between consumer sentiment and stock shares. He tries to find out whether markets increase due to an increment in stock shares as a consequence of individuals' perceives of economic activities, and potential labour force income. According to findings, individuals use stock price movement as a leadership indicator for their perception based on Michigan University survey.

Acemoğlu and Scott (1994) point out that forward looking attitude of consumer confidence and its consistent explanatory feature is associated with greater optimism about the level of consumption. Matsusaka and Sbordone (1995) investigate the relationship between economic fluctuations and consumer confidence. Consumers' pessimistic perception excites deceleration in production level by reducing consumption expenditures. Hollanders and Vliegenthart (2011) draw attention to media factor over real economy and consumer confidence from this aspect. Negative news creates a real economic consequence by decreasing consumer confidence.

Tsai et al. (2015) examine the relationship between consumer confidence index and macroeconomic factors from 2006–2011 with weekly data for Taiwan. They use GARCH model for estimation. According to findings, consumer confidence index is one of the important factors for foreign exchange rate forecasting. Kuzmanovic and Sanfey (2012) deal with the case from the aspect of consumer confidence and real variables for the period of 2005–2012 monthly data for Croatia. They see that consumer confidence is helpful to predict and explain real economic activity based on Granger causality tests.

Görmüş and Güneş (2010) investigate the relationship between consumer confidence, stock prices, and exchange rate for the period of 2002:1–2008:12 in Turkey. They use CNBC-e represented consumer confidence index, real exchange rate, consumer price index, world and Turkey stock market index, industrial production index, and their differences. They use ARDL method, GARCH-M, and Granger causality for this period. According to their findings, stock prices and real exchange rate are Granger cause of consumer confidence. Güneş and Çelik (2009) use the same index for the relationship between consumer confidence and financial variables for the period of 2003:1–2007:12. They find cointegration among variables, which emphasize the importance between consumer confidence and financial variables in Turkey.

Yıldırım and Zeren (2014) asses the relationship between consumer confidence and credit card usage for the period 2008:1–2012:12. They see that variables are cointegrated according to Hatemi-J cointegration test, and they find causality relationship from consumer confidence to credit card usage according to Toda and Yamamoto (1995) causality test. Alacahan and Yavuz (2017) asses the relationship between consumer confidence and the real exchange rate for the period 2008:1–2015:04. According to their findings based on Granger VECM model, consumer confidence is a cause of real exchange rate in the short term. İbicioğlu et al. (2013) investigates the relationship between consumer confidence index and exchange rate for the period of 2003:12–2011:12 for Turkey. According to findings, exchange rate is one way Granger cause of consumer confidence based on VAR model Granger causality and impulse-response results. Çelik (2010) evaluates the functional identity of consumer sentiment. According to findings, the movement in consumer confidence depends on exchange rate, stock index, business indexes, and manufacturing industry index.

3 Data Set and Methodology

Monthly data for the period of 2004:1–2018:6 are arranged from Turkish Statistical Institute and Central Bank of Republic of Turkey. Consumer confidence index values are taken from Turkstat. Real exchange rate is taken from CBRT, and consumer price index basis real effective exchange rate (2003=100) is determined with monthly average values at level.

First of all, unit root structure of the variables is particularly examined. Then, variables are determined endogenously, and VAR model is decided for their relationship whether consumer confidence triggers real exchange rate movements, or real exchange rate explains the consumer confidence of Turkey.

$$y_t = \rho y_{t-1} + \varepsilon_t, \quad t = 1,2,\ldots \tag{1}$$

Simple AR(1) model of random walk unit root is represented at equation 1. If $\rho = 1$, then unit root emerges at the series (Wooldridge, 2013: pp.639). Unit root structure of series takes importance. When a shock arises at series, it becomes continuous for a random walk process.

Tab. 1: The Definition of Variables and Data Sources

Variables	Series	Sources
CCI=	Consumer Confidence Index	TurkStat
REX=	Real Exchange Rate	CBRT

$$CCI_t = \sum_{i=1}^{k} \alpha_i CCI_{t-i} + \sum_{i=1}^{k} \beta_i REX_{t-i} + \mu_{1t} \tag{2}$$

or

$$REX_t = \sum_{i=1}^{k} \alpha_i REX_{t-i} + \sum_{i=1}^{k} \beta_i CCI_{t-i} + \mu_{2t} \tag{3}$$

If past values of consumer confidence index can be used to predict unexplained part of the real exchange rate, then consumer confidence index can be prima facie cause of real exchange rate for equation 2, and vice versa for equation 3 (Granger, 1980: pp.349). k is the lag length extent for equation 2 and 3. If $\beta_i = 0$ (i= 1,2,......,n), then real exchange rate fails to cause consumer confidence index for equation 2, and vice versa for equation 3 (Maddala, 1992: pp.393). So, main purpose of the analysis is to see Granger causality relationship between these two variables for Turkey based on unit root features and cointegration relationship. After identifying lag length extent for VAR model, Toda and Yamamoto (1995: pp.245–246) proposed (k+d_{max}) order estimation. d_{max} is the maximum order of integration of unit roots. As a result, VAR model is estimated without having to test unit roots and cointegration ranks in Toda and Yamamoto (1995) causality estimation.

4 Empirical Findings

Unit root features of series are examined based on ADF and PP tests at first. After, further unit root structure is discussed for structural shift situation of series based on Zivot and Andrews (1992), and Lee and Strazicich (2013) test statistics.

Unit root test findings of variables are displayed at Tab. 2. According to results, CCI and REX are not stationary at level, but they both get stationary at first difference in series even if treated constant, or constant and trend.

Chart of variables are demonstrated at Graph 1. It is seen that both variables have a trend at this period. Therefore, constant and trend model is seen more appropriate for estimations. Moreover, structural break creates suspicion at series, thus structural break unit root tests needs to be analysed for both variables.

Zivot and Andrews (1992) ADF test and Lee and Strazicich (2013) LM tests are applied to series. It is considered as both CCI and REX have a unit root leaning on structural break testing. Besides, 2009:12 and 2007:11 dates are appointed as break dates respectively for consumer confidence index. 2010:9 and 2007:10 dates are appointed as break dates for real exchange rate for this period. Those dates can be interpreted as the 2008 Financial Crisis impact over series, which reflects the sensitivity of variables to external effects. Moreover, these break dates can also be considered for the 2009 Europa Debt Crisis. Therefore, it can be made as an inference that these series are fragile to external shocks.

After unit root investigation, first step is to find out cointegration relationship existence before passing the step of causality analysis (Nazlıoğlu and Soytaş,

Tab. 2: Unit Root Structure of Variables

Variables	**Level**		**First Difference**	
	Constant	**Constant and Trend**	**Constant**	**Constant and Trend**
CCI-ADF	−1.884	−3.125	−3.857***	−3.889**
-PP	−2.107	−3.077	12.398***	−12.616***
REX-ADF	−0.751	−2.588	−7.376***	−7.619***
-PP	−0.991	−2.403	−9.973***	−10.016***

Note: *The maximum lag length is taken as 12 for ADF test, and Akaike information criterion is used to determine optimal lag length. "Barlett Kernel" method is used for PP test and band width is determined according to "Newey West Bandwith" method. ***,** imply significance at 1, 5 percent, respectively.*

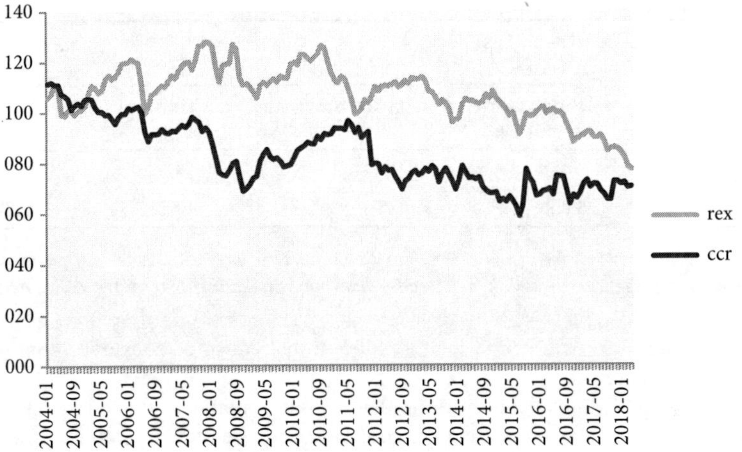

Graph 1: Chart of Variables

2011: pp.491). Johansen Cointegration test is applied based on trace test in order to see whether variables are cointegrated with each other in the long run. According to findings, there is no any cointegration relationship between variables.

Causality test results are demonstrated with Chi-square and bootstrap probability values at Tab. 5. According to findings, past values of consumer confidence index is not a Granger cause of real exchange rate, but past values of real exchange rate is a Granger cause of consumer confidence based on both standard causality and Toda and Yamamoto causality test results. So, it demonstrates that

Tab. 3: Structural Break Unit Root Test Results

Structural Break Tests	Model: One Break in level and trend			
	Test Stat	**Fraction (λ)**	**Lag**	**Break date**
Zivot and Andrews-ADF				
CCI	−4.282	0.414	9	2009m12
REX	−4.507	0.466	3	2010m09
Lee and Strazicich-LM				
CCI	−3.616	0.270	9	2007m11
REX	−4.114	0.402	4	2009m10

Note: *The maximum lag length is taken as 12 to determine optimal lag length by using Akaike information crieria.*

Tab. 4: *Johansen Cointegration Test Result*

Hypothesized No. of CE(s)	Trace Test			
	Eigenvalue	**Trace Statistics**	**Critical Value (%5)**	**p-value**
None	0.069	21.921	25.872	0.144
At Most 1	0.056	9.798	12.518	0.137

Note: *Lag interval is taken from 1 to 4 based on Akaike information criteria. Demeaned and detrended cointegration equation is determined without deterministic term for VAR model.*

real exchange rate is a prima facie unidirectional cause of consumer confidence index for this period.

If obtained findings deal with impulse-response analysis, active impact of real exchange rate shocks over consumer confidence can be seen at Graph 2. One standard shock given to real exchange rate creates remarkable impact over consumer confidence, especially in the short run (Tarı and Bozkurt, 2006: pp.24).

5 Conclusion

Nowadays, Turkey's exchange rate market has an upward trend, and it is creating real impact over economic activity. It is discussed whether the exchange rate movement is one of the soft belly of Turkish economy, or not. Purchasing power of consumers and their willingness to purchase are together important concepts, and reflecting the consumer's reactions over economic developments. Therefore, consumer confidence index measurements represent consumer's position and psychologic reflexes leaning on their optimistic and pessimistic tendency. Thereby,

Tab. 5: Causality Test Results

Tests	Wald Statistics	Lag	Chi-square p-value	Bootstrap p-value
Standard Granger				
CCI->REX	6.055	4	0.195	0.199
REX->CCI	15.275***	4	0.004	0.006
Toda and Yamamoto				
CCI->REX	3.330	5	0.649	0.639
REX->CCI	16.713***	5	0.005	0.006

Note: *The maximum lag length is taken as 12, and optimal lag length is determined according to Akaike information criteria.* d_{max} *is taken as 1 for Toda and Yamamoto, and bootstrap p-values are obtained from 10.000 replications.* *** *imply significance at 1 percent.*

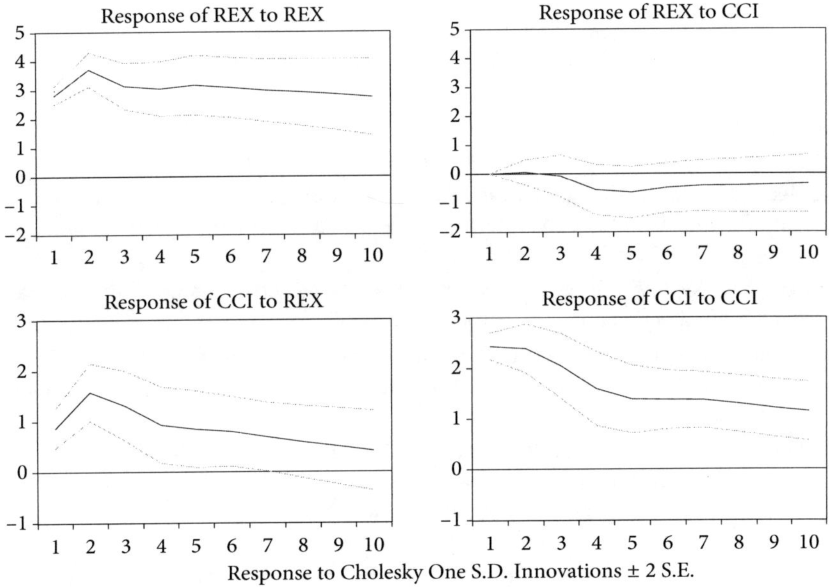

Graph 2: Impulse-Response Chart of VAR Model

we asked whether these two important economic variables have a relationship with each other, or not. First of all, unit root structure is examined, and it is seen that both variables are not stationary at level, which reflects persistency of shocks over series. After that causality relationship of variables are investigated with bootstrap standard errors based on standard causality, and Toda and Yamamoto (1995) causality. According to findings, it is seen that past values of real exchange rate has a casual impact over consumer confidence, but not vice versa. So that, consumers' confidence is sensitive to real exchange rate movements in Turkey based on selected period.

Bibliography

Acemoğlu, D., and Scott, A. (1994). Consumer Confidence and Rational Expectations: Are Agents Beliefs Consistent with the Theory?. Economic Journal, 1–19.

Alacahan, N. D., and Yavuz, R. A. (2017). The Relationship of Consumer Confidence with Real Exchange Rates: Analysis of Turkey. International Refereed Academic Social Sciences Journal, 22–44.

Bram, J., and Ludvigson, S. (1998). Does Consumer Confidence Forecast Household Expenditure? A Sentiment Index Horse Race. Economic Policy Review, 59–78.

CBRT. (2018). EVDS Data Central. Retrieved July 5, 2018, from Central Bank of Republic of Turkey: https://evds2.tcmb.gov.tr/index.php?/evds/serieMarket

Çelik, S. (2010). An Unconventional Analysis of Consumer Confidence Index for The Turkish Economy. International Journal of Economics and Finance Studies, 1(2), 121–129.

Granger, C. W. (1980, June). Testing for Causality: A Personal Viewpoint. Journal of Economic Dynamics and Control, 2, 329–352.

Görmüş, Ş., and Güneş, S. (2010). Consumer Confidence, Stock Prices and Exchange Rates: The Case of Turkey. Applied Econometrics and International Development, 2(10), 103–114.

Güneş, H., and Çelik, S. (2009). Consumer Confidence and Financial Market Variables in an Emerging Economy: The Case of Turkey. 15th International Conference on Computing in Economics and Finance (pp. 1–28). Sydney: Society for Computational Economics.

Hollanders, D., and Vliegenthart, R. (2011). The Influence of Negative Newspaper Coverage on Consumer Confidence: The Dutch Case. Journal of Economic Psychology, 32, 367–373.

İbicioğlu, M., Kapusuzoğlu, A., and Karan, M. B. (2013). Türkiye'deki Tüketici Güven Endeksi ile Döviz Kuru Arasındaki İlişkinin Ampirik Analizi. İşletme Araştırmaları Dergisi, 5(1), 5–16.

Karagöz, D., and Aktaş, S. (2015). Evaluation of Consumer Confidence Index of Central Bank of Turkey Consumer Tendency Survey. The Online Journal of Science and Technology Volume 5 Issue 3, 31–36.

Katona, G. (1968). Consumer Behaviour: Theory and Findings on Expectations and Aspiraitons. American Economic Association, 58(2), 19–30.

Kuzmanovic, M., and Sanfey, P. (2013). Can Consumer Confidence Data Predict Real Variables?. Croatian Economic Survey, 15(1), 5–24.

Lee, J., and Strazicich, M. C. (2013). Minimum LM Unit Root Test with One Structural Break. Economics Bulletin, 33(4), 2483–2492.

Maddala, G. S. (1992). Introduction to Econometrics (2. ed.). New York: Macmillan Publishing Company.

Matsusaka, J. G., and Sbordone, A. M. (1995). Consumer Confidence and Economic Fluctuations. Economic Inguiry, 2(33), 296–318.

Nazlıoğlu, Ş., and Soytaş, U. (2011). World Oil Prices and Agricultural Commodity Prices: Evidence from an Emerging Market. Energy Economics, 33, 488–496.

Otoo, M. W. (1999). Consumer Sentiment and Stock Market. Washington D.C: Board of Governors of the Federal Reserve System.

Özsağır, A. (2007). Ekonomide Güven Faktörü. Elektronik Sosyal Bilimler Dergisi, 6(20), 46–62.

Roos, M. W. (2008). Willingness to consume and ability to consume. Journal of Economic Behavior &Organization, 66, 387–402.

Tarı, R., and Bozkurt, H. (2006). Türkiye'de İstikrarsız Büyümenin VAR Modelleri ile Analizi. Istanbul University Econometrics and Statistics Journal, 4, 12–28.

Toda, H. Y., and Yamamoto, T. (1995). Statistical Inferences in Vector Autoregressions with Possibly Integrated Processes. Journal of Econometrics, 66, 225–250.

Tsai, P.-W., Liu, C.-H., Liao, L.-C., and Chang, J.-F. (2015). Using Consumer Confidence Index in the Foreign Exchange Rate Forecasting. International Conference on Intelligent Information Hiding and Multimedia Signal Processing (pp. 360–363). Adelaide: IEEE.

TurkStat. (2017, May 18). Türkiye İstatistik Kurumu Haber Bülteni. Retrieved May 22, 2017, from www.tuik.gov.tr: http://www.tuik.gov.tr/PreHaberBultenleri.do?id=24909

TurkStat. (2018). Indicator. Retrieved July 6, 2018, from Turkish Statistical Institute: https://biruni.tuik.gov.tr/gosterge/?locale=en

Wooldridge, J. M. (2013). Introductory Econometrics: A Modern Approach (5. ed.). Ohio: South-Western Cengage Learning.

Yıldırım, E., and Zeren, F. (2014). The Relationship Between Consumer Confidence Index and Online Credit Card Using in Turkey: New Evidence From Frequency Domain Causality Test. Journal of Internet Banking and Commerce, 19(1), 1–13.

Zivot, E., and Andrews, D. W. (1992). Further Evidence on the Great Crash, the Oil-Price Shock, and the Unit-Root Hypothesis. Journal of Business & Economic Statistics, 10(3), 251–270.

Aycan Hepsag

Asymmetric Stochastic Volatility in Nordic Stock Markets[1]

1 Introduction

The volatility of asset returns is still one of the major issues of financial econometrics. The understanding of volatility in stock markets matters because volatility has an important role in option pricing, portfolio management and asset allocation. It is well known that stock market volatility, defined as the conditional variance or standard deviation of stock returns, changes over time.

The relationship between a stock market index (or a stock price) and its volatility has been studied widely in market economies and also it is well documented that a negative shock increases the stock market volatility more than the positive shock at the same magnitude and this circumstance is described as "asymmetry". As mentioned in Cappiello et al. (2006), asymmetric volatility could be explained in two ways: "leverage effect" and "volatility feedback effect". The leverage effect is described as the notion that a fall in stock price causes an increase in the debt-equity ratio (financial leverage) of the firm and the risk (volatility) of the firm increases right after (Selçuk, 2005). On the other hand, volatility feedback effect is specified as the notion that once volatility is priced, an expected increase in volatility enhances the required return on equity, leading to an urgent stock price downfall. The main difference between leverage effect and volatility feedback effect is the direction of causality between stock returns and volatility. In the leverage effect, the direction of causality is running from the stock returns to volatility whilst the volatility feedback effect implies that the causality running from the volatility to stock returns.

The main goal of the present paper is to investigate the asymmetric impact of innovations on volatility and the relationship between the stock return and volatility dynamics in the case of Nordic markets, which have been researched far less than the other markets, using univariate asymmetric stochastic volatility approach. Although stock return and its volatility in advanced markets have been well studied, there exist relatively few contributions to return and volatility dynamics in Nordic region.

The volatility in the Nordic stock markets tends to be relatively higher in comparison with advanced stock markets. Also, the trading volume and the number

1 This paper was presented at the EconWorld 2016 conference held at Rome, Italy, January, 25–27, 2017

of traded firms of the Nordic stock markets are relatively low but are growing at a greater rate than advanced markets.

The present paper differs from the extant literature in the following way: to the best of our knowledge, it is the first study that examines the stock returns and volatility dynamics and asymmetric innovations to volatility in the stock markets from the Nordic region using the framework of the asymmetric stochastic volatility models.

The remainder of the paper is organized as follows: in section 2 we discuss the literature review and in section 3 we present the econometric methodology. Section 4 contains the data description and empirical results of the study. The 5th and last section includes conclusions.

2 Literature Review

As mentioned above, there exist few empirical studies on the Nordic region and the empirical findings on asymmetric volatility are conflicted. Booth et al. (1997) investigated the volatility in the stock markets of Nordic region, i.e. Denmark, Finland, Norway and Sweden using EGARCH model and they reached the findings on the persistency of volatility and also findings on asymmetric impact of innovation on volatility for the Nordic stock markets.

Kulp-Tag (2007a) also explored the volatility in the stock markets of Nordic region, i.e. Denmark, Finland, Norway and Sweden using EGARCH model and reported that negative innovations have a higher impact on volatility than positive innovations, so the asymmetric volatility exists in Nordic stock markets.

Kulp-Tag (2007b) examined the volatility in the stock markets of Nordic region, i.e. Denmark, Finland, Norway and Sweden using GARCH model and its extensions and found out weak evidence of asymmetric volatility in Nordic stock markets.

Urooj et al. (2009) used ARCH and GARCH models in their empirical study and found out the persistency of volatility and volatility clustering in the stock market of Finland.

3 Econometric Methodology

A general representation of a volatility model for a stationary series of returns r_t takes the form:

$$\begin{aligned} r_t &= \mu_t + y_t \\ y_t &= \sigma_t \varepsilon_t \end{aligned} \tag{1}$$

where ε_t is i.i.d. random variable with zero mean and unit variance and σ_t is either a deterministic or stochastic random process which depends on the past values of returns. μ_t denotes either a constant or an autoregressive variable with a parameter close to zero and y_t denotes a stochastic process i.e. demeaned returns.

The main issue is related to which process σ_t follows; if σ_t is expressed as a deterministic function of lagged (squared) returns, we are within the ARCH models (Engle, 1982; Bollerslev, 1986), which have achieved widespread popularity in applied empirical research (Pellegrini and Rodriguez, 2007). On the other hand, when σ_t is expressed as a stochastic function of an unobserved latent variable, we introduce the stochastic volatility model proposed by Taylor (1986). Stochastic volatility models are attractive because they are close to the models often used in Financial Theory to represent the behaviour of financial prices and their statistical properties are easy to derive using well-known results on log-normal distributions (Broto and Luiz, 2004). The main relative advantages of stochastic volatility models are discussed by Carnero et al. (2004) and also Das et al. (2009) emphasise that stochastic volatility models have the capability to provide one-step-ahead prediction and to better harmonise with excess kurtosis and leverage effects compared to GARCH models.

The stochastic volatility model is represented as the following form;

$$\begin{aligned} y_t &= \exp(h_t/2)\varepsilon_t \\ h_t &= \gamma + \phi h_{t-1} + \eta_t \end{aligned} \tag{2}$$

where h_t is latent stochastic volatility which equals to $\ln\sigma_t^2$. ε_t is i.i.d. random variable with zero mean and unit variance and also η_t is i.i.d. random variable with zero mean and variance σ_η^2, independent of ε_t. σ_η^2 indicates the volatility (variability) of volatility and measures the uncertainty about future volatility. The parameter ϕ is described as a measure of the persistence of shocks to the volatility. There is such a trade-off relationship between σ_η^2 and ϕ; namely when ϕ approximates to one, σ_η^2 tends to approximate to zero.

As mentioned Ghysels et al. (1996), it can be noticed that if ε_t and η_t are allowed to be correlated with each other, the model can pick up the kind of asymmetric behaviour observed on stock prices. Indeed a negative correlation between ε_t and η_t induces a leverage effect. Harvey and Shephard (1996), propose a specification which considers contemporaneous dependence and allows the correlation between ε_t and η_t as $corr(\varepsilon_t, \eta_t) = \rho$. In other respects, Jacquier et al. (2004) propose a specification which considers intertemporal dependence and allows the correlation between ε_t and η_{t-1} as $corr(\varepsilon_t, \eta_{t-1}) = \rho$.

Asai and McAleer (2005) present a specification that captures asymmetry in "dynamic leverage" model through the direct negative correlation between returns and volatility innovations as the following form:

$$\begin{aligned} y_t &= \exp(h_t/2)\varepsilon_t \\ h_{t+1} &= \mu + \phi h_t + \eta_t \quad \varepsilon_t \sim \mathrm{N}(0, 1) \quad \eta_t \sim \mathrm{N}(0, \sigma_\eta^2) \\ E(\varepsilon_t \eta_t) &= \rho\sigma_\eta \end{aligned} \tag{3}$$

We could describe this type of asymmetry, namely when $\rho < 0$, as the Dynamic Leverage Stochastic Volatility model. When $\rho = 0$, there exists no dynamic leverage between the innovations to returns and volatility (Asai and McAleer, 2005).

4 Data and Empirical Results

The data set involves daily closing price indices of four Nordic countries for the period from January 2, 2009 to September 30, 2016 (post-2008 Global financial crisis period) and consists of stock indices of Denmark (KFX Index), Finland (HEX Index), Norway (OBX Index) and Sweden (OMX Index). The source of data is the Bloomberg Database. Finally, we calculate the stock returns from the stock market indices of the selected countries using the $\ln(P_t/P_{t-1})\times 100$ formula where P_t denotes the value of the stock price indices of each country at time t.

The descriptive statistics for the stock returns of each stock market indices are reported in Tab. 1.

All of the stock return series have small means and the standard deviations of the stock returns are greater than the means of stock returns, indicating that the stock market of Nordic countries follow a random walk process. Additionally, the stock return series have negative skewness and the excess kurtosis for each is significantly positive, indicating that they have heavy tails relative to the normal distribution, which is also typical in these financial data (Ding and Vo, 2012).

The stochastic volatility models can be estimated using different techniques. The most popular approaches are the quasi-maximum likelihood method as proposed by Harvey and Shephard (1996) and the Markov Chain Monte Carlo (MCMC) method which was introduced by Jacquier et. al. (1994). In this study, we employ the MCMC approach for estimating Dynamic Leverage model and we use the code provided by Yasuhiro Omori[(1)] utilized for the WinBUGS software. In MCMC estimation strategy, we determine the prior values as μ~Inverse-Normal$(-10,1)$, ρ~Inverse-Uniform$(-1,1)$, σ_η^2~Inverse-Gamma$(2.5,0.025)$ and ϕ~Inverse-Beta$(20,1.5)$ following Yasuhiro Omori and MCMC sampler is also initialized by setting the values $\mu=-9$, $\sigma_\eta^2=100$,

Tab. 1: Descriptive Statistics of the Stock Returns

	Denmark	Finland	Norway	Sweden
Mean	0.07202	0.03162	0.05988	0.04659
Median	0.09882	0.05341	0.07564	0.06063
Maximum	6.36103	7.39165	7.45211	6.43374
Minimum	−6.55617	−7.83603	−6.71443	−8.42423
Std. Dev.	1.26198	1.36927	1.45405	1.34654
Skewness	−0.01181	−0.07234	−0.08221	−0.16030
Kurtosis	5.15024	5.54899	5.24386	5.75986
Jarque-Bera	372.43	529.07	410.23	625.61
Probability	0.00000	0.00000	0.00000	0.00000
Observations	1933	1948	1945	1945

$\phi = 0.95$ and $\rho = -0.4$ following also Yasuhiro Omori. We obtain the posterior means of the coefficients ignoring the first 10.000 iterations and utilizing the following 90.000 iterations in all cases. The posterior means of parameter estimates with 95 % posterior credibility intervals are presented in Tab. 2.

The estimation results shown in Tab. 2 indicate that the volatility persistence coefficients ϕ are in between 0.939 (Denmark) and 0.987 (Norway) and the empirical findings imply that there exists a remarkable volatility persistence and strong evidence of volatility clustering in the Nordic stock markets.

The posterior means of the coefficient $\hat{\rho}$, indicating the correlation between innovations to returns and volatility, are negative and statistically significant at the 5 % level for all of Nordic stock markets. The smallest value is -0.514 for Denmark and the highest value is -0.779 for Norway. It can be concluded that there is a high leverage effect in the stock markets of Denmark, Finland, Norway and Sweden so a negative shock increases the stock market volatility more than the positive shock at the same magnitude in these markets.

In other respects, the posterior means of the volatility of volatility coefficient $\hat{\sigma}_\eta$, indicating the measure of uncertainty about the future volatility are within the range of 0.164 (Finland) and 0.263 (Denmark). It can be concluded that the Nordic stock markets exhibit a low variability of volatility and also the future volatility is relatively certain in these stock markets.

Tab. 2: The Estimation Results of the Posterior Means of Parameters

	$\hat{\mu}$		$\hat{\phi}$		$\hat{\rho}$		$\hat{\sigma}_\eta$	
Denmark	−8.935*		0.939*		−0.514*		0.263*	
	(0.097)		(0.013)		(0.059)		(0.031)	
	[−9.121	−8.738]	[0.910	0.962]	[−0.620	−0.389]	[0.207	0.329]
Finland	−8.843*		0.978*		−0.669*		0.164*	
	(0.134)		(0.006)		(0.065)		(0.021)	
	[−9.105	−8.577]	[0.964	0.988]	[−0.784	−0.534]	[0.126	0.208]
Norway	−8.725*		0.987*		−0.779*		0.169*	
	(0.194)		(0.004)		(0.050)		(0.016)	
	[−9.100	−8.331]	[0.979	0.993]	[−0.861	−0.670]	[0.139	0.203]
Sweden	−8.898*		0.973*		−0.744*		0.205*	
	(0.130)		(0.006)		(0.046)		(0.023)	
	[−9.149	−8.633]	[0.961	0.985]	[−0.833	−0.651]	[0.165	0.254]

Notes: The posterior standard deviations and 95 % posterior credibility intervals are presented in the parentheses and brackets, respectively. * denotes statistical significance at the 5 % level.

5 Conclusions

The present paper is a first attempt to find out stock market volatility dynamics in the Nordic economies using the framework of asymmetric stochastic volatility models. The data set involves daily closing price indices of four Nordic countries and consists of stock indices of Denmark (KFX Index), Finland (HEX Index), Norway (OBX Index) and Sweden (OMX Index).

The empirical findings provide strong evidence of asymmetry for all of the Nordic stock markets. The estimation results display that there is a high leverage effect in the stock markets of Denmark, Finland, Norway and Sweden so a negative shock increases stock market volatility more than a positive shock at the same magnitude in these markets.

Also it is shown that the Nordic stock markets have significant and high volatility persistence. It can be implied that the volatility clustering occurs in the stock markets of Denmark, Finland, Norway and Sweden. Moreover, the empirical results demonstrate that there exists a low variability of the volatility in stock markets of the Nordic region which are Denmark, Finland, Norway and Sweden.

The most interesting and unique results obtained from the present paper are that there is both a low variability of volatility and a high volatility persistence in the stock markets of Denmark, Finland, Norway and Sweden. Additionally, we can conclude that the stock markets of Denmark, Finland, Norway and Sweden, which have leverage effect, have lower variability of volatility and in these markets the future volatility is relatively certain. The results presented in this paper could be a guide for the investors who are planning to invest in stock markets from the Nordic region.

Notes

(1) Code used in MCMC estimations of the parameters can be downloaded from Professor Yasuhiro Omori's web site http://www.omori.e.u-tokyo.ac.jp/WinBUGS/index.htm

Bibliography

Asai, M. and McAleer, M. (2005). Dynamic Asymmetric Leverage in Stochastic Volatility Models, *Econometric Reviews*, 24(3): 317–332.

Bollerslev, T. (1986). Generalized Autoregressive Conditional Heteroskedasticity, *Journal of Econometrics*, 31(3): 307–327.

Booth, G. G., Martikainen, T. and Tse, Y. (1997). Price and Volatility Spillovers in Scandinavian Stock Markets, *Journal of Banking & Finance*, 21(6): 811–823.

Broto, C. and Luiz, E. (2004). Estimation Methods for Stochastic Volatility Models: A Survey, *Journal of Economic Survey*, 18(5): 613–649.

Cappiello, L., Engle, R. F. and Sheppard, K. (2006). Asymmetric Dynamics in the Correlations of Global Equity and Bond Returns, *Journal of Financial Econometrics*, 4(4): 537–572.

Carnero, M. A., Pena, D. and Ruiz, E. (2004). Persistence and Kurtosis in GARCH and Stochastic Volatility Models, *Journal of Financial Econometrics*, 2(2): 319–342.

Das, A., Ghoshal, T. K. and Basu, P. N. (2009). A Review of on Recent Trends of Stochastic Volatility Models, *International Review of Applied Financial Issues and Economics*, 1(1): 83–116.

Ding, L. and Vo, M. (2012). Exchange Rates and Oil Prices: A Multivariate Stochastic Volatility Analysis, *The Quarterly Review of Economics and Finance*, 52(1): 15–37.

Engle, R. F. (1982). Autoregressive Conditional Heteroskedasticity with Estimates of the Variance of United Kingdom Inflation, *Econometrica*, 50(4): 987–1007.

Ghysels, E., Harvey A. C. and Renault, E. (1996). Stochastic Volatility, In: Maddala, G.S. and Rao C.R., eds. *Handbook of Statistics 14: Statistical Methods in Finance.* Amsterdam: 119–191.

Harvey, A. C. and Shephard, N. (1996). Estimation of an Asymmetric Stochastic Volatility Model for Asset Returns, *Journal of Business and Economics Statistics*, 14(4): 429–434.

Jacquier, E., Polson, N. G. and Rossi, P. E. (1994). Bayesian Analysis of Stochastic Volatility Models, *Journal of Business and Economic Statistics*, 12(4): 371–389.

Jacquier, E., Polson, N. G. and Rossi, P. E. (2004). Bayesian Analysis of Stochastic Volatility Models with Fat-tails and Correlated Errors, *Journal of Econometrics*, 122(1): 185–212.

Kulp-Tag, S. (2007a). Short-Horizon Asymmetric Mean-Reversion and Overreactions: Evidence from the Nordic Stock Markets, *Meddelanden Working Papers*, 524: 1–25.

Kulp-Tag, S. (2007b). An Empirical Comparison of Linear and Nonlinear Volatility Models for Nordic Stock Returns, *Meddelanden Working Papers*, 525: 1–25.

Pellegrini, S. and Rodrigez, A. (2007). Financial Econometrics and SV models, Available at: <http://halweb.uc3m.es/esp/Personal/personas/spellegr/esp/Curso_Cordoba/Tutorial_Guide.pdf> [Accessed on 15 October 2016].

Selçuk, F. (2005). Asymmetric Stochastic Volatility in Emerging Markets, Applied Financial Economics, 15(12): 867–874.

Taylor, S. J. (1986). *Modelling Financial Time Series*, U.K.: John Wiley.

Urooj, S. F., Zafar, N., Durrani, T. K. and MAJU, I. (2009). Finding the Stock Return Volatility: A Case of KSE-100 Index, *Interdisciplinary Journal of Contemporary Research in Business*, 1(4): 65–80.

Ayşegül Çimen and Yağmur Sağlam

Testing Life-Cycle Hypothesis for Emerging Markets

1 Introduction

John Maynard Keynes mentioned about some motive behind savings in his book named "General Theory of Employment, Interest and Money". Because in his period, it was popular to work on national saving but not enough attention was paid to its reasons. One of the motives was "Foresight" that provides an expected future relation between income and individual needs such as; in relation to old age, family education etc. which explains the characteristic of current saving depends on future consumption via dissaving (Modigliani, 1988: 15). Importance of saving and the sources of wealth were also studied by Harrod in 1948 and called "hump saving" because of people will save more for their retirement when they are in their middle ages. Finally Modigliani and his student Brumberg combined this idea with Classical Theory of consumer choice in 1950's and worked out a theory which is called Life Cycle Theory.

Zhu (2011,) says that according to the life cycle theory of Modigliani, young people will save for future consumption because savings mean future consumption whereas an aging population dissave. As a demographic indicator, higher dependency ratio means higher consumption. Naturally it is expected that the correlation between total dependency ratio and savings rate will be negative. Higgins (1998) claims that according to literature there are substantial demographic effects of aging because of the increases in both the youth and old-age dependency ratios related with lower saving rates. Colae and Hoover (1958) point that developing countries which have high degree of integration with capitals markets suffer from youth dependency. Because the relationship between youth dependency and current account balance limits to sustain those countries domestic capital formation and economic growth.

Jaffri et al. (2012), points that population growth is a crucial determinant of current account balance. Because if inactive population grows faster than national savings rate will reduce and the deviation from savings to investments will perish. As life cycle theory explains households have different tendencies in each stage of their lives. Prati et al. (2011) mentions that especially in developing countries inactive population (old and young ages) spends more money from their future income because of high demand for imported goods and it worsened current account balance via distortion of foreign exchange rates. He confirms that population growth and fertility have an impact on current account balance as life cycle theory points out. Bloom et al. (2011) shows that consumption behaviour of people differs in their life cycle. The tendency of consumption is higher for youth, and elderly people. Because according to official definition they are outside of the working age society. That means the rate of economic growth will decrease in countries with young and old population because of the main drivers of economic growth such as labour, efficiency, productivity and savings are decreasing. It ends with the deterioration of current account balance.

Researchers tried to answer the question that if current account balance is correlated with demographic structure of an economy under the light of Modigliani's Life Cycle Hypothesis. In an open economy, savings are the sum of internal (domestic) and external savings (current account surplus). If the answer of this question is yes, then saving rate is an important explanatory variable of current account balance (CAB). In addition to that demographic changes have direct or indirect impacts on it. This is why in this study we tested the causality between current account balance (%of GDP) and age dependency [sum of old (over 65) and young (0–15) age dependency – % of working age population] with Hatemi-J (2011) asymmetric panel causality test. Also we take into account gross saving rates (%of GDP) as a control variable to strengthen the direction the relationship. The contribution of this study to the literature can be divided into two; firstly it includes BRICS and Next Eleven emerging-developing economies with a wide span of time period (1981–2016). Secondly there is no study that analyzed life cycle hypothesis with a panel asymmetric causality test and takes into account different reactions of households to positive and negative shocks in different economies.

The paper consists of five sections. First section gives information about Life Cycle Theory and the second section contains empirical studies from the current literature. The third and fourth part consists of econometric methodology, model and data. The last section interprets findings of study and draws a conclusion.

2 Empirical Literature

A number of empirical studies focus on the effect of demographic changes on savings rate and the current account balance. For instance, Kim and Lee (2007) examine the effects of demographic changes on saving and current account balance in 10 East Asian countries between 1981 and 2003. The panel Vector-Auto Regressive (VAR) model shows that an increase in the dependency rate lowers saving rates and worsens current account balances. The results indicate that the aging of the population and increase in dependency rate in East Asia might have a significant impact on savings rate and current account in the next decade. Zhu (2011) analyses the impact of demographic structure on internal and external savings within the scope of strict family planning policy in China between 1978 and 2007. Engle Granger cointegration test results show that the savings rate and total dependency ratio are cointegrated and support life cycle theory.

Thomas et al. (2010) examines current account balance for eleven emerging markets from 1970 to 2008 by using OLS technique. Results confirm that both old and young dependency negatively affect current account balance and higher fiscal deficit results in decrease in national savings. Higgins (1998) analyses the relationship between demographics, national savings and the current account balance by using time-series and cross-section data for 100 countries. The findings show that substantial increase in both the youth and old age dependency ratios results in lower saving rates.

3 Methodology

Asymmetric causality test has been proposed by Hatemi-J (2011) and later developed by others. This test allows researcher to take into account possible effects of the elements that causes instability such as; structural breaks, positive and negative shocks.

Granger causality approach is criticised because of its concept which bases on the notion of whether or not the past values of one variable can increase the precession of the forecast of another one and it has neglected asymmetric causal impacts (Hatemi-J et al., 2015: 3).

No asymmetry means being too restrictive about assumptions of the study. For example, there is almost no market that is characterized by symmetric information. In practice agents are giving different reactions to negative shocks than the positive ones even if they have the same magnitude. Panel data analysis has two dimensions; cross-sections and time series. It helps researchers to increase the degrees of freedom especially for developing and emerging market studies where time dimension (T) is shorter than number of observations (N) or taking into account spillover effects between cross-sections. This is why combining asymmetric causality with panel data analysis is much more efficient in a globalized era where all the economies are linked to each other and crossed borders (Hatemi-J, 2011: 2–3). Also the empirical studies show that in general, a potential asymmetry in the causality testing has crucial indirect effects for the underlying causal inference between elated variables.

This test focused on nexus between two variables such as w_1 *and* w_2. The integration between variables can be shown as follow (Hatemi-J et al., 2015:9);

$$w_{i1,t} = w_{i1,t} + e_{i1,t} = w_{i1,0} + \sum_{j=1}^{t} ei1,j \tag{1}$$

$$w_{i2,t} = w_{i2,t} + e_{i2,t} = w_{i2,0} + \sum_{j=1}^{t} ei2,j \tag{2}$$

N represents the number of cross-sections and t represents time. Error term (e) has white noise, zero mean and no correlation with its past values. For all $i = 1,\dots,N$ positive and negative shocks are defined as follow respectively; $e_{i1,t}^{+} := \max\left(e_{i1,t},0\right), e_{i2,t}^{+} := \max\left(e_{i2,t},0\right) and\, e_{i1,t}^{-} := \min\left(e_{i1,t},0\right), e_{i2,t}^{-} := \min\left(e_{i2,t},0\right)$. These equations are used to obtain cumulative sums of the shocks.

Hatemi-J (2015) asymmetric panel causality test is using VAR-SUR (p) – Vector Autoregressive Seemingly Unrelated Regression model. p signify lag order of the model which explains a trend in the data and it is important because it takes into account that error terms might be independent and that helps describing the data and predicting a response accurately. The optimal lag order is determined by information criteria (minimum one has chosen).

The null hypothesis "$w_{i2,t}^{+}$ does not cause $w_{i1,t}^{+}$" is tested via Wald test statistic and Wald test is based on normality assumption and has asymptotic chi-square χ^2 distribution (Hatemi-J and El-Khatib, 2016: 4036). If the negative components are tested than ($w_{i1,t}^{-}$ $w_{i2,t}^{-}$) vector might be used. Cumulative sums of shocks are calculated by an algorithm which is written in Gauss program by Hatemi-J.

4 Model and Data

The data has been taken from World Bank Development Indicators for twelve emerging markets (BRICS+Next Eleven; Brazil, India, China and South Korea, Indonesia, Philippines, Turkey, Bangladesh, Egypt, Mexico, Nigeria, Pakistan) during 1981–2016. Due to the lack of data, four countries (Russia, South Africa Republic, Vietnam, Iran) could not be included to the model. Theoretically current account balance is equal to excess of national savings according to equation 3 written below (Graff et al., 2012: 2);

$$CAB = (T - G) + S - I = Y - (C + I + G) \tag{3}$$

T,G,S,I,C,Y respectively represent tax revenue, government spending, private saving, domestic investment, private consumption and output. According to equation 3 demography is hypothesised to impact (directly or indirectly) the current account balance. Modigliani (1970) life cycle hypothesis claims that households at working age are the main savers of societies, while young society are likely to be borrowers and elderly people are dissavers. Naturally, economies with a relative young or old population consume more than what they produce. So it results with a current account deficit or vice versa.

Our study assumes that in an emerging economy current account balance (%of GDP) is a function of total age dependency – TD (%of working age population) and gross savings – GS (%of GDP).

$$CAB = f(TD, GS) \tag{4}$$

The asymmetric causality between variables tested one by one such as; TD *to* CAB and GS *to* CAB.

Tab. 1 shows the summary statistics of CAB, TD, GS. J-B represents the probability value of normality and less than 0.05. According to Jarque Bera (J-B) test results variables are normal.

Panel data analysis considers dependence between countries (cross-sections) because an economic shock in one country can affect the other one easily thanks

Tab. 1: Summary Statistics of Variables

Variables	Mean	Median	Maximum	Minimum	Std.Dev.	Skewness	Kurtosis	J-B
CAB	-0.405	-0.993	32.543	-14,167	4.396	2.010	14.235	0.00000
TD	65.469	65.023	94.581	35.590	15.651	-0.032	2.057	0.00000
GS	24.668	21.826	51.965	-5.604	10.029	0.644	3.034	0.000323

Tab. 2: Homegeneity and Cross-Section Dependence

Test	Statistics	Prob.
$\tilde{\Delta}$	8.910	0.000
$\tilde{\Delta}_{adj}$	9.435	0.000
CD_{LM1}	166.333	0.000
CD_{LM2}	8.733	0.000
CD_{LM}	5.328	0.000

to globalization. We first test the homogeneity and cross-sectional dependency between individual units by order of Delta test developed by Pesaran and Yamagata (2008) and later CD_{LM} test firstly developed by Breusch, Pagan (1980) – CD_{LM1} than Pesaran (2004) $-CD_{LM2}, CD_{LM}$.

$\tilde{\Delta}$ represents Delta test statistic for small samples and $\tilde{\Delta}_{adj}$ represents augmented Delta test statistic for big samples. According to Tab. 2, given variables are heterogeneous because the calculated probability value is under 0.05 for both level. So null hypothesis has rejected. Also probability values of CD_{LM} test for all variables are significant. The null hypothesis which claims that there is no cross-sectional dependency is rejected.

Maximum length is taken as 4 and optimal lag length for each section is determined by the Schwarz information criteria. CADF unit root test's critical values for the level with constant are as follows; -4.00 (%1), -3.30 (%5) ve -2.95 (%10) (in Pesaran 2007, table I(b), p.275); for model with constant and trend -4.51 (%1), -3.79 (%5) and -3.44 (%10) (in Pesaran 2007, table I(c), p.276).

Panel critical values for the first difference are as follows; for model with constant -2.44 (%1), -2.25 (%5) and -2.14 (%10) (in Pesaran 2007, table II(b), p.280); for model with constant and trend -2.93 (%1), -2.76 (%5) and -2.66 (%10) (in Pesaran 2007, table II(c), p.281).

CIPS (adjusted Im-Pesaran-Shin statistic) is the average of the t-values calculated for each cross-section unit. For negative serial correlation CADF(0), CIPS critical values for model with constant 0.795 and CADF(1), 0.041 in Pesaran 2007, p. 291. For model with constant and trend; CADF(0), 0.058 and CADF(1), 0.075.

The *CADF* test maintains its validity even when the time dimension (T) is larger or smaller than the observation (N) size (Güloğlu ve İvrendi, 2010: 383). According to Tab. 3, calculated test statistic are in general (* represents t-statistics in level and ** represents t-statistics in first level) higher than Pesaran (2007) critical values. So

Tab. 3: Cross-Sectionally Augmented Dicky-Fuller Unit Root Test

Countries	*CAB*		*TD*		*GS*	
	Constant	**Constant and Trend**	**Constant**	**Constant and Trend**	**Constant**	**Constant and Trend**
Brazil	−1.892 (level)*	−1.987*	−1.975*	0.067*	−1.556*	−1.341*
	−2.93 (1st *dif.*)	−2.690**	−3.398	−4.414	−2.250**	−2.730**
Bangladesh	−3.945	−4.636	−4.666	−4.649	−3.241	−3.478*
	−5.32	−5.328	−4.499	−4.493	−6.717	−6.607
China	−3.106	−2.753*	−1.629*	−0.280*	−0.339*	−1.672*
	−4.99	−5.008	−8.026	−7.939	−3.752	−6.332
India	−5.532	−5.675	−4.297	−4.927	−1.015*	−2.456*
	−4.43	−4.294	−3.234	−3.291	−5.176	−4.168
Indonesia	−2.377*	−2.880*	0.407*	−1.822*	−0.896*	−1.242*
	−5.73	−5.661	−5.417	−5.462	−4.710	−5.101
Egypt	−4.007	−4.022	−4.096	−4.176	−0.531*	−4.754
	−6.00	−5.845	−4.537	−4.463	−6.066	−4.630
S. Korea	−2.506*	−3.347*	1.926*	0.205*	−3.843	−3.741*
	−4.92	−4.830	−3.592	−4.349	−6.794	−5.958
Mexico	−3.614	−3.681	−4.310	−4.251	−1.603*	−1.534*
	−5.64	−5.612	−6.303	−6.219	−5.316	−6.676
Nigeria	−1.398*	−2.134*	−1.188*	−3.499*	−1.867*	−2.540*
	−3.72	−3.702	−5.655	−5.723	−8.428	−5.261
Pakistan	−3.452	−3.409*	−6.015	−6.040	−3.888	−3.936
	−2.34	−2.281	−7.825	−7.735	−3.712	−8.952
Philippines	−1.124*	−1.472*	3.245*	1.242*	−1.615*	−1.516*
	−6.02	−6.202	−1.589**	−3.315	−3.712	−3.633
Turkey	−4.319	−4.186	−3.247	−3.788*	−4.845	−4.957
	−7.38	−7.244	−5.855	−5.817	−5.822	−5.745
CIPS	−3.106	−3.348	−2.154	−2.660	−2.103	−2.764
	−4.95	−4.891	−4.994	−5.817	−5.421	−5.483

Tab. 4: Asymmetric Panel Causality Test

Countries	Null Hypothesis	P. value	Casual Parameter	Null Hypothesis	P. value	Casual Pa.
Brazil	$TD \neq> CAB$	0.134	–	$GS \neq> CAB$	0.190	–
	$TD^- \neq> CAB^-$	0.474	–	$GS^- \neq> CAB^-$	0.001*	2.583
	$TD^+ \neq> CAB^+$	0.849	–	$GS^+ \neq> CAB^+$	0.096	–
Bangladesh	$TD \neq> CAB$	0.014*	−2.600	$GS \neq> CAB$	0.909	–
	$TD^- \neq> CAB^-$	0.040*	2.344	$GS^- \neq> CAB^-$	0.048*	2.583
	$TD^+ \neq> CAB^+$	0.642	–	$GS^+ \neq> CAB^+$	0.082	–
China	$TD \neq> CAB$	0.309	–	$GS \neq> CAB$	0.000*	6.131
	$TD^- \neq> CAB^-$	0.001*	−10.389	$GS^- \neq> CAB^-$	0.043*	0.713
	$TD^+ \neq> CAB^+$	0.928	–	$GS^+ \neq> CAB^+$	0.488	–
India	$TD \neq> CAB$	0.817	–	$GS \neq> CAB$	0.000*	4.843
	$TD^- \neq> CAB^-$	0.160	–	$GS^- \neq> CAB^-$	0.370	–
	$TD^+ \neq> CAB^+$	0.000*	0.047	$GS^+ \neq> CAB^+$	0.213	–
Indonesia	$TD \neq> CAB$	0.239	–	$GS \neq> CAB$	0.809	–
	$TD^- \neq> CAB^-$	0.021*	6.995	$GS^- \neq> CAB^-$	0.391	–
	$TD^+ \neq> CAB^+$	0.005*	−1.320	$GS^+ \neq> CAB^+$	0.070	–
Egypt	$TD \neq> CAB$	0.999	–	$GS \neq> CAB$	0.246	–
	$TD^- \neq> CAB^-$	0.784	–	$GS^- \neq> CAB^-$	0.493	–
	$TD^+ \neq> CAB^+$	0.907	–	$GS^+ \neq> CAB^+$	0.002*	0.547
S. Korea	$TD \neq> CAB$	0.078	–	$GS \neq> CAB$	0.000*	3.326
	$TD^- \neq> CAB^-$	0.120	–	$GS^- \neq> CAB^-$	0.598	–
	$TD^+ \neq> CAB^+$	0.721	–	$GS^+ \neq> CAB^+$	0.740	–
Mexico	$TD \neq> CAB$	0.931	–	$GS \neq> CAB$	0.873	–
	$TD^- \neq> CAB^-$	0.932	–	$GS^- \neq> CAB^-$	0.232	–
	$TD^+ \neq> CAB^+$	0.003*	0.187	$GS^+ \neq> CAB^+$	0.043*	−0.781
Nigeria	$TD \neq> CAB$	0.188	–	$GS \neq> CAB$	0.992	–
	$TD^- \neq> CAB^-$	0.928	–	$GS^- \neq> CAB^-$	0.626	–
	$TD^+ \neq> CAB^+$	0.971	–	$GS^+ \neq> CAB^+$	0.724	–
Pakistan	$TD \neq> CAB$	0.681	–	$GS \neq> CAB$	0.051	–
	$TD^- \neq> CAB^-$	0.903	–	$GS^- \neq> CAB^-$	0.355	–
	$TD^+ \neq> CAB^+$	0.481	–	$GS^+ \neq> CAB^+$	0.810	–
Phillipines	$TD \neq> CAB$	0.002*	1.860	$GS \neq> CAB$	0.004*	0.756
	$TD^- \neq> CAB^-$	0.774	–	$GS^- \neq> CAB^-$	0.981	–
	$TD^+ \neq> CAB^+$	0.000*	3.626	$GS^+ \neq> CAB^+$	0.179	–
Turkey	$TD \neq> CAB$	0.000*	−0.018	$GS \neq> CAB$	0.884	–
	$TD^- \neq> CAB^-$	0.274	–	$GS^- \neq> CAB^-$	0.069	–
	$TD^+ \neq> CAB^+$	0.414	–	$GS^+ \neq> CAB^+$	0.261	–

null hypothesis is accepted in level but rejected for the first differences. Variables are I(1).

The demonstration $TD \neq> CAB$ means that total age dependency ratio does not Granger cause current account balance. The demonstration $GS \neq> CAB$ means that gross savings (% of GDP) does not Granger vause current account balance (% of GDP). The vectors (TD^{+}, CAB^{+}) and (GS^{+}, CAB^{+}) show the cumulative positive shocks. The vectors (TD^{-}, CAB^{-}) and (GS^{-}, CAB^{-}) represent the cumulative negative shocks. Hatemi-J (2011) asymmetric panel causality test has been analyzed with Gauss 10.0. According to Tab. 4, nonasymmetric causality ($TD \neq> CAB$) signifies that the null hypothesis is not causing current account balance and cannot be rejected except for Bangladesh, Philippines and Turkey. * represents significant probability values in % 5 level. ($GS \neq> CAB$) cannot be rejected except for China, India, S. Korea and Philippines.

The null hypothesis of positive shock in total age dependency ratio not causing similar shocks in current account balance cannot be rejected except for India, Indonesia, Mexico, Philippines. The null hypothesis of positive shock in gross savings not causing similar shocks in current account balance cannot be rejected except for Egypt and Mexico. For instance, estimated casual parameter for Mexico is 0.187, which means a 1 % increase in total age dependency ratio will cause 0.187 % current account surplus opposite to life cycle hypothesis. Meanwhile a 1 % increase in gross savings will cause -0.781 % current account deficit in the same country.

The null hypothesis that negative total age dependency ratio or gross savings shocks do not cause negative shocks in current account balance cannot be rejected except for respectively; Bangladesh, China, Indonesia and Brazil, Bangladesh, China. For example, a 1 % increase in total age dependency ratio will cause -10.389 % current account deficit in China and a 1 % increase in gross savings will cause 0.713 % current account surplus.

These results confirm that in general, life cycle hypothesis is rejected for emerging economies. On the other hand, an increase in gross savings can cause current account surplus but as we can see from the table increases in gross saving rates are smaller than increases in total age dependency ratio.

5 Conclusion

In this paper, the impact of total age dependency and gross savings on current account balance is analysed. The contribution of this paper to the literature can be divided into two; firstly it includes BRICS and Next Eleven emerging-developing economies with a wide span of time period (1981–2016). Secondly there is no study that analyzed life cycle hypothesis with a panel asymmetric causality test and takes into account different reactions of households to positive and negative shocks in different economies. Hatemi-J (2015) asymmetric panel causality test results indicate that the significance of life cycle hypothesis is rejected for emerging economies. On contrary to the hypothesis, the results show that increase in total age dependency cause current account surplus.

Bibliography

Bloom D. E, Canning D. F., (2011). Implications of Population Aging for Economic Growth. PGDA Working Paper No.64.

Breusch, T. S. and Pagan, A. R. (1980). The Lagrange Multiplier Test and Its Application to Model Specifications in Econometrics. Review of Economic Studies, 47: 239–253.

Coale, A. and Hoover, E. (1958). Population Growth and Economic Development in Low-Income Countries, Princeton: Princeton Univ. Press.

Graff, M., Tang, K. and Zhang J. (2012). Does Demographic Change Affect the Current Account? A Reconsideration. Global Economy Journal, 12(4): 1–24.

Güloğlu, B. and İvrendi, M. (2010). Output Fluctuations: Transitory or Permanent? the case of Latin America. Applied Economics Letters, 17: 381–386.

Hatemi-J, A. (2011). Asymmetric Panel Causality Tests with an Application to the Impact of Fiscal Policy on Economic Performance in Scandinavia, Munich Personal RePEc Archive. https://mpra.ub.uni-muenchen.de/55527/1/MPRA_paper_55527.pdf (Date of access, 26.03.2018).

Hatemi-j, A., Ajmi, N. A., Montanasser, G. Inglesi-Lots, R. and Gupta, R. (2015). Research Output and Economic Growth in G7 Countries: New Evidence from Asymmetric Panel Causality Testing. Applied Economics, 2301–2308.

Hatemi-J, A., Chang, T., Chen, W., Lin, F. and Gupta, R. (2015). Asymmetric Granger Causality between Military Expenditures and Economic Growth in Top Six Defense Suppliers, University of Pretoria, Department of Economics Working Paper Series, September.

Hatemi-J, A. and El-Khatib, Y. (2016). An Extension of the Asymmetric Causality Tests for Dealing with Deterministic Trend Components. Applied Economics, 48(42): 4033–4041.

Higgins, M. (1998). Demography, National Savings and International Capital Flows. International Economic Review, 39(2): 343–369.

Jaffri, A. A., Naveed, T. A., Asjed, R., and Khatoon, I. (2012). Impact of Population Growth on Current Account Balance of Pakistan. Journal of Managerial Sciences, 6(2): 178.

Kim, S., and Lee, J. (2007). Demographic Changes, Saving, and Current Account in East Asia. Asian Economic Papers, 22–53.

Modigliani, F. (1970). The Life Cycle Hypothesis of Consumption. in: W. A. Eltis, M. F. G. Scott, and J. N. Wolfe, eds., Induction, Growth, and Trade: Essays in Honour of Sir Roy Harrod, Oxford University Press: 197–225.

Modigliani, F. (1988). The Role of Intergenerational Transfers and Life Cycle Saving in the Accumulation of Wealth. Journal of Economic Perspectives, 2(2): 15–40.

Modigliani, F. and Brumberg, R. (1954). Utility Analysis and the Consumption Function: An Interpretation of Cross-Section Data. in K. Kurihara, ed., Post-Keynesian Economics, New Brunswick: Rutgers University Press.Obstfeld, M. and Rogoff, K. (2000). The Six Major Puzzles in International Macroeconomics: Is There a Common Cause?. NBER Macroeconomics Annual. The MIT Press.Pesaran, H. M. (2004). General Diagnostic Tests for Cross Section Dependence in Panels, Working Paper No: 0435, University of Cambridge.

Pesaran, H. M. (2007). A Simple Panel Unit Root Test in the Presence of Cross Section Dependence. Journal of Applied Econometrics, 22(2): 265–312.

Prati, A., Ricci, L. A., Christiansen, L., Tokarick, S., and Tressel, T. (2011). External Performance in Low Income Countries. International Monetary Fund, Occasional Paper, 272

Thomas, A., Prat, J. and Medina, L, (2010). Current Account Estimates for Emerging Market Economies, IMF Working Paper No 10/43.

Zhu, C. (2011). China's Saving and Current Account Balance: A Demographic Transition Perspective, Modern Economy, 2: 804–813.

Esra N. Kilci

Analysis of the Relationship between Interest Rates and Non-Performing Loans Ratio in the Framework of Adverse Selection Problem; Turkey Case[1]

1 Introduction

Financial stability in general and banking sector soundness in particular has great role in facilitating high and sustainable economic growth rates. Among several indicators of financial stability, non-performing loans ratio in banking sector has critical importance as it indicates to deterioration in loan portfolio thereby asset quality which is a crucial factor leading to insolvency and illiquidity in banking sector by jeopardizing bank capital and increasing the probability of financial distress. In several studies that examine the determinants of NPLs, generally referring to loans which do not generate income for a relatively long period of time, at least 90 days or more (Joseph et al, 2012), either macroeconomic or bank-specific determinants are used as explanatory variables. Of the bank-specific determinants, interest rate changes are highly considered to have impact on NPLs. Besides, high real interest rates with the excessive credit growth are closely correlated with systemic banking crises (Demirgüç-Kunt and Detragiache, 1998; Borio and Lowe, 2002).

Interest rate is defined as the price that borrowers have to pay to the banks for the use of funding provided (Collins and Wanjau, 2011). Therefore, interest income charged in return for funding is an important source which supports bank profitability and is there is a high dependence between interest income and performing loans. Interest revenue come from loans and all advances extended by a bank such as working capital overdrafts and it also contains interest received on bank's deposits kept with other financial institutions. Growth in non-performing loans which do not yield income results in erosion of interest income (Ugoani, 2016).

Hence, while loan repayments improve profitability of banks, if the borrowers cannot make the payments properly, the consequence would be increase in NPLs. Interest rate rises are generally correlated to increases in NPLs. At first, rising

1 This paper is a revised and expanded version of a paper entitled ***'Analysis of the Relationship between Interest Rates and Non-Performing Loans Ratio in the Framework of Adverse Selection Problem; Turkey Case'*** presented at the 3rd International Conference on Economics, Business Management and Social Sciences (ICEBSS 2018) which was held on August 07–11, 2018 in Skopje, Macedonia.

interest rates directly affect borrower's lending capacity, if the share of variable-rate interest rate loans is significant, the effect will be greater (Nkusu, 2011; Beck et al, 2013; Love and Ariss, 2013). High interest rates charged to borrowers may trigger adverse selection problem[2] due to the rising cost of borrowing (Stiglitz and Weiss, 1981). The market is characterized by adverse selection if riskier firms are more likely to borrow and these borrowers take loans with an intention not to repay. In this case, increase in interest rates aggravates adverse selection problem, inducing a deterioration in the quality of borrowers (Crawford et al, 2015).

It is impossible to sustain the profitability of banking sector without having proper flows of interest incomes as a result of the intermediation role of banks. Since banks could not generate appropriate interest incomes from their loans and NPLs hurt the reserve provision of the banks in a sense that banks have to keep provisions set aside from their earnings according to regulations, erosion of capital will occur which hits negatively on their profitability.

There will be increases in non-performing loans, since potential bad credit risks are the ones who most actively seek out a loan in the market. Increases in NPLs put pressures on banks' balance sheets preventing them from maintaining their traditional intermadiation role of giving credits thereby negatively affecting aggregate demand, investments and economic activity. Hence, identifying the determinants of the NPLs is of great importance for the banking system to produce adequate policies.

These problem loans also have potential for reducing private consumption, and if there is no deposit guarantee mechanism to protect depositors, they can become a source of economic contraction, especially when along with declining gross capital formation in the context of a credit crunch caused by erosion of banks' equity and assets. During the late 1980s and most of the 1990s, a large number of countries including Mexico, Argentina and East-Asian countries experienced systemic crises. These crises were largely characterized by the poor performance of banking and financial institutions. They were largely associated with a rapid accumulation of non-performing loans in the banking sector and a deterioration of asset quality due to increases in credit risk (Fofack, 2005; pp. 3–5).

The increase in NPLs is frequently associated with several factors, including macroeconomic performance (Espinoza and Prasad, 2010), business failures (Williamson, 1987), macro-financial conditions (Caprio and Klingebiel, 1996;

2 Adverse selection is an asymmetric information problem that occurs when the parties who want to take on big risks are likely to be the most eager to take out a loan. Thus, the parties who are the most likely to produce an undesirable outcome are most likely to be selected. Since adverse selection makes it more likely that loans might be made to bad credit risks and uncertainty increases, banks become reluctant to function their traditional role of lending even though there are good credit risks in the market (Mishkin, 1996; p. 2).

Kaminsky and Reinhart, 1999), real interest rates and credit conditions (Jimenez and Saurina, 2006), credit market frictions and macro-financial vulnerability (Nkusu, 2011), large exposures to highly procyclical credit types, managerial inefficiency (Louzis et al, 2010), credit growth, capital ratio, bank size, market power (Salas and Saurina, 2002), and moral hazard problems (Goldstein and Turner, 1996). Exploring the determinants of NPLs which derivates from ex-post credit has great importance in terms of actions and regulations that the financial system and authorities would implement to maintain banking sector thereby financial stability. As most of these studies support, interest rates increases are one of the macroeconomic factors triggering NPLs ratio.

In Turkey, the rising trend in levels of NPLs in the period of 2014–2018 brings concerns, given that experiences from 2000–2001 Crises caused big harm to the banking sector and the reforming and restructuring processes took a long time. The purpose of this study is to analyze the relationship between consumer credit interest rates and non-performing loans ratio in Turkish banking sector by using monthly data which range from 2005:01 to 2018:03. The results of econometric analysis indicate that there is a causality relationship between consumer credit interest rates and NPLs ratio.

2 A Brief Review of Banking Sector in Turkey

The Turkish banking sector experienced critical consolidation in the five year period after 1999–2001 disinflation programme failed and the Turkish 2000–01 Crises devastated to the Turkish economy. At the beginning of 2004, the banking sector was able to move to the second stage of consolidation and growth, leaving behind a very jittery period (Steinherr et al, 2004; p. 1). Another important crucial point in Turkey has been the 2008–09 Global Financial Crisis. A major restructuring program was followed to protect the banking sector from the adverse effects of the global financial crisis. This crisis has changed the structure of Turkish banking sector and ownership has played a key role in this change. Since the banking sector constitutes a large part of the financial system, Central Bank of the Republic of Turkey (CBRT) has taken measures to reduce the probability of financial distress and has adopted financial stability as an additional goal (Us, 2015; p. 1).

The banking sector which has a dominant role in the financial sector constitutes more than %90 of the financial system in terms of asset size and has great significance for financial stability. Compared to similar emerging market economies, the share of non-bank financial institutions in the financial system is small and capital market intermediation remains insignificant. The financial system which accounts for % 118 of 2015 GDP in terms of asset size, has grown much faster than GDP size since 2008. It is seen that the concentration in the sector is low and the market share is equally distributed among state-owned, private-domestic and foreign-owned banks. Entries provided by foreign banks through acquisition-based transactions has led to a large increase in their asset ownership share (IMF, 2016; p. 10).

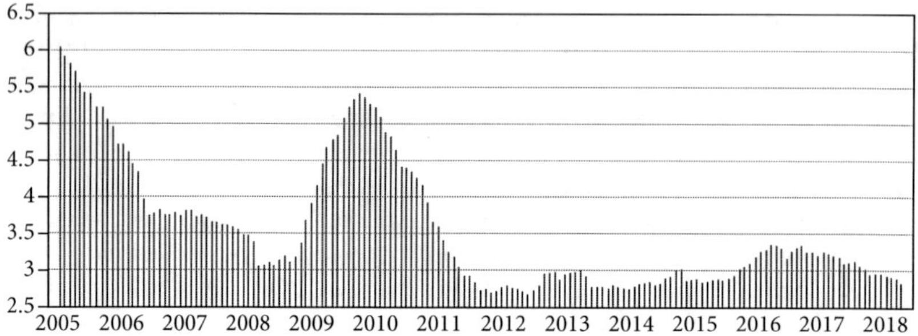

Graph 1: Non-performing Loans Ratio; 2005–2018 (As of March). Source: www.ceicdata.com

Development of the banking sector in Turkey has contributed significantly to the overall growth of the economy. As of 2016, the number of banks operating in the sector was 52 and deposit banks with a total number of 34 had the largest weight. Excluding stocks traded in the Istanbul stockmarket (BIST), the ratio of assets of the banks owned by foreign banks to total assets was approximately % 25 (TBB, 2017).

When the NPLs ratios are examined in the period of 2005–2018 period, it can be inferred from the graph below that the ratio seems to take its maximum values in the years of 2005 (%6.0), 2009 (%5.3) and 2016 (%3.4). By the year 2017 (As of December), the NPLs ratio realizes as % 3.0 and the ratio stands at 2.9 percent as of March 2018 (Ministry of Treasury and Finance, 2018).

3 Literature Review

Several researches related to the determinants of NPLs have been conducted in many countries with conclusions which indicate to significant relationships between NPLs and the factors including macroeconomic and bank-specific factors. Of them, the relationship between interest rates and NPLs in the banking system has been subject to a great amount of interest in both theoretical and empirical literature.

Demirgüç-Kunt and Detragiache (1998) studied the factors which could be associated with the rise of systemic banking crises in a large sample of developed and developing countries in the period of 1980–94 by using a multivariate logit econometric model. They indicated that banks faced insolvency owing to falling asset values when bank borrowers were unable to repay their debt due to high interest rates. Shu (2002) examined the impact of macroeconomic developments on the asset quality of the banking sector by using NPLs ratio in Hong Kong by using regression analysis. The results showed that both asset quality and the increasing NPLs ratios are influenced by macroeconomic factors such as economic growth, inflation and interest rates and by variables demonstrating financial fragility such as property prices and bankruptcies.

Ranjan and Dahl (2003) analysed the determinants of NPLs in commercial banks in India by employing panel regression model. The empirical analysis assessed that how NPLs in the banking sector were influenced by three major sets of economic and financial factors including terms of credit, bank size induced risk preferences and macroeconomic shocks. The empirical results suggested that terms of credit variable had significant impact on the banks' NPLs in the presence of bank size induced risk preferences and macroeconomic shocks. Concurrently, the changes in the cost of credit in terms of expectations of higher interest rates led to a rise in NPLs.

Berge and Boye (2007) investigated macroeconomic factors that acted as driving forces behind the developments in NPLs in Norway over the period of 1993–2005. They found that problem loans are highly sensitive to developments in real interest rates in Norway. They also proved that housing prices and unemployment made a significant contribution to the NPLs. Glogowski (2008) examined the relationship between macroeconomic variables such as GDP growth, real interest rates and unemployment and NPLs as well as loan loss provisions for the 108 bank operating in Polish banking sector. They found that loan loss provisions were positively correlated to the unemployment rates and real interest rates and negatively correlated to the GDP growth, that is, while increases in real interest rates and unemployment rates led to increases in the loan losses of banks, increases in GDP growth resulted in decreases in the loan loss provisions.

Espinoza and Prasad (2010) employed a dynamic panel over 1995–2008 on nearly 80 banks in the Gulf Corporation Council region including the countries such as Bahrain, Qatar, and Saudi Arabia. They found that both macroeconomic and bank-specific determinants had impact on NPLs. Their results also showed that the NPL ratio was deteriorated as economic growth got lower and interest rates increased. Nkusu (2011) investigated the macroeconomic determinants of NPLs by using panel regressions for 26 developed economies. They found that higher interest rates and unemployment rates, slower GDP growth and falling asset prices led to rise in NPLs.

Louzis et al (2011) anayzed both macroeconomic and bank-specific determinants of NPLs in Greece by using dynamic panel data sets. Their results showed that the Greek banking sector and NPLs were influenced by macroeconomic variables including GDP growth, unemployment, interest rates and public debt and by bank-specific determinants. They also found that the management performance and efficiency had also impact on NPLs. Saba et al (2012) examined the determinants of NPLs in U.S banking sector for the period of 1985–2010. In their study, they took the real GDP per capita, inflation and total loans as independent variables and NPLs as dependent variable. They found that although the impacts were not highly significant, all independent variables had significant impact on NPLs.

Messai and Jouini (2013) tried to find the factors that could affect NPLS for a sample consisting of 85 banks in Greece, Italy and Spain during the period of 2004–2008.

The results indicated that GDP growth and profitability of banks' assets had negative impact on NPLs. On the other hand, the unemployment rate, loan loss reserves to total loans ratio and the real interest rates had positive impact on NPLs. Beck et al (2013) studied the macroeconomic determinants of NPLs for 75 advanced and emerging economies in the period from 2000 to 2010 by using a novel panel data set. According to their dynamic panel estimates, the exchange rate, real GDP growth, share prices and the lending interest rate were found to significantly impact NPL ratios.

Chaibi and Ftiti (2015) examined the determinants of NPLs of commercial banks in France and Germany for the period of 2005–2011 by using dynamic panel data approach. The results indicated that except for the inflation rate, the set of macroeconomic variables including inflation, GDP growth, interest rate and exchange rate used in the study influenced the NPLs of both France and Germany. They also found that bank-specific determinants such as inefficiency, loan loss provisions, leverage and bank size had significant impact on NPLs.

Pullicino (2016) tested the impact of macroeconomic variables on the level of NPLs for commercial banks in Malta, Italy, Spain, France and UK by using a multiple linear regression model for each country during the period of 2002–2014. Their results showed that some macroeconomic variables had impact on NPLs. For instance, GDP and money supply were significant in Malta, the interest rate was significant in case of Spain and the exchange rate was significant in the U.K. Gabeshi (2017) studied the determinants of NPLs for Albania by using multiple linear regression during the period of 2005–2014. The results indicated that NPLs were significantly affected by macroeconomic and financial factors. According to their findings, credit risk increased when GDP growth, credit growth rate and the share price indices decreased and it became lower when interest rates and loan to deposit ratio decreased.

4 Econometric Analysis

4.1 Data and Methodology

In this study, the causality relationship between interest rates and non-performing loans ratio is analyzed using Fourier Approach. The period ranges from 2005:01 to 2018:03. The period covers the period 2016–2017 which are the years market interest rates have an upward trend because of increasing uncertainty in the financial markets as a result of both domestic and external factors. In investigation of the relationship between variables, consumer credit interest rates to approximate interest rates and NPLs ratio to approximate the ratio of problem loans, which are obtained from Bloomberg, Banking Regulation and Supervision Authority (BRSA) and Ministry of Treasury and Finance have been used.

In the first stage, Fourier KPSS Stationary Test has been employed to test the stationary of the variables. The Fourier test developed by Becker et al (2006) can detect not only sudden changes but also slow changes and the position, number and form of structural changes do not affect the power of the test. Subsequently,

Tab. 1: Variables and Expected Relationship

	Variables	Measure	Expected Relationship
Dependent Variable	Problem Loans	Non-Performing Loans Ratio (NPLs Ratio)	(+)
Independent Variable	Interest Rate	Consumer Credit Interest Rates	

Fourier Granger Causality Test has been employed to test the causality relationship between variables. The VAR with Fourier Frequencies which has been employed by Enders and Jones (2015) that uses Flexible Fourier Form yields powerful results. After introducing trigonometric functions into the model, they found a richer set of interactions between the variables.

4.2 Analysis and Results

Since there is generally no specific information relating to the definite nature of the breaks and no practical knowledge about the location and the number of breaks to use in testing for stationary, using an incorrect specification for the number or form of breaks might create some dilemma such as ignoring the breaks together. Becker et al (2006) developed a stationary test in which a chosen frequency component of a Fourier function was used to estimate the deterministic components of the model. A Fourier series could effectively model the behavior of an unknown function even though this function is not regular. In this stationary test, that the Fourier function capturing the movements of the unknown function is the primary reason for applying it. The Fourier test developed by Becker et al (2006) can detect not only sudden changes but also slow changes and the position, number and form of structural changes do not affect the power of the test. For this reason, the performance of the tests was substantially robust to several kinds of structural breaks often seen in economic analysis, including the breaks of opposite signs (Tsong, 2016).

The methodology developed by Becker et al (2006) seems strong to notice sharp and u-shaped breaks as well as smooth breaks near the end of a series and it functions best when breaks are gradual. Becker et al (2006) employ trigonometric terms to capture unknown nonlinearities. The test they developed is a KPSS-type stationary test (Becker et al, 2006).

Becker et al (2006) take into account the following DGP;

$$y_t = Xt'\beta + Zt'\gamma + r_t + \varepsilon_t$$
$$r_t = r_{t-1} + u_t, \quad (1)$$

where ε_t are stationary errors and u_t are independent and identically distributed with variance σ_u^2. It is chosen $Z_t = [sin(2\pi kt/T), cos(2\pi kt/T)]'$ to capture a break in the deterministic term, where k represents the frequency and T is the sample size. Here, to test whether y_t is stationary or not, it is defined as X_t = [1] for a level-stationary process for y_t and $X_t = [1, t]'$ for a trend-stationary process.

At the start, one of the models described below is estimated and the residuals are obtained, in order to acquire the t-statistic required for testing the null hypothesis $(H_0 = \sigma_u^2 = 0)$;

$$y_t = \propto_0 + \gamma_1 \sin\left(\frac{2\pi kt}{T}\right) + \gamma_2 \cos\left(\frac{2\pi kt}{T}\right) + e_t \tag{2}$$

$$y_t = \propto_0 + \beta t + \gamma_1 \sin\left(\frac{2\pi kt}{T}\right) + \gamma_2 \cos\left(\frac{2\pi kt}{T}\right) + e_t \tag{3}$$

The following test statistics is obtained;

$$\tau_\mu(k) \; or \; \tau_\tau(k) = \frac{1}{T^2} \frac{\sum_{t=1}^{T} \tilde{S}_t(k)^2}{\tilde{\sigma}^2} \tag{4}$$

where $\tilde{S}_t(k) = \sum_{j=1}^{t} \tilde{e}_j$ and $\tilde{e}_j$ are the OLS residuals from the regression (2) for $\tau_\mu(k)$ or (3) for $\tau_\tau(k)$. As in KPSS, a nonparametric estimate $\tilde{\sigma}^2$ of the long-run variance could be obtained by choosing a truncation lag parameter l and a set of weights w_j, j = 1,…,l;

$$\tilde{\sigma}^2 = \tilde{\gamma}_0 + 2\sum w_j \tilde{\gamma}_j, \tag{5}$$

where $\tilde{\gamma}_j$ is the jth sample auto-covariance of the residuals $\tilde{e}_t$ from equation (2) or (3).

To determine the optimal number of k, the value which gives the minimum sum of residuals (OLS) is being selected. In case the non-linear trend is not present in DGP, it can be applied the standard KPSS test in order to obtain increased power. As it seems useful to test for the absence of a non-linear trend, Becker et al (2006) proposed that F-test statistic to be used. Therefore, the following F-test statistic for this hypothesis (absence of a nonlinear trend (i.e. $\gamma_1 = \gamma_2 = 0$) can be calculated against the alternative of a nonlinear trend with a given frequency k.

$$F_i(k) = \frac{(SSR_0 - SSR_1(k)/2}{SSR_1(k)/(T-q)} \quad i = \mu, \tau, \tag{6}$$

The F-test could be used only if the null of stationary is rejected. The standard KPSS test statistic would be used in case trigonometric terms are not significant. In comparison with the critical values related to Fourier Test which are shown in the study of Becker et al (2006), the results of the stationary test are stated below;

Tab. 2: Stationary Test Results

Variable	Frequency	MinSSR	FKPSS	F-Statistic
NPLs Ratio	1	78,14355	0,165197	42,165
Consumer Credit Interest Rate	1	986,2413	0,112867	107,0348
	FKPSS Critical Values			**F-Statistic Critical Values**
1 %	0,2709			6,281
5 %	0,1696			4,651
10 %	0,1294			3,935

As seen in the Tab. 2, the NPLs ratio and Consumer Credit Interest Rate variables are stationary. According to the F-Test results which are used to test the significancy of the trigonometric terms, it seems that trigonometric terms for both variables are significant when the values are compared with the F-Statistic Critical Values which are shown in the study of Becker et al (2006).

In the second stage, it is employed Fourier Granger Causality Test proposed by Enders and Jones (2015) in this study in order to investigate the causal linkages between consumer credit interest rates and NPLs ratio. Since the linkages between the variables have been subjected to gradual shifts and linear specifications are mostly inappropriate to capture the relationships, econometric examinations are not generally direct and simple. Enders and Jones (2015) allows the Flexible Fourier form to capture the multiple smooth mean shifts that are likely to be present in the VAR system. In one respect, their results complement those of Enders and Holt (2014) who estimate a VAR with LSTAR mean shifts. While they focus on long-run mean shifts, Enders and Jones focus on Granger causality tests and on the short-run dynamics of the system.

Instead of estimating the number, form, and the size of the breaks, Enders and Jones tried the Flexible Fourier Form to control for breaks in a VAR and after they tested the non-stationary of variables, they considered the linear VAR as following;

$$z_t = \delta + \sum_{i=1}^{11} A_i z_{t-i} + e_t \tag{7}$$

where δ is a (4x1) vector of intercepts, A_i is a (4×4) coefficient vector and e_t is the vector of innovations. Although the responses seem reasonable, they have some problems for two reasons. First, to the extent that there are neglected structural breaks, the system given by (7) is misspecified. Second, given that an unrestricted VAR is likely to be over parameterized, the confidence intervals shown in the figure may be unnecessarily large. In order to show how neglected breaks can interfere with Granger causality tests, they followed a standard recommendation and limited the VAR by imposing the restrictions implied by the Granger causality tests. Their results indicated that there is very little interaction among the variables. The significant responses are such that series tend to respond only to their own shocks.

Then, Enders and Jones allowed the deterministic regressors be as following, instead of the VAR given by (7);

$$z_t = \delta(t) + \sum_{i=1}^{11} A_i z_{t-i} + e_t \tag{8}$$

$$\delta(t) = \left[\delta_1(t), \delta_2(t), \delta_3(t), \delta_4(t)\right]' \tag{9}$$

and each intercept δ_{it} depends on n Fourier frequencies such that;

$$\delta_i(t) = a_i + b_i t + \sum_{k=1}^{n} a_{ik} \sin\left(\frac{2\pi kt}{T}\right) + b_{ik} cos\left(\frac{2\pi kt}{T}\right) \tag{10}$$

When the Fourier terms are used to control for breaks, the Granger causality results change from those documented before in several important ways. In contrast to the Granger causality results indicated by the linear VAR, when Enders and Jones (2015) put trigonometric functions into the model, they detected stronger relations and richer sets of interactions between the variables.

Tab. 3 shows the results of Fourier Granger Causality Test. According to the results, as asymptotic p-value is less than 0.05 in both directions, there seems to be a causality relationship between Consumer Credit Interest Rate and the NPLs Ratio. The findings indicate that both the changes in Consumer Credit Interest Rates do have impacts on NPLs Ratio and the changes in NPLs ratio have impacts on Consumer Credit Interest Rates.

Tab. 3: Causality Test Results

Optimal Frequency	**Wald-stat**	**Asymptotic p-value**	**Bootstrap p-value**	**Optimal Lag**
3	32.665	0,000***	0,001	7
3	22.595	0,002**	0,002	7

Consumer Credit Interest Rates → NPLs Ratio
NPLs Ratio → Consumer Credit İnterest Rates
Notes: → denotes to causality. Optimal k (frequency) and p (lag) are determined by Akaike information criterion. Bootstrap p-values are based on 1000 replications. ***, **, and * denote %1, %5, and %10 levels of statistical significance, respectively. Because n>50 in this study, we will take asymptotic p-value in comparison.

5 Conclusion

As NPLs ratio serves as one of major indicators to the health of banking sector in general and refers to asset quality in particular, adequate assessment of credit risk and identifying the determinants of NPLs by policy makers has great importance in terms of macro-prudential analysis. Of the bank-specific determinants, interest rate changes are highly considered to have impact on NPLs. When the negative effects of the increases in the interest rates are examined in the academic literature, it comes out that adverse selection problems and effects of interest rates rises in the market are outstanding.

Adverse selection problem expresses that the interest rates have impacts on loan quality and higher interest rates might lead to withdrawal of high-quality borrowers from the market. Thus, the parties who are the most likely to produce an undesirable outcome are most likely to be selected. Therefore, both the decline in the loans and the increase in the non-performing loans might occur. As a result of adverse selection problem and increasing uncertainty, that banks become reluctant to function their traditional role of lending leads to slowdown in investments and economic activity.

Because of its importance, there have been several studies carried out to determine the impact of interest rates on NPLs ratio in the literature. In Turkey, after the 2000–01 Crises, there has been seen a significant improvement in macro-financial indicators and as a result interest rates recorded remarkable declines due to the structural reforms, fiscal discipline and inflation targetting program. However, in the last two-year period, the interest rates has an upward trend as a result of deterioration in risk perception which arises from political uncertainty and negative outlook in macro-financial indicators such as inflation and real exchange rate. There has been also a slightly upward movement in non-performing loans ratio at the same period.

This study based on monthly data over the period from 2005:01 to 2018:03 provides an empirical analysis as to the relationship between interest rates and NPL ration in Turkish banking sector. The findings implies that there is a causality relationship between consumer credit interest rates and NPLs ratio. It can be inferred from the results that if interest rates continue to rise in the following period, it seems highly probable that the increase in NPLs ratio will accelerate gradually. As known, uncertainty and risk perception has great importance in terms of economic outlook. As stated above, in especially last two-year period, it has been witnessed there has been increase in uncertainty and negative risk perception which has worsened economic outlook in Turkey. As a result of increase in financial volatility, both upward trend in foreign exchange rates and interest rates have occurred. In order to improve economic confidence and reduce negative risk perception and thereby to be able to lower interest rates, it seems that adopting reforms and taking actions correctly in both real sector and financial sector is required. Therefore, as economic outlook becomes healthier, it is expected that the improvements in interest rates will bring with the positive performance in NPLs ratio.

Bibliography

Beck, R., Jakubik, P. and Piloiu, A. (2013). *Non-Performing Loans, What Matters in Addition to the Economic Cycle?*, Working Paper Series, No. 1515, 1–34.

Becker, R., Enders, W. and Lee, J. (2006). *A Stationarity Test in the Presence of an Unknown Number of Smooth Breaks*, Journal of Time Series Analysis, Vol. 3, No. 5, 381–409.

Berger, A.N. and DeYoung, R. (1997), *Problem Loans and Cost Efficiency in Commercial Banks*, Journal of Banking and Finance, Vol. 21, No. 6, 849–870.

Berger, T.O. and Boye, K.G. (2007). *An Analysis of Bank's Problem Loans*, Norges Bank Economic Bulletin, 65–76.

Borio, C. and Lowe, P. (2002). *Asset Prices, Financial and Monetary Stability: Exploring the Nexus*, BIS Working Papers, No. 114, 1–43.

Caprio, G. and Klingebiel, D. (1996), *Bank Insolvencies: Cross Country Experience, World Bank Policy and Research*, Working Paper, No. 1620, 1–60.

Chaibi, H. and Ftiti, Z. (2015). *Credit Risk Determinants: Evidence from a Cross-country Study*, Research in International Business and Finance, Vol. 33, 1–16.

Collins, N. J. and Wanjau, K. (2011). *The Effects of Interest Rate Spread on the Level of Non-Performing Assets: A Case of Commercial Banks in Kenya*, International Journal of Business and Public Management, 58–65.

Crawford, G., Pavanini, N. and Schivardi F. (2015). *Asymmetric Information and Imperfect Competition in Lending Markets*, University of Zurich, Working Paper Series, No. 192, 1–48.

Demirgüç-Kunt, A. and Detragiache, E. (1998). *The Determinants of Banking Crises in Developing and Developed Countries*, IMF Staff Papers, Vol. 45, No. 1, 81–109.

Enders, W. and Jones, P. (2016). Grain Prices, Oil Prices, and Multiple Smooth Breaks in a VAR, Studies in Nonlinear Dynamics & Econometrics, 2016, Vol. 20, Issue 4, 399–419.

Espinoza, R. and Prasad, A. (2010). Nonperforming Loans in the GCC Banking Systems and their Macroeconomic Effects, IMF Working Paper Vol. 10, No. 224, 1–25.

Fofack, H. (2005). Non-performing Loans in Sub-Saharan Africa: Causal Analysis and Macroeconomic Implications, World Bank Policy Research Working Papers, No. 3769, 1–36.

Gabeshi, K. (2017). The Impact of Macroeconomic and Bank Specific Factors on Albanian Non-Performing Loans, European Journal of Sustainable Development Research, Vol. 2, No. 1, 95–102.

Glogowski, A. (2008). Macroeconomic Determinants of Polish Banks' Loan Losses-Results of a Panel Data Study, National Bank of Poland Working Papers, No. 53, 1–28.

Goldstein, M. and Turner, P. (1996). Banking Crises in Emerging Economies: Origins and Policy Options, BIS Economic Papers, No. 46, 1–67.

Hu, J.L., Li, Y. and Chiu, Y.H. (2004). Ownership and Non-performing loans: Evidence from Taiwan's Banks, The Developing Economies, Vol. 42, No. 3, 405–420.

IMF (2016) Turkey Financial System Stability Assessment, IMF Country Report, No. Vol. 17, No. 35, 1–109.

Jimenez, G. and Saurina J. (2006). Credit Cycles, Credit Risk and Prudential Regulation, International Journal of Central Banking, Vol. 2, No. 2, 65–98.

Joseph, M.T., Edson, G., Manuere, F., Clifford, M. and Michael, K. (2012). Non-Performing Loans in Commercial Banks: A Case of CBZ Bank Limited in Zimbabwe, Interdisciplinary Journal of Contemporary Research in Business, Vol. 4, No. 7, 467–488.

Kaminsky, G. and Reinhart, C. (1999). The Twin Crises: the Causes of Banking and Balance of Payments Problems, The American Economic Review, Vol. 89, No. 3, 473–500.

Louzis, D.P., Vouldis, A.T. and Metaxas, V.L. (2010). Macroeconomic and Bank Specific Determinants of Non-performing Loans in Greece: A Comparative Study of Mortgage, Business and Consumer Loan Portfolios, Bank of Greece, Working Papers, No.118, 1–44.

Love, I., and Ariss, R. T. (2013). Macro-Financial Linkages in Egypt: A Panel Analysis of Economic Shocks and Loan Portfolio Quality, IMF Working Papers, 1–40.

Messai, A.S. and Jouni, F. (2013). Micro and Macro Determinants of Non-performing Loans, International Journal of Economics and Financial Issues, Vol. 3, No. 4, 852–860.

Mishkin, F. (1996). Understanding Financial Crises: A Developing Country Perspective, NBER Working Papers, No. 5600, 1–65.

Nkusu, M. (2011). Nonperforming Loans and Macrofinancial Vulnerabilities in Advanced Economies, IMF Working Paper, Vol. 11, No. 161, 1–28.

Pullicino, Katya (2016). Impact of Macroeconomic Variables on Non-performing Loans: An Empirical Study of Commercial Banks in Malta, Italy, Spain, France and UK, University of Malta, https://www.um.edu.mt/library/oar//handle/123456789/14036

Ranjan, R. and Dhal, S.C. (2003). Non-performing Loans and Terms of Credit of Public Sector Banks in India: An Empirical Assessment, Reserve Bank of India, Occasional Papers, Vol. 24, No. 3, 81–121.

Saba, I., Kouser, R. and Azeem, M. (2012). Determinants of Non Performing Loans: Case of US Banking Sector, Romanian Economic Journal, Vol. 15, No. 44, 125–136.

Salas, V. and Saurina, J. (2002). Credit Risk in Two Institutional Regimes: Spanish Commercial and Savings Banks, Journal of Financial Services Research, Vol. 22, No. 3, 203–224.

Shu, C., (2002). The Impact of Macroeconomic Environment on the Asset Quality of Hong Kong's Banking Sector, Hong Kong Monetary Authority Research Papers, 1–26.

Skarica, B. (2014). Determinants of Non-performing Loans in Central and Eastern European Countries, Financial Theory and Practice, Institute of Public Finance, Vol. 38, No. 1, 37–59.

Steinherr, A., Tükel, A. and Üçer, M. (2004). *The Turkish Banking Sector Challenges and Outlook in Transition to EU Membership*, Bruges European Economic Policy Briefings, No. 9, 1–39.

Stiglitz, J. E. and Weiss, A. (1981). Credit Rationing in Markets with Imperfect Information, American Economic Review, Vol. 71, No. 3, 393–410.

Ugoani, J. (2016). Nonperforming Loans Portfolio and Its Effect on Bank Profitability in Nigeria, Independent Journal Of Management & Production, Vol. 7, No. 2, 303–319.

Us, V. (2015). The Turkish Banking Sector Before and After the Global Crisis: An Ownership Breakdown, CBRT, Research Notes in Economics, No: 2015–02, 1–17.

TBB (2017). Banks in Turkey 2016, Publication No: 322, June 2017, 1–322.

Treasury of Ministry and Finance (2018). Economic Indicators Statistics, https://www.treasury.gov.tr/economic-indicators-statistics

Tsong, C.C., Lee, C.F., Tsai, L.J. and Hu, T.C. (2016). The Fourier Approximation and Testing for the Null of Cointegration, Empirical Economics, 51(3), 1085–1113.

Williamson, S. (1987). *Fi*nancial Intermediation, Business Failures and Real Business Cycles, Journal of Political Economy, Vol. 95, No. 6, 1196–1216.

Esra Balli

Russia's Macroeconomic Performance during the Transition Process

1 Introduction

The transition process is characterized by a sum of radical changes in social, cultural and political structure. The inability to reach reliable data at the beginning of the transition period from the command economy to the market economy, as well as the difficulties that arise from the system itself, leads to great difficulties in understanding and evaluating this period. Moreover, the limited experience of international corporations in transition economies and process has not been enough to solve the problems that have arisen with the disintegration of the control economies. In addition, transitional policies have been implemented regardless of the local conditions, historical backgrounds and institutional structures of transition economies (Güler, 2012). In the development of the socialist model, heavy industrialization and major monopoly corporations have come to the forefront under the centralized management, and international trade has been organized through agreements made by states and not by the market (Fisher and Gelb, 1991). According to Ericson (1991), there are nine characteristics of the Soviet-type socialist economic system. These include: hierarchical structure, distribution and planning of production centrally and rigidly, pressure on planning to maximize use of resources, collection of physical or non-physical distribution of goods and services on one hand, excessive price control, lack of flexibility and liquidity in the goods or financial markets in the system, lack of legal alternatives in economic relations, absolute control over the agreed plan and lack of initiative beyond that plan. According to the IMF, the transition process takes occurs through liberalization, macroeconomic stability, restructuring, privatization and legal and institutional reforms. Liberalization means the effort of integration with the world market economies by allowing the prices to be set in free market and removing trade barriers. In macroeconomic stability, it is aimed primarily to take inflation under control and to ensure that credit growth is brought under discipline. With restructuring and privatization, a healthy financial sector is created in these economies, ensuring that enterprises can produce goods at free markets and transfer these enterprises into private sectors. Legal and institutional reforms are meant to redefine the role of the state in these economies, as well as the creation of legal rules and competition policies.

According to the World Bank Development Report in 1996, countries entering the transition period have different starting points and major economic reforms. The initial conditions of the transition countries may vary in each country. The countries' level of economic liberalization, democratization period before the collapse communist regime and command economy, the share of the private sector in the economy, the openness of the economy in comparison to capitalist countries, the existence of natural resources that may be subject to trade, the level of internal and external macroeconomic balance, the strength of anti-communist and independence movements in past, and ethnic homogeneity or differences make the economic and political transition period of each country different. The length of the transition recession, characterized by sharp declines in production and high rates of unemployment, in Russia and Ukraine, covers periods of 9 and 10 years, respectively (Mickiewicz, 2005).

Donnorummo (2006) argues that three important factors such as the historical background, the policies the countries have made from the 1990s onwards and the existence of external and / or internal conflicts influences the transition process. According to Russia's neoliberal transition strategy called "shock therapy", liberalization, stabilization and privatization are three important policies. Liberalization refers to the removal of state restrictions on prices; stabilization refers to the control of inflation by reducing government expenditures; and privatization refers to the privatization of state-owned enterprises by selling them (Kotz, 2000). In his study of the economic transformation of Russia in 1999, Aslund explains that the failure of the radical economic reforms in the country is due to the pursuit of profit by former enterprise managers. According to Aslund (1999), the lack of economic elitism and economic distortions in Russia after the dissolution of the Soviet Union led to the strengthening of the old rulers. If democratic institutions were fast-paced and the West provided rapid financial support for the realization of reforms from the beginning of 1992, it would have provided the necessary reinforcements for reforms. Despite the fact that rents have begun to decline over time, the institutions that Russia owns have suffered serious damage due to corruption. This competition on the rent is also one of the factors that caused the crisis in August 1998. At the same time, Aslund (1999) suggests that limiting the level of rent is a precondition for successful reforms. Ahrend and Tompson (2005) point out that when Russia's market transformation process is examined, it first needs to focus on crises experienced by the Soviet system. Along with this, the radical reforms initiated by the creation of new independent states along with the collapse of the Soviet Union have gained importance in this process. External shocks such as the long-term decline in the growth rate of the Soviet Socialist Republics since 1950, the Chernobyl accident, the decline in international oil prices in 1986, and the rapid depreciation of oil between the years 1986–1987 have all contributed to the collapse of the Soviet control economy. The loose economic reforms that took place in the late 1980s were unsuccessful due to the traditional constellation and command economy feature. According to Dąbrowski and Antczak (1995), Central and Eastern Europe and the former Soviet Union countries seem to meet serious economic problems from the communist era. These include factors like explicit prohibitions or serious restrictions on the private investment, monopoly market structure, price adjustments carried out by the government, structural distortions due to central investment decisions, excess social welfare obligations relative to the level of economic development, and internal and external macroeconomic imbalances.

Many scholars agree that the initial conditions are of importance during the transition from the command economy to the market economy. The paper is organized as follows: The second section covers the literature review, the third section examines the macroeconomic performances of Russia. Finally, the fourth section concludes.

2 Literature Review

There are many studies on the economies in the transition period. In their study in 1995, Dąbrowski and Antczak analyzed why Russia, Ukraine and Belarus lag behind other Baltic and Central and Eastern European countries during the transition process. Accordingly, in their comparative analysis, among these reasons, they found a strong correlation between political change and economic success. In their study that De Melo et al. (1996) examined the transition process of Central and Eastern European countries and the former Soviet Union countries, they noted that although the initial conditions of the countries were different, countries with the same stages in reform process showed common characteristics. In the study that the researchers measured the political reforms and initial conditions through the liberalization index they developed by themselves, they showed that the capital and the labor force shifted from the industrial sector to the service sector and the previously oppressed sectors achieved positive development with the rapid reforms being undertaken. In the study that Dabrowski (1998) examined the relationship between the economic transformation in the former Soviet Union countries and the aid the West provided between the years 1990 and 1994, he suggested the most important aid in the first stages of the transformation process came from the IMF and that IMF-financed programs played a vital role for each country involved in the transformation process.

According to Popov (2000), the impact of good or bad economic policies on the output in the transition period and the success and failure of macroeconomic stability policies were measured by the liberalization index and the inflation rate, respectively. Popov (2000) assessed the performances of the different countries in the transition period by going through an alternative explanation for the transition process. Accordingly, the causes of supply-side recession may include central planning disturbances and disproportion in the distribution of resources. In addition, he noted that 60 % of the economic performance differences between countries in the transition period stemmed from unequal initial conditions. Popov (2007) examined the transition recession in two parts. According to this, the transition recession that continued till the mid-1990s constituted the first part of the transition period. During this period, there was a decline in the productions of transition economies. In the later stages of the transition period, the economic growth process began to be seen. In his study that he examined 28 transition economies, Popov (2007) noted that the production crashes that occurred during the transition period were due to adverse impacts of supply shocks triggered by changes in the relative price differences caused by trade patterns and industrial structure distortions during central planning. In their study of 28 transition countries covering East Asia, Central and Eastern Europe and the former Soviet Union, De Melo et al. (2001) examined growth and initial conditions, political change and reforms. As a result of the study, they found that there was a relationship between initial conditions and liberalization index and growth.

The World Bank's report (2002) on the transition period of the former Soviet Union and Eastern European countries between the years 1991 and 2000, revealed that countries showed different growth performances. According to this report, prices should first be released in the process of transition to the market economy and in the reform process, but due to high inflation, which can be the result of price liberalization, policy makers must implement tight monetary and fiscal policies. Non-governmental organizations should play an important role in the implementation of reform policies. In addition, the method of privatization is of great importance. State-owned investments should be directed towards productive areas and privatization should take place in this way. To ensure economic growth, policy-makers should discipline old enterprises and create an environment that encourages new investments. The creation of legal and institutional structures is also of great importance in terms of reforms.

Hamm, King, and Stuckler (2012) investigated the reasons why the transition from socialism to capitalism led to growth in some countries while it caused economic decline in others. Studies in this field focused on three principles. The first is that the successful countries were the ones that rapidly performed neoliberal policies, the second is that the failures were based on institutional structures rather than policies, the third and final one is that the politics had the opposite effect because it harmed the state. In the study that they examined the possible impact of neoliberal policies on a poor economic performance from a state-centered perspective, they found that countries experiencing large-scale privatization programs have experienced severe financial shocks, thereby the private-sector management capability was severely limited and the impact of resurgence in transition was deepened. In the study they examined 25 post-communist countries, they used some dependent variables like the effects of government activity, weak contracts, unofficial payments, real government expenditures, per capita GDP between the years 1990–2000 and they also used some independent ones like large privatization, price liberalization, democratization, oil, war, urbanization, education and being a member of the Soviet Union or not. The findings of the study showed that large-scale privatizations affected economic growth, government capacity, and defense of property rights in the negative direction.

Within the framework of the Big Bang vs. Gradualist approach, Dell'Anno and Villa (2013) examined the speed of transition reforms on economic growth in 25 transition economies on the basis of the years 1990–2008. In this study, the pace of transition reforms was calculated within the framework of a three-dimensional analysis of key components and with a new indicator developed by them.

Accordingly, while the pace of transition process reforms was a Granger cause of economic growth, no adverse effect was observed. Besides, while the simultaneous pace of transitional reforms had a negative impact on economic growth, this had become positive in the long term. Finally they came to the conclusion that the initial conditions and macroeconomic stability programs affected the economic growth.

In their work, Walder, Isaacson, and Lu (2015) argued that the initial recessions could be interpreted as a direct expression of political turmoil, which might be deepened by the regime change. In this regard, the most common confusion occurs when a nation state is divided into many independent states. This can lead to hyperinflation, civil wars, and armed conflicts at the border of the nation. In their study they examined the impact of the initial conditions on many aspects, the authors primarily dealt with the market reforms, the political developments in the initial conditions, and the pace and scope of privatization prior to the breakdown. Accordingly, they investigated 31 old socialist economies based on the years 1989–2007 by using the variables of armed conflict, hyperinflation, economic conditions, geographical advantages, per capita oil output, initial agricultural activities, per capita national income, industrialization policy, political economy, liberalization, massive privatization, democratization and rule of law. The authors came to the conclusion that these variables they used reveal little of the recessions that took place in the 1990s.

3 Macroeconomic Performance

In this section, the economic situation in Russia revealed during the transition period by examining GDP per capita Income, growth rate, unemployment rate, inflation Rate, human development index (HDI) and Gini Coefficient. The examination of some economic and social indicators of Russia is important in terms of giving information about the changes that took place during the transition period. Human Development Index is composed of dimensions of long and healthy life, information access and human life standards. In addition, the human development index has a highest level of human development (between 1–49), a high level of human development (between 50–105), a medium level of human development (between 106–143) and a low level of human development (between 145 -188). According to the UNCTAD (2015) report, Russia is ranked from 0.798 to 50th place in terms of the Human Development Index. Considering that the Human Development Index of the European and Central Asian region rose from 0.651 in the 1980s to 0.771 today, Russia is above the average. When we look at the Gini coefficient it was found to be 0.77 in 1973 and 0.61 in 1979 in Ofer and Vinkour (1992)'s study based on the Soviet immigrants (Transporter Alexeev, 1999). In Russia this ratio was 0.48 in 1993, 0.37 in 1999, 0.40 in 2009 and 0.37 in 2015. This suggests that at the beginning of the transition period income inequality was higher in Russia. It is possible to say one of its main reasons was that it could not be distributed equitably through privatizations. Fig. 1 shows Russia's GDP per capita. Russia ranks first among the members of the

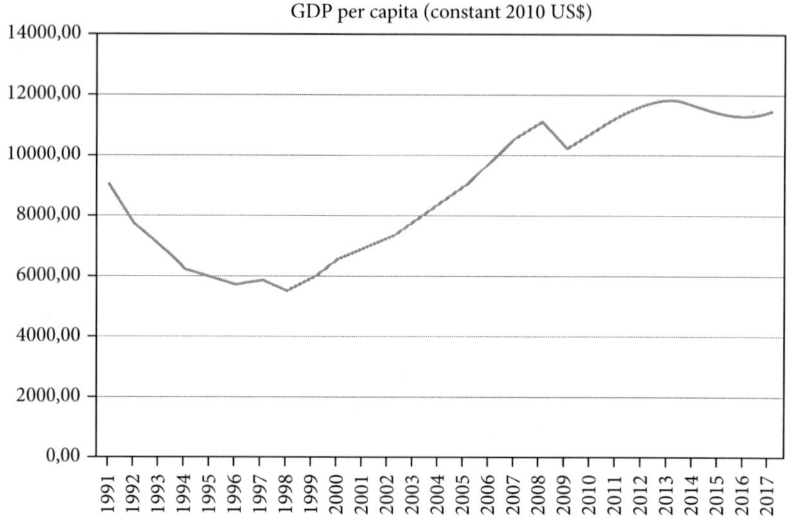

Fig. 1: GDP per capita (Source: World Bank)

Independent State Community. One of the main reasons for this is that Russia is the world's largest natural gas exporter and second largest oil exporter (EIAa, 2013). At the beginning of the 1990s, while the oil price was 18 US dollars, this figure started to rise in 2001 and became 28 US dollars in 2003, and with the price of 132.72 US dollars it reached at its top in July 2008. Finally, it went into a rapid decline and became 30 US dollars in January 2016 (EIAb, 2016). In related to this, Russia's export revenues, which are tied to exports of gross national natural resources, have also declined. As shown in Fig. 1, this situation, according to calculations made on the basis of 2010-based USD, while the GDP per capita in Russia was 9033 USD in 1991, it declined to 5505 USD in 1998. Due to the increase in oil prices, in 2008 Russia's GDP per capita was USD 11089, and the effects of the 2008 global crisis were felt in 2009 largely, too. However, due to the increase in oil and natural gas prices after 2010, Russia's GDP per capita has started to increase again.

Fig. 2 shows the growth rates of Russia between the years 1991–2014. Accordingly, the growth rate of Russia has shown itself in a structure that has been following a negative course from the beginning of the transition period until the year 2000. The lowest level of production was in Russia at 45.1 % in 1998 (Fischer and Sahay, 2000). In addition, these rates affected by the Russian economic crisis that took place in August 1998.

Fig. 3 shows the inflation rates of Russia between the years 1996–2014. Accordingly, we can see that countries face very high inflation rates during the transition period. In 1991, when the State Bank of the USSR was liquidated, the so-called State Bank of the Russian Soviet Federated Socialist Republic became the Russian

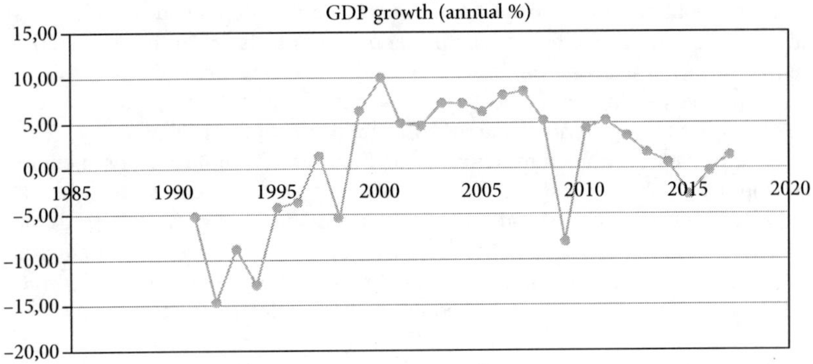

Fig. 2: Growth rate (annual %) (Source: World Bank)

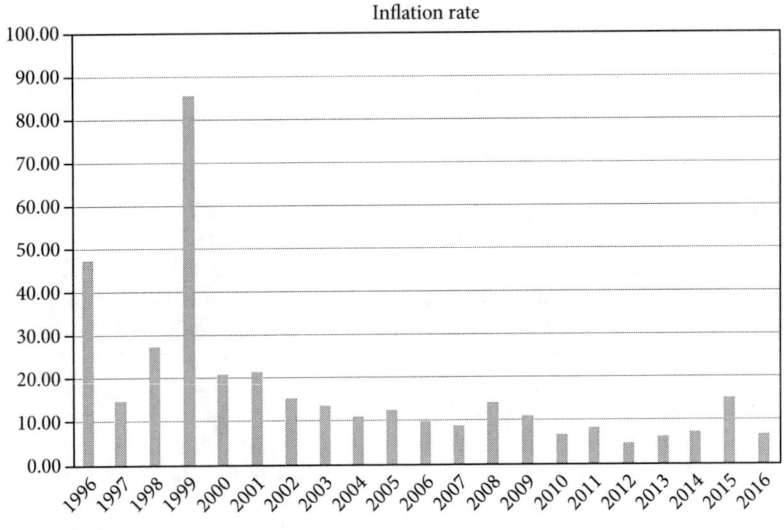

Fig. 3: Inflation rate (%) (Source: World Bank)

Central Bank. In the study that Loungani and Sheets (1997) examined the impact of the Central Bank on inflation and the effects of inflation on economic growth in 12 former Soviet countries including Russia and Ukraine, they found that there is a relationship between the Central Bank's independence and low inflation rates. In their study of 26 former socialist economies, Cukierman, Miller and Neyapti (2002) noted that central banks were unconcerned with the high inflation in the first stages of the liberalization process and central bank independence could not stop the strong inflationary effect on the initial price controls. With the acceleration of the liberalization process, the legal independence of the Central Bank influenced the decline in the inflation rates. The shortage of institutions caused the transitional process to be extended and necessary reforms not to be made.

According to the transition report of the European Bank for Reconstruction and Development in 2017 that stated the levels of energy, infrastructure, financial sectors in the transition countries and showed transition indicators from 1 (little or no change) to 4 (industrialized market economy standard), it is seen that among these transition countries in the capital market Russia is in the best position as agricultural trade, real estate sector, banking telecommunication, electricity and railways.

4 Conclusion

The countries established after the dissolution of the Soviet Union deeply affected by the process of transition from the socialist economy to the market economy in spite of the strong industrial heritage infrastructure and well-educated human power left over from the Soviet Socialist Republics (USSR) era. The duration of transition recessions in these countries varied. This period was 9 years in Russia that is wealth of natural resources. With the recession that took place during the transition to the market economy, the transition economies saw a sharp decline in their production levels, followed by a negative economic growth trend, unemployment and hyperinflation. The privatizations that took place at the beginning of the transition period created an imbalance in the distribution of the wealth, causing it to be collected only in some hands, and income inequality increased at high rates. The fact that the policies recommended for the old socialist block were not adapted separately for each country's conditions, the lack of institutional structures that could implement the proposed policies and the inadequacy of support for making reforms made the transition period challenging and painful. Besides, the institutional shortage in the transition period is of great importance. The lack of institutions that would prepare the country for the transition process from the command economy to the market economy was one of the main factors that caused the transition period to be long and painful. When compared to the initial period, it is seen that the inflation rate has fallen; the growth rate and GDP per capita have increased in Russia over 27 years. Due to its socio-economic and economic infrastructures, Russia has started its transition process in a better position than other countries and has succeeded in maintaining this position.

Bibliography

Ahrend, R., & Tompson, W. (2005). Fifteen Years of Economic Reform in Russia: What has been Achieved? What Remains to be Done?. OECD Economics Department Working Paper, No. 430, http://papers.ssrn.com/sol3/papers.cfm?abstract_id=881547

Aslund, A. (2000). Why Has Russia's Economic Transition Been So Arduous?. 21837 Ain, 399. Carnegie Endowment for International Peace.Cukierman, A., Miller, G. P., & Neyapti, B. (2002). Central Bank Reform, Liberalization and Inflation in Transition Economies—An International Perspective. Journal of Monetary Economics, 49(2), 237–264.

Dabrowski, M., & Antczak, R. (1995). Economic Transition in Russia, the Ukraine and Belarus in Comparative Perspective. Center for Social and Economic Research (CASE), Warsaw, Poland

Dabrowski, M. (1999). Different Strategies of Transition to a Market Economy: How Do They Work in Practice?. The World Bank.

Dabrowski, M. (1998). Western Aid Conditionality and the Post-Communist Transition 1990–19941. The Journal of Policy Reform, 2(2), 169–193.

De Melo, M., Denizer, C., & Gelb, A. H. (1996). From Plan to Market--Pattern of Transition. World Bank Publications.

Gelb, A., Melo, M., Denizer, C., & Tenev, S. (1999). Circumstance and choice: The role of Initial Conditions and Policies in Transition Economies. The World Bank.

Dell'Anno, R., & Villa, S. (2013). Growth in Transition Countries: Big Bang Versus Gradualism. Economics of transition, 21(3), 381–417.

Donnorummo, B. (2006). The Political and Economic Complexities of Transition. Zagreb International Review of Economics & Business, (1), 13–27.

Energy Information Administration (EIAa). 2013. Country Analysis Brief. http://www.eia.doe.gov/countries/country-data.cfm?fips=RS.

Energy Information Administration (EIAb). 2016. http://www.eia.gov/dnav/pet/pet_pri_spt_s1_d.htm.

Ericson, R. E. (1991). The Classical Soviet-Type Economy: Nature of the System and Implications for Reform. Journal of Economic perspectives, 5(4), 11–27.

European Bank for Reconstruction and Development (EBRD). Transition Report (2016–2017).

Fischer, S., & Gelb, A. (1991). The Process of Socialist Economic Transformation. Journal of Economic Perspectives, 5(4), 91–105.

Fischer, S., & Sahay, R. (2000). The Transition Economies After Ten Years (No. w7664). National Bureau of Economic Research.

Güler, E. (2012). Sosyalizmden Kapitalizme Geçiş Sürecinde Rusya: Nasıl Bir Kapitalizm?. Business & Economics Research Journal, 3(3).

Hamm, P., King, L. P., & Stuckler, D. (2012). Mass Privatization, State Capacity, and Economic Growth in Post-Communist Countries. American Sociological Review, 77(2), 295–324.

International Monetary Fund. 2013. World Economic Outlook Database. http://www.imf.org/external/pubs/ft/weo/2013/01/weodata/index.aspx.

Kaymak, H. (2005). Yabancı Doğrudan Yatırımları Artırmak İçin Teşvikler Gerekli ve/veya Yeterli mi?. Maliye Dergisi, 149, 74–104.

Kotz, D. M.; (2000); "Lessons from Economic Transition in Russia and China Political Economy and Contemporary Capitalism: Radical Perspectives on Economic Theory and Policy" edited by Ron Baiman, Heather Boushey, and Dawn Saunders, M.E. Sharpe, Armonk, 210–217.

Loungani, P., & Sheets, N. (1997). Central Bank Independence, Inflation, and Growth in Transition Economies. Journal of Money, Credit, and Banking, 381–399.

Mickiewicz, T. (2005). Post-communist Recessions Re-examined. In Economic Transition in Central Europe and the Commonwealth of Independent States. Palgrave Macmillan, London. pp. 99–118.

National Bank of Ukraine. http://www.bank.gov.ua.

Popov, V. (2000). Shock Therapy Versus Gradualism: The End of the Debate (Explaining the Magnitude of Transformational Recession). Comparative Economic Studies, 42(1), 1–57.

Syrquin, M., & Chenery, H. B. (1989). Patterns of Development, 1950 to 1983. World Bank, Washington, DC.

The Central Bank of Russian Federation. www.cbr.ru

Walder, A. G., Isaacson, A., & Lu, Q. (2015). After State Socialism: The Political Origins of Transitional Recessions. American Sociological Review, 80(2), 444–468.

World Bank .2014. World Development Indicators. World Bank, Washington, D.C.

World Bank .2002. Transition – The First Ten Years: Analysis and Lesson or Eastern Europe and the Former Soviet Union. World Bank, Washington D.C.

World Bank. 1996. World Development Report: From Plan to Market. Oxford University Press, London.

United Nations. 2015 .International Human Development Indicators.

Niyazi Kurnaz and Ali Kestane

Effect of the Culture on Internal Audit: Application for Participation Banks

1 Introduction

Accounting scandals and briberies have increased the importance of cultural values in accounting cases. The effect of cultural values on accounting systems and internal audit activities of enterprises in relevant countries has been an issue of concern.

This research aimed to determine whether Hofstede's cultural values as ***Power Distance, Avoidance of Uncertainty and Individualism-Collectivism*** have an effect on internal audit activities of participation banks of Turkey in 2017. Determining whether the culture has an impact on internal audit activities of participation banks of Turkey and also specifying how auditors are affected by cultural values for their decisions show the importance of this research. The scope of this study is composed of the participation banks that are in service in Turkey as of 2017. Since obtaining data is difficult in practice, internal auditors of **XXX** banks constitute the research sample to make healthy comments and explain more reliable and consistent information to the information users. It was used a coding as XXX because of the absence of the permission from the relevant banks. Information and data were reviewed and coded in line with the research objective. **50** questionnaire forms were distributed for application; **40** of them were answered and finally, **33** of these forms were evaluated. The data obtained were transferred into "SPSS (Statistical Package for the Social Sciences) 22.0" by coding in "Microsoft Excel 2010" program. Proper analyses ***(reliability analysis, descriptive statistics, average standard deviation)*** were performed in this program. Moreover, ***correlation and regression analyses*** were conducted for making healthy comments as a result of confirming the assumption of normal distribution of error terms that is one of the essential assumptions of the classical regression analysis. The research has two main parts. The first chapter includes the introduction the research; studies realized in the relevant field in literature; internal audit concept and Hofstede cultural values. In the second chapter, the application towards determining the effect of cultural values on internal audit activities of banks in Turkey; the results were commented.

2 Literature

Cultural values and internal audit activities have an extensive application area as well as they have subjected to several academic studies in different sectors. The studies mentioned in literature are explained below.

Tosunoğlu and Yeşilçelebi (2016, s. 73) reviewed the effect of culture on internal audit towards members of accounting professions who operate in TR90 region of Turkey. It is pointed at the end of the research that avoidance of uncertainty has a negative impact on the internal audit; power distance, individualism, and collectivism have no effect on the internal audit. Dicle and Usluer (2016, s. 45) analyzed the effect of culture on the internal audit quality towards internal auditors operate in 46 countries including Turkey within the scope of Hofstede's cultural variables. They mentioned at the end of the study that there is a negative relationship between masculinity and the quality of internal audit function. Okaro and Okafor, (2015, p. 17) researched how the quality of audit activities are affected by cultural values for members of accounting professions in Nigeria. They revealed the negative effect of the culture by confirming that accountants accept bribe during the duty term by endangering the quality of the audit.

Alzeban (2015, p. 57) researched the relationship between cultural dimensions and internal audit quality within the scope of 67 enterprises that are listed on the stock exchange in Saudi Arabia. With reference to the research results, internal audit quality is low in companies in which the power distance and avoidance of uncertainty ratios are high; moreover, there is a positive relationship between individualism and internal audit quality. Abdolmohammadi and Sarens (2011, p. 384) analyzed the relationship between adaptation to internal audit standards/use of internal audit standards and cultural dimensions as part of internal auditors operate in 19 countries that are classified such as Anglo, East and German Europe, Latin America and Latin Europe. According to the evaluation, there is an inverse relationship between avoidance of uncertainty that is one of the cultural dimensions and adaptation to internal audit standards/use of internal audit standards. Hell and Wang (2009, pp. 48–49) surveyed the effect of cultural values on the studies of auditors operate in China and France. They mentioned at the end of the survey that cultural differences do not affect the studies of auditors. Moreover, with reference to their emphasis, the auditors in France may attach more importance to components relating to audit evidence evaluation and control environment in comparison with the auditors in China. Hope et al. (2008, pp. 357) research the relationship between auditor selection and national culture by analyzing companies that operate in 37 countries. It is pointed out at the end of the study that the national culture affects the auditor selection in a good part of the relevant companies; this circumstance shows us there may be a connection between national culture and financial reporting quality. Sander et al. (2008, pp. 12–13) researched the effect of avoidance of uncertainty, power distance and individualism factors on the audit system. They revealed that the factors mentioned have an impact on risk assessment operations. Kosmala (2007, pp. 336–337) focused on Eastern Europe and analyzed the effect of culture on audit independence. According to the results, there are significant connections between components like power distance, individualism and uncovering the tricks. Erturan (2007, ss. 133–157) reviewed the effect of culture on the audit and audit process toward the behaviors of auditors operate in companies ride on Capital Markets Boards (CMB) in Turkey. He revealed based on the research results that cultural values affect the auditor about objective acting during performing the audit activities. The effect of culture on the behaviors of auditors operate in multinational companies in Hong-Kong was also reviewed by Tsui and Gul (1996, p. 41). They mentioned that ethical values and culture significantly affect the decisions made by the auditors.

3 Internal Audit Concept, Goal, and Scope of Internal Audit

Internal audit can be defined as being guided the operating activities to increase the productivity and competitive capacity; being managed the reserves rationally; investment and management consultation. Besides, internal audit is the control that is conducted by independent auditors to prohibit mistakes and tricks (Kurnaz and Çetinoğlu, 2010, s. 31). The internal audit that is an independent evaluation function is performing the tasks about reviewing and evaluating the operating activities to serve the enterprise (Pickett, 2005, p. 5; Sağlar and Tuan, 2009, s. 344). The internal audit that is a control activity analyzes the efficiency and biddability of other intrabusiness controls (Sevim and Eliuz, 2007, s. 62). According to the current definition of internal audit concept by International Internal Audit Institute; Internal audit is an independent and impartial consulting and assurance activity to improve the activities of an institution. Internal audit helps to reach the goals of an institution by bringing a systematic and disciplined approach to evaluate and develop the efficacy of risk management, control and governance processes (Özbek, 2012, s. 3; Tüm, 2013, s. 103). The goals of internal audit can be aligned with reference to the definitions as follows; creating values for the institution (Akçay, 2013 s. 59); providing assurance and consulting service (Arcagök et al, 2006, ss. 192); providing to actualize audit activities fit to the standards (Kösea, 2007, s. 50); helping senior management and board members to fulfill their responsibilities productively (Sevim and Eliuz, 2007, s. 62). Analyzing and evaluating the success quality in fulfilling the duties and efficacy of internal audit system of the enterprise constitute the scope of the internal audit in line with the goals mentioned (Yılancı and Sevim, 1991, ss. 132). At the present time, this scope can be extended in the way that controlling the corporate governance and risk management processes, evaluating the appropriateness of activities to the legislation, auditing information technologies and consulting activities (Özbek, 2012, ss. 20–21). From this point of view, below functions can be accepted as the parts of the internal audit (Kurnaz and Çetinoğlu, 2010, ss. 33–34; Yılancı and Sevim, 1991, s. 132);

- To reveal the financial and operational information; to also reveal the accuracy and reliability of that information mentioned. To analyze the instruments used for measuring, classifying and reporting,
- To analyze the system that is established to provide the appropriateness of laws, regulations, plan, and policies that produce a significant effect on activities and

reports to the official activities and reports. To determine whether the enterprise is in accord with the factors mentioned,

- To review the methods of protecting the assets; to evaluate the sources are used as economical and efficient,
- To research or evaluate whether the conclusions are fit to the goals.
- Internal audit activities have importance about improving the business process of institutions, using the sources productively, prohibiting the mistake and tricks, reducing the losses arising from the risks. Internal audit plays a key role as the guarantee of corporate governance and corporate reputation (Yurtsever, 2015, s. 96).

4 Hofstede's Cultural Values

Hofstede's cultural values (Hofstede 1980, pp. 44; Kurnaz and Kestane 2016, ss. 3) have been evaluated under "Power Distance, Avoidance of Uncertainty and Individualism/Collectivism" dimensions within the scope of the theme of core values of national culture that is highly benefited for culture studies (Reimann et al 2008, p. 65),

Power Distance: This concept shows the difference between the power distribution in society. This concept that is benefited (Ding et al. 2005, p. 332; Hofstede 1984, p. 390) to express the non-powerful individuals' espousing levels about the power does not distribute equally also shows the endpoint that is acceptable for unequally distribution of power in relationships, organization or structures (Hofstede 2001, p. 151).

Avoidance of Uncertainty: This concept that means to measure the coping status with uncertainties also means the coping levels of individuals with uncertainty when they face an unknown circumstance (Hofstede 2001, p. 145). While the rules matter (Franke and Nadler 2008, p. 256) in societies with a high level of avoidance of uncertainty, an informal structure becomes prominent in societies with a low level of avoidance of uncertainty as well as the rules are more flexible (Ay 2013, s.77).

Individualism-Collectivism: In individualism, the person considers the needs of his own and his family; on the other hand, his loyalism to social requirements is poor at the same time (Soares et al. 2008, 280). In collectivism, the individual deals with the needs of both his family, his own and the society (Varıcı and Özdemir 2013, ss. 26–27).

5 Application

In this chapter of the research, it is tried to determine whether ***Power Distance, avoidance of Uncertainty and Individualism-Collectivism*** dimensions of Hofstede's cultural values have an effect on ***internal audit*** activities of participation banks operate in Turkey as of 2017. The expressions about the goal and importance of the research can be seen in this chapter. Moreover, the information about the content is relayed by specifying the scope.

5.1 Goal and Importance of the Research

This research aimed to determine whether Hofstede's cultural values as ***Power Distance Avoidance of Uncertainty and Individualism-Collectivism*** have an effect on internal audit activities of participation banks of Turkey in 2017.

Determining whether the culture has the impact on internal audit activities of participation banks of Turkey and also specifying how auditors are affected from cultural values for their decisions show the importance of this research.

5.2 Population and Sample Selection

The scope of the research is composed of the participation banks operate in Turkey as of 2017. Since obtaining data is difficult in practice, internal auditors of XXX banks constitute the research sample to make healthy comments and explain more reliable and consistent information to the information users. It was used a coding as XXX because of the absence of the permission from the relevant banks.

5.3 Obtaining Data and Creating Hypotheses

The data in research was applied via survey technique as face to face with the internal auditors operated in XXX banks between **12/08/2017 – 30/09/2017**. Since the absence of the permission, XXX expression was used. The studies **(Alzeban, 2015, pp. 57–77; Tosunoğlu and Yeşilçelebi, 2016, ss. 73–87; Soba et al., 2015, ss. 485–496)** whose validity was confirmed before was utilized to create the content of the surveys. There are 26 questions and 2 groups of questions in questionnaire form. 21 statements can be seen in the first group of the questions toward determining the effect of the culture on the audit. The second group of questions has statements relating to the position, age, gender, and educational background of the answerer to determine their demographic and descriptive characteristics of the participants. Each of the statements is coded from 1 one 5; the participation levels are as follows; **"Strongly Disagree" "Disagree" " Neither Agree or Disagree" "Agree" and "Agree Strongly".**

This research aimed to determine whether Hofstede's cultural values as ***Power Distance, Avoidance of Uncertainty and Individualism-Collectivism*** have an effect on internal audit activities of participation banks of Turkey in 2017. The main hypothesis called as "***H: The culture has an effect on internal audit activities of participation banks***" was constituted as is suitable for the purpose of the study.

H_1 : Power distance has a ***positive effect*** on the internal audit.
H_2 : Avoidance of uncertainty has a ***positive effect*** on the internal audit.
H_3 : Individualism has a ***positive effect*** on the internal audit.
H_4 : Collectivism has a ***positive effect*** on the internal audit.

5.4 Analyzing and Commenting the Data

Information and data that were reached by the survey were organized and coded in parallel with the purpose of the research. **50** questionnaire forms were distributed for application; **40** of them were answered and finally, **33** of these forms were evaluated. The data obtained were transferred into ***"SPSS (Statistical Package for the Social Sciences) 22.0"*** by coding in "Microsoft Excel 2010" program. Proper analyses ***(reliability analysis, descriptive statistics, average standard deviation)*** were performed in this program. Reliability analysis was made to determine whether the data obtained by survey technique is accidental or consistent. The data obtained from the sample is accepted as reliable at a normal level in case of Cronbach's Alpha (reliability coefficient value-∝) is found as 0,60–0,79 (Tanrıöğen, 2012, ss. 176). In this research, Cronbach's Alpha value was found as 0, 631; this shows that the study is reliable at the normal level. With reference to the information obtained during the data collection process, correlation and regression analyses were performed for making healthy comments as a result of confirming the assumption of normal distribution of error terms that is one of the essential assumptions of the classical regression analysis. In addition, because the reliability score of the expressions of the individuality dimension of the participants for the internal audit effect of the culture was not sufficient only mean and standard deviation values were calculated and not included in the correlation and regression analysis.

5.5 Research Findings

In this chapter of research, following items are commented by summarizing; (i) reliability of the survey used in research; (ii) distribution of roles of participants; (iii) information about the demographic attributes of participants; (iv) results relating to average standard deviation values about the statements on the effect of the culture on the internal audit; (v) correlation and regression analyses results. Tab. 1 shows the reliability analysis results.

It is seen when the reliability analysis results of questions are analyzed that the power distance is ∝= 0,631; avoidance of uncertainty is ∝= 0,559; individualism is ∝= 0,0375; collectivism is ∝= 0,707; internal audit dimension is ∝= 0,754. The average of answers for relevant dimensions is in the Tab. 2.

Distribution of tasks and percentages are as follows; 0,12 % of them are the lead auditors, 0,03 % of them are the lead auditor assistants, 57 % of them are the internal auditors, 28 % of them are the internal auditor assistants. It is seen when the subject is evaluated in terms of the working time that the auditors who have 1–5 years experience are in 54 % ratio; the auditors who have 6–10 years of experience are in 29 % ratio; finally, the auditors who have 10 years and above of experience are in 17 % ratio. Tab. 3 shows the information on age, gender and educational levels of attendees.

As is seen in the table, 60 % of the participants are in 26–30 age range. Furthermore, 40 % of the participants are females; 69 % of them took master degree. Tab. 4 describes the participants' expressions on the effect of culture on internal audit.

Tab. 1: Reliability Analysis Results

		Power Distance	
No	**∝ = 0,631**	**Average: 2,80**	**% Var: 0,283**
1	Directors can make decisions without taking subordinates' advice.		
2	Directors need to frequently use their authority and power for the subordinates.		
3	Directors should rarely ask employees' opinion.		
4	Employees should not present an opinion in management decisions.		
5	Directors should not transfer the significant duties to the employees.		
		Avoidance of Uncertainty	
No	**∝ = 0,559**	**Average: 4,18**	**% Var: 0,140**
6	Mentioning the job specifications and orders in detail is important for employees to know what is expected from themselves.		
7	Directors want employees to closely follow the procedures and orders.		
8	Since the rules and regulations inform employees about the expectations, rules and regulations are accepted as important.		
9	Standard working procedures help employees.		
10	Job orders are essential for employees.		
		Individualism	
No	**∝ = 0,375**	**Average: 2,69**	**% Var: 0,228**
11	Employees believe that they are independent from the organization; according to them, bringing their unique characteristics and skills to the organization is crucial.		
12	Employees develop short-dated relationships and change their workplaces based on their own decide.		
13	Companies firstly concern the working performance of their employees; their personal or family happiness does not primarily interest the companies.		
14	Important decisions are made by the individuals.		
15	Works are designed as personal to maximize the independency of the employees.		
		Collectivism	
No	**∝ = 0,707**	**Average: 3,94**	**% Var: 0,473**
16	Group welfare is more important than personal rewarding.		
17	Group success is more important that personal success.		
18	Employees should pursue the goal by considering the group's welfare		
		Internal Audit	
No	**∝ = 0,754**	**Average: 4,34**	**% Var: 0,260**
19	Internal audit systems in enterprises are independent.		
20	Internal audit system provides consulting and assurance service for the enterprises.		
21	Internal audit system contributes to enterprises in risk management.		

Tab. 2: Duty and Working Period of Participants

Distribution of Tasks	n	%	Working Time	n	%
Lead Auditor	4	0,12	*1 – 5 Years*	18	0,54
Lead Auditor Assistant	1	0,03	*6 – 10 Years*	11	0,29
Internal Auditor	19	0,57	*10 Years and Above*	4	0,17
Internal Auditor Assistant	9	0,28			
TOTAL	**33**	**100**	TOTAL	**33**	**100**

Tab. 3: Distribution of Demographic Attributes of Participants

	Explanation	n	%		Explanation	N	%
Age	**Between 20–25**	6	0,19	**Educational Level**	**Undergraduate**	23	**0,69**
	Between 26–30	20	**0,60**		**Post Graduate**	9	0,27
	Between 31–35	3	0,09		**Doctorate**	1	0,04
	36 and older	4	0,12		*TOTAL*	**33**	**100**
	TOTAL	**33**	**100**				
Gender	**Female**	13	0,40				
	Male	20	**0,60**				
	TOTAL	**33**	**100**				

Four foremost items for the participants are as follows; "Internal audit system provides consulting and assurance service for enterprises" (4,48 ± 0,088); "Internal audit system contributes to enterprises in risk management" "Job orders are important for employees" (4,30 ± 0,102); "Since the rules and regulations inform employees about the expectations, rules, and regulations are accepted as important" (4,27 ± 0,079). Three items with the least importance are as follows; "Employees develop short-dated relationships and change their workplaces based on their own decide" (2,58 ± 0,163); "Important decisions are made by the individuals" (2,33 ± 0,172); Works are designed as personal to maximize the independence of the employees (2,18 ± 0,154). Tab. 5 describes the results of correlation analysis between variables.

As is seen in Tab. 8, there is a so weak and positive relationship ($0,00 < r < 0,30$; $p < 0,01$) between internal audit activity and power distance dimension that is the sub-dimension of the cultural value. There is one more so weak and positive relationship ($0,00 < r < 0,30$; $p < 0,01$) between avoidance of uncertainty and internal audit activity. There is significant relationship at medium-level ($0,30 < r < 0,70$; $p < 0,01$) between collectivism and internal audit activity (Köseb, 2017: 2). It can be

Tab. 4: Participants' Statements about the Efficacy of Internal Audit System

Participants' Statements About the Effect of the Culture on the Internal Audit	Ort.	Std. Sp.
Directors can make decisions without taking subordinates' advice.	3,36	0,150
Directors need to frequently use their authority and power for the subordinates.	**2,33**	**0,128**
Directors should rarely ask employees' opinion.	2,73	0,159
Employees should not present an opinion in management decisions.	2,70	0,141
Directors should not transfer the significant duties to the employees.	2,88	0,149
Power Distance	**2,80**	**0,145**
Mentioning the job specifications and orders in detail is important for employees to know what is expected from themselves.	4,15	0,108
Directors want employees to closely follow the procedures and orders.	4,15	0,108
Since the rules and regulations inform employees about the expectations, rules and regulations are accepted as important.	**4,27**	**0,079**
Standard working procedures help employees.	4,06	0,137
Job orders are essential for employees.	**4,30**	**0,102**
Avoidance of Uncertainty	**4,18**	**0,106**
Employees believe that they are independent from the organization; according to them, bringing their unique characteristics and skills to the organization is crucial.	3,27	0,152
Employees develop short-dated relationships and change their workplaces based on their own decide.	**2,58**	**0,163**
Companies firstly concern the working performance of their employees; their personal or family happiness does not primarily interest the companies.	3,09	0,133
Important decisions are made by the individuals.	**2,33**	**0,172**
Works are designed as personal to maximize the independency of the employees.	**2,18**	**0,154**
Individualism	2,69	0,154
Group welfare is more important than personal rewarding.	3,73	0,159
Group success is more important that personal success.	4,00	0,151
Employees should pursue the goal by considering the group's welfare	4,12	0,143
Collectivism	**3,94**	**0,151**
Internal audit systems in enterprises are independent.	4,24	0,131
Internal audit system provides consulting and assurance service for the enterprises.	**4,48**	**0,088**
Internal audit system contributes to enterprises in risk management.	**4,30**	**0,102**
Internal Audit	**4,34**	**0,107**

Tab. 5: Correlation Analysis Results Between Variables

		Power Distance	Internal Audit
Power Distance	Pearson Correlation	1	**,046**
	Sig. (2-tailed)		,799
	N	33	33
Internal Audit	Pearson Correlation	**,046**	1
	Sig. (2-tailed)	,799	
	N	33	33
		Avoidance of Uncertainty	**Internal Audit**
Avoidance of Uncertainty	Pearson Correlation	1	**,197**
	Sig. (2-tailed)		,271
	N	33	33
Internal Audit	Pearson Correlation	**,197**	1
	Sig. (2-tailed)	,271	
	N	33	33
		Individualism	**Internal Audit**
		Collectivism	**Internal Audit**
Collectivism	Pearson Correlation	1	**,516****
	Sig. (2-tailed)		,002
	N	33	33
Internal Audit	Pearson Correlation	**,516****	1
	Sig. (2-tailed)	,002	
	N	33	33

** Correlation is significant at the 0.01 level (2-tailed)

Tab. 6: Multiple Regression Analysis Results

Model Summary				
Model	**R**	**R Square**	**Adjusted R Square**	**Std. Error of the Estimate**
1	,566[a]	,320	,223	,44972

[a] Predictors: (Constant), Power Distance, Avoiding of Uncertainty, Individualism, Collectivism

Tab. 7: ANOVA Results

ANOVA[a]						
Model		**Sum of Squares**	**df**	**Mean Square**	**F**	**Sig.**
1	Regression	2,667	4	,667	3,297	,025[b]
	Residual	5,663	28	,202		
	Total	8,330	32			

[a] Dependent Variable: Internal Audit
[b] Predictors: (Constant), Power Distance, Avoidance of Uncertainty, Individualism, Collectivism

Tab. 8: Results Toward the Effect of Cultural Dimensions on Internal Audit

Coefficients[a]						
Model		**Unstandardized Coefficients**		**Standardized Coefficients**	**t**	**Sig.**
		B	**Std. Error**	**Beta**		
1	**(Constant)**	1,262	1,252		1,008	,322
	Power Distance	,104	,168	,108	,616	,543
	Avoidance of Uncertainty	,246	,228	,181	1,079	,290
	Individualism	,142	,182	,133	,783	,440
	Collectivism	**,349**	,121	**,470**	2,874	**,008**

[a] Dependent Variable: Internal Audit

said when the correlation coefficients are generally analyzed that the direction of relationships of all the dimensions except collectivism is weak. Tab. 6 shows the results of multiple regression analysis.

The dimensions (Power Distance, Avoidance of Uncertainty, Individualism, Collectivism) that are discussed as independent variable relating to the cultural values explain the internal audit activities at 22,3 % level (corrected R^2= 0,22,3). In other words, the internal audit activities take shape based on the cultural values by 22,3 %. Tab. 7 shows the anova results.

The value in significance column of ANOVA table shows that the relationship between Power Distance, Avoidance of Uncertainty, Individualism, Collectivism and the internal audit activity is statistically significant at **F= 3,297; p<0,05** level.

It is seen when looking at Tab. 8 that only the collectivism dimension that is the independent variable positively affects **(β= 0,470)** internal audit activities of banks.

According to the coefficient **(B value)** in the standardized regression equation, a unit of positive increment in collectivism dimension creates **0,349** units of increment on internal audit activities **(p<0,05).** These findings support hypothesis by satisfactory evidence. The only hypothesis is accepted, other ones below are denied;

H_1 : Power distance has a ***positive effect*** on internal audit
H_2 : Avoidance of uncertainty has a ***positive effect*** on the internal audit.
H_3 : Individualism has a ***positive effect*** on internal audit.
H_4 : Collectivism has a ***positive effect*** on the internal audit.

6 Conclusion

Accounting scandals and briberies have caused being queried the cultural values in accounting cases. The effect of cultural values on internal audit mechanisms of enterprises operate in relevant countries have been the issue of concern. Integrating the information technologies into accounting systems and settling these technologies in accounting systems enabled authorities to develop new tools about transparency and objectivity of applications mentioned. However, since the auditing mechanism is in the focus of human, the importance of cultural values in auditing implementations have increased.

This research aimed to determine whether Hofstede's cultural values as Power Distance, Avoidance of Uncertainty and Individualism-Collectivism have an effect on internal audit activities of participation banks of Turkey in 2017. Determining whether the culture has an impact on internal audit activities of participation banks of Turkey and also specifying how auditors are affected by cultural values for their decisions show the importance of this research. The scope of this study is composed of the participation banks that are in service in Turkey as of 2017. Since obtaining data is difficult in practice, internal auditors of XXX banks constitute the research sample to make healthy comments and explain more reliable and consistent information to the information users. It was used a coding as XXX because of the absence of the permission from the relevant banks. 50 questionnaire forms were distributed for application; 40 of them were answered and finally, 33 of these forms were evaluated. The data obtained were transferred into "SPSS (Statistical Package for the Social Sciences) 22.0" by coding in "Microsoft Excel 2010" program. Proper analyses (reliability analysis, descriptive statistics, average standard deviation) were performed in this program. Moreover, correlation and regression analyses were performed for making healthy comments as a result of confirming the assumption of normal distribution of error terms that is one of the essential assumptions of the classical regression analysis.

Participants have below socio-demographic attributes;

- They are composed of internal auditors in terms of duties,
- 54 % of them have 1–5 years of experience in terms of working time,
- 60 % of them are in 26–30 age range,

- 40 % of them are females,
- 69 % of them are bachelors.

Below items are found when the participants' information about the effect of the culture on internal audit activity is analyzed;

- ***Internal audit activities*** provide consulting and assurance service for enterprises; these same activities contribute to the risk management,
- ***About Avoidance of uncertainty,*** Job orders are important in terms of the employees; the legislation is crucial because of informing employees about expectations,
- ***About Individualism;*** The employees develop short-dated relationships and change their workplaces based on their own decisions. The participants show a negative tendency about being designed the works as personal to maximize the independence of employees. Another reason to show a negative tendency is that the important decisions can be made by the individuals.
- ***About the Power Distance;*** Directors do not need to frequently use authority and power for subordinates.
- ***Below items are found towards the effect of culture on the internal audit activities;***
- It is seen when the relationship between cultural value dimensions and internal audit is analyzed that there is a low and positively significant relationship between Power Distance, Avoidance of Uncertainty and Individualism dimensions. There is a positive significant relationship at medium-level can be seen in collectivism dimension.
- Power Distance, Avoidance of Uncertainty, Individualism and Collectivism dimensions shape the internal audit activities at 22,3 % level ***at the end of the regression analysis***.
- It is clear that there are imperfections about changing workplaces based on decisions of employees, making important decisions and keeping the independence during the business. This circumstance may reflect the internal audit affairs as well. Since the employees cannot act independently about the job, the internal auditor may not make the right decisions and reach reliable information through the employees. On the other hand, the natural risk of auditor will increase on financial accounts prepared; accordingly, the reliability of those financial accounts will be queried. There is a need for improving the working environment and conditions during performing the internal audit activities. New instrument and methods should be developed by considering the cultural values of internal auditors to avoid the mistake and tricks. Improving the internal audit mechanisms and considering the cultural values by the senior management of the banks; specifying performance criteria and making evaluations about the applications can contribute to determining efficacy and productivity of the activities performed. Accordingly, the reliability of the information obtained will increase. For the next studies, revealing the effect of cultural values by evaluating the cultural values on internal audit system can bring a different perspective in the literature.

Bibliography

Abdolmohammadi, Mohammad. J. Ve Gerrit, Sarens (2011). "An Investigation of The Association Between Cultural Dimensions and Variations İn Perceived Use Of And Compliance With Internal Auditing Standards İn 19 Countries", The International Journal of Accounting, sayı. 46, ss. 365–389.

Akçay, Serkan, (2013). "Türkiye'de İç Denetim Sürecinin Kamu Kurumlarının Faaliyet Sonuçları Üzerindeki Etkinliği: Belediyeler Üzerine Bir Uygulama", Afyon Kocatepe Üniversitesi, İİBF Dergisi (C. XV, S. I), ss: 57–77.

Alzeban, Abdulaziz, (2015). "The Impact of Culture on the Quality of Internal Audit: An Empirical Study, Journal of Accounting", Auditing & Finance, cilt. 30, sayı. 1, ss: 57–77.

Arcagök, M.Sait Ve Erüz, Ertan (2006). Kamu Mali Yönetimi ve Kontrol Sistemi, Maliye Hesap Uzmanları Derneği Yayını, İstanbul.

Ay, A. F. 2013. Ulusal Kültürün Motivasyona Etkisi: Sivas İlinde Bir Araştırma. Cumhuriyet Üniversitesi Sosyal Bilimler Enstitüsü: Doktora Tezi, Sivas.

Dicle, Ülkü ve Tolga Usluer, (2016). The Relationship between Culture and Effectiveness of Internal Auditing, an Empirical Study, International Journal of Contemporary Applied Sciences, Cilt. 3, sayı. 1, ss. 34–52.

Ding, Y., Jeanjean, T. ve S. Hervé. (2005) "Why Do National Gaap Differ From Ias? The Role of Culture", The International Journal Of Accounting, Vol. 40, No.4: pp. 325 – 350.

Erturan, İlkay Ejder, (2007). Kültürün Denetçi ve Denetim Sürecine Etkileri: Türkiye'deki Denetçiler Üzerine Bir Araştırma, Doktora Tezi, Anadolu Üniversitesi Sosyal Bilimler Enstitüsü, Eskişehir.

Franke, G. R. Ve Nadler S. Scott. (2008). "Culture, Economic Development, And National Ethical Attitudes", Journal of Business Research, Vol. 61, No. 3: ss. 254–264.

Gürsoy, D. Ve W.T. Umbreit. (2004). "Tourist Information Search Behavior: Crosscultural Comparison Of European Union Member States", Hospitality Management, Vol. 23, pp: 55–70.

Hell, Regis Emmanuel, ve Danni, WANG, (2009). Cultural impact on the auditing planning phase: An Empirical Study In China And Finance, Yüksek Lisans Tezi, Umea University, İsveç.Hofstede, Geert. (1980). "Motivation, Leadership, And Organization: Do American Theories Apply Abroad?. Organizational Dynamics", Amacom, A Division of American Management Associations. Summer. pp. 42–63.

Hofstede, Geert. (1984). Cultural Dimensions In Management and Planning, Asia Pacific Journal of Management, ss. 81–99.

Hofstede, Geert. (2001). Cultures Consequences: Comparing Values, Behavior, Institutions And Organizations Across Nations, 2nd Edition, Sage Publications, Thousand Oaks.

Hope, Ole-Kristian, Kang, Tony, Thomas, Wayne, Ve Yong Keun Yoo, (2008). Culture and Auditor Choice: A Test of the Secrecy Hypothesis, Journal Account Public Policy, Sayı. 27, ss. 357–373.

KOSMALA, Katarzyna, (2007). (Un)realised Independence in the CEE Region: Insights from Interpretive Cultural Theory, Critical Perspectives on Accounting, No. 18, ss. 315–342.

KÖSEa, Hacı Ömer (2007) Dünyada ve Türkiye'de Yüksek Denetim, Sayıştay 145. Kuruluş Yıldönümü Yayınları, Ankara.

Köseb, S. Kenan (2017), Korelasyon Ve Regresyon Analizi, http://file. toraks. org. tr/ TORAK SFD 23NJ KL4 NJ4H 3BG3JH /mse-ppt-pdf/Kenan_KOSE3.pdf.

Kurnaz, Niyazi ve Ali Kestane, (2016). "Afro-Avrasya Ülkelerinde Ulusal Kültür Ve Sermaye Yapısı İlişkisi Kriz Sonrası Dönem: Karşılaştırmalı Bir Bakış", I. Uluslararası Afro-Avrasya Araştırmaları Kongresi, 15–15 Ekim 2016 Almatı/ Kazakistan.

Kurnaz, Niyazi ve Tansel, Çetinoğlu, (2010). İç Denetim Güncel Yaklaşımlar, 1. Baskı, Umuttepe Yayınları, Kocaeli.

Okaro, Sunday C. Ve Gloria O. Okafor, (2015), "Cultural Factors and Audit Quality Evidence from Nigeria", International Journal of Academic Research in Accounting, Finance and Management Sciences, cilt. 5, sayı. 2, ss. 17–22.

ÖZBEK, Çetin (2012). İç Denetim, Kurumsal Yönetim, Risk Yönetimi, İç Kontrol, Türkiye İç Denetim Enstitüsü Yayınları, Yayın No. 3.

Pickett, K.H. Spencer (2005). The Internal Auditing Handbook, John Willey and Sons, England.

Reimann, M., Lünemann, U.F. Ve R. B. Chase. (2008). "Uncertainty Avoidance As A Moderator of The Relationship Between Perceived Service Quality and Customer Satisfaction", Journal of Service Research, Vol. 11 No. 1, ss. 63–73.

Sander, James F., Hughes, Susan B., Higgs, Scott D. and Charles P. Cullinan, (2009). The Impact of Cultural Environment on Entry-Level Auditors' Abilities to Perform Analytical Procedures, Journal of International Accounting, Auditing and Taxation, No. 18, pp: 29–43.

Sağlar, Jale ve Koray Tuan, (2009). "İşletmelerde İç Denetim Fonksiyonunun Bağımsız Dış Denetim Maliyeti Üzerindeki Etkileri", Ç.Ü. Sosyal Bilimler Enstitüsü Dergisi, Cilt. 18, Sayı. 1, ss. 343–358.

Sevim, Şerafettin Ve Ayşenur Eliuz, (2007). "Denetim Komitelerinin İç Denetimin Etkinliği Üzerindeki Rolleri ve İMKB'de Bir Araştırma", Journal of MUFAD, No. 36, ss. 60–70.

Soares, A. Maria, Farhangmehr, M. Ve S. Aviv. (2008). "Hofstede's Dimensions Of Culture In International Marketing Studies", Journal of Business Research, Vol. 60, No. 3, ss. 277–284.

Soba, M., Bayhan, M., Şimşek, A. Ve Kestane, A. (2015). "Safha Maliyet Sistemi Ve Tam Zamanında Stok Yönetimi (JIT) İlişkisinin Üretim İşletmelerinin Üzerine Etkisi: Uşak İlinde Bir Uygulama", Üretim Araştırmaları Sempozyumu, Ege Üniversitesi, Vol. 15, 14–16 Ekim 2015, İzmir: 485–496.

Tanriöğen, A. (2012). Bilimsel Araştırma Yöntemleri. 3. Baskı, Ankara: Anı Yayıncılık.

Tosunoğlu, Büşra veGül Yeşilçelebi, (2016). "Kültürün İç Denetim Üzerindeki Etkisinin Muhasebe Meslek Mensupları Açısından Değerlendirilmesi", Journal of Accounting, Finance and Auditing Studies, Cilt. 2, Sayı. 1, ss. 73–87.

Tsui, Judy S. L. VeFerdinand A. Gul, (1996), "Auditors' Behaviour In An Audit Conflict Situation: A Research Note On The Role Of Locus Of Control And Ethical Reasoning", Accounting Organizations Society, Vol. 21, No. 1, pp. 41–51.

Tüm, Kayahan, (2013). "Kurumsal Yönetim, İç Denetim ve İç Denetimin Kalitesi: Kalite Güvence ve Geliştirme Programı", Çukurova Üniversitesi İİBF Dergisi, Cilt. 17, Sayı. 2, ss. 93–112.

Varıcı, İdris veFevzi Serkan Özdemir, (2013). "Uluslararası Finansal Raporlama Standartlarına Yönelişin Kültür Bağlamında Değerlendirilmesi", Mali Çözüm Dergisi, Eylül-Ekim Sayısı, ss. 15–41.

Wu, Yi Ming. (2008). "Comparing Expected Leadership Styles in Taiwan and the United States: A Study of University Employees", China Media Research, Vol. 4, No. 1, ss. 36–46.

Yilanci, Münevver ve Sevim, Şerafettin, (1991). "İşletmelerde İç Kontrol Sistemi ve İç Denetim Fonksiyonu, İşletmecinin El Kitabı", BİAR Eğitim Yayınları, No. 13, Ankara.

Yurtsever, Gürdoğan, (2015). "İç Denetimin Fonksiyonları ve Katma Değeri", Finans Politik & Ekonomik Yorumlar Dergisi, Cilt. 52, Sayı. 602, ss. 89–101.

Altan Fahri Gülerci

Financial Consumer Protection and Party Autonomy: Is Laissez-Fare Really Dead?

1 Consumer Law and It's Effect to the Party Autonomy

In one of a cartoon that I've seen, a cow and a banker make a contract. The cow reads the contract and asks the man the question, "As far as I see it in the contract that, you can benefit from my milk. But here it's writing that you can also benefit from my meat!" The bank manager replies, "It's not important. they are routine words, like all the contract terms. Let's sign it, please!" Indeed, the idea of restricting freedom of contract is not fundamentally different from the idea that voiced in that cartoon. If the cow signs the contract, it is deemed to have accepted to be cut off. If it does not sign, loses the benefit, that it hopes getting from the contract. This is the main idea underlying many contracts today.

The most important limitations on the basis of party autonomy are, consumer law regulations that force the field of freedom of contract with a growing intensity of violence. Consumer law regulations inevitably emerges as a specific form of view of the law of obligations. From the sociological point of view, consumer is a mass. With the birth of the consumer society, the states were indifferent to the initiatives of consumer movements and activist consumers that first appeared in the USA and then in the European countries. After this period, countries were put into effect the systems which were abolished freedom of contract of the strong side. Today, though the freedom of contract is a product of the basic philosophy of the law of obligations, is confined to a narrow application space because of the consumer law regulations.

As it seen, consumer law is separating from the law of obligations day by day, because the main element of classic contract doctrine is party autonomy in liberal economies. But when one part of the contract is a consumer, the legislators have started to put the party autonomy aside.

It is a fact that in the 19th century and much of the twentieth century, in the field of the law of obligations, freedom of contract was the dominant theory. Freedom of contract was at the height of its power and during this long honeymoon period it knew to enjoy of its power. However, after the emergence of the consumer society and together with the globalization process this honeymoon period ended. Especially with the globalization of financial markets, everybody understood that when an event occurred in one side of the world, it could affect the other side of the world easily and rapidly. Thus freedom of contract has begun to decline. These attacks were actually directed to capitalism under the name of contract freedom. The end of the capitalism age is now beginning. Nowadays, the widespread opinion in the academy is that the capitalist system's dying day by day and alarm bells start to ring with the subprime crisis. People were afraid to disclosure this reality, but now this truth is become openly defended.

Indeed, it appears that the intervention to freedom of contract continues to increase at an accelerated rate in particular with the mortgage crisis. All of us witness that freedom of contract is increasingly confined to a narrow space. It is now clear that even in the US, which is the motherland of liberalism and free market economy, the interventions that have deeply affected the freedom of the contract have been successively occurred. It's clear that the truck of the contract freedom has been swiftly thrown away from a great downhill with an empty gear. In short, the king is naked!

Of course, to advocate whether the freedom of contract will end soon or to be condemned to cell imprisonment will force the boundaries of this short work. But I would like to underline, it is an undeniable reality that the existence of consumer law itself is a very important and powerful threat to the future of contract freedom.

For this reason, I think that the social state is coming in the form of a bottom wave which is gradually turning into a tsunami and freedom of contract is going to stay under this tsunami. As a result, it is necessary to anticipate that the upcoming periods will cause great difficulty for contract freedom. We also have to remember that; each intervention to the consumer contract is an attack on the party autonomy.

2 Financial Consumer and Scope of the Financial Consumer Protection

Financial institutions especially banks, are the main economic actors in all of our daily life. They are the symbols of capitalist power and the pathological structure of financial transactions requires to involve standard terms in its contracts. The consumer is generally a weak party among other parties in financial transactions. Maybe, the half of the problems of consumers concerning law arised from financial transactions and financial contracts. In financial contracts, the need for protection of the consumer is at the highest level because of the nature of the strong party.

The financial crisis highlighted that financial protection of consumers is necessary for the long term stability. But who is the financial consumer and how can we protect them? The financial consumer is a consumer who uses financial product or service. I must mention that financial consumer protection is different from consumer financial protection. They're strictly associated with each other. Sometimes these have the same meaning, sometimes mingled. It's not easy to say financial consumer means consumer financial protection especially when the protected consumer is not a financial consumer. For example Title X of the Dodd-Frank Act is named as "Consumer Financial Protection Act" but it contains the protection of consumer from financial products and services and systems of the consumer financial protection.

Financial consumer is a new concept. But it was known as a term, before the subprime mortgage crisis. However it became a famous subject after the financial meltdown. Because during the financial crisis of 2007, financial consumer played leading role and gave everybody (legislators, scholars...) food for thought. So it was understood that financial consumer and protection of financial consumer are the building blocks of the consumer society and sustainable capitalist system.

Financial consumer protection aims consumers to be enlightened and be informed during they are taking their decisions. To provide access to information, not to be a subject of unfair practices, and access to dispute channels are also the other aims of financial consumer protection[1]. So the scope of financial consumer protection must be educating the consumer on how to use financial products and legal rights[2]. Thus consumers can be gain skills to understand the results of their risky decisions. Another aim of the financial consumer protection must be to establish fair rules for financial institutions.

3 Recent Developments About the Topic in the Positive Law Field

3.1 Some of International Documents

The complex problems of the financial consumer are not be unconcerned the international economic organizations. For example OECD has published a document named "High Level Principles on Financial Consumer" in October 2011. We can also mention the "Effective Approaches to Support The Implementation of the Remaining G 20/ OECD High Level Principles on Financial Consumer" that published in September 2014. The other example is World Bank Good Practices. In June 2012 The World Bank published a document named Good Practices for Financial Consumer Protection. These international documents are not obligatory. Unlike this, they're advisory. For them, we can say that they are parts of international soft law.

In October 2011 with the attemption of finance ministers and governors of central bank establish common provisions on consumer protection from financial products[3]. These principles consist of basic principles that can be used not only in the G 20 countries but also in other relevant economies. In other words, effective approaches emerge as a common product of common problems that concern both developed and developing countries[4]. Moreover, these Effective Approaches have

1 The World Bank (2012). Good Practices for Financial Consumer Protection. http://siteresources.worldbank.org/EXTFINANCIALSECTOR/Resources/Good_Practices_for_Financial_CP.pdf . Washington: The World Bank, 1

2 World Bank, 1

3 OECD (2011). G20 High Level Principles on Financial Consumer Protection. http://www.oecd.org/daf/fin/financial-markets/48892010.pdf. France: OECD

4 OECD (2014). Effective Approaches to Support The Implementation of The Remaining G20/OECD High-Level Principles on Financial Consumer Protection. http://www.

a comprehensive nature (consisting of banking and credit; securities; investment; insurance and pensions). This text is also designed to guide the interest of every group in the financial consumer[5].

In June 2012 The World Bank published a document named Good Practices for Financial Consumer Protection. One of the main objectives of good practices is to provide comprehensive solutions to the players in financial markets. World Bank Good Practices divided financial consumers into four main sector (banking sector, securities sector, insurance sector and non-bank credit institutions). Good Practices have two main parts. The General Part proposes at least 39 common good practices that are applied all consumer financial services[6]. This text, which was published by the World Bank in 2012, has been off the agenda in a short time and has updated and re-published in 2017[7]. In the new text, there are main chapters (on deposit and credit products and services, insurance, private pensions, securities) and additional chapters (on retail payment systems, credit reporting systems and financial capability).

3.2 Financial Consumer Revolution in the USA

Although the US has experienced many financial crises, it is clear that the outcome of the subprime mortgage crisis is the most important crisis after the Great Depression[8]. The vital result of the subprime mortgage crisis was to be reveal of

---

oecd.org/daf/fin/financial-education/G20-OECD-Financial-Consumer-Protection-Principles-Implementation-2014.pdf . France: OECD

5 Effective approaches covers the principles that, every sector, can take into account from implementers to consumers and from policy makers to regulators. Practically, it can be expressed as a solution-oriented text that has the ability to be practiced in different legal circles and different conditions. The OECD likens the effective approaches, to a "toolbox" in the field of consumer protection. Through effective approaches, consumers will be able to conduct their transactions safely, knowledge based, in privacy, thus, effective consumer protection can be provided. In this way confidence in financial products and services will reestablished again; Effective Approaches, 4.

6 Topics of the Common Good Practices are as follows: Consumer protection institutions (Art. 1-6), disclosure and sales practices (Art. 7-14), privacy and data protection (Art. 20-24), dispute resolution mechanisms (Art. 25-28), guarantee and compensation schemes (Art. 29-31), financial literacy and consumer empowerment (Art. 32-36), competition policy in financial services and consumer welfare (Art. 37-39).

7 The World Bank (2017). Good Practices for Financial Consumer Protection. https://openknowledge.worldbank.org/bitstream/handle/10986/28996/122011-PUBLIC-GoodPractices-WebFinal.pdf?sequence=1&isAllowed=y. Washington: The World Bank

8 Kennedy L.J, McCoy P and Bernstein E (2012). The Consumer Financial Protection Bureau: Financial Regulation For The Twenty-First Century. Cornell L. Rev, 97: 1141

the deficiency of the federal regulatory system[9]. After the subprime mortgage crisis Congress made massive and radical revolution on the financial system with a Dodd-Frank Wall Street Reform and Consumer Protection Act of 2010.

There isn't any definition of financial consumer in the Dodd-Frank Act. But the Act identified the consumer as "an individual or an agent, trustee, or representative acting on behalf of an individual" and gives a very comprehensive definition of financial products and services via the consumer[10]. Dodd-Frank Act covers comprehensive financial regulatory issues. However, the most important reform was the creation of the Consumer Financial Protection Bureau[11]. With the Dodd-Frank Act, a new regulatory agency named CFPB established which is aimed to build a new and steady system on sector and protect the financial consumer[12]. The objectives of the CFPB are the enlightenment the consumer, protecting the consumer from unfair practices, to eliminate the outdated regulations and to provide a fair financial products sector[13]. When we look to the Powers of the CFPB, we can see that it has rulemaking, supervision and enforcement powers[14].

---

9 Kennedy, McCoy, & Bernstein, 1141

10 USC, 12, § 5481, 15, A

11 The purpose of the CFPB see USC 12, § 5511, a

12 Why USA needs to establish a new regulatory agency named CFPB should be examined well. In American doctrine, Levitin mentions about three important and major structural problem about the pre-CFPB period According to Levitin, all of the regulatory agencies were authorized on protecting financial consumer but none of them has authorized. In other words there wasn't a primary agency. All had liabilities about CFP but their main goal was to provide soundness of financial system indeed; to look the panorama of pre CFPB period see Levitin A.J. (2012-2013). The Consumer Financial Protection Bureau: An Introduction. Rev. Banking & Fin. L., 32: 329-334.

13 USC 12, § 5511, b. According to the Act, CFPB has six primary functions. See USC 12, § 5511, c.

14 First and vital power of the CFPB is rulemaking authority (see USC, 12, § 5514, b, 1); for covered persons look also USC, 12, § 5514, a, 1); As a rulemaking authority, CFPB has authority on Federal Consumer Financial Law (USC, 12, § 5491, a). Federal Consumer Financial Law consist of two main parts. The first one is the authority that is given by the Title X of Dodd-Frank Act to the CFPB; the second is the authority on Federal statutes (named enumerated consumer laws), that is transferred to the CFPB; see Levitin, 344. If CFPB's regulations creates systemic risk, Financial Stability Oversight Council (FSOC) has a veto authority (see USC, 12, §, 5513, c, 3, A, B). CFPB cannot force financial institutions to submit any financial product to the consumer. CFPB has also a supervision authority. As a supervision authority, CFPB has supervisory authority to investigate the institutions' commercial books and other recorded documents. Indeed, the Bureau shall require reports and conduct examinations on a periodic basis of covered persons described in the Act. While the supervision, CFPB can learn confidential information. But this information is confidential and cannot be shared; see Levitin, 355. It is crucial to state that CFPB's supervisory authority has covered only to specific persons like residential mortgage loan provider, payday lender, private student lender, depositary covered person, banks etc; See Levitin, 356.

Giving detailed information about the CFPB forces the boundaries of this work. Briefly, we can say that; At first glance, it appears that the CFPB has, perform a much more regulatory function. But it's a reality that it has essentially had authorities to may deeply influence to contract freedom. Undoubtedly, the underlying philosophy that lies behind this must be the last crises.

3.3 Financial Consumer Protection and It's Effect to Party Autonomy in Turkish Law

In Turkish law, the interference to the freedom of contract by the way of imposing mandatory rules in consumer contracts was first realized by the Consumer Protection Act of 1995 which was accepted by the Turkish parliament GNAT[15]. This Act then went through significant changes in 2003. Finally, the New Consumer Protection Act of 2013[16] represents the last point reached in terms of consumer protection. The purpose of the act, in Consumer Protection Act has been determined in a very comprehensive way. In line with the article 1 of the Consumer Protection Act, aims of the act are as follows:

- To protect the health, safety and economic interests of the consumer in accordance with the public interest.
- To compensate the losses of the consumer.
- To ensure that consumers are protected from environmental hazards.
- To take measures to enlighten the consumer and raise awareness of consumer.
- To encourage the consumers to protect themselves.
- To encourage to establish voluntary organizations in the creation of policies on consumer issues.

It is explained in the preamble of the new Code of Consumer Protection that how and when there is an intervention to the freedom of contract as follows:

"As the need to protect consumers depends on various reasons, the tools that must be used to protect the consumer are also different. One of the reasons for the necessity of protection of the consumer also is that the consumer does not have the information he needs to establish the legal transaction with the most appropriate content. In these cases because of the information asymmetry between the parties, mandatory measures must be taken to eliminate this asymmetry.

At the end, USC 12, § 5564/a is about the enforcement authority of the Bureau. In line with this article if there is a breach of financial consumer regulations, Bureau has been authorized to take a civil suit and take necessary measures.

15 Grand National Assembly of Turkey. This Code is mentioned as the Code of Consumer Protection of Number 4077. Publishing date in the Official Gazette: 8th March 1995; Volume: 22221

16 This Code is mentioned as the Code of Consumer Protection of Number 6502. Publishing date in the Official Gazette: 28th November 2013; Volume: 28835

As a matter of fact, in all cases where there is an obligation to inform the consumer before or during the establishment of the contract in the new Act the aim is to eliminate this unbalanced situation between the parties. Thus, it is residual possible for the consumer to establish an informed contract. The EU legislation attaches particular importance to the obligation to inform the consumer. That's why, the intervention to the freedom of contract will be decreased.

In some cases, make a written contract is necessary as a precondition to the obligation to inform the consumer. The sanction of make a nonwritten contract is absolute nullity. In some cases it is anticipated that the contract will be set up despite the lack of information. However, in cases where the consumer is not informed about the conditions of the contract, it will be interpreted against the writer of the condition. Thus, there is a matter of a boomerang effect in the presence of an unjust condition will be involved.

The problem with a number of contracts is that the consumer signs them without much thought, either because of the characteristics of the marketing techniques or the appeal of the process. In such cases, generally the usual situation is that the consumer regrets because of being a part of a contract. In these situations, the Act is recognising the consumer has a right of withdrawal from the contract. Right to withdrawal is the right to take back the declaration aimed to the will to make a contract. Indeed, the Act recognized this right for a number of contracts (like timeshare vacation and long-term holiday service contracts, out of office – off-premises contracts distance contracts, distance contracts of financial services etc.). Generally withdrawing time is fourteen days. Thus, the consumer will have the opportunity to get rid of the contract when he make a contract without thinking.

The most serious interventions to the contract freedom are the situations of when the content of the contract is filled by a judge or by an Act. In such cases, the law establishes a mandatory contractual content or authorize the judge to about to intervene the contract. For example, mandatory provisions on installment contracts or on consumer credit contracts directly shape contractual content. On the other hand, the auditing mechanism regarding unfair conditions in the consumer contracts get the judge to intervene in the content of the contract according to the characteristics of the concrete case or if there are provisions against the consumer, the judge have also the authority to make the contract provisions absolutely void."

For the law of obligations, the essential problem is the application area of the Consumer Protection Act. In other words, the scope of the Consumer Protection Act is an important problem for the law of obligations. In this sense, Art. 3/1-k of the Consumer Protection Act has defined the consumer as a natural or legal person acting for non-commercial or non-professional purposes. In line with the Art. 3/1-l of the Consumer Protection Act all of the contracts and legal transactions including contract of work, transport agreement, brokerage contract, insurance transactions, agency, banking can be a consumer transaction. But one party of this transactions must be a consumer. The other party can be a real person or legal entities (including public entities) that acts with a commercial or professional purposes or on these persons behalf.

If we evaluate both definitions together, it seems that the application area of Code of Obligations has been narrowed considerably.

Article 4 of the Consumer Protection Act is setting out the basic principles of consumer contracts. The first sub-article of the Art. 4 is related to the form of the written consumer contracts. Accordingly, the contracts and notifications must be comprehensible, simple and readable. The type size shall be minimum 12 points. The contract must be given to the consumer with a paper based form or with permanent storage device. The lack of some mandatory conditions in the contract does not affect the validity of the contract. However the regulator party shall immediately make up for this deficiency.

In Turkish Law, there is no definition of financial consumer in the new Turkish Consumer Protection Act of 2013. Consumer Protection Act of 2013 identified consumer as a natural person and a legal entity who acts with noncommercial or nonprofessional purposes. The Act established a consumer council, board of advertisement, arbitration committees on consumer problems and consumer courts. But there isn't any definition and direct provision of financial consumer.

Although there is no definition of the subject, there are comprehensive provisions on financial consumer transactions like unfair contract terms, consumer credit, mortgage loans, distance contracts on financial products and services. In Turkish Law debit and credit cards are regulated in a separate Code, named the Bank Cards and Credit Card Act of 2006. This act and related regulations contain important provisions on credit card contracts.

In addition, the Consumer Protection Act foresees a different regulation on the products or services offered to consumers by banks, financial institutions issuing consumer loans and card issuing organizations. Indeed, in accordance with the second sentence of the Consumer Protection Code's article 4/3, all kinds of fees, charges, expenses that is demanded from the banks and financial institutions must be taken, out of the interest of the consumer. On the purpose of this the Code of Consumer Protection has had authority to the Banking Regulation and Supervision Authority to make a regulation. With the aim of consumer protection by Turkish BRSA a website called http://www.finansaltuketici.gov.tr/ was established. In addition, the action plan and background paper for the protection of the financial consumer by the BRSA were prepared and publicly announced[17]. And then a Regulation on the Procedures and Principles Regarding the Fees to be Obtained from the Financial Consumer has published[18].

In line with the Consumer Protection Act article 4/4, it is compulsory to provide information on all kinds of fees and charges that to be demanded from the

---

17 There is also a prime ministers' circular (after 24th June 2018, presidency circular) on financial consumer protection.

18 Publishing date in the Official Gazette Date: 3rd October 2014; Volume: 29138

consumers in respect of the consumer contracts arranged in the Consumer Protection Code in a written paper form. This paper is generally an additional part of the contract.

In contracts established by means of remote communication, this information shall be given in accordance with the remote communication medium used. The burden of proof whether or not this information gives or not, belongs to the contract drafter party.

Financial consumer is identified in the regulation of bank charges which was made by the financial supervision authority of Turkey. According to this regulation, financial consumer is the consumer identified in the Consumer Protection Act and offered a financial product and service from a financial institution like banks, consumer credit institutions, debit or credit cart institutions

The other important document is the Financial Consumer Protection Action Plan. The Prime Minister's office published "The Strategy and Action Plan of Financial Access, Financial Education and Protection of Financial Consumer" in the official gazette dated June 5, 2014. After this document, Banking Regulation and Supervision Agency published a document named the background of financial consumer protection action plan.

The most important problem in Turkey is the lack of expert regulatory and supervisory agency like Consumer Financial Protection Bureau[19]. In Turkish Law like pre CFPB period in U.S., the authority is divided between regulatory agencies (Banking Regulation and Supervision Authority, Capital Markets Board, Central Bank) and Directorate General of Consumer Protection and Market Surveillance (that is only a sub unit in the Ministry of Customs and Trade). The Consumer Protection Act gives authority to Banking Regulation and Supervision Agency to make regulations on bank charges in favor of the consumer. But some important provisions of the regulations are against the consumer and these regulations were cancelled by the Council of the State.

4 Conclusion: Is Laissez-Fare Really Dead?

I think, there is an interesting dichotomy on party autonomy. We mentioned above that the end of contract freedom is now beginning because of the consumer

---

19 This problem is also mentioned in the prime ministers' circular with the following statements: "In Turkey, responsibility for the protection of financial consumer is distributing in a functional mode between banking, capital markets, insurance and payment systems. There is no specific administrative department for the protection of the financial consumer. In this framework, there is a need for the development of coordination and cooperation between organizations with authority and responsibility for the protection of the financial consumer. And also there is a need to improve the enhancement of the resources allocated for the protection of the consumer by these organizations and active participation in international platforms."

law regulations. But in my opinion nobody ask the question of "Did the freedom of contract really existed?" Indeed, freedom of contract never existed. The only thing that existed was the hegemony of the strong party. In another words party autonomy is the slogan of the classical Laissez-Fare doctrine. So, what can we do?

It appears that the effect of consumer law regulations on contract freedom has increased rapidly, especially with the birth of the concept of financial consumers. The need for protection of the consumer in financial products and services is based on several reasons. First of all financial institutions that offer financial products and services are much more likely to impose their own contract conditions. Consumers are in a stronger situation in this respect vis-à-vis to other institutions. Secondly, the wrong decisions made by consumers about financial products and services not only affect the consumer itself. It can also affect businesses (financial institutions) providing financial products and services. For this reason, protection of financial consumer is especially important.

Another issue that needs to be discussed is how to control consumer financial contracts. We must think the party autonomy again and in financial contracts we must improve consumer rights and protect the consumer from wrong economic decisions. In this respect, the first option is to intervene in the contract directly. However, it is clear that this method is quite repressive and carries the risk of completely abolishing the freedom of contract. The second way is to create processes that will enable the consumer to be a reasonable and act in his/her favor. To provide this the consumer shall be enlightened and educated. It is also difficult for the consumer to find a interlocutor at the financial institutions to solve his/her problems of himself/ herself. For this reason, the creation of new and effective dispute resolution channels is also important.

To legislate or establish regulations does not mean to have effective consumer protection regime in financial transactions. We must establish an effective, sustainable, viable consumer protection regime because of financial institutions are the strong party in financial contracts.

Bibliography

Kennedy L.J, McCoy P and Bernstein E (2012). The Consumer Financial Protection Bureau: Financial Regulation For The Twenty-First Century. Cornell L. Rev, 97: 1141–1175

Levitin A.J. (2012–2013). The Consumer Financial Protection Bureau: An Introduction. Rev. Banking & Fin. L., 32: 321–369.

OECD (2011). G20 High Level Principles on Financial Consumer Protection. http://www.oecd.org/daf/fin/financial-markets/48892010.pdf. France: OECD

OECD (2014). Effective Approaches to Support The Implementation of The Remaining G20/OECD High-Level Principles on Financial Consumer Protection. http://www.oecd.org/daf/fin/financial-education/

G20-OECD-Financial-Consumer-Protection-Principles-Implementation-2014.pdf . France: OECD

The World Bank (2012). Good Practices for Financial Consumer Protection. http://siteresources.worldbank.org/EXTFINANCIALSECTOR/Resources/Good_Practices_for_Financial_CP.pdf . Washington: The World Bank

The World Bank (2017). Good Practices for Financial Consumer Protection. https://openknowledge.worldbank.org/bitstream/handle/10986/28996/122011-PUBLIC-GoodPractices-WebFinal.pdf?sequence=1&isAllowed=y. Washington: The World Bank

Ahmet Fethi Durmuş and Figen Canbay Çiğdem

Evaluation of Orchards Within the Scope of Tms 41: Apricot Garden Sample

1 Introductıon

Agricultural activities, that its past goes back thousands years and have fundamental role for humanity's adopting sedentary life, has shown regular development and evaluation with the advancing technology. Agriculture sector that was associated just with the production of staple foods in the past is today considered in a wide range condition as fruit and vegetable growing, viticulture, green housing, meat and milk products production, forestry, aquaculture, poultry farming and bee culture.

Agriculture sector is a very important sector because of some reasons such as being source of raw material, wide employment opportunities, addition to national dividend and its impact on economic development. Especially with investments done to agriculture sector by developed countries, agricultural activities have shown tendency to be commercial activities instead of small and medium sized activities done for obtaining family income recently. With all these developments, financial information needs of the ones in agricultural activities have increased and accounting standardization regarding agricultural activities is necessitated. For this purpose, UMS 41 Agricultural Activity Standard that is published in December 2000 and would be applied for accounting periods after 1 January 2003 went into effect. In our country, TMS 42 Agricultural Activity Standard is published in 24.02.2006 dated 26090 numbered Official Gazette as it would be applied in accounting periods starting after 31.12.2015 date. Then, different updates are made to standard according to the changes occurred in UFRS in 2007, 200 and 2009 dates.

Turkey is a very rich country in terms of climate and soil characteristics, underground and aboveground sources. Its best example is growing and exporting varieties of fruit and vegetables in appropriate ecological conditions of Anatolia. Thus, our country is ranked as among important fruit producer countries of the world in terms of both number of kind and type and amount of production. Anatolia is homeland of apple, pear, quince, plum, cherry, berry, cranberry, nut, peanut, almond, walnut, chestnut, olives, fig, pomegranate and grapes. Except from these fruits, there are many kinds of fruits that their trees are benefited in different ways such as thorn apple, rose hip, blackberry, cherry laurel, oleaster, locust, hackberry, terebinth, buttum tree and citronella. One of the fruits that being produced and its commerce is made in Anatolia is apricot. Today, apricot trees can be seen in Siberia's very cold fields, subtropical fields of North Africa, deserts of Middle Asia, damp fields of Japan and Eastern China and the world's most qualified apricots and grown in Anatolia. A very rich genetically variety occurred in terms of shape, massiveness and color in apricot that its agriculture has been made for nearly 2500 years in fertile fields of Anatolia (Asma, 2011:17).

Past of the apricot and information about its being cultivated plant are very limited. Most extensive information about this task is found in China. The oldest records regarding growing apricot as cultivated plant is belonging to approximately four thousand years ago and how apricot agriculture is made in China Imperial Yu period is mentioned (BC 2205 – 2198). Chinese philosopher and scholar Confucius (BC 551 – 479) taught his philosophy to his students in Apricot Tree Temple (Xing Tan Ge) in Qufu city. Today, there are different ideas regarding how apricot spread from Middle Asia to West. Many experts claim that the apricot came to Anatolia during the Asia journey of Alexander the Great. According to this opinion, Macedonia king Alexander the Great brought apricot to Anatolia from Iran and Trans Caucasus ways during the Asia journeys started in BC 334 with his troops. According to some other people, it was expanded to West by silk dealers from origin centers. When Europe met with well-known silk and spices of Fareast, great demand to these products occurred. In 2nd century BC, Silk Road, which starts in Xian city of China, passes Turkistan, Afghanistan, Iran and reaches Anatolia, ends in Rome by passing different cities of Anatolia. This road that protects its importance in terms of commercial and military for seventeen centuries is the unique connect of Europe with Far East. According to the third and final opinion, Rome soldiers had an important role for the spread of the apricot. Romans had great effort after 2nd century to hegemonies Syria, Iran and Caucasus, even called Near East. Roman soldiers, working in Near east that is regularly moving in terms of military, provided the spread of apricot by taking it along (Ministry of Food, Agriculture and Livestock, 2015:11–12)

2 Production of Apricot in Turkey and Malatya

Production of fresh apricot is done in Iran, Uzbekistan, Pakistan, Ukraine and Algeria with the countries covering Mediterranean such as Spain, France, Italy, Turkey and Algeria in the world. In addition to these countries, Japan has great share in the production of apricot.

In the production of fresh apricot, Turkey is at first rank with between 350.00 and 800.000 tons of production amount. Production of apricot in Turkey's big part is done in Malatya province. Within the years, production of apricot has shown increase with fluctuations. The basic reason of fluctuations is spring season late frosts that are fundamental for apricot fruit.

Malatya province is almost identified with apricot fruit. Due to the fact that the economy of Malatya is highly based on agriculture and animal breeding and apricot has big importance in terms of economical income within the agricultural products; apricot fruit is very fundamental for Malatya province. Number of apricot tree number and fields of total orchards has shown increase within years in Malatya province. Since 2016, 380.551 tons of apricot production with approximately 50 kg yield per tree from more than 8 million trees is done in Malatya.

Tab. 1: Apricot Production in Malatya Between 2004–2016 Years. Source: TUİK, https://biruni.tuik.gov.tr/bitkiselapp/bitkisel.zul, Date Accessed: 08.04.2017

Year	Fields of total orchards (decare)	Production (tones)	Average yield per tree (kg)	Number of trees at age of giving fruit	Number of trees at age of not giving fruits	Total tree number
2004	636.980	84.706	14	6.055.500	546.400	6.601.900
2005	645.320	500.269	78	6.400.300	466.290	6.866.590
2006	675.920	242.871	37	6.648.770	428.313	7.077.083
2007	679.990	267.733	40	6.740.050	471.490	7.211.540
2008	688.290	362.873	53	6.803.250	486.480	7.289.730
2009	700.150	340.085	49	6.889.000	501.280	7.390.280
2010	709.880	220.927	32	6.912.350	539.850	7.452.200
2011	729.100	409.646	59	6.971.800	565.600	7.537.400
2012	742.800	510.000	72	7.068.060	576.900	7.644.960
2013	754.320	411.825	58	7.135.350	552.150	7.687.500
2014	768.000	38.654	5	7.287.000	531.000	7.818.000
2015	801.100	336.000	45	7.475.000	501.000	7.976.000
2016	810.970	380.551	50	7.558.000	498.040	8.056.040

Tab. 2: Turkey and Malatya Apricot Production (tones) 2004–2016. Source: TUİK, https://biruni.tuik.gov.tr/bitkiselapp/bitkisel.zul, Date Accessed: 08.04.2017

Years /Apricot production (ton)	Turkey	Malatya
2004	320.000	84.706
2005	860.000	500.269
2006	460.182	242.871
2007	557.572	267.733
2008	716.415	362.873
2009	660.894	340.085
2010	450.000	220.927
2011	650.000	409.646
2012	760.000	510.000
2013	780.000	411.825
2014	270.000	38.654
2015	680.000	336.000
2016	730.000	380.551

City of Malatya takes the first place in terms of apricot production in Turkey. The amount of apricot production in Malatya is even more than half of the Turkey's apricot production. But still, the late spring frosts are playing an important role in the fluctuation of apricot production in Malatya.

Around the City of Malatya, Baskil (Elazığ), Elbistan (Kahramanmaraş), Gölbaşı (Adıyaman), Gürün (Sivas) are the other districts whereby apricot production is being done densely and the amount of apricot which are being harvested in those districts is an addition amount for Malatya's apricot market figures, but in terms of figures that amount is apart from Malatya's production figures. Since these districts are geographically similar to City of Malatya, the apricot harvests from these regions have almost the same qualifications with the apricot harvest of Malatya. Accordingly, they can be used as dried fruits. Other cities where apricot production is done are Erzincan, Kahramanmaraş, Kayseri, Elazığ, İçel, Konya, Ankara, Sivas, Iğdır and Nevşehir. As well as City of Malatya, Erzincan, Elazığ, Nevşehir and Niğde are the other cities where dried apricot production is being done. Edible apricot production is being done in other cities (Ünal, 2010:20–21).

3 TMS 41 Standards of Agricultural Activities

Agriculture is an important sector of the global economy. However, for a long time accounting in agriculture was not a priority for researchers and standard issuers (Feleaga & others, 2016: 32). Agricultural activity is transformation of assets to be recycled or to be sold to living assets or agricultural goods and management of harvesting goods by an enterprise (TMS 41, m., 5). TMS 41 Standards of Agricultural Activities has been published in 26090 numbered Official Gazette by the date of 24.02.2006 to be applicable from the 31.12.2005 dated account terms. Above mentioned standards are updated seven times by the notifications in different Official Gazettes in the period between the dates of 15.07.2007 and 12.11.2014. The main reasons which are important in the process of establishing the standards are; the share of agricultural sector is noticeable in gross national product figures for many countries, uncertainty of when and how accountancy of living assets and related events of agricultural enterprises which consist main asset structure will be done and the existence of disagreements in preparing the financial statements for displaying living assets of those agricultural enterprises (Yazarkan, 2016:412).

Most enterprises from the agriculture branch do not belong to the users' circle of IFRS. If they do belong, the measurement of the biological assets and agricultural produce according to IAS 41 means a change in paradigm. This happens because while the provisions of the accounting law, namely the accounting principles, require that such assets should be evaluated through guiding percents or standard production costs, IAS 41 requires recognition at fair value less the estimated point-of-sale costs. Unlike many other IFRS standards, the changes in fair value are immediately recognized in the profit or loss account, with an influence on the result (Lefter and Roman, 2007:21). With the increase of commercial

Tab. 3: Live Assets, Agricultural Products and Post-Harvest Agricultural Products

Live Assets	Agricultural products	Products grown after harvest as result of proceeding
Sheep	Wool	Wool yarn, carpet
Tree	Log	Lumber
Sugar beet plant	Sugar beet	Sugar
Fruit garden	Fruit	Fruit juice or proceeded fruit
Grapevine	Grape	Wine
Tea garden	Tea leaf	Tea
Dairy animal	Milk	Cheese
Cow	Meat	Sausage, salami, bologna
Cow	Milk	Cheese

enterprises which are active in agricultural sector in recent years, basic accounting applications on these enterprises started to be more important. Because, similar to other enterprising sectors, also in agricultural sectors, the data which are given from accounting departments help management on the managerial decisions. (Hatunoğlu and Kıllı, 2016: 48). And that's where standards of agricultural activities come into prominence.

3.1 The Aim and Scope of Standards

The aim of this standard is determination of methods of accountancy and basics of reporting for related agricultural activities. This standard will be applied on accounting process of the mentioned assets when the following assets are related with any agricultural activity.

(a) Living assets;
(b) Agricultural goods during harvesting season
(c) Related with governmental incentives which take place in Paragraph 34–35

This standard is applied on only harvested agricultural goods, which are the living assets of an enterprise, during harvest season. It is not applicable for the goods after the harvest season. In the below given table, information is given about related samples of agricultural goods and other processed goods after the harvest season (Örten, Kaval and Karapınar, 2016: 601)

Agricultural activity involves wide group of activities; for example, livestock rising, forestry, yearly or perennial (longer period) agricultural cultivation, fruit orchard and sapling planting, flowering and aqua cultural work facilities (aquaculture is included).

3.2 Recognition of Agricultural Products and Living Assets

The required conditions for recognition of a living asset or an agricultural product in enterprises mentioned in the standards are presented as following (TMS 41, paragraph.10):

a) An enterprise is to control living assets or agricultural products as a result of past activities,
b) Being probable of transferring of the promising benefits related with living assets or agricultural goods, c) Trusted Calculation of real price or value of a living property or an agricultural product. In terms of agricultural activities, for example; purchasing cattle according to laws and stigmatizing during the process of giving birth or ablactating are the signs that there is a control system relating living assets (TMS 41, paragraph.11)

Living assets which have the above given qualifications (in case of trusted and secure value calculation) are evaluated with remaining value after the deduction of real approximated expenses for the following evaluations, since it is accepted that the real price which is accordingly evaluated and calculated with respect to the above mentioned standards so the values of agricultural products are evaluated in that way (Örten, Kaval and Karapınar, 2016: 602).

3.3 Evaluation of Agricultural Products and Living Properties

According to the standards, except the situations whereby unsafe calculations are done for real values of goods, evaluations for those living assets are done after the real expenses deductions made from real prices during the period of first recognition date and by the end of each reporting term (TMS 41, Paragraph.12). And also in the standard it was mentioned that agricultural products which are processed through living assets will be measured after the sale expenses are deducted from their real values. The above mentioned measurement is the cost on the date of when "TMS 2 Stocks" as a mentioned standard or another proper standard which is applicable (TMS 41, Paragraph.13). It is also suggested in the standard that to make the measurement of the approximated real value of a living asset or agricultural product easier, above mentioned living assets and agricultural products will be categorized according to their ages and qualities. The enterprise will determine the mentioned qualifications according to basics of determination of prices in the market. According to the standard, the costs of agricultural products and living assets will approach to their real values (TMS 41, Paragraph.24): a) since a little biologic conversion has taken place after the determination of first owning cost. Plantation of seedling and owning the living animals which take place just before the end of the reporting term can be an exemplary for this situation. b) Not expecting the effect of biological conversion on the process of pricing. For example, the first growth in the process of production of a 30 years pine forest. Some studies on agricultural activity standard are as follows.

Herbohn, K., Herbohn, J. (2006) investigates the implications of International Accounting Standard 41 (IAS 41) for European Union (EU) entities reporting on material holdings of forest assets. Evidence suggests that constituents' key concerns with IAS 41 relate to the measurement of biological assets at fair value and the inclusion in income of unrealised gains or losses from measuring these assets at fair value.

Aryanto (2011) to analyze the theoretical aspects of IAS 41: Agriculture. Based on the results of several other empirical studies, it turns out that the adoption impact of IAS 41 is not as good as expected. In addition, rejection on IAS 41 are appear as it causes volatility of income and misleading on taxation-related decisions. Also, other research states that IAS 41 has failed in achieving its objectives, which is to increase financial statement comparability in agricultural sector. These findings lead to a variety of questions, whether the principle of arrangement in IAS 41: Agriculture is theoretically correct?

Gonçalves and Lopes (2014), analyzed disclosures practices of accounting in agriculture under the International Accounting Standard (IAS) 41 – Agriculture of 270 listed firms worldwide that have adopted International Financial Reporting Standards (IFRS) until 2010. . In order to extend previous research on disclosure practices under the IAS 41, an index of the disclosure of biological assets is constructed and calculated based on the notes of financial statements included in the 2011 annual report. This paper tests several hypotheses relating the index and firm-level determinants – biological assets intensity, ownership concentration, firm size, auditor type, internationalization level, listing status, profitability and sector – and country-level determinant – legal status. This variable is measured using two different proxies, following institutional country classification, namely the dichotomy common law versus code law countries and cluster classification. It was found that the mandatory and voluntary disclosure of biological assets is influenced by biological assets intensity, ownership concentration, firm size, sector and legal status.

Klychova, Mavlieva, Klychova and Kulikova,(2014), analyzed In the current economic environment, both external (financial) and internal accounting reporting are the main sources of information for assessing the solvency and creditworthiness of potential business entities, management decision-making in evaluation and optimization of structural units, business processes, and other segments of agricultural organization. Using this information in the field of supply, the selection of suppliers and contractors is made, the ways of transporting and delivery of raw materials, components, semi-finished products to the organization and directly to the production units are determined. Biological assets from the investor's perspective as a user of accounting data require special user skills, that is, the rules of evaluation and recognition in reporting, in view of their special economic function as a property that cannot serve as collateral for obligations of the company, when its financial position corresponding to the principle of continuity of operations, but for this it is a major potential of profitability of appropriate enterprises. On this basis, a possible way to improve the content of accounting reporting in Russian agricultural enterprises should be adaptation of method of biological assets accounting, determined by international accounting standards, with a view to the possibility of its use in Russian accounting practice.

4 Evaluation and Recognition of Fruit Orchards According to TMS 41

Our country has a wide variety of fruit orchards and in addition to that, in different regions of City of Malatya different species of fruits are grown. However, apricot orchards are well-known with the city of Malatya and apricot comes to the minds firstly when Malatya is mentioned. Our country is in the first place in terms of apricot production and 80 % of the country's apricot production belongs to Malatya. So, in terms of economic matters, apricot production is an important income source for Malatya. That's why apricot orchards are observed in our study. Cost data for plantation area of 1 decare for 10 trees is used. In the fifth harvest year, minimum 19kgs, maximum 38kgs of crop can be gained from one tree. To consider a fruit orchard efficient, there must be 500 trees in a 50 decares of a fruit orchard. And issue price of apricot is considered as 2 TL.

4.1 Costs Paid at the Stage of Preparation

COSTS	AMOUNT	UNIT PRICE (TL)	FIRST YEAR (ESTABLISHMENT YEAR 2014)
A. labor – watering costs			
Field cleaning and leveling	1	50,00	50,00
Fertilization (workmanship)	1	50,00	16,00
Soil cultivation	1	35,00	35,00
Bush area spotting	0,1	75,00	7,50
Bush scooping	1	45,00	27,00
Sapling planting pruning	0,3	50,00	6,50
Sapling planting and watering + water costs (22 TL)	1	45,00	77,00
Prop planting and tying	0,18	30,00	4,00
Circlet projection unsnapping digging	2	50,00+35,00	13,00
Disinfection	1	25,00+40,00	8,50
Pruning	0,1	75,00	7,50

Continued

COSTS	AMOUNT	UNIT PRICE (TL)	FIRST YEAR (ESTABLISHMENT YEAR 2014)
B. material costs			
Bush cost (10m*10m)	10	5,00	50,00
Farm Manure	0,3	40,00	12,00
Chemical manure		1,10	8,00
Prop	10	0,25	2,50
Medicine			8,00
C. Other costs			
Management costs (%3)			9,98
Unexpected costs (%10)			16,63
Capital interest (%10)			16,63
Field lease			90,00
Total costs (A+B+C)			**456,73**

TMS-41 has brought an important innovation to current agricultural applications in our country. This standard has adopted evaluation of the values agricultural products and harvested goods with proper valuing method (Aksoylu, 2013:76). The reason why this standard has been adopted by the system is fair value model is; it is the best method in terms of reflecting the effects of changes and variances. Changes in the fair value of biological assets directly vary the future expectations of the enterpriser (Timurtaş 2016:157). When it comes to uniform accounting policies, living assets are considered as non-living properties. So changes in the living assets (growth, gaining weight, etc …) are not taken into consideration. In Turkish Recognition Standards, number 41 standard (TMS-41) regulated biological changes on living assets and predicted and stipulated that biological changes may bring forward some evaluation differences, so profit or loss may occur from those changes during a term, so it should be added to the values of goods (Hacıhasanoğlu and Ünlü, 2017:409).

According to Standards of Agricultural Activities, as per article 30, value evaluation of fair value measurement can be done secure. But this assumption can be non-existent during first recognition of living assets whereby related alternative value prediction can be no secure, since market value or price can't be found. In such a situation, the above mentioned living assets' values can be measured after deductions are made according to accumulated depreciation and decrease of accumulated values. In the situation of the fact that the fair value of the asset can be reliably determined, the value of the assets is measured by deducting sales costs from fair value (İçöz, 2015:1234–1235).

After the literature researches on our study, recognition upon categorization according to option 7/B has been decided to be used since costs are more appropriate to the soul of standards. Expenses which occur in an apricot orchard are classified upon the data that is received from the specialists of provincial directorate of agriculture and according to option 7/B, it has been recorded as following. The expenses are mainly grouped under three titles and some expenses are even detailed in themselves.

4.1.1 *Preparation Stage Accounting Records (Establishment Year, 2014)*

790 Raw Materials and Supplies Costs	80,50	
791 Worker Wages and Expenses	230,00	
793 External Supplied Benefit and Services	22	
794 Other Expenses	116,61	
797 Finance Costs	16,63	
100 Cash Account		465,74
Apricot trees purchase costs, water and planting costs		
799 production cost account	465,74	
798 Cost Varieties Reclassification Account		
Transfer of costs tolerated for trees to related account		465,74
31.12.2014		
211 Vegetative Assets	465,74	
799 Production Cost Account		465,74
Transfer of costs to vegetative assets account		
31.12.2014		
211 Vegetative Assets	69,26	
605 Living Assets Evaluation Differences		69,26
End of 2014 year record of fair value difference		

In our study, by the end of year 2014, fair value of an apricot tree is evaluated as 535 TL. Total expenses are 465,74 TL. The difference of 69,26 is between the two figures is considered and recorded as fair value difference.

Reasonable Value expresses a figure in case of during mutual bargaining environment, the exchange of a presence among knowledgeable and willing groups or payment of debts (Kırlıoğlu and Gökgöz, 2012:111). If there is an active market, then fair value (reasonable value) can be determined according to market prices, even if there is no active market, then fair value will be evaluated according to the value of value of agricultural goods in fruit orchards or according to the area of the fruit orchards. If small biological conversions appear during the first recording step, for example plantation of fruit tree seedlings to be done before financial statement, it can be used as cost-effective fair value (TMS 41.24).

4.2 Maturing Stage

COSTS	AMOUNT	UNIT PRICE	2.Year 2015	3. Year 2016	4. Year 2017
A. Workmanship-Leasing costs					
Fertilization	1	50,00	18,00	19,00	21,00
Soil cultivation	1	35,00	35,00	35,00	35,00
Bush area spotting	1	45,00	2,70	0,00	0,00
Bush scooping	0,3	50,00	0,65	0,00	0,00
Sapling planting and watering + water costs (20 – 21–25 TL)	1	45,00	65,00	66,00	70,00
Prop planting and tying	0,18	30,00	0,65	4,00	0,65
Circlet projection unsnapping digging	2	50,00+35,00	15,00	17,00	19,00
Disinfection	1	25,00+40,00	10,00	12,50	14,00
Pruning	0,1	75,00	8,50	10,00	12,50
B. Material Costs					
Farm Manure	0,3	40,00	14,00	15,00	18,00
Chemical manure		1,10	10,00	11,00	14,00
Prop	10	0,25	0,25	2,50	0,25
Medicine			10,00	12,00	13,50
C. Other Costs					
Management costs (%3)			5,84	6,12	6,53
Unexpected costs (%10)			9,74	10,20	10,90
Capital interest (%10)			9,74	10,20	10,90
Field lease			90,00	90,00	90,00
Total Costs (A+B+C)			**305,07**	**320,52**	**336,23**

By the end of year 2015, fair value of an apricot tree is 965 TL. By the end of year 2016, fair value of an apricot tree is 1.500 TL. By the end of year 2017, fair value of an apricot tree is valued as 2.150 TL.

4.2.1 2015 Year Records

790 Raw Materials and Supplies Costs	34,25	
791 Worker Wages and Expenses	135,50	
793 External Supplied Benefit and Services	20	
794 Other Expenses	105,58	
797 Finance Fosts	9,74	
100 Cash Account		305,07
Costs tolerated for apricot trees		
799 Production Cost Account	305,07	
798 Cost Varieties Reclassification Account		305,07
Transfer of costs tolerated for trees to related account		
31.12.2015		
211 Vegetative Assets	305,07	
799 Production Cost Account		305,07
Transfer of costs to vegetative assets account		
31.12.2015		
211 Vegetative Assets	124,93	
605 Living Assets Evaluation Differences		124,93
End of 2015 year record of fair value difference		

4.2.2 2016 Year Records

790 Raw Materials and Supplies Costs	40,50	
791 Worker Wages and Expenses	142,50	
793 External Supplied Benefit and Services	21,00	
794 Other Expenses	106,32	
797 Finance Fosts	10,20	
100 Cash Account		320,52
Costs tolerated for apricot trees		
799 Production Cost Account	320,52	
798 Cost Varieties Reclassification Account		320,52
Transfer of costs tolerated for trees to related account		

Continued

31.12.2016		
211 Vegetative Assets	320,52	
799 Production Cost Account		320,52
Transfer of costs to vegetative assets account		
31.12.2016		
211 Vegetative Assets	214,48	
605 Living Assets Evaluation Differences		214,48
End of 2016 year record of fair value difference		

4.2.3 2017 Year Records

790 Raw Materials and Supplies Costs	45,75	
791 Worker Wages and Expenses	147,15	
793 External Supplied Benefit and Services	25,00	
794 Other Expenses	107,43	
797 Finance Fosts	10,90	
100 Cash Account		336,23
Costs tolerated for apricot trees		
799 Production Cost Account	336,23	
798 Cost Varieties Reclassification Account		336,23
Transfer of costs tolerated for trees to related account		
31.12.2017		
211 Vegetative Assets	336,23	
799 Production Cost Account		336,23
Transfer of costs to vegetative assets account		
31.12.2017		
211 Vegetative Assets	313,77	
605 Living Assets Evaluation Differences		313,77
End of 2017 year record of fair value difference		

4.3 Product Stage

COSTS	AMOUNT	UNIT PRICE	5.year (2018)
A. Workmanship-Leasing costs			
Fertilization	1	50,00	23,00
Soil cultivation	1	35,00	35,00
Sapling planting and watering + water costs (30 TL)	1	45,00	75,00
Prop planting and tying	0,18	30,00	0,65
Circlet projection unsnapping digging	2	50,00+35,00	21,00
Disinfection	1	25,00+40,00	17,00
Harvest, crating and transportation		140+70	210,00
Pruning	0,1	75,00	15,00
B. Material Costs			
Farm Manure	0,3	40,00	20,00
Chemical manure		1,10	18,00
Prop	10	0,25	0,25
Medicine			15,00
Total			**53,25**
C. Other costs			
Management costs (%3)			13,49
Unexpected costs (%10)			22,49
Capital interest (%10)			44,99
Field lease			90,00
Total			**170,97**
Total Costs (A+B+C)			**620,87**

Fair value of apricot garden is defined as 3,200 TL after end of 2018 year.

4.3.1 2018 Year Records

790 Raw Materials and Supplies Costs	53,25
791 Worker Wages and Expenses	366,65
793 External Supplied Benefit and Services	30,00
794 Other Expenses	125,98

Continued

797 Finance Costs	44,99	
100 Cash Account		620,87
Costs tolerated for apricot trees		
799 Production Cost Account	620,87	
798 Cost Varieties Reclassification Account		620,87
Transfer of costs tolerated for trees to related account		
31.12.2018		
211 Vegetative Assets	620,87	
799 Production Cost Account		620,87
Transfer of costs to vegetative assets account		
31.12.2018		
211 Vegetative Assets	429,13	
05 Living Assets Evaluation Differences		429,13
End of 2018 year record of fair value difference		

This standard relates to the registration (recording) and valuation of the living asset and its agricultural product at the harvest point. It is not interested with the harvested products. So, just because the harvest season for apricot fruit is between months of June and July, during the calculations of end of 2018 balance calculations, the amount of harvested products were not taken into considerations and recognitions. The harvested apricots will be assessed and accounted for according to the standard of stocks.

According to tax legislation, the tree asset and the earth asset values in the fruit orchards must be capitalized and depreciated over the cost basis. The amortization time in the fruit orchards will begin on the date that the fruit orchards are removed from the account of the construction in progress and taken to the account of the related asset (Tunçez, 2011:315). In order to start depreciation from a tangible fixed asset, the period of capitalization of this fixed asset must be completed. And also, the condition for this asset to be ready to be used is another condition to start for depreciation application. What should be understood from the saying starting of fruit orchards is starting to see fruits on the trees of those fruit orchards. However, it is not enough to start giving fruit for those fruit orchards, because even the same year when planted as seedlings, a seedling can give fruit. In this case, a fruit tree needs to start to yield enough fruit to be amortized. What must we understand from the saying 'giving enough fruit'? Starting from the year when fruit is purchased on a level that meets the cost of a tree for one year, the amortization is calculated by calculating the amount subject to depreciation for that tree (Taştan, 2013:29). However, according to TMS 41, since fruit orchards are evaluated over the fair value (reasonable value), no amortization will be applied on them.

Regarding standard gains and losses, it stated that earnings and losses could be born in two ways. The first is the gains and losses resulting from lowering the cost of sales at fair value during the initial recognition of a living asset by the entity. And the second is the gains and losses that occur in time at the fair value of living beings. In both cases, losses and gains arising are recognized in the period of profit or loss (UMS.41.26).

5 Conclusion

Today, especially developed countries are making great investments in technological innovation, productivity increase and organic agriculture fields in order to improve the agricultural sector by understanding the importance of agricultural activities more seriously. In our country too, there are serious problems in the field of agriculture recently and urgent solutions are waiting to be handled by making new arrangements for them. Increased emphasis on the agricultural sector and the increased need for information in this sector is creating a constant search for changes and new regulations in both standard and uniform accounting systems.

In this context, our study held an assessment of apricot orchards was carried out according to the TMS 41 standard of agricultural activities. Since living entities are exposed to the biological conversion process, TMS 41 standard of agricultural activities determine the standard for the recognition and valuation principles of living assets. In this context, the fair value approach is used by the standard in the valuation of biological assets. According to the Tax Procedure Law (VUK), agricultural activities are valued at cost. However, TMS adopts the fact that the agricultural activities are evaluated at the fair value instead of cost, and thus provides a basis for the formation of more realistic valuations about living assets.

Apricot orchards are one of the important agricultural activities related to fruit gardening. The evaluation of apricot gardens in the apricot activity, which is one of the most important income items for city of Malatya, is covered in TAS 41 in this study. Five years have passed since the planting phase (from first planting) in the apricot trees (the time of giving fruit here is determined as the time to reach the level of exceeding the costs of the product produced).In our study, apricot orchards were assessed at their fair value because they were able to determine their true values during this period of time. By observing the literature studies, the records have been realized by varying the expenditures in terms of the recommendations of the experts according to the 7/B option most frequently encountered in applications.

In the current literature, especially with the uniform chart of accounts in order to eliminate the differences between Turkey Accounting Standards uniform set of recommendations regarding the creation of new accounts in the accounting system of agricultural activity it is repeated widely. In this way, the valuation differences between tax laws and standards are considered to be abolished.

Bibliography

Aksoylu, S., (2013). "Tarımsal Faaliyetlerin Türkiye Muhasebe Standardı 41 (Tms-41)'E Göre Muhasebeleştirilmesi: Gerçeğe Uygun Değer Muhasebesi", Muhasebe ve denetime Bakış Dergisi, S.39, s.65–78.

Aryanto, Y.H., (2011) "Theoretical Failure of IAS 41" Electronic copy available at: http://ssrn.com/abstract=1808413

Asma, B.M., (2011). "Her Yönüyle Kayısı", Ankara, Uyum Ajans Anıt Matbaası.

Asma, B.M., (2015). "Tarihsel Süreçte Kayısıcılık", Ankara, Uyum Ajans Anıt Matbaası.

Feleaga, L., Feleaga, N., Raileanu, V., (2016). "Theoretical Considerations about Implementation of IAS 41 in Romania", Theoretical and Applied Economics Volume XIX (2012), Vol. 2, No. 567, pp. 31–38.

Gonçalves, R., Lopes, P., (2014). "Firm-Specific Determinants of Agricultural Financial Reporting", Procedia – Social and Behavioral Sciences, Volume: 110, pp 470–481.

Hacıhasanoğlu, T., Ünlü, A., (2017). "Canlı Varlıkların TMS 41 Ve Tekdüzen Muhasebe Sistemine Göre Muhasebeleştirilmesi: Süt Üretim İşletmesi Uygulaması", International Journal of Academic Value Studies, cilt: 3, S.9, s. 394–410.

Hatunoğlu, Z., Kıllı, M., (2016). "Tarım İşletmelerinde Bitkisel Üretim Maliyetlerinin TMS 41 Çerçevesinde Muhasebeleştirilmesi", KSÜ Sosyal Bilimler Dergisi, Cilt:13 (1), s.47–68.

Herbohn, K., Herbohn, J., (2006). "International Accounting Standard (IAS) 41: What are the Implications for Reporting Forest Assets?", Small-scale Forest Economics, Management and Policy, Volume: 5, No. 2, pp 175–189.

İçöz, A., (2015). "In The Framework Of IAS 41 Accounting Problems In The Agricultural Actions And Solutions Recommendations", The Journal of International Social Research, Volume: 8, No. 41, p. 1230–1235.

Kırlıoğlu, H., Gökgöz, A., (2012). "Tms 41 Çerçevesinde Tarımsal Faaliyetlerin Muhasebeleştirilmesi: Su Ürünleri Sektörü Uygulaması", Atatürk Üniversitesi İktisadi ve İdari Bilimler Dergisi, Cilt: 26, S.2, s. 107–127.

Klychova, G.S., Mavlieva, L.M., Klychova, A.S., Kulikova, L.I., (2014). "Organization of Accounting in Fur Farming According to IAS", Mediterranean Journal of Social Sciences, Volume: 5, No: 24, pp 84–90

Lefter, V., Roman, A.G., (2007). "IAS 41 Agriculture: Fair Value Accounting", Theoretical and Applied Economics Review, Volume: 5, pp. 15–22

Örten, R., Kaval, H., Karapınar, A., (2016). Türkiye Muhasebe-Finansal raporlama Standartları, Ankara, Gazi Kitabevi.

Taştan, H., (2013). "Ceviz Bahçelerinde Türkiye Muhasebe Standartları – 41 Ve Vergi Usul Kanunu Uyarınca Amortisman Ayrılması Ve Değerlemesinin Karşılaştırmalı İncelenmesi", Muhasebe ve Finansman Dergisi, Ekim, s.25–37.

Timurtaş, E. E., (2016). "Tarımsal Faaliyetlerin TMS 41 Kapsamında Muhasebeleştirilmesi Ve Borsa İstanbul'da İşlem Gören Tarım İşletmelerinin İncelenmesi", Muhasebe ve Denetim Dünyası Dergisi, S.3, s.153–177.

TMS 41 Tarımsal Faaliyetler Standardı.http://www.resmigazete.gov.tr/eskiler/2006/02/20060224-16.htm

TUİK, https://biruni.tuik.gov.tr/bitkiselapp/bitkisel.zul, Erişim Tarihi: 08.04.2017

Tunçez, H.A., (2011). "Tarımsal Faaliyetlerin Muhasebeleştirilmesinin Türkiye Muhasebe Standardı-41 Çerçevesinde İncelenmesi: Bir Tarım İşletmesinde Örnek Uygulama", Selçuk Üniversitesi sosyal Bilgiler Meslek Yüksek Okulu Dergisi, Cilt: 14, S. 1–2, s. 311–328.

Ulusal Kayısı Çalıştayı, 18–19 Kasım 2014 Malatya, Ankara, TC. Gıda Tarım ve Hayvancılık Bakanlığı Bitkisel Üretim Genel Müdürlüğü, 2015.

Ünal, M. R., (2010). Kayısı Araştırma Raporu, Malatya, Fırat Kalkınma Ajansı.

Yazarkan, H., (2016). "Üretim İşletmelerine Ait Fındık Bahçelerine İlişkin Mali İşlemlerin Türkiye Muhasebe Standartları (TMS) Çerçevesinde Muhasebeleştirilmesi: Durak Fındık A.Ş. Örneği", Yönetim ve Ekonomi Dergisi, Cilt: 23, S. 2, s. 409–434

Tansel Çetinoğlu

The Independent Auditing Profession in Turkey: Theoretical an Investigation

1 Introduction

Independent auditing in the world has emerged due to the diversification of companies' activities, increased competition, technological developments and speeding up of international trade, as well as the necessity of providing information users with reliable and transparent information and information. Although auditing of the credibility and accuracy of information appears to be a good tool, it is also important to investigate whether auditing work has been carried out in accordance with legal regulations and whether it has been conducted independently. (Özulucan, Keles and Arslan, 2016, p.25).

Independent audit scandals in the United States (USA) and elsewhere in the early 2000s have led to confidence losses on the audit results of financial users. In order to compensate for these losses, fundamental arrangements have been made in the United States, mainly in the United States, by authorities in some other countries developed economically, in the establishment of institutions to carry out independent auditing and preparation of new laws relating to independent auditing.

International arrangements made in this area in Turkey in the European Union (EU) integration process has necessitated the need to make a variety of changes. For this purpose, the existing Turkish Commercial Code (TTK) was revisited and the rules and standards related to the supervision of capital companies were reorganized, especially with the entry into force of the Turkish Commercial Code numbered 6102. These new regulations are crucial for the institutionalization of companies, sustainability, the creation of public trust and the transparency of financial information. 6102 numbered TTK has taken the independent auditing duty from the supervisory board within the company and gave an independent auditor outside the company. Accordingly, will be subject to independent auditing companies 19 December 2012 and 2012/4213 No. of Ministers is determined by the Council, Turkey Auditing Standards of the companies in this context (TDS) is based on monitoring by independent external auditors is adopted. Those external auditors who are to carry out independent auditing shall have the title of Sworn-in Certified Public Accountant (Sworn-in CPA) and Certified Public Accountant (CPA) who are licensed according to Law No. 3568. In addition, regulations have been made concerning the supervision of the commercial life, in particular in order to ensure a more reliable structure of the independent audit. The Public Oversight, Accounting and Auditing Standards Authority (KGK), which is similar to the examples in the Western countries, has been established with the Decree Law on the Organization and Duties of the Public Oversight, Accounting and Auditing Standards Institution 660 prepared in this framework. With the establishment of this Institution, supervisory authorities on the supervision bodies of the Capital Markets Board (SPK), Energy Market Regulatory Authority (EMRA), Banking Regulation and Supervision Agency (BDDK) and Undersecretariat of Treasury have ended. (Özulucan et al., 2016, p. 40) According to the Independent Auditing Regulation prepared by the Public Oversight, Accounting and Auditing Standards Authority, it is aimed to obtain sufficient and appropriate independent audit evidence to ensure reasonable assurance about the appropriateness and accuracy of the independent audit, financial statements and other financial information to the financial reporting standards. For this purpose, it refers to the auditing of the necessary audit techniques required by the auditing standards and to the audit, evaluation and connection to the report through the books, records and documents. (Köse and Ertan, 2016, p.292) In our study, it is aimed to Introducing the theoretical meaning of the auditing profession in Turkey, changes in the past and present in relation to the profession of independent auditing, determination of relevant institutions and laws, As a result, as a result of the literature review, it has been found that in the universities providing independent auditing training, the information about the accounting profession of the students and related to the independent audit profession is inadequate. In addition, according to the results of the co-examination of the authors, the fact that the authorization of the independent auditor is made only by the independent audit examination made by the Public Oversight Accounting and Auditing Standards Institution causes disturbance among the professional accountants. The workload on the independent audit profession is less than the accounting profession, but it is stated that the income and the image in the society are higher. In the future, with the increase in the areas in which the company operates, the independent audit profession will become more widespread and the success of the financial transactions and the decisions will be increased.

2 Development of Independent Auditing Profession in Turkey (The Period Until the New Turkish Commercial Code)

In Turkey, controls the size of the accounting profession began with expertise activities in the first court. Expertise in accounting is a traditional practice that has continued from the foundation years of the Ottomans to this day. In fact, the first auditing begins with granting the authority to conduct tax audits in accordance with the tax laws for some professionals well-known and honest in the accounting profession between 1926 and 1934 (Bezirci and Karasioğlu, 2011, p.571).

The start of the independent auditing profession in Turkey and the wishes of the most important factors in the development has been operating in the financial markets, banks and other financial institutions. Since the mid-1960s, banks operating in financial markets and institutions providing funds abroad have started independent auditing of financial statements at the request of foreign fund resources. Initially, these studies conducted by independent audit companies that are built abroad began to be realized by resident member firms of international audit company in Turkey since the 1970s (Bezirci and Karasioğlu, 2011, p.572).

In Turkish law, audits of companies have come into effect until 1987, in the form of an audit conducted by public authorities in order to secure public revenues under the Turkish Commercial Code and tax legislation. After 1987, there was a tendency to use independent auditors as well as public auditors, and along with this tendency, independent audit took place under the audit of companies (Selimoğlu and Göktepe, 2007, p.22). The auditing of the financial statements until 1987 in Turkey was carried out by the Turkish Commercial Code and Tax Legislation and the in our country audit concept for the first time took place in the Turkish Commercial Code (Bayazitli, 1991, p.64).

Independent auditing relevant institutions in Turkey, in chronological order, are as follows. (Fırat and Şahin, http: //www.kgkuzder.org.tr, 2018)

- Capital Markets Board Audit (CMB) (1987)
- Law No. 3568 on Certified Public Accountants and Sworn-in Certified Public Accountants (1989)
- Certified Public Accountant and Turkey Union of Chambers of Sworn-in Certified Public Accountants (TURMOB) (1989)
- Independent Audit of Insurance Supervisory Board and Insurance Companies (1994) – Undersecretariat of Treasury
- Banking Regulation and Supervision Agency (BRSA) (1999)
- Turkey Accounting Standards Board (TASB) (2002)
- Energy Market Regulatory Authority and Energy Market Independent Auditing (EMRA) (2001)
- The Required Audit According to The New Turkish Commercial Code (2011)
- Ministry of Customs, Industry and Commerce
- Public Oversight Accounting and Auditing Standards Authority (POA) (2011)

The obligation to carry out independent external auditing in our country was first introduced by the supervision of banks in 1987, but the principles and rules of auditing became legal by the communiques issued by the Capital Markets Board in 1988 (Kutukız and Öncü, 2009, p.133).

In this process, 19 companies of national and foreign origin were registered. These companies came together to establish "Independent Audit Association" (Bezirci and Karasioğlu, 2011, p.571).

The system of audit and accounting professions has been established with the Law No. 3568 on Certified Public Accountants and Sworn-in Certified Public Accountants, which entered into force in 1989. Union of Chambers of Certified Public Accountants and Sworn-In Certified Public Accountants of Turkey (TURMOB) was established by determining the targets and activity fields of the audit with this law. TURMOB, in accordance with the Capital Markets Law 22 /

d, has been cooperating with the CMB on the sharing of the disciplinary status of the members of the independent auditing institutions. Furthermore, in accordance with Article 13 of the Regulation on the Authorization and Activities of the Institutions to Perform Independent Audit with the BRSA, it has carried out joint activities related to the quality assurance system (Sayar, 2013.55). The Insurance Supervisory Board, which was established in 1963, was authorized to examine the transactions made by the insurance companies and was named as the Insurance Supervisory Board in 1994. The Board has started to operate as a supervisory unit under the Treasury Undersecretariat to carry out the supervision of the transactions of the insurance companies. The board's duties, insurance and reinsurance companies established in Turkey with the insurance and reinsurance companies established in foreign countries, within the insurance legislation by branches in Turkey to oversee the financial statements will be published by independent audit firms; their qualifications, their authorization to be exercised, their temporary or permanent abolition, and the procedures and principles concerning the contents of the independent audit contract and the obligations of the parties to the independent audit contract.

Auditing of banks with the Banking Law no 3182 held in 1985 the Central Bank is distributed between the Treasury Undersecretariat and the Banks Association of Turkey. The Banking Regulation and Supervision Board was made autonomous by the Banking Law No. 4389 which entered into force on 18 June 1999. After the crisis in the banking sector that lived in the 2000s, the legislation was changed. The Energy Market Regulatory Authority (EMRA) is engaged in "Regulation on the Auditing of Real Legal Entities by Independent Audit Firms" with respect to independent audit. This arrangement is parallel to the regulations of the CMB. (Fırat and Şahin, http: //www.kgkuzder.org.tr, 2018)

3 Development of Independent Auditing Profession in Turkey (The Next Period from the Entry into Force of the New Turkish Commercial Code)

The rapid change in the capital markets and the technology has brought the countries closer together and the world has become a single market. This change, called globalization, has quickly emerged contained in the integrated and work to comply with EU law has begun to show the effects in Turkey and the need to make some changes in the various economies (Güler, 2012, p.82). Turkey also began some work to meet this needs and as result TCC no 6102 entered into force. The Turkish Commercial Code introduces a number of innovations for corporate law within the framework of public disclosure and transparency (Altaş,2012,p.143). These innovations brought by the TCC numbered 6102 will affect trade life and accounting practices to the finest detail. With the entry into force of the new TCC, basic commercial transactions, accounting process, registrations and valuation issues were reconsidered. The new TCC incorporates regulations that will provide significant benefits and contributions to the areas they are relevant to, providing a significant opportunity and ground for institutionalization, sustainability, increasing competitive power, creation of public trust and transparency of Turkish companies. Therefore, it is necessary to evaluate this opportunity in the best way and to adopt the new TCC as an important change project which will enable the Turkish companies to grow healthy and confidently in the future (Uluşahin, Eren and Köylü, 2012, p.12). With the new Turkish Commercial Code, independent auditing has gained a new dimension. The newly prepared TCC, which is in the process of harmonization with the European Union, has been prepared in accordance with the EU Directive on Corporate Law 8. With the new arrangement, the independent auditing mechanism, which is now under the supervision of an auditor who is among the compulsory organs of the company and which is not subject matter experts, has to be carried out by independent auditing firms (Fırat and Şahin, http://www.kgkuzder.org.tr, 2018). Within this scope, Public Oversight, Accounting and Auditing Standards Authority (POA) was established with Decree Law No. 660 published in the Official Gazette dated November 2, 2011 and numbered 28103, and a public oversight system was introduced for independent auditing. (Özulucan, Keles and Arslan, 2016, p.25)

The powers and duties of the Public Oversight Authority in Article 9 of the Decree Law No. 660 are determined as follows (www.kgkuzder.org.tr, 2018).

- Create and publish Turkey Accounting Standards,
- Creating and publishing National Independent Auditing Standards,
- Determining the establishment conditions and working principles of independent auditors and independent audit firms, and publicizing the authorized professional members to the public.
- Auditing of the activities of the independent auditors and independent audit firms
- Establishing examinations, authorization and registration for independent auditors, continuing education standards and professional ethics rules

The Public Oversight Authority under the Decree Law No. 660 also has the authority and responsibility to establish the necessary standards of auditing and to provide the necessary confidence and quality in independent auditing as well as to authorize independent auditors and supervise public surveillance. The Public Oversight Agency has published the Independent Audit Code (IAC) to fulfill this authority and responsibility. The independent auditing code published in the Official Gazette No. 28509 dated December 26, 2012 contains the regulations for independent audit. In addition, the public oversight authority regulates the authorization of independent auditors, creation of registry records and the inspection thereof (Özulucan, Keles and Arslan, 2016, p.55) The decision on the determination of the companies subject to independent testing is renewed every year by the Council of Ministers. (www.istanbulymmo.org.tr, 2018). In 2018, according to Article 397 of the Turkish Commercial Code No. 6102 on the letter dated 22/3/2018 of the Ministry of Finance dated 22/3/2018, the Council of Ministers decided on 26/3/2018 and published the official gazette dated 26 May 2018 has published and has entered into force. (www.resmigazete.gov.tr, 2018)

The following companies are subject to independent audit within the provisions of the Law No. 6102 and the Decree Law on the Organization and Duties of the Public Oversight, Accounting and Auditing Standards Institution dated 26/9/2011 and No. 660. (www.resmigazete.gov.tr, 2018) Companies listed in the attached list (I) without regard to any measure. (www.resmigazete.gov.tr, 2018) Other companies exceeding the thresholds values of at least two of the following three criteria in two consecutive accounting periods: Thresholds values for companies that are not traded on a stock exchange or other organized markets but are publicly traded under the Capital Markets Law dated 6/12/2012 and numbered 6362: Total assets are 15 million Turkish Liras, annual net sales revenue is 20 million Turkish Liras and the number of employees is 50 persons. Thresholds values for companies listed in the attached list (II): (www.resmigazete.gov.tr, 2018) Total assets are TL 30 million, annual net sales revenue is TL 40 million and the number of employees is 125 persons. Thresholds values for companies not covered by the subsections 1 and 2 no (www.resmigazete.gov.tr, 2018): Total assets are TL 35 million, annual net sales revenue TL 70 million, number of employees is 175 persons. Companies outside the scope of this Decision are also noted in the relevant decision. Public Oversight Accounting and Auditing Standards Authority (POA) is empowered to determine the principles and procedures for the implementation of this decision and to avoid any hesitations that may arise (www.istanbulymmo.org.tr, 2018).

4 Features Required for Those Who Want to Become Independent Auditor in Turkey and Independent Auditor Examination

According to the independent audit regulation prepared by the Public Oversight Authority, those who want to conduct the audit activity must first fulfill the following conditions. It is necessary to obtain diplomas from faculties and higher education institutions that provide education in law, economics, finance, business, accounting, banking, public administration and political Sciences or it is necessary to obtain at least a bachelor's degree from a foreign higher education institution approved by the Council of Higher Education. Even if you graduate from other education branches with a bachelor's degree, you should have received at least the master degree at the level of the above mentioned science branches. (Özulucan, Keles and Arslan 2016, p.30) In addition, being a member of the profession, living in Turkey, having the competence to use civil rights, to be completed practical training is need to be successful in the independent auditor exam. Members of the profession who provide all of the above conditions must apply to the POA with the information and documentation indicating these conditions. The applicants who are determined to have the required conditions as a result of the examination made by the Public Oversight Authority are declared by POA by registering to the independent auditor registry in case of payment of necessary fees and expenses. After registration, these persons are given an auditor's certificate, an auditor's identity and an auditor's seal. In addition, those who want to become auditors have the obligation to participate in applied vocational training according to the Independent Auditing Code. Accordingly, there is a requirement that those who want to become auditors must have practical training in professional matters, including financial statement audit for at least three years, in the audit firm. Participants in applied vocational training are considered to be assistant auditors in the period of applied vocational training and can participate in the supervision work under supervision of auditors. Auditors or audit firms who employ an auditor assistant must take all necessary precautions to acquire the necessary professional competence of auditor assistants in order to put the theoretical information into practice. In addition, information and documents indicating that the necessary conditions are met in order to start practical vocational training should be notified to the POA by the audit agency, auditor or auditor assistant (www.kgk.gov.tr, 2018). Article 15 of the independent audit regulation, which regulates the requirements for applied vocational training, also includes arrangements for matters to be considered during the period of applied vocational training. According to this, for professional accountants who have 15 years of professional experience, no practical vocational training condition is required (www.kgk.gov.tr, 2018) Those who want to be an independent auditor must take independent audit examination other than practical vocational training and be successful as a result of this examination.

For those who have fulfilled the training requirement, the issues that are responsible for the audit examination to be made by the Public Oversight Board (www.kgk.gov.tr, 2018). Accounting (General Accounting, Cost Accounting, Management Accounting), Accounting Standards, Corporate Governance Principles and Financial Management, Audit (Turkey Auditing Standards, Code of Professional Ethics, Independence, Risk Management, Other Related Legislation with the Internal Control and Audit,) are subjects. In addition, the General Law Legislation (Trade Law, Debts Law, Execution and Bankruptcy Law, Civil Law, Tax Law, Social Security Legislation, Administrative Law), Capital Markets, Banking, Insurance and Private Pension Legislation. According to the independent audit examination notification (IAEN) prepared for the evaluation of the exam to be made, at least 60 points out of 100 points must be taken from each of the exam subjects in order to be considered as successful and there is a condition that the arithmetic average of the grades taken from all examination subjects is at least 70 points (http: //kgk.gov.tr, 2018)

5 Conclusion

In early the 2000s significant adjustments have been made by authorities in several economically developed countries led by the United States, to relieve the loss of confidence in the audit results of financial users due to the independent audit scandals that took place in the United States (USA) and various countries. Very important regulations have been made by the authorities in various economically developed countries under the leadership of the United States in order to overcome the confidence losses associated with the audit results of financial information users. Establishment of institutions to carry out the preparation of new laws related to independent auditing and oversight of independent auditing can be counted among these regulations. Independent audit is carried out in Turkey since 1988. Independent auditing, which was previously valid for companies affiliated to regulatory agencies such as CMB, BRSA, EMRA, is now carried out for Joint Stock Companies and Limited Companies, as determined by POA, according to TTK No. 6102. POA, established in accordance with the Decree Law No. 660, collects independent audit practices in one place. Independent Auditing Standards (BDS) and (TFRS) Turkey Financial Reporting Standards issued by the POA again published with a new approach and has entered into force. It has been stated in the Turkish Commercial Code No. 6102 that independent auditing should be in accordance with TFRS and that TFRS should be in accordance with International Financial Reporting Standards (IFRS). As a result of the literature review, it has been found that in the universities providing independent audit training, the information about the accounting profession of the students and related to the independent audit profession is inadequate. As a result of the literature review, it has been found that in the universities providing independent audit training, the information about the accounting profession of the students and related to the independent audit profession is inadequate. Moreover, according to the results of the co-examination of the authors, the fact that the authorization of the independent auditor is made only through the independent audit examination conducted by the Public Oversight Accounting and Auditing Standards Authority leads to disturbance among professional accountants. The workload on the independent audit profession is less than the professional accountants, but it has been determined that the income and the image in the society are higher. In the future, as the field of activity increases, the independent audit profession will become more widespread and an increase in the success of the financial transactions of the enterprises and the decisions to be taken will be ensured. It will be useful to extend and implement regulations related to independent audit by interested parties so that the expected benefit from the Independent Audit activities can be at the highest level and in particular the expectations of professional members of the auditor candidates can be met at the highest level. Thus, due to future regulations, implementation differences from developed countries will be abolished and more transparent, more reliable information will be obtained through independent auditing activities to be done in high quality. In addition, the inclusion of all of the capital companies, regardless of size measures, rather than the capital companies that meet certain criteria in the future within the scope of independent audit, will be more accurate at the point of providing the expected benefit from the audit.

Bibliography

Altaş, S. (2012). Yeni Türk Ticaret Kanunu'na Göre Şirket Denetimi. Ankara: Seçkin Yayınları.

Bayazıtlı E. (1991). "Uluslararası Bağımsız Dış Denetim Standartları ve Türkiye Uygulaması". Ankara Üniversitesi Sosyal Bilimler Enstitüsü, İşletme Anabilim Dalı Yayınlanmamış Doktora Tezi, Ankara.

Bezirci M. ve Karasioğlu F.,(2011)."Türkiye'de Denetimin Tarihsel Gelişimi", Sosyal Ekonomik Araştırmalar Dergisi, Cilt 11, Sayı 21, s.571–592.

Demir M., Çiçekay H., Arslan Ö.,ve Arslan E. (2016)."Muhasebe Meslek Mensuplarının Bağımsız Denetçilik Mesleği Hakkındaki Düşünceleri", Celal Bayar Üniversitesi İktisadi ve İdari Bilimler Dergisi, Cilt 17, Sayı 1, s.37–56.

Fırat A. ve Şahin M. "Muhasebe ve Denetim Dünyası", http://www.kgkuzder.org.tr/upload/ files/Turkiyede_Bagimsiz_Denetimin_Gelisimi.pdf (Accessed: 18.07.2018).

Güler, E. (2012). "Muhasebe Mensuplarının Yeni TTK'da Yer Alan Denetim Uygulamaları Hakkındaki Farkındalıklarına Yönelik Bir Araştırma", Muhasebe ve Vergi Uygulamaları Dergisi, Cilt: 5, Sayı: 3, s. 81–104.

Resmi Gazete (2013), "Bağımsız Denetçilik Sınav Tebliği" http://kgk.gov.tr/Portalv2Uploads/files/Duyurular/v1/Teblig/Ba%C4%9F%C4%B1ms%C4%B1z%20Denet%C3%A7ilik%20S%C4%B1nav%20Tebli%C4%9F.pdf (Accessed: 17.07.2018).

İstanbul Yeminli Mali Müşavirler Odası (2017), "Bağımsız Denetim Uygulamalarına Genel Bakış (TFRS,BOBİ TFRS,KOBİ TFRS)" http://www.istanbulymmo.org.tr/Data/Platform/2017_EK%C4%B0M_29.pdf (Accessed: 19.07.2018).

Kamu Gözetimi Kurumu (2018), "Bağımsız Denetim Yönetmeliği" http://www.kgk.gov.tr/Portalv2Uploads/files/Duyurular/v1/BDY/BDYGuncel22Aralik2015.pdf (Accessed: 15.07.2018).

Resmi Gazete (2018), "Bağımsız Denetime Tabi Şirketlerin Belirlenmesine Dair Bakanlar Kurulu Kararı" http://www.resmigazete.gov.tr/eskiler/2018/05/20180526-2.pdf (Accessed: 19.07.2018).

Köse Y. ve Ertan S. (2016)."Türkiye'de Bağımsız Denetçilik ve Bağımsız Denetçinin Sorumluluğu", Uluslararası Yönetim İktisat ve İşletme Dergisi, Uluslararası Muhasebe ve Finans Araştırmaları Kongresi Özel Sayısı, s.290–307.

Kutukız, D. ve Öncü, M.A. (2009). "Bağımsız Denetimin Anonim Ortaklıklarda Kurumsal Yönetimin Gelişmesine Etkisi", Muhasebe ve Finansman Dergisi, Sayı 41, s.131–139.

Özulucan A., Keleş D. ve Arslan S.(2016)."Muhasebe Meslek Mensuplarının 6102 Sayılı Türk Ticaret Kanunu'nda Yer Alan Bağımsız Denetimle İlgili Hususlar Hakkındaki Görüşlerine Yönelik Ordu İlinde Bir Araştırma", Niğde Üniversitesi İktisadi ve İdari Bilimler Fakültesi Dergisi, Cilt 9, Sayı 1, s.25–42.

Sayar Z.(2013).Bağımsız Denetimin Kamu Gözetiminde Dünya Uygulamaları, Ankara, Türmob Yayınları.

Selimoğlu S.ve Göktepe H., (2007). "Türk Ticaret Kanunu Tasarısındaki Bağımsız Denetimle İlgili Yeni Düzenlemeler.", Mali Çözüm Dergisi, Sayı 81, s.17–44.

Uluşahin, H., Eren, E. ve Köylü, Ç. (2012)."6102 Sayılı Yeni Türk Ticaret Kanunu (TTK)'Nun Muhasebe Ve Denetim Uygulamalarına Getirdiği Yenilikler Üzerine Bir Araştırma", Muhasebe ve Finansman Dergisi, Sayı 55, s.11–34.

Yanık R. (2013). "6102 Sayılı Türk Ticaret Kanunu Kapsamında Denetçi Sorumluluğu ve Borç-Alacak Hesaplarının Denetimine İlişkin Bir Öneri", Atatürk Üniversitesi İktisadi ve İdari Bilimler Fakültesi Dergisi, Cilt 27, Sayı 4, s.358–367.

M. Murat, Aktaş

Belated Innovative Financial Instrument for Turkish Capital Markets: Mortgage-Backed Securities

1 Introduction

Mortgage-backed securities (MBS) issuances regulated under the Capital Market Law No. 6362[1] Article 58 and the Capital Markets Board (CMB)[2] Communiqué on Asset-Backed and Mortgage-Backed Securities (Serial No: III -58.1)[3]. Firstly, we will briefly examine securitization as the theoretical base of the MBS issuance process/structure. Secondly, we will shortly explain selected issues of the aforesaid Turkish legal framework.

2 Mortgage-Backed Securities and Securitization

MBS or so-called "mortgage-backed bonds"[4] are the solution and the purpose of a mortgage securitization process. In other words, MBS issuance is a mortgage securitization. Historically, MBS are the first application of the securitization (in Europe called as "securitisation") as an invention of a new financial method in United States (U.S.)[5] at

1 Capital Market Law No. 6362 published in the Official Gazette edition 28513 on 30.12.2012. Hereinafter the Capital Market Law No. 6362 will be stated as "Law".

2 Article 58 of the Law gives CMB the authority to determine the principles and procedures regarding the issuers and issuance of MBS.

3 Hereinafter it will be referred to as "the Communiqué". CMB published the Communiqué on Asset-Backed and Mortgage-Backed Securities (III -58.1) in the Official Gazette edition 28877 on 09.01.2014.

4 Securities Industry and Financial Markets Association-SIFMA Investor's Guide, Mortgage-Backed Securities (MBS) and Collateralized Mortgage Obligations (CMOs), https://www.rbcwm-usa.com/file-588373.pdf. MBS, technically cannot be defined as bonds. MBS are an alternative financial tools of the on-balance sheet debt securities like bonds and covered-bonds. Covered bonds have been part of European finance since the time of Frederick the Great, **(Schwarcz, S. L.** (May 2011). "The Conundrum of Covered Bonds". Business Lawyer, Vol. 66: p. 562).Covered bonds are mostly issued in Europe, with Germany and Denmark being the largest issuers. Covered-bonds and also the mortgage covered bonds are regulated in Turkey by the Law Article 59 and the CMB Communıqué On Covered Bonds (Serial No: III-59.1) which is published in the Official Gazette dated 21.01.2014 and numbered 28889.

5 U.S. securitizations regulated by Securities and Exchange Commission-SEC "Regulation AB" that took effect on 01.01.2006 and it covered four major areas: Registration,

1970's[6]. Mortgage securitization is a type of existing asset securitizations[7]. In an existing asset securitization, the cash flow from the asset exists and there is an existing claim to value[8]. In a typical securitization, a bank or another credit institution (usually referred to as the "originator"[9]) pools[10] and sells ("true sale") rights to payment in income-producing or financial assets[11] (such as mortgage loans, account receivables, instruments, lease rentals, franchise and license fees, and other intangible rights to payment) to a special purpose vehicle (SPV)[12]. In other words, originators don't directly issue MBS and they have to use an intermediary vehicle. SPV sometimes interchangeably called a special-purpose entity or SPE. In U.S. practice, the "pooling", sale and the other subjects of the MBS issuance provisions generally stated under an agreement which is usually called as Pooling and Servicing Agreement (PSA)[13].

---

disclosure, communication practices, and periodic reporting, (https://www.sec.gov/divisions/corpfin/guidance/regulation-ab-interps.htm). SEC later revised the aforesaid regulation under the provisions called as "Regulation AB II".

6 The era of securitization began in the United States of America (U.S.) back in the 1970s with the Government National Mortgage Association (Ginnie Mae) issuance of the securities which are backed by a portfolio of mortgage loans. In 1971 the first conventional loan securitization was issued and in 1977 the first private label residential mortgage pass-through bond was created.

7 In a future flow securitization, there is no existing claim or contractual right to a cash flow; such contractual rights will be created in the future, (**Kothari, V.** (2006). Securitization The Financial Instrument of the Future. Singapore. p. 73).

8 **Kothari**, p. 73.

9 According to the Communique "originator" shall mean the legal entities, institutions and organizations that will transfer their assets to the fund portfolio or to mortgage finance institutions/corporations (MFI), (Article 3).

10 Securitization is the process of creating securities by "pooling" together various cash-flow producing assets. Originator bundle the assets into (mortgage loan receivables) separate pools (this transaction referred as "pooling") to "back" the issuance of different type MBS

11 Any asset can be securitized as long as it is a cash flow producing.

12 **Stone, C. A./Zissu, A.** (2012). The Securitization Markets Handbook, Structures and Dynamics of Mortgage- and Asset-backed Securities. New Jersey. p. 3; **Simkovic, M.** (2013). "Competition and Crisis in Mortgage Securitization". Indiana Law Journal, Vol. 88: p. 214; **Frankel, T./Fagan, M.** (2009). Law and the Financial System, Securitization and Asset Backed Securities: Law, Process, Case Studies, and Simulations, Florida. p. 17; **Kothari**, p. 4; **Schwarcz, S. L.** (1994). "The Alchemy of Asset Securitization Stanford Journal of Law". Business, and Finance, Vol. 1: p. 133.

13 Pooling and sale of the mortgages stated under the agreement called as PSA. PSA is the legal document that lays out the rights and obligations of certain parties over a pool of securitized mortgage loans, (https://www.sec.gov/Archives/edgar/data/1550120/000119312512283969/d371026dex41.htm).

SPV issues securities to capital market investors and use the proceeds to make the payment to the originator for the assets. "True sale"[14] nature of the assignment of assets to the SPV (Communiqué Article 15(2))[15], makes securitization is a category of off-balance financing transactions. Here, the main goal is to separate the assets (pool) from the risks generally associated with the originator to distinguish it from the SPV. The investors, who are repaid from collections of the assets, buy the securities based on their assessment of the value of the assets. Because the SPV (and no longer the originator) owns the assets, their investment decision often can be made without concern for the originator's financial condition.

3 Historical Development of Mortgage-Backed Securities in Turkey

The legal historical development of MBS in Turkish capital market law can be divided into three phases: Law No. 3794[16] changes[17] at the Capital Market Law No. 2499[18]; Law No.

---

14 True sale is a buzz word in the securitization industry, (**Kothari**, s. 578–579).

15 Asset transfer agreement between the originator and the Fund (SPV) is regulated as "True sale" according to the Communiqué. The Fund shall acquire the assets listed in the Article 15(1)(b) by an written agreement to be executed. As a result of such acquisition, all rights of ownership and title of the relevant assets shall be transferred to the fund and this will be stated in the agreement to be executed, (Communiqué Article 15(2)).

16 Law No. 3794 ("Sermaye Piyasası Kanununda Değişiklik Yapılmasına, Bankalar Kanunu'nun Bir maddesinin Değiştirilmesine ve 35 sayılı KHK'nın Bazı maddelerinin Yürürlükten Kaldırılmasına Dair Kanun") is published in the Official Gazette edition 21227 on 13.05.1992. Law No. 3794 defines the ABS and regulates the issuance of ABS by the changes at the Articles 13/A, 22/c, 32 and 39 of the Capital Markets law No. 2499.

17 The frontiers of the securitizations and MBS issuances were regulated under the asset-backed securities (ABS) regulations in Turkish capital market law. This ABS legislation came in force by the Law No. 3794 provisions which made changes in the articles of Capital Market Law No. 2499. In this term, MBS was regulated under the Article 13/A of Law. No. 2499 and the Capital Markets Board (CMB) Communiqué of Serial: III, No: 14, (**Öcal, N.** (1994). Türkiye'de Menkul Kıymetleştirme Uygulaması, Etkileri, Sorunlar ve Çözüm Önerileri. Yüksek Lisans Tezi, Ankara. pp. 59–60). Communıqué Serial: III, No: 14, Communıqué on Principles Regarding Registration of Asset Backed Securities with the Board and Principles Regarding the Establishment and Activıties of General Financial Companies ("Varlığa Dayalı Menkul Kıymetlerin Kurul Kaydına Alınmasına ve Genel Finans Ortaklıklarının Kuruluş ve Faaliyet İlkelerine Dair Esaslar Tebliği) published in the Official Gazette number 21301 on 31.07.1992.

18 Capital Market Law No. 2499 published in the Official Gazette number 17416 on 30.07.1981.

5582[19] changes in the Capital Market Law No. 2499; the Capital Market Law No. 6362 era.

The very first "real" MBS legal framework introduced by the Law No. 5582 (so-called "mortgage law") changes at the Capital Markets Law No. 2499 and other related Laws[20]. Afterwards the establishing the legal base of MBS issaunces by the Law No. 5582, the CMB made the very first Turkish MBS regulation: "Serial: III, No: 34, Communiqué regarding the Principles related to Housing finance Funds and Mortgage-Backed Securities"[21].

The Law repealed the Capital Market Law No. 2499. Current legal basis of the MBS issuances regulated under the article 58 of the Law and the CMB[22] and the Communiqué on Asset-Backed and Mortgage-Backed Securities (Serial No: III -58.1)[23]. The Communiqué, bundled the Turkish securitization securities into one simple regulation and repeal the old Communiqué on Asset Financing Funds and Asset Backed Securities (Serial: III, No: 35) and the Communiqué on House Financing Funds and Mortgage Backed Securities (Serial: III, No: 34).

4 Definition and Basic Legal Features of Mortgage-Backed Securities

4.1 Definition

Definition of the MBS takes place at the Article 58 of the Law and the Article 3 of the Communique. Under the Article 58, MBS are defined as capital market instruments issued by putting as contingency the assets taking place in the portfolios of the related funds or mortgage institutions. According to the section 3(1)(g) of the Communiqué, MBS defined as "...issued and backed by the assets that will be acquired by the housing finance fund or mortgage finance institution".

19 Law No. 5582 published in the Official Gazette number 26454 on 06.03.2007.

20 Law No. 5582 ("The Law Amending the Laws Related to Housing Finance System") also made changes in several other Laws: Law of Foreclosure No. 2004; Law of Legal Interest and Default Interest No. 3095; Law on Protection of Consumers No. 4077; Leasing Law No. 3226; Law on Mass Housing No. 2985; Law of Income Tax No. 193; Expenditure Taxes Law No. 6802; Duties Law No. 492; Stamp Duty Law No. 488; Value Added Tax Law No. 3065. Because of its extensive scope, the Law No. 5582 is called as "Turkish mortgage system Law" or the "Housing Finance System Law" in practice.

21 Published in the Official Gazette dated 04.08. 2007 and numbered 2660.

22 Article 58 of the Law gives CMB the authority to determine the principles and procedures regarding the issuers and issuance of MBS.

23 Hereinafter it will be stated as "the Communiqué". CMB published the Communiqué on Asset-Backed and Mortgage-Backed Securities (III -58.1) in the Official Gazette edition 28877 on 09.01.2014.

4.2 Basic Legal Features

MBS are also debt securities and they are specified as "Mortgaged Capital Market Instrument"[24] (İpotekli Sermaye Piyasası Aracı) under the Article 3 of the Law. As mentioned above, under the Communiqué Article 15(2) MBS are true-sale securitization tools. As a result of being mortgage securitizations, MBS are off-balance sheet financial instruments as well. MBS represent claims on the principal and interest payments made by borrowers on the loans (Communiqué section 15(b)) in the pool[25]. Typically, MBS holders has no recourse right to the originator and issuer SPV[26]. Interest and principal payment to MBS holders arises from the cash-flows generated by the underlying loans. In other words, securitization investors have no claim on those assets of the originator that were not transferred to the SPV.

Unfortunately, there is no outstanding MBS issuance in Turkey. Because of the aforesaid reason, considerations on the issuance of possible types of MBS under the provisions of the Communique is theoretical. Under the Communiqué Article 9(2) it is possible to form MBS "tranches"[27] within the same tenor that offering different rights according to these criteria's: Maturity of the assets, principal or interest payment dates of the assets, type of interest or return to be obtained from the assets, priority claims in principal, interest or revenue payments, rights relating to liquidation procedures, credit risks, and others may be defined by the CMB. Under the Communiqué art. 17(3) the Fund shall be managed either by "pass through" or by "pay through methods". So, both "pass through method"[28] and "pay through method"[29] can be used in the issuances of MBS. But, because of the mandatory

24 Mortgaged capital market instrument: Mortgage covered securities, mortgage-backed securities, capital market instruments other than shares issue d by mortgage finance institutions and other capital market instruments which are backed by the receivables derived from housing finance or under the guarantee of these receivables.

25 https://www.sec.gov/fast-answers/answersmortgagesecuritieshtm.html.

26 The core difference between securitization and borrowing transactions is that while borrowing transactions are based on a promise of the borrower to pay, securitization transactions are, in a way, pre-paid at the very beginning as the originator transfers assets to the SPV up front. As an issuer of MBS, even the obligation of the SPV or the trustees is essentially obligation to distribute (under the issuance documents) and not obligation, (**Kothari**, p. 577).

27 The word "tranche" comes from the French trancher, which means "to cut". In securitization terminology tranches means "bond" classes in a CMO that differ from one another either by priority of the receipt of cash flows or in some other way.

28 Communiqué defines this method as "...after the deductions required under this Communiqué are made, the cash flows obtained from the assets included in the fund portfolio, which may or may not be based on a payment plan, are transferred directly to the investors without holding them in the fund".

29 Under the Communiqué the "pay through method" described as "...after the deductions required under this Communiqué are made, the cash flows obtained from the assets included in the fund portfolio may be held in the fund in accordance

true sale provision (Communiqué section 15(2)) there cannot be made MBS likely issuances[30] under the Communiqué. Different classes of MBS with different rights may be issued for credit enhancement (CE) according to Communiqué Article 19(1)(b) as well.

5 Issuance of Mortgage-Backed Securities

5.1 Related Legal Framework

Housing Finance Funds (HFF-Fund)[31] and the Mortgage Finance Institutions/ Corporations (MFI) are the entities that can issue MBS under the Law and the Communiqué (Communiqué Article 4). MBS issuances shall be made under the special provisions of the Communiqué and the general capital market instrument issuance regulations that are the Serial No: II-5.1-Communiqué on Prospectus[32] and Issue Document and the Serial No: II-5.2-Communiqué on Sales of Capital Market Instruments[33].

For the CMB fees (Communiqué Article 29) that apply to MBS issuances, the third, fourth, and fifth paragraphs of Article 12 of the Serial No: II-31.1 Debt Securities Communiqué[34] shall be applied *mutatis mutandis* as well. Another regulation that related to MBS issuances is the No: III-60.1 Communique on Mortgage Finance Institutions[35].

5.2 Issuance and Redeem Process in General

As mentioned above MBS issuances can be made by only two kind of issuers: the Fund and MFI. MFI can issue MBS directly itself or by establishing a Fund.

---

with the principles set forth in the prospectus or the issue document, before they are transferred to the investors at the determined maturity dates".

30 The main types of mortgage related securities can be classified as mortgage pass-through securities (MPTs), mortgage-backed bonds (MBBs), mortgage pay-through bonds (MPTBs), collateralized mortgage obligations (CMOs), residential mortgage-backed securities (RMBS) and commercial mortgage-backed securities (CMBS). MPT is the basic form of MBS and also bears the basic features of true MBSs like to be off-balance sheet (true sale) instrument. CMO can be off-balance sheet instrument as well. MPT is also defined as equity type security but the MBBs, MPTBs and MBBs are debt securities, (**Brueggeman, W./Fisher, J.** (2011). Real Estate Finance & Investments. New York, NY. p. 659).

31 Hereinafter HFF will be referred to as "Fund".

32 Serial No: II-5.1 Prospectus and Issue Document Communiqué published in the Official Gazette dated 22/6/2013, numbered 28685.

33 Serial No: II-5.2 Communiqué on Sale of Capital Market Instruments published in the Official Gazette dated 28/6/2013, numbered 28691.

34 Published in the Official Gazette dated 07.06.2013 numbered 28670.

35 Published in the Official Gazette dated 17.07.2014 and numbered 29063.

Communiqué provisions based on the Fund issuance[36] model and the special provisions on MFI issuances regulated incorporated (Article 30) to the model Fund issuance provisions of the Communiqué mutatis mutandis. The core documents of the MBS issaunces are the prospectus or issue documents and the Fund statute (MFI statute). In principle, the application for the establishment of a Fund (by Fund statute) should be evaluated together with the application for approval of the prospectus or issue document of MBS (model issuance type). However, upon the request of the founder, such applications may also be evaluated separately, (section 7(1))[37].

36 In case of the issuance is carried out by the Fund, the Fund shall be deemed as issuer for the purpose of implementation of such regulations of the CMB, and the responsibilities of the issuer shall be fulfilled by the Fund board (Communiqué section 7(8)). According to the Article 7 of the Communiqué, MBS may be issued by a public offering or be sold to qualified investors solely or be sold by private placement provided that the unit nominal value is minimum TL 100,000. In case of issuance by public offering, MBS issuance should be made as a single issuance, and the prospectus shall be prepared as a single document. MBS which will be issued without public offering or abroad, may be sold in tenors within the time frame and the issue ceiling set by the CMB. In public offerings, it is required for MBS to be traded at the stock exchange (Stock exchange defined in the Law Article 3(1)(ç)).According to the Communiqué the rating agencies are required to provide credit rating for each tenor of MBS, and if any, for MBS tranches, that will be offered to the public, (section 9(3)). So, if MBS will not be issued in public credit rating score of the security is not mandatory by law. But, in practice, every MBS issuance must have a credit rating score to get attention of institutional investors. The credit ratings that are given or updated by rating agencies for MBS shall be announced through the Public Disclosure Platform (PDP) and in the founder's website within six business days following the notification to the founder or the fund board (section 21(1)(d)).In principle, all capital market instruments and also the MBS (both domestic and the international offerings) shall be issued in the dematerialised form in the electronic environment, without certificates and registered with the Central Registry Agency (Agency) which is defined in the Law Article 3. In case of the international offerings, the CMB may grant an exemption from the electronic registration requirement. Dematerialisation of capital market instruments can be made under the provisions of the Article 13 of Law and the Communiqué Serial: II-13.1 on Recordings of the Dematerialisation of Capital Market Instruments that published in Official Gazette edition 29081 on 07.08.2014. The provisions set out in the Serial No: II- 31.1 Communiqué regarding Debt Securities shall be applied mutatis mutandis for issuances of MBS by the Fund or the MFI.

37 Communiqué regulates the principles about issuance of MBS and the establishment of the Fund together Article 7 et seq. In principle, the application for the establishment of a Fund should be evaluated together (section 7(2)) with the application for approval of the prospectus or issue document of MBS. However, upon the request of the founder, such applications may also be evaluated separately (section 7(3)).

In case of the model issuance type (Fund and the MBS issuance application bundled) the Founder shall apply to the CMB along with the documents specified in Annex 2 and Annex 3[38]. The applications shall be finalized by the CMB within twenty days following submission of necessary documentation in full. If the decision with regard to the application is affirmative, the Fund statute, as approved by the CMB, shall be registered with the trade registry, and shall be announced in the Turkish Trade Registry Gazette (TTRG) within six business days following receipt of CMB approval by the founder. Upon registration of the Fund statutes, the fund establishment procedures shall be deemed complete.

Following the submission of documents evidencing that the Fund statute have been registered with the trade registry; and agreements (like servicing) executed, as set forth under the Communiqué, the prospectus or the issue document will be approved by the CMB. Such documents and agreements are required to be sent to the CMB within ten business days following registration of the fund statute with the trade registry (Article 7).

According to the principles set out in Communiqué the Part Five, the Fund portfolio shall be set up with the MBS proceeds collected from the investors following the issuance (section 9(1)). So, Fund portfolio shall be defined and pooled under the issuance documents following the MBS issuance.

MBS shall be redeemed in accordance with the principles set forth in the prospectus or the issue document, (section 9(5)). The payments that will be made to investors regarding the MBS issuance, shall be covered by the cash flow deriving from the assets of the Fund. In order to cover the cash flows, the founders and legal entities qualified as founders may provide partial or full guarantee while the insurance companies defined under Insurance Law dated 03.06.2007 and numbered 5684 may provide insurance coverage prior to the issuance, (Article 9(1)).

5.3 Risk Retention Liability or Skin-in the Game Regulation

Securitization is a credit risk transfer process from originators/founders (securitizers) to the investors. As seen in the 2008 global financial crisis, the full credit risk transfer of the assets by the true sale of receivables to the SPV may cause a moral hazard for securitizers. To solve[39] this potential moral hazard, Communiqué to Article 10 ("Risk Retention Liability") regulates that the originator or founder

38 In case of the separately applications, only the specified documents of the Annex 2 have to be added to application. In the event of separate application the Founder or the Fund board shall, within six months following registration of the "Fund statute" with the trade registry, submit the application for approval of the prospectus or the issue document of the MBS to the CMB, along with the documents listed in Annex-3 (Article 7).

39 In U.S, Dodd-Frank Act section 941 et seq. "Subtitle D—Improvements to the Asset-Backed Securitization Process" make the provisions called as "Regulation of Credit Risk Retention (sec. 941)" to fix this problem.

is required to repurchase MBS corresponding to 5 % (maximum %10[40]) of the nominal value of the MBS issued and retain this value until the end of maturity. In our opinion, “Risk Retention Liability” or so-called “Skin in the game” provisions may help to lower the moral hazard risks causes from risk transferring nature of securitization but it also has a side-effect to maintain the “true sale” and attraction of mortgage securitization to alternative securities.

6 Issuers of Mortgage-Backed Securities

6.1 Housing Finance Funds

6.1.1 Definition

Issuer SPV can be established in many legal forms but it’s main legal form is trust. The Funds are also SPVs which formed as a trust like legal structure under the Communique. Housing Finance Fund (Fund) shall mean the fund, without a legal entity, established on account of MBS holders, by using the proceeds collected from the issuance of MBS, in accordance with the fund statutes, based on the principle of fiduciary ownership (Communiqué Article 3). Fund term is defined at the Article 58 of the Law as “...a property established by means of the funds collected in return for mortgage-backed securities, on behalf of the mortgage-backed securities’ holders, while the asset finance fund is a property established by means of the funds collected in return for asset-backed securities, on behalf of the asset-backed securities’ holders; both funds are established in accordance with the principle of fiduciary ownership with the fund rules and do not have a legal identity”.

6.1.2 Fund Statute

Core legal text of the Fund is the “Fund Statute” which is defined under the Article 5 of the Communiqué. The Fund statute[41] constitute an adhesion contract between the investors, the founder and the fund board[42], destined to ensure that the fund portfolio is kept in accordance with the principles of fiduciary ownership and is managed in accordance with principles applicable to agency agreements (Communiqué Article 5). According to this definition it can be easily said that

---

40 CMB is authorized to vary the ratio, depending on the type of assets or to increase on the basis of originators or founders provided that the ratio will not exceed 10 %.

41 CMB determined the minimum requirements or the standards of the Fund statute by the Annex-1 of the Communiqué.

42 The Fund board represents and manages the fund so as to protect the right of the MBS’ holders. The Fund board shall be responsible from the accuracy of records related to assets included in the fund portfolio as well as for the protection and keeping of these assets (Law Article 58(3)).

the Fund is structured similar to U.S. trust SPVs. In the event that no provision takes place in the Law, in the related legislation and in the fund rules, provisions of article 502 to 514 of the Law (provisions on agency contract) numbered 6098 (Turkish Law of Obligations)[43] shall be implemented by analogy to the relations between the fund board and the holders of mortgage-backed or asset-backed securities (Law Article 58(4)). The minimum requirements or standard for fund statutes determined by the CMB which is provided under Annex-1[44] of the Communiqué. CMB also published a standardized Fund statute on its website[45].

The Founder is responsible for filing an application for establishment of the Fund, determining the Fund board members and preparing the Fund statutes. But, preparing the amendments to the fund statutes, preparation, registration and announcement of the documents in relation to issuance is Fund board's (likely trustee) responsibility, (Communiqué section 11(3)(4)).

The amendments to the Fund statute shall be approved within the framework of Communiqué section 7(3)(b),(c) and (ç), following the submission of the application to the CMB and shall be registered with the trade registry and announced in the TTRG by the Fund board (Communiqué section 7(6)). The Fund shall be terminated under the following conditions defined in the Communiqué Article 28.

6.1.3 Fund Portfolio (Pool) Coverage

Provisions regarding the Fund portfolio are mainly set up by the Communiqué Part Five (Article 15 et. Seq). The asset[46] types[47] that can be included into the Fund portfolio are regulated under the Communiqué Article 15(1)(b). There are six main categories of assets can be included to MBS pools: Receivables of banks and financing corporations, arising from "housing finance"[48] as, which have been secured by establishing mortgage at the relevant registry; Receivables arising from financial

43 Published in the Official Gazette numbered 27836 on 11.01.2011.

44 Communiqué Annex-1 the "Minimum Elements To Be Included in The Fund Statute": The trade name and term of the fund; general principles in relation to the fund; method of liquidation of the fund; other elements to be determined by the CMB.

45 http://www.spk.gov.tr/Duyuru/Goster/20140424/1; http://www.spk.gov.tr/Sayfa/Dosya/1026.

46 At the Comminuque Article 3 "asset" defined as "the receivables, loans, rights, collaterals and other assets which may be included into the fund portfolio as mentioned in first paragraph of Article 15".

47 These assets must fulfill the "characteristics of assets" conditions at the date of inclusion to portfolio which are defined at the Communiqué art. 16.

48 According to Law section 57(1) "Housing finance" defined as loans to consumers to acquire houses; leasing of houses to the consumers through financial leasing; extension of loans to consumers under the guarantee of the houses that the consumer owns and the extension of loans for the refinancing of these loans. The transactions performed by housing finance institutions (Law section 57(2)), Funds and MFI on the basis of these loans and receivables or under their guarantee are also in this scope.

leasing agreements entered into within the framework of the Law numbered 6361, provided that such arise from "housing finance"; commercial loans and receivables of banks, financial leasing companies and financing corporations, which have been secured by establishing mortgage at the relevant registry; Receivables based on installments and contracts, which result from house sales by the Housing Development Agency of Turkey (TOKİ); assets within the scope of subsections (5), (6) and (7) of subparagraph (a); Rights and obligations arising from derivative instruments.

6.1.4 Segregation and Protection of Fund Assets

The assets of the funds (or MFI) cannot be used as collateral or be pledged, except being used for taking credits, performing derivative instrument transactions, short selling transactions, or similar transactions realized as a party in the name of the fund, provided that they are on the account of the fund and that a provision exists in the fund rules. The assets of the fund are separate from the assets of the founder/servicer/originator, the assets of those providing services to the fund and of those transferring their receivables or assets to the fund portfolio. Until issued outstanding MBS have been redeemed; the fund assets cannot be disposed of with another purpose, even when the management or audit of the founder, of those carrying out services to the fund and of those who transferred their receivables and assets to the fund portfolio is transferred to public institutions, they cannot be attached even for the purpose of collecting the public receivables, they cannot be included in the bankruptcy estate and cannot be subject to a cautionary injunction (Law section 58(2); Communiqué 6(1),(2),(3)).This mentioned legal and regulatory provisions on the segregation of the SPV assets from the originator/founder/servicer and the "safe harbor", all supports the "true sale" and "bankruptcy remote"[49] natures of the MBS issuances which are the cornerstones of the whole process.

6.2 Mortgage Finance Corporations

6.2.1 Definition and Legal Framework

MFI are formed as corporations and it is regulated under the Article 60 of the Law and the CMB Communiqué Serial No: III-60.1[50]. According to the Law Article 60(1), MFI are joint stock corporations which established[51] in the context of housing and

49 If a securitization transaction is not treated for legal purposes as a true or valid securitization, it may cause a "recharacterization of the transaction" which takes place in a judicial proceeding relating to the nature of the transaction. Recharacterization, is a big threat for securitizations, because in the event of a bankruptcy of the originator/founder, it will place the SPV asset (mortgage) pools back to the originators property (bankruptcy estate). (**Kothari**, p. 577, 590, 592).

50 Published in the Official Gazette numbered 29063 on 17.07.2014.

51 Founder institutions of the MFI is defined at section 5(1)(a) of the Communiqué No: III-60.1: Housing finance institutions, intermediary institutions with a broad

asset finance (Law Article 57) for the purpose of taking over the assets the types and qualities of which are determined by the CMB, transferring them, managing the assets taken over and taking the assets as collateral as well as performing the other activities deemed appropriate by the CMB.

Under the Communiqué No: III-60.1 art. 18 et seq. MFI's line of business is regulated with wide scope. In this manner MFI can be act as a liquidity facility, servicer, security issuer (covered bonds and ABS/MBS), Fund (AFF/HFF) or MFI founder. This regulative wide scope can be determined as irrelevant to the naming of the MFI. Because, the regulative scope of the MFI line of business includes elements of "asset finance"[52] which is out of the "mortgage finance".

6.2.2 Special Provisions Regarding to MBS Issuances by MFI

MFI can issue MBS either establishing a Fund or directly without establishing a Fund. MFI's directly issuances regulated incorporated with the Fund related provisions of the Communiqué. In case of the MBS issuances made by MFI without the establishment of a Fund; the provisions of the Communiqué regarding the Founder or the Fund shall be applied in for MFI, the provisions of the Communiqué regarding Fund portfolio shall be applied to the assets of MFI, and the provisions of this Communiqué regarding the Fund board shall be applied to the board of directors of the MFI mutatis mutandis. In such case, the minimum elements to be included in the fund statute determined in Annex-1 shall be included in the articles of association of the MFI mutatis mutandis, (Communiqué section 30(1)).

The regulations of the CMB regarding MFI and the issuance of MBS by MFIs are reserved, (Communiqué section 30(2)). According to the Communiqué No: III-60.1 section 18(3), in the event of MFI MBS issuances without establishing the Fund, there have to be a mandatory provision at the article of incorporation of the MFI which states that the MFI's sole line of business must be restricted to MBS/ABS issuances. Under this provision the MFI's itself became a "Corporation SPV". For MBS issuances made by MFI without establishment of a Fund, a new tenor of MBS may not be issued unless the issued MBS have been fully redeemed (section 7(14)).

6.2.3 Protection of MFI Assets

Assets of the MFI is protected from the recourses arises from other institutions especially in the event that a resource has been procured from MFI by putting up

---

scope of authority, asset leasing corporations (Law Article 61), Housing Development Agency of Turkey (TOKİ), Collective Investment Schemes (Regulated under Fourth Chapter of the Law) and other institutions that have CMB's approval..

52 Under the Communiqué No: III-60.1 Article 18, MFI can made such activities under the asset financing: Fund resource for other institutions on asset financing; servicing activities of ABS; issue ABS, lease certificates (Law Article 61); can be founder of "Asset Financing Fund"; can be party of secured asset financing transactions.

as “collateral” the assets mentioned in the Article 60(1) of Law (Law Article 60(3)). In case of directly MBS issuances (without establishing a Fund) by the MFI, MFI’s assets will be protected under the Communiqué Fund regulations will be applied mutatis mutandis.

Bibliography

Brueggeman, W./Fısher, J. (2011). Real Estate Finance & Investments. New York.

Frankel, T./Fagan, M. (2009). Law and the Financial System, Securitization and Asset Backed Securities: Law, Process, Case Studies, and Simulations. Florida.

Kotharı, V. (2006). Securitization The Financial Instrument of the Future. Singapore. https://www.rbcwm-usa.com/file-588373.pdf, https://www.sec.gov/

Öcal, N. (1994). Türkiye’de Menkul Kıymetleştirme Uygulaması, Etkileri, Sorunlar ve Çözüm Önerileri. Yüksek Lisans Tezi, Ankara.Schwarcz, S. L. (1994). “The Alchemy of Asset Securitization Stanford Journal of Law”. Business, and Finance, Vol 1: p. 133

Schwarcz, S. L. (May 2011). “The Conundrum of Covered Bonds”. Business Lawyer, Vol. 66: p. 562

Sımkovıc, M. (2013). “Competition and Crisis in Mortgage Securitization”. Indiana Law Journal, V. 88: p. 214

Stone, C. A./ZISSU, A. (2012). The Securitization Markets Handbook, Structures and Dynamics of Mortgage- and Asset-backed Securities. New Jersey.

Arif Saldanlı and Hakan Bektaş

Performance Measurement of the Enterprises Traded at the BIST 50 Index Using the Moora Method

1 Introduction

The primary purpose of all decisions, whether for financing or investment purposes, should be to maximize the value of the enterprise. According to profit maximization, the most important advantage of maximizing company value is to take time and risk dimension into account. When considered in terms of business finance, the three decisions with respect to three basic functions, i.e. the Investment decisions, Financing decisions and Dividend decisions need be taken in this direction in order for this objective to be realized. The value maximization discussed at this point can be defined as the present value of the cash inflows that the enterprise can realize both today and in the future. Therefore, its meaning is different from the balance sheet size.

Measuring financial performance is one of the steps necessary to ensure continuity of enterprises and to achieve value maximization objective. Financial performance tries to measure the achievement of the financial targets set by the enterprises. As a measure of financial performance, a number of financial ratios could be used that could be obtained from the balance sheet. When we look at literature, it is seen that criteria such as Profitability, Balance Sheet Size and Cash Flow are used frequently.

There are various internal and external factors that affect the financial performance of enterprises. An analysis of the level of attainment of the financial targets set as required for the decisions to be taken by financial statement information users could be difficult due to excess data and the complex structure of the relationships between them.

Although discussed by many economists in economics literature, the concept of alternative cost was first described by G. Haberler (Haberler, 1936). Alternative cost or opportunity cost can be expressed as the most valuable option you have to give up when you make a preference. When evaluated in terms of financial decisions, the alternative cost is quite significant. For example, an enterprise's decision to increase the liquidity needed to maintain its day-to-day operations more easily may have a negative impact on potential profitability in the sense that assets are valued in short-term investments rather than long-term investments. Similarly, in order to reduce the weighted average cost of capital in asset financing, the borrowing costs will increase because the foreign-funded enterprise will have a riskier financial structure. There are a number of criteria that need to be addressed in order to be able to make decisions in such complex situations.

Multi-criteria decision-making techniques allow decision makers to optimize their preferences by jointly evaluating multiple contradictory criteria. For example, it is assumed that there is a positive correlation between an increase in the risk of an asset for financial decision-makers and its expected outcome. The question of up to what risk level investors should increase their return expectations can be determined using multi-criteria decision-making techniques.

In this study, 33 enterprises which are traded at the Stock Exchange Istanbul (BIST) 50 Index for the year 2017 will be analyzed based on 9 criteria identified. The performance measurement of the said enterprises will be made using the MOORA method. In the first section, a summary of the literature on the application of multi-criteria decision-making methods used in banking and finance will be given. The MOORA method which will be used for performance measurement of the enterprises will be introduced in the second section. The third section will contain the dataset and findings; the results of the study will be given in the fourth and last section.

2 Literature Review

Yurdakul and İç (2003) used the data for the period 1998–2001 of the Automotive Sector companies in their study. The seven ratios determined were analyzed using the TOPSIS method and it was observed that the ranking results obtained were in parallel with the stock performance of companies in the overall analysis period. (Yurdakul & İç, 2003)

Opricovic and Tzeng (2004) conducted a comparative analysis on VIKOR and TOPSIS methods. They concluded that while the VIKOR method uses linear normalization and the normalized value does not depend on a decision criterion, the TOPSIS method uses Vector normalization and the normalized value may depend on the evaluation criterion. (Opricovic & Tzeng, 2004)

Eleren and Karakul (2008) evaluated the performance of Turkish economy for the period 1986–2006 using the TOPSIS method. Seven separate macro variables covering a period of 21 years were used in the study. According to achievement scores obtained for each year, the best year was 1986, followed by 1990, 1987 and 1993 respectively. (Eleren & Karagül, 2008)

Demireli (2010) measured the performance of publicly owned banks for the period 2001–2007 using the TOPSIS method. In the study, the evaluation was made by giving equal weight to the criteria. According to the results obtained, it was determined that public sector banks operating widely in Turkey are affected by local and global financial crises, performance scores fluctuate constantly based on foreign data, and there is no significant improvement in the banking sector. (Demireli, 2010)

Çetin and Çetin (2010) analyzed the performance of banks in the Turkish banking sector using the VIKOR method and analyzed 13 banks using 27 ratios. According to the results obtained, it was concluded that the weight to be used is very important for the method to be successful. (Çetin & Çetin, 2010)

Dinçer and Görener (2011) conducted a study on the Turkish banking sector and classified the banks as public, private and foreign capital. For the purpose of determining the financial performance of these groups, the AHP method was used first and then the performance comparison between the groups was performed using the VIKOR method. (Dinçer & Görener, 2011)

Within the scope of the study conducted by Bülbül and Köse (2011), the financial ratios of the financial performances of the companies in the Turkish food sector were utilized and graded according to TOPSIS and ELECTRE methods. According to the results obtained, it is stated that both methods can be used for performance measurement. (Bülbül & Köse, 2011)

Şahin and Akkaya (2013) used the PROMETHEE method for portfolio creation with the shares of the companies included in the BIST 50 index for the year 2011. According to the results obtained, PROMETHEE ranking method is a tool that can provide a solution for portfolio creation. (Şahin & Akkaya, 2013)

Akyüz and Rock (2013) used the TOPSIS method which is a multi-criteria decision-making method to evaluate ay the sectoral level the financial performance of non-life and life insurance/pension companies in Turkey for the period 2007–2011. Performance rankings were made for the relevant years using 10 equally weighted evaluation criteria.

In the study conducted by Güneysu, Er and Ar (2015) aiming to determine the financial performance of the banks operating in the Turkish Banking System for the period 2010–2014, 16 ratios were used. In the first part, the proportions and importance ratios were determined using the AHP method. In the second part, the GIA method was used to rank the banks according to their financial performances separately as banks with private, public and foreign capital. (Güneysu,Er,& Ar, 2015)

Kula, Kandemir and Baykut (2016) examined the financial performance of seven insurance companies and one pension company traded at the Istanbul Stock Exchange (BIST) for the year 2013 using the Gray Relational Analysis. Based on the results obtained, it was determined that the capital structure of half of the companies is effective and that the efficiency levels of companies with low current ratio and profitability ratios (net profit margin, earnings per share, return on equity and return on assets) are low according to the GIA method and rank among the last in the ranking. (Kula, Kandemir , & Baykut, 2016)

Güney and Kaya (2017) assessed the financial performances of brokerage houses traded in the BIST for the period 2014–2015 using 11 financial ratios and ELECTRE, ORIENT and TOPSIS methods. It was seen that the methods used as a result of the analyzes performed gave similar results. (Güney & Kaya, 2017)

Ege and Yaman (2018) used the TOPSIS and MOORA methods to measure the financial performance of companies based on 10 financial ratios used as criteria. The 6-month data of the cement-concrete industry companies traded in the BIST for the period 2010–2016 were used. In general, the ranking of the two methods is close to one other. However, it is seen that there is a great difference in the ranking of some enterprises. The performance measures obtained from these methods are considered as a variable and the panel data analysis was performed. According to the results of this analysis, it was stated that the TOPSIS method may be more suitable for performance measurement. (Ege & Yaman, 2018)

3 Methodology

Decision is a choice among a number of alternatives. This choice is made as if the preferred alternative is best among other options. However, the decision process is not always easy since there are usually multiple alternatives and many criteria in this process. Therefore, instead of evaluating the performance of alternatives at each criterion level, it is necessary to make a general evaluation considering all the criteria. The multi-criteria decision making (MCDM) methods play an important role in this process. The MCDM is designed to consider the alternatives and criteria of decision makers, to identify the preferred alternative, to classify the alternatives under a small number of categories and/or to rank the alternatives in an order of preference. (Lootsma, 1999). Many methods have been developed in order to solve the problems in question. These methods are presented in Tab. 1 based on five properties.

When Tab. 1 is examined, the Multi-Objective Optimization by Ratio Analysis (MOORA) is computationally very simple, easily comprehendible and robust. Thus, in case the required conditions are met in order to apply the multi-criteria decision-making methods, it is understood that the use of the MOORA method is more appropriate. Therefore, the MOORA method was used in this study.

The implementation of the MOORA method developed by Brauers and Zavadskas (2006) starts with a decision matrix showing the performance of different alternatives with respect to various criteria.

Tab. 1: Comparative Performance of Some Popular MCDM Methods. Source: Shankar Chakraborty, Applications of the MOORA method for Decision-Making in Manufacturing Environment, *The International Journal of Advanced Manufacturing Technology*, *54*(9–12), 2011, p.1165.

MCDM	Computational time	Simplicity	Mathematical calculations	Stability	Information type
MOORA	Very less	Very simple	Minimum	Good	Quantitative
AHP	Very high	Very critical	Maximum	Poor	Mixed
TOPSIS	Moderate	Moderately critical	Moderate	Medium	Quantitative
VIKOR	Less	Simple	Moderate	Medium	Quantitative
ELECTRE	High	Moderately critical	Moderate	Medium	Mixed
PROMETHEE	High	Moderately critical	Moderate	Medium	Mixed

$$X = \begin{bmatrix} x_{11} & \cdots & x_{1n} \\ \vdots & \ddots & \vdots \\ x_{m1} & \cdots & x_{mn} \end{bmatrix} \tag{1}$$

In order to show alternatives and column criteria in the decision matrix; where x_{ij} is the performance measure of *i*th alternative on *j*th attribute, m is the number of alternatives, and n is the number of criteria.

The decision matrix is normalized in the following step. At this stage, the square root of the sum of the squares of the values of the alternatives for each criterion in the decision matrix is calculated, and then the value of the alternatives is divided by the calculated value.

$$x_{ij}^{*} = \frac{x_{ij}}{\sqrt{\sum_{i=1}^{m} x_{ij}^{2}}} \tag{2}$$

In this step, Equation 2 is applied irrespective of whether the criterion is to be maximized or minimized.

In the following step, performance values of alternatives are calculated and alternatives are listed. In the normalized decision matrix, the sum of the performance values to be minimized is subtracted from the sum of the performance values to be maximized.

$$y_i^{*} = \sum_{j=1}^{g} x_{ij}^{*} - \sum_{j=g+1}^{n} x_{ij}^{*} \tag{3}$$

j =1,2, ..., g for the objectives to be maximized, j = g+1, g+2, ..., n for the objectives to be minimized, y_i^{*} is the normalized assessment of alternative i with respect to all objectives. An ordinal ranking of y_i^{*} shows the final preference (Brauers & Zavadskas, 2006). Thus, the alternatives are listed according to the MOORA method. Although there are several approaches to the MOORA method, the MOORA-the ratio system approach, which consists of the three steps mentioned in this study, is used.

4 Dataset and Findings

In this study, the MOORA method was applied using the financial ratios of the companies listed in the Istanbul Stock Exchange (BIST) index for 2017. BIST 50 consists of 50 shares (BIST, 2018) selected from the companies listed on the Star Market and the Main Market, real estate partnerships and venture capital investment trusts traded in the Collective Investment Products and Structured Products Market. Within the scope of this study, sports clubs, financial institutions and real estate investment trusts within the scope of BIST 50 are excluded from the analysis, the dataset of 33 enterprises, which are continuous in the stock market

Tab. 2: Enterprises Included in the Analysis in the Study

Transaction Code	Transaction Code
AKSA	MGROS
ALARKO	NTHOL
ARCLK	PETKM
ASLSN	PGSUS
BIMAS	SAHOL
CCOLA	SASA
ECILC	SISE
ENJSA	TAVHL
ENKAI	TRCELL
EREGL	THYAO
FROTO	TEKFEN
IPEKE	TOASO
KARSN	TTKOM
KCHOL	TUPRS
KOZAA	VESTEL
KOZAL	ZOREN
KRDMD	–

and can be accessed regularly, are examined. This dataset was created by making the calculations using the financial statements obtained from the web pages of the related companies.

The enterprises surveyed in the study are presented in Tab. 2 in alphabetical order according to the transaction code.

The growth rates, activity ratios, financial structure ratios, profitability ratios and liquidity ratios were taken into consideration when measuring the financial performance of the companies listed in Tab. 2. Literature search was carried out in order to determine the appropriate variables when measuring the titles. In this context, 9 variables were determined: asset growth (%), stock turnover rate, debt turnover rate, asset turnover rate, equity/assets, asset profitability (%), gross operating profit margin (%), equity profitability (%) and current ratio. These variables are shown in Tab. 3.

Tab. 4 shows the decision matrix for the first step of the MOORA method, which is applied to assess the performance of the enterprises covered in the study in terms of the criteria presented in Tab. 3.

In the second step of the MOORA method, the decision matrix is normalized. Therefore, based on the decision matrix in Tab. 4, the data matrix is normalized

Tab. 3: Variables Used in the Study

Variable	Abbreviation	Ideal Situation
Asset Growth (%)	K1	Maximum
Stock Turnover Rate	K2	Maximum
Debt Turnover Rate	K3	Maximum
Asset Turnover Rate	K4	Maximum
Equity/Assets	K5	Maximum
Asset Profitability (%)	K6	Maximum
Gross Operating Profit Margin (%)	K7	Maximum
Equity Profitability (%)	K8	Maximum
Current Ratio	K9	Maximum

using the formula in Equation 2. The calculated version of the values in the denominator of this formula are presented in Tab. 5.

The alternative value in the decision matrix is given in Tab. 6, it is the normalized matrix obtained calculated by dividing to the relevant value in Tab. 5.

Enterprises are shown in the rows and criteria are shown in the columns in Tab. 6. In this computed matrix, row totals are calculated taking into consideration whether the criteria are to be maximized or minimized. However, since the criteria discussed in this study are to be maximized, it is sufficient to take row totals on an alternative basis. The performance value calculated for each alternative is given under the column Total in Tab. 6. As a result of ranking the values in this column from high to low, it can be said that the enterprise with the highest value is the best alternative in terms of the criteria taken into consideration for the year 2017. Tab. 7 presents the top 10 enterprises in terms of performance value.

Tab. 7 shows that the best alternative for the year 2017 is the MIGROS Inc. Co. with the transaction code MGROS among the enterprises analyzed in terms of the criteria handled in line with the purpose of the study.

5 Conclusion

In this study, the performance of the BIST 50 enterprises was analyzed based on certain criteria by using the MOORA method which is one of the multi-criteria decision making methods. Within this scope, 33 enterprises were analyzed using 9 criteria namely asset growth (%), stock turnover rate, turnover rate, turnover rate, equity/asset, asset profitability (%), gross operating profit margin (%), equity profitability and current ratio respectively. The findings show that the performance value of MIGROS Inc. Co with the transaction code MGROS is the highest. The findings in the study have shown that the MOORA method can be a good tool

Tab. 4: Decision Matrix

	K1	K2	K3	K4	K5	K6	K7	K8	K9
AKSA	25,49	7,99	7,54	0,77	30,87	7,63	8,76	35,76	0,69
ALARKO	10,63	4,21	9,9	0,28	48,69	8,06	17,72	16,68	1,9
ARCLK	20,86	3,95	3,25	1,12	33,67	4,51	31,22	13,11	1,62
ASLSN	35,37	2,4	3,33	0,53	40,96	13,72	25,28	32,81	1,66
BIMAS	40,82	14,92	32,81	4,12	42,1	14,37	17,05	35,52	0,94
CCOLA	28,1	8,7	9,21	0,71	35,36	1,99	34,05	5,26	1,38
ECILC	-4,04	4	2,92	0,15	90,84	3,73	39,21	4,34	3,53
ENJSA	22,83	82,89	5,43	0,73	31,64	5,86	31,86	18,59	0,84
ENKAI	13,46	8,11	7,8	0,37	77,29	9,01	25,89	11,84	2,2
EREGL	19,98	2,78	8,68	0,72	65,85	14,43	27,69	22,15	2,69
FROTO	29,35	19,25	9,81	2,38	30,77	13,99	10,41	43,44	1,13
IPEKE	14,88	2,54	28,05	0,31	24,08	2,56	53,17	10,49	8,77
KARSN	13,65	6,39	2,58	0,56	19,44	0,4	15,08	1,96	1,51
KCHOL	18,16	8,2	6,9	1,02	28,8	5,11	16,56	17,59	1,49
KOZAA	14,95	2,45	28,97	0,31	46,17	5,79	54,71	12,44	9,38
KOZAL	19,86	2,24	68,9	0,33	91,82	19,08	58,43	21,06	10,62
KRDMD	22,49	4,21	6,69	0,63	35,33	4	16,9	10,74	0,97
MGROS	64,14	6,49	176,51	1,85	14,27	6,18	26,6	61,69	0,68
NTHOL	43,1	13,08	3,24	0,17	65	8,35	38,66	15,42	1,47
PETKM	24,25	7,49	9,02	1,05	48,71	19,95	25,23	41,26	1,79

PGSUS	43,97	164,54	12,26	0,78	30,98	7,33	14,49	24,61	1,66
SAHOL	14,88	4,79	7,98	0,04	7,51	1,05	112,2	14	0,66
SASA	130,38	5,7	4,14	0,97	47,85	11,94	19,29	24,44	1,91
SİSE	11,25	3,67	5,08	0,56	46,16	6,06	32,07	13,33	2,22
TAVHL	17,83	64,28	7,06	0,37	29,76	5,73	43,95	20,43	0,91
TRCELL	7,54	91,08	5,92	0,52	44,11	6,04	36,89	12,77	1,53
THYAO	5,49	41,4	19,3	0,59	29,38	0,96	19,7	3,36	0,85
TEKFEN	40,46	6,86	5,06	0,93	31,77	9,62	13,74	28,97	1,26
TOASO	17,11	14,82	10,87	1,36	25,82	9,97	11,6	39,23	1,13
TTKOM	8,46	31,61	3,95	0,65	15,63	4,05	44,71	28,6	1,22
TUPRS	22,25	10,41	11,69	1,56	27,18	10,99	11,52	41,29	1,15
VESTEL	43,46	3,55	3,91	1,03	15,93	0,47	20,06	2,77	0,88
ZOREN	64,82	220,39	10,38	0,43	14,93	0,57	20,52	4,83	0,58

Tab. 5: The Square Root of the Sum of the Squares Per Criterion

K1	K2	K3	K4	K5	K6	K7	K8	K9
208,751	315,257	201,1506	6,527051	249,667	51,59395	203,8902	144,7763	18,71281

Tab. 6: Normalized Matrix

	K1	K2	K3	K4	K5	K6	K7	K8	K9	Total
AKSA	0,12	0,03	0,04	0,12	0,12	0,15	0,04	0,25	0,04	0,90
ALARKO	0,05	0,01	0,05	0,04	0,20	0,16	0,09	0,12	0,10	0,81
ARCLK	0,10	0,01	0,02	0,17	0,13	0,09	0,15	0,09	0,09	0,85
ASLSN	0,17	0,01	0,02	0,08	0,16	0,27	0,12	0,23	0,09	1,14
BIMAS	0,20	0,05	0,16	0,63	0,17	0,28	0,08	0,25	0,05	1,86
CCOLA	0,13	0,03	0,05	0,11	0,14	0,04	0,17	0,04	0,07	0,77
ECILC	−0,02	0,01	0,01	0,02	0,36	0,07	0,19	0,03	0,19	0,88
ENJSA	0,11	0,26	0,03	0,11	0,13	0,11	0,16	0,13	0,04	1,08
ENKAI	0,06	0,03	0,04	0,06	0,31	0,17	0,13	0,08	0,12	1,00
EREGL	0,10	0,01	0,04	0,11	0,26	0,28	0,14	0,15	0,14	1,23
FROTO	0,14	0,06	0,05	0,36	0,12	0,27	0,05	0,30	0,06	1,42
IPEKE	0,07	0,01	0,14	0,05	0,10	0,05	0,26	0,07	0,47	1,21
KARSN	0,07	0,02	0,01	0,09	0,08	0,01	0,07	0,01	0,08	0,44
KCHOL	0,09	0,03	0,03	0,16	0,12	0,10	0,08	0,12	0,08	0,80
KOZAA	0,07	0,01	0,14	0,05	0,18	0,11	0,27	0,09	0,50	1,42
KOZAL	0,10	0,01	0,34	0,05	0,37	0,37	0,29	0,15	0,57	2,23
KRDMD	0,11	0,01	0,03	0,10	0,14	0,08	0,08	0,07	0,05	0,68
MGROS	0,31	0,02	0,88	0,28	0,06	0,12	0,13	0,43	0,04	2,26
NTHOL	0,21	0,04	0,02	0,03	0,26	0,16	0,19	0,11	0,08	1,09
PETKM	0,12	0,02	0,04	0,16	0,20	0,39	0,12	0,28	0,10	1,43
PGSUS	0,21	0,52	0,06	0,12	0,12	0,14	0,07	0,17	0,09	1,51
SAHOL	0,07	0,02	0,04	0,01	0,03	0,02	0,55	0,10	0,04	0,86
SASA	0,62	0,02	0,02	0,15	0,19	0,23	0,09	0,17	0,10	1,60
SİSE	0,05	0,01	0,03	0,09	0,18	0,12	0,16	0,09	0,12	0,85
TAVHL	0,09	0,20	0,04	0,06	0,12	0,11	0,22	0,14	0,05	1,02
TRCELL	0,04	0,29	0,03	0,08	0,18	0,12	0,18	0,09	0,08	1,08
THYAO	0,03	0,13	0,10	0,09	0,12	0,02	0,10	0,02	0,05	0,65
TEKFEN	0,19	0,02	0,03	0,14	0,13	0,19	0,07	0,20	0,07	1,03

Tab. 6: Continued

	K1	K2	K3	K4	K5	K6	K7	K8	K9	Total
TOASO	0,08	0,05	0,05	0,21	0,10	0,19	0,06	0,27	0,06	1,08
TTKOM	0,04	0,10	0,02	0,10	0,06	0,08	0,22	0,20	0,07	0,88
TUPRS	0,11	0,03	0,06	0,24	0,11	0,21	0,06	0,29	0,06	1,16
VESTEL	0,21	0,01	0,02	0,16	0,06	0,01	0,10	0,02	0,05	0,63
ZOREN	0,31	0,70	0,05	0,07	0,06	0,01	0,10	0,03	0,03	1,36

Tab. 7: Performance Value

No.	Transaction Code	Performance Value
1	MGROS	2,26
2	KOZAL	2,23
3	BIMAS	1,86
4	SASA	1,60
5	PGSUS	1,51
6	PETKM	1,43
7	KOZAA	1,42
8	FROTO	1,42
9	ZOREN	1,36
10	EREGL	1,23

for studies on performance measurement and evaluation. However, only the use of the 2017 dataset and the use of 9 criteria should be mentioned as a limitation of this study. Researchers can analyze different data periods or sectors using the MOORA method in the studies focusing on performance assessment. Hence, future studies can compare the results of the MOORA method and other multi-criteria decision-making methods. Thus, the performance of these methods could also be evaluated.

Bibliography

Akyüz, Y., & Kaya, Z. (2013). Türkiye'de Hayat Dışı ve Hayat/Emeklilik Sigorta Sektörünün Finansal Performans Analiz ve Değerlendirmesi. Selçuk Üniversitesi İktisadi İdari Bilimler Fakültesi Sosyal ve Ekonomik Araştırmalar Dergisi, 356–371.

BIST. (2018). BIST Pay Endeksleri Temel Kuralları. Retrieved August 28, 2018 from Borsa İstanbul: http://www.borsaistanbul.com/docs/default-source/endeksler/bist-pay-endeksleri-temel-kurallari-haziran-2018.pdf?sfvrsn=4.

Brauers, W. K., & Zavadskas, E. K. (2006). The MOORA Method and Its Application To Privatization In A Transition Economy. *Control and Cybernetics*, 445–469.

Bülbül, S., & Köse, A. (2011). Türk Gıda Şirketlerinin Finansal Performansının Çok Amaçlı Karar Verme Yöntemleriyle Değerlendirilmesi. *Atatürk Üniversitesi İktisadi ve İdari Bilimler Fakültesi Dergisi*, 71–97.

Chakraborty, S. (2011). Applications Of The MOORA Method For Decision Making In Manufacturing Environment. *The International Journal of Advanced Manufacturing Technology*, 1155–1166.

Çetin, K., & Çetin, E. İ. (2010). Multi Criteria Analysis Of Banks' Performances. *International Journal Of Economics And Finance Studies*, 73–78.

Demireli, E. (2010). TOPSIS Çok Kriterli Karar Verme Sistemi: Türkiye'deki Kamu Bankaları Üzerine Bir Uygulama. *Girişimcilik ve Kalkınma Dergisi*, 101–112.

Dinçer, H., & Görener, A. (2011). Analitik Hiyerarşi Süreci ve VIKOR Tekniği ile Dinamik Performans Analizi: Bankacılık Sektöründe Bir Uygulama. *İstanbul Ticaret Üniversitesi Sosyal Bilimler Dergisi*, 109–127.

Ege, İ., & Yaman, S. (2018). TOPSIS ve Moora Yöntemleri ile Ölçülen Finansal Performansın Pay Getirilerine Etkisi: Bist Çimento Beton İşletmeleri Üzerine Bir Panel Veri Uygulaması. *Al-Farabi Uluslararası Sosyal Bilimler Dergisi*, 75–94.

Eleren, A., & Karagül, M. (2008). 1986–2006 Türkiye Ekonomisinin Performans Değerlendirmesi. *Yönetim ve Ekonomi*, 1–14.

Günay, B., & Kaya, İ. (2017). Borsa İstanbul'da Yer Alan Aracı Kurumların Performansının Çok Kriterli Karar Verme Yöntemleri ile Değerlendirilmesi. *Manisa Celal Bayar Üniversitesi Sosyal Bilimler Dergisi*, 141–164.

Güneysu, Y., Er, B., & Ar, İ. (2015). Türkiye'deki Ticari Bankaların Performanslarının AHS ve GİA Yöntemleri ile İncelenmesi. *Karadeniz Teknik Üniversitesi Sosyal Bilimler Dergisi*, 71–93.

Haberler, G. v. (1936). *The Theory of International Trade With Its Applications to Commercial Policy.* (A. Stonier, & F. Benham, Trans.) London: William Hodge & Company.

Kula, V., Kandemir , T., & Baykut, E. (2016). Borsa İstanbul'da İşlem Gören Sigorta ve BES Şirketlerinin Finansal Performansının Gri İlişkisel Analiz Yöntemi İle İncelenmesi. *Afyon Kocatepe Üniversitesi İktisadi ve İdari Bilimler Fakültesi Dergisi*, 18(1), 37–53.

Lootsma, F. A. (1999). *Multi-Criteria Decision Analysis via Ratio And Difference Judgement.* Kluwer Academic Publishers.

Opricovic, S., Gwo-Hshiung , T. (2004). Compromise Solution by MCDM Methods: A comparative Analysis of VIKOR and TOPSIS. *European Journal of Operational Research,* 445–455.

Şahin, A., & Akkaya, C. (2013). PROMETHEE Sıralama Yöntemi ile Portföy Oluşturma Üzerine Bir Uygulama. *Ekonomi ve Yönetim Araştırmaları Dergisi,* 67–81.

Yurdakul, M., & İç, Y. T. (2003). Türk Otomotiv Firmalarının Performans Ölçümü ve Analizine Yönelik TOPSİS Yöntemini Kullanan Bir Örnek Çalışma. *Gazi Üniversitesi Mühendislik Mimarlık Fakültesi Dergisi,* 1–18.

Yusuf Kaya

Changing Risk Management and Updated Risk Frameworks/Standards: Coso & ISO 31.000

1 Introduction

Looking at the concept of risk management, it is observed that significant changes have been experienced in international financial markets and financial systems, which are the main items of these markets, when the last twenty years' time frame is examined. The rapid application of the financial sector in the field of information technologies has resulted with a rapid increase in sectoral activity and profits. However, the fact that the institutional structures of the enterprises, operating in the sector, and even the regulatory authorities, cannot keep up with these developments caused structural weaknesses (Bolak, 2004). This situation causes the question of traditional risk management approach.

Traditional risk management has focused solely on financial risks, by identifying the silo approach in enterprises, not taking non-financial risks too much into consideration. In addition, each department prepared its own risk reports and presented them to management. This has resulted in the preparation of different reports in different languages; It has caused the enterprise not to have a general language of reporting. More than one departments have been involved in the same risk, causing unnecessary time and job loss. For this reason, a risk management approach involving all departments and employees who adopt the portfolio approach has been needed. According to Küçük (2007), what an enterprise needs is an ERM approach that creates a holistic picture.

ERM is an integrated management process that affects all departments of the business, its employees and managers. In 2004, the Treadway Commission (COSO) formed the framework of Enterprise Risk Management and published its revisions in 2013 and 2017. The International Organization for Standardization (ISO) first published ISO 31.000 Risk Management Standard in 2009 and revised this standard in 2018. In this study, the history of risk management is described and new updates and differences of generally accepted standards are mentioned.

2 History of Risk Management and Transition from Traditional Risk Management to Enterprise Risk Management

After the industrial revolution, mass production brought risks together and managing risks became important. In the modern sense, it is clear that the history of risk management is not very old. The term was first introduced in the 1950s. Risk management was first introduced in the insurance sector.

The raw material crisis and oil crises that took place in the 1970s led to the understanding of the importance and necessity of risk management. The bankruptcies and losses experienced in the crisis have put the companies and investors in a difficult situation, showed necessity of the pursuit of new quests. For the first time these years, the foundations of the rating agencies have begun to be established. Managers have begun to demand more information about the risks to which they are confronted and the more risks they have to face for the unexpected consequences of their decisions since the 1990's, while only the credit risk, loss risk and market risk were taken into account in the 1980's. Risk management has begun to shift to "business risk management," aimed at assessing the risks arising from increased competition in the market and growing enterprises. Institutions are now beginning to worry about the risks that may cause the bankruptcy. Studies at the end of the 1990's showed that the risks involved in managing enterprises increased, and in time the scope continued to expand. This expansion is taken as a basis of risk management. In the 2000's, enterprise risk management has now become a tool that all enterprises use to manage risk. Scope of the risk has become the largest in history. Now, not only lost and financial risks, but also strategic and operational risks are included. Risk has now begun to be carried out as a whole within the enterprise rather than in a specific department or function. Tab. 1 shows the developments in risk management from the 1950's to the present day;

Before modern risk management and insights emerged, traditional risk management systems were used by enterprises. Traditional risk management is known as a method in which each department plans risk separately, rather than introducing a general risk plan that measures risk using static methods. One of the biggest criticisms was that the measurements were not objective enough and subjective evaluations were made.

The economic crises that have been intensifying since the beginning of the 1990's have led to an increase in the risk perception of the enterprises, the traditional risk management approach is not sufficient and new and more effective management approaches are required. In the last 20 years, they have realized that enterprise risk management should be a more systematic structure in which employees at all levels are involved, with more integrated, strategic and institutional widespread activities.

In 2000, integrated risk management concept was introduced by Colquitt, after which Dickinson became the first scientist in 2001 to gain the concept of Enterprise Risk Management (ERM). ERM is a contemporary risk management approach in which all risks are systematically and coordinated in a way that predetermines, classifies and evaluates the risks that enterprises may incur as they continue their operations. In Tab. 2, the risk-based approach, the differences between traditional risk management and ERM, are shown comparatively;

Tab. 1: Developments in Risk Management between the 1950's and 2018

Date	Events
1950–1960's	Traditional Risk Management
1970's	Risk Management systems was beginning to be accepted
1977	Law on Bribery and Corruption Prevention in America
1985	Risk departments and internal audit units started to be established. In 1985, Treadway Commission was established.
1988	Basel I
1992	1992 the Coso published the Internal Control Integrated Framework report.
1999 (revision 2004)	Australia/New Zealand Risk Management Standard AS/NZS 4360 Risk Management Process
2002	Sarbanes Oxley Act was signed in America.
2004	Coso published the Enterprise Risk Management Framework.
2004	Basel II
2009	ISO published 31.000 Risk Management Standard
2010	Basel III
2013	COSO Internal Control Revision
2017	COSO Enterprise Risk Management Revision: Integrating with Strategy and Performance
2018	ISO 31.000:2018 Revision

3 Updated COSO and ISO 31.000

3.1 COSO Updates (2013–2017)

The Committee of Sponsoring Organizations of the Treadway Commission (COSO) published two frameworks: Internal Control-Integrated Framework, published in 1992 and revised in 2013, and the other, the Enterprise Risk Enterprise Risk Management – Integrated Framework COSO published the revised Enterprise Risk Management Framework on September 6, 2017 in the name of "Enterprise Risk Management-Aligning Risk with Strategy and Performance".

3.1.1 COSO 2013 Update

COSO first published its internal control framework in 1992. Since its publication, the framework has become the most widely accepted and applied framework of internal control throughout the world. Since 1992, because of following reasons it was needed to be updated;

Tab. 2: Comparatively Indication of the differences between Traditional Risk Management and ERM. **Source:** Pehlivanlı D. (2008), "Kurumsal Risk Yönetimi Temelli İçi Denetim ve Türkiye Uygulamaları" Kocaeli Üniversitesi Social Sciences Institute, Phd Thesis, 2008

Factor	**Risk-Focused Activities**	**Traditional Risk Management**	**Enterprise Risk Management**
Perspective	Physical Threats	All Threats	Opportunities and Threats
Focus	Special Projects	Special Activities	Enterprise General And Enterprise Partners Basis
Responsible	Specialists	Administrators	All Employees
Level of Details	Complex Analysis	Detailed Analysis	General Assessment
Timing	Once	Regular	Continuous
Language	Different Terms	Similar Terms But Different Angles	General Language and Perspective
Reporting	Once Detailed	Divided at the high level	Integrated Business reports
Focus of Control	Based On Security And Probability Planning	Individual Control Mechanisms Temelli	Based on Control Frames
Tools	Data Analysis	Control Risk and Self-Assessment and questionnaires	Control Risk and Self-Assessment questionnaires and tools for integrating ERM with business processes
Target	Low-level Assurance	Risk Identification and Management for Risk Registration	Access to Institutional Purposes
Scope	Conformity	Operational	Strategic
Standards	Dependent on the expert	Dependent on the manager	Dependent on Institutional Risk Policy
Vision	Protection of Institutional Resources	Preservation of the Board of Directors and Management	Establishment of Integrated Risk Management Framework and Improvement of Institution's Reputation
System directors	External Threats	CEO VE CFO	Shareholders, CEOVE CFO

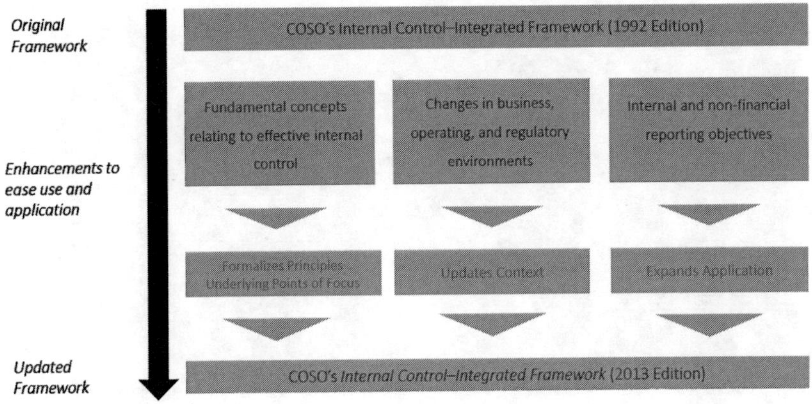

Fig. 1: COSO Update 2013. Source: http://g31000.org/wp-content/uploads/2014/08/G31000-PwC-presentation-on-COSO-ISO-at-the-IIA-SA-conference-11-Aug-2014.pdf

- Increasing and becoming more complicated risks
- Increased emphasis on corporate governance
- Development of technology
- Complexity of institutions and business life
- Renewed legal obligations, etc. (http://www.tide.org.tr/uploads/TI%CC%87DE-COSO%20Sunumu %202013%20son.pdf)

Fig. 1 reveals the changes in COSO update 2013 framework;

What has been changed with COSO 2013 IC?

- The increased importance of technology has been taken more into account.
- The importance of the concept of governance was emphasized.
- Non-financial reporting was also important.
- More space was allocated to fighting mischief.
- The principles that make up the components were clearly defined
- It was transformed from a complex structure to a more understandable structure.

With the enhanced focus on risk, the ERM framework expands the internal control framework's risk assessment, creating three components: event identification, risk assessment, and risk response. Fig. 2 shows the Coso IC 2013 comparison with Coso ERM

3.1.2 COSO 2017 Update

COSO was first published its Enterprise Risk Management – Integrated Framework back in 2004. Since its publication, the framework has been received wide

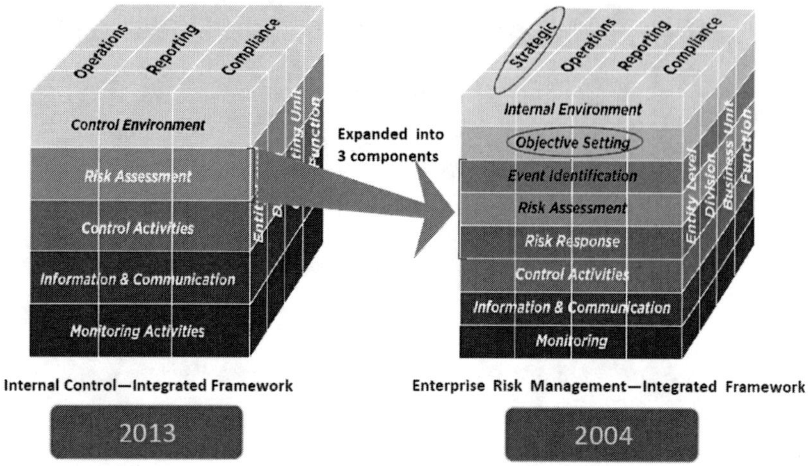

Fig. 2: COSO 2013 Cube. **Source**: http://g31000.org/wp-content/uploads/2014/08/G31000-PwC-presentation-on-COSO-ISO-at-the-IIA-SA-conference-11-Aug-2014.pdf

acceptance and participation, especially in the United States. However, over the past 13 years, the emergence of new risks, the need to make existing risks more complex, the need for better risk reporting, and new developments in risk management have necessitated the creation of a new framework.

The new framework, presented in 2017, was published with the name of COSO ERM-Integrating with Strategy and Performance.

What has been changed with COSO 2017 ERM?

- With the new framework, the name ERM-Integrating with Strategy and Performance is being used instead of the name ERM-Integrated Framework. This name change was emphasized that the strategy and performance of the new framework were significantly related to ERM.
- Instead of COSO cubes, which have been known since 2004 and composed of 8 components, the COSO helix, consisting of 5 components, as seen in Figs. 3 and 4, came. These 5 components are also expressed in 20 terms.
- For the stakeholders who want more transparency with the new framework, more simple understandable risk reporting systems are emphasized.
- It is emphasized that the system should be used and integrated within all processes of the enterprise.
- It is emphasized that the purpose of risk management is to add value to the company, to preserve the current value, to realize and to determine the strategies and to be an integrated application. It is also stated that ERM will only help

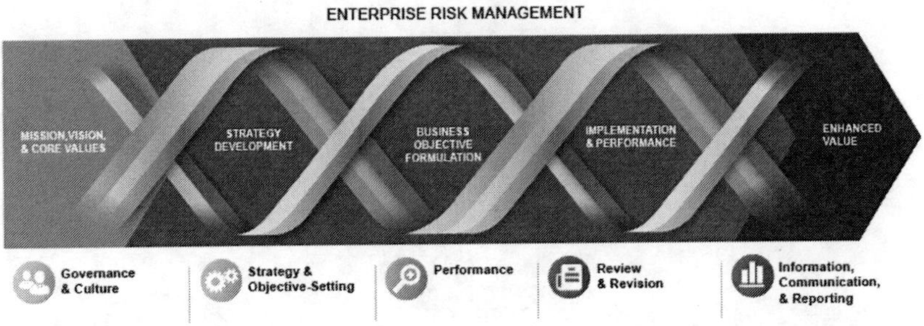

Fig. 3: COSO 2017-ERM. **Source:** 2017 COSO ERM-Integrating with Strategy and Performance Executive Summary

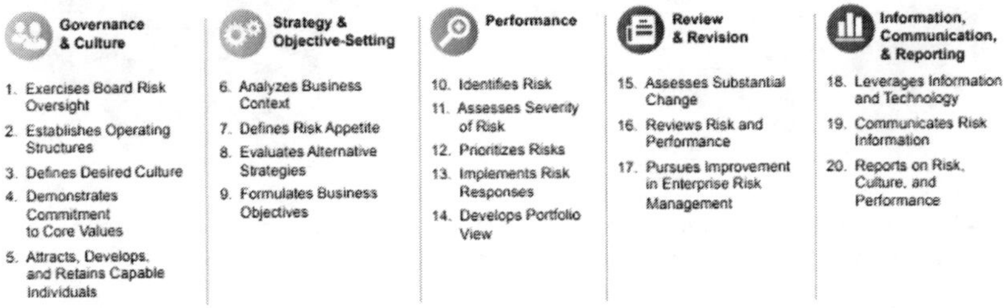

Fig. 4: Five Components and Principles. **Source:** 2017 COSO ERM-Integrating with Strategy and Performance Executive Summary

to create opportunities for value enhancement and sustainability, integrating with strategy determination, not focusing on reducing value and lowering risks to an acceptable level. (https://nazifburca.com/2017/09/20/yenilenen-coso-kurumsal-risk-yonetimi-cercevesi/).

The five components of the framework and a description of each from COSO are listed below:

3.2 ISO 31.000–2018 Update

International Organization for Standardization (ISO) is an independent, non-governmental international organization with a membership of 161 national standards bodies (https://www.iso.org/about-us.html). Initially published as ISO 31.000 Risk Management in 2009, the standard was revised in 2018.

The ISO has revised the standard in 2018 to maintain the general status of the standard and has not made a comprehensive change in the frame. Compared with COSO's revision of 2017, ISO made a smaller change. Basically, the three-part

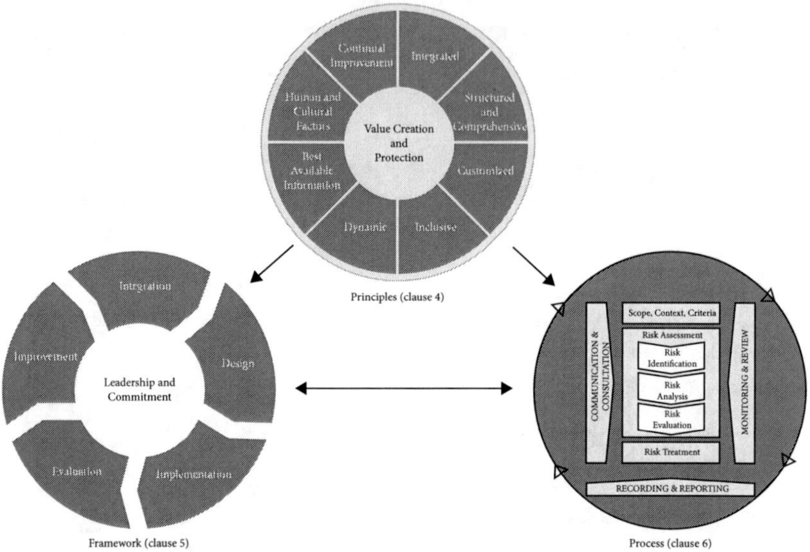

Fig. 5: ISO 31.000:2018 Principles, Framework, Process. Source: https://nazifburca.com/2018/02/27/yenilenen-iso-31000-risk-yonetimi-rehberi/

standard, Principles, Framework and Process, keeps this form in 2018. The new version emphasizes the importance of integrating risk management into all the activities and processes of organizations and the participation and leadership of top management in risk management. The number of pages has been reduced to 16, drawn from 11 to 8 in Principles. It can be said that the overall objective is to set a more easily understandable and applicable standard. Fig. 5 shows the basic 3 parts of the standard;

What has been changed with ISO 31.000:2018

- More focuses on the integration
- Leaders responsibility
- Risk was defined "the effect of uncertainty on objectives". It highlights the impact of incomplete knowledge of circumstances on an organisation's decision making
- Focus on "creating and protecting value"

4 Conclusion

The time and complexity of risk management has necessitated the updating of existing frameworks and standards. COSO ERM and ISO 31000 frameworks/standards are the most used guides in the world over the last 10 years in terms of risk management. The main points of the updates of both organizations are to determine the risks more accurately, to integrate the system, to make the frameworks more understandable.

As the technology and the markets are changing day by day, the enterprises should get precautions in order to adopt the new risks. Although new updated COSO and ISO guides meet the requirements, new revisions and risk models should be considered for the enterprises.

Bibliography

Bolak, M. (2004). Risk ve Yönetimi, Birsen Publishing, İstanbul, page: 3–36.

COSO (2004) "Enterprise Risk Management-Integrated Framework" Executive Summary.

COSO (2017). COSO ERM-Integrating with Strategy and Performance, Executive Summary.

Küçük, A. (2007). Havaalanlarında Kurumsal Risk Yönetimi Örneği: Atatürk Havalimanı Terminalleri İşletmesi İçin Kurumsal Risk Yönetimi Modelleri, (Unpublished Phd Thesis), Anadolu Üniversitesi Social Sciences Institute, Eskişehir.

Pehlivanlı D. (2008), "Kurumsal Risk Yönetimi Temelli İçi Denetim ve Türkiye Uygulamaları" " Kocaeli Üniversitesi Social Sciences Institute, Phd Thesis, 2008

http://www.tide.org.tr/uploads/TI%CC%87DE-COSO%20Sunumu%202013%20son.pdf (Accessed: 16.06.2018)

http://g31000.org/wp-content/uploads/2014/08/G31000-PwC-presentation-on-COSO-ISO-at-the-IIA-SA-conference-11-Aug-2014.pdf (Accessed: 14.07.2018)

https://nazifburca.com/2018/02/27/yenilenen-iso-31000-risk-yonetimi-rehberi (Accessed: 15.07.2018).

https://nazifburca.com/2017/09/20/yenilenen-coso-kurumsal-risk-yonetimi-cercevesi/. (Accessed: 15.07.2018)

https://www.iso.org/about-us.html (Accessed: 25.07.2018)

https://www.iso.org/iso-31000-risk-management.html (Accessed: 25.07.2018)

Ferit Karahan

Reactions of Football Investors: Analysis of Turkish 3 Bigs Derbies

1 Introduction

Today football has become a global industry with a huge economic volume. Successes of major football teams are important for a society and its morale. Football, as well as all over the world to drag after the masses in Turkey and is closely related to people's psychology. There is a supporter and team relationship in the football rarely seen. In general, fans tend not to change their soccer team, and even if they lose the match they lose their support. There is a serious stability in team keeping between fans in Football. When their teams win, supporters feel proud and happy when teams lost they feel depressed and unhappy. The performances of football clubs occupy an important place in the lives of their supporters.

On the other hand, being a fan on the football and being an investor are different concepts. Many football clubs are in the form of public corporations of which stocks are traded in stock markets. Investors should not be as emotional as fans, and rational in their investment decisions, which points to the effectiveness of the markets. Consequently, many investors in the Stock Exchange make their buy/sell decisions according to performance of the football clubs they support.

According to the effective market hypothesis, all information on the market is known to investors and this information is reflected in asset prices. For this reason investors are not able to get a return on the market. However, in some studies, it has been determined that despite the effective market hypothesis, it is possible to obtain a return above normal using other publicly disclosed information and insider learned information

The link between the results of football matches and stock returns has been investigated by many researchers, and the findings of some of these studies revealed a relationship between them. The aim of this study is to investigate whether the matches results of sports organizations (Türkiye Süper Ligi) among Beşiktaş, Fenerbahçe, Galatasaray (derby games in Turkey) that are traded in Istanbul Stock Exchange after they go public are causing the abnormal return will investigated. With this purpose we used event study method to show performances of Turkish football teams on derby matches have impact on stock returns.

Especially football clubs, going public of sport clubs is important for investors also company management. On Turkey, the public offerings of soccer clubs began since 2000s. Beşiktaş and Galatasaray sold their stocks in 2002 and Fenerbahçe in 2004 and Trabzonspor in 2005. These teams are named "4 big" in Turkey and these teams lead the football innovations in Turkey. But in this study we investigate 3 big Istanbul city teams because of classification of derby matches.

2 Literature Review

In the past decade the relationship between sports matches' performances and stock returns has been investigated in economics and finance literature. In early studies Stadtmann (2003) investigated country index, game result, contract duration of players, new transfers, sold players variables of Borussia Dortmund team between 1999–2002 and find low explanatory power of regression model on these variables. On the other hand at the same year (2003) Ashton et al investigated the relationship between FTSE index and game results of all British clubs between 1984–2002 years with ARCH- GARCH models. Results show that the ARCH-GARCH models are high explanatory power.

Berument et al.(2006a) investigated the effect of soccer success on stock market returns after certain characteristics of the stock market are controlled for on Turkish Clubs. They used GARCH analysis in this research and evidence suggests that Beşiktaş's win against foreign rivals in the Winners' Cup increased the stock market returns. The same effect is not present for the other two major Turkish teams (Fenerbahçe and Galatasaray). The day of the week effect on the stock market and the relationship between risk and return are also presented.

Berument at al. (2006b) studied the connection between Turkish industrial production growth and the success of Beşiktaş. The empirical evidence provided that industrial production growth tends to increase with the success of Beşiktaş in European cups. Moreover, if the winnings are in displacement, the increase in industrial production is higher than if the winnings are in the home field. On the other hand, findings on the effects of domestic games on industrial performance are not statistically significant.

Aygören at al.(2008) investigated whether performances of football clubs have impact on stock returns. The findings shows investors are able to get abnormal returns during the event window interval both in derbies and European football matches. In derbies, only in the case of defeat, there is an abnormal return on the day after the match.

Baur and McKeating (2009) evaluated 27 European clubs in Dow Jones STOXX index to investigate the effects of public offerings between 1990 and 2008. They used panel data regression and achieved that the public offerings had no positive effect on big clubs whereas they were beneficial to those clubs in lower leagues.

Uludağ and Varan (2013) examined the impact of football matches performances on financial performance. The event study methodology is applied and the findings reveal the fact that defeats and draws significantly affect the market value of 4 Bigs. The investors' reactions to defeats are negative and stronger than those to draws. In particular, in the case of defeats and draws, the investors of Beşiktaş and Fenerbahçe lose more than those of Galatasaray and Trabzonspor.

Demirhan (2013) studied whether the sporting success of Turkish national football team affects Borsa Istanbul (BIST) stock index returns. In this study, GARCH analysis is used. According to the findings, the wins of the national team are not affecting the BIST-100 index return, whereas the failures (losses and draws) have a negative effect.

3 Data

In this study we used derby match scores and stock prices on BIST of Galatasaray, Beşiktaş and Fenerbahçe football teams (known as three big's). Match scores are taken on website of three teams and daily closing stock prices are taken on BIST databases. Used sample data's are chosen after clubs go public dates. (Last going public date for Fenerbahçe team on 2004) Beşiktaş and Galatasaray sold their stocks in 20.02.2002 and Fenerbahçe in 20.02.2004 on BIST. In this period 74 derby matches played among three team. Galatasaray- Fenerbahçe played against 25 times, Fenerbahçe-Beşiktaş played against 25 times and Galatasaray Beşiktaş played against 24 times in this period. And to compare the market return we used BIST index. Daily data taken from BIST website.

4 Methodology

We use the event study methodology to analyze the effect of the results in the football matches on the stock market return of the 3 big's football team. In this football matches, there exist abnormal returns in (-1, +1) event window regardless of the match results. This methodology can be used to analyze the price reaction of a share from a specific event. Brown and Warner (1980, 1985) and Campbell et al. (1997) give a through overview of this methodology. The event in our case is the result of the football match. The outcome is either a win, loss or a draw. The normal return of the share R_{jt} is calculated as,

$$R_{jt} = log\left[\left(P_{jt} + D_{jt}\right) / P_{jt-1}\right]$$

where
P_{jt} is the price of firm j at the end of period t;
D_{jt} is the dividend given to the shareholder during period t;
P_{jt-1} is the price of firm j at the end of period t – 1.

5 Results

In this context we have exhibited 3 main tables. Tab. 1 shows the match results between Fenerbahçe and Galatasaray, the event window returns and volumes of 3 bigs and BIST, and abnormal returns. After the time period of the match (-1,+1) average abnormal return of the stocks are GS -0,014647017, FB -0,010682692 and BJK -0,003289159.

Tab. 2 shows the match results between Fenerbahçe and Beşiktaş, the event window returns and volumes of 3 bigs and BIST, and abnormal returns. After the time period of the match (-1,+1) average abnormal return of the stocks are GS 0,0054513, FB 0,0055445 and BJK -0,0113977.

Tab. 3 shows the match results between Beşiktaş and Galatasaray, the event window returns and volumes of 3 bigs and BIST, and abnormal returns. After the

Tab. 1:

					GS			FB			BJK			BIST
	Match Date	H	Score	Win	Return	Vol	Ab Returns	Return	Vol	Ab Returns	Return	Vol	Ab Returns	Returns
1	29.02.2004	FB	2–1	FB	−0,008	−0,161	−0,038	−0,028	0,994	−0,058	−0,037	−0,098	−0,067	0,030
2	12.12.2004	GS	0–1	GS	−0,014	1,200	−0,009	−0,009	0,134	−0,004	0,013	−0,014	0,018	−0,005
3	22.05.2005	FB	1–0	FB	−0,053	−0,150	−0,008	−0,090	1,746	−0,046	−0,067	−0,273	−0,022	−0,045
4	27.11.2005	GS	1–0	FB	−0,082	1,574	−0,078	0,000	0,018	0,004	0,000	−0,234	0,004	−0,004
5	22.04.2006	FB	4–0	FB	−0,037	−0,189	−0,042	0,000	0,733	−0,004	0,000	1,625	−0,004	0,004
6	03.12.2006	FB	2–1	FB	−0,008	2,138	0,007	0,010	0,157	0,024	−0,008	7,140	0,006	−0,014
7	19.05.2007	GS	2–1	FB	−0,005	0,869	−0,008	−0,013	−0,103	−0,016	−0,005	0,331	−0,008	0,003
8	08.12.2007	FB	2–0	FB	0,000	1,555	0,000	0,024	0,045	0,024	0,000	−0,176	0,000	0,000
9	27.04.2008	GS	0–1	GS	0,040	12,043	0,040	−0,009	0,673	−0,010	−0,017	−0,406	−0,017	0,000
10	09.11.2008	FB	4–1	FB	−0,025	−0,794	−0,030	−0,011	−0,070	−0,017	0,000	−0,584	−0,006	0,006
11	12.04.2009	GS	0–0	B	−0,008	−0,694	0,005	−0,006	−0,617	0,008	0,174	0,576	0,187	−0,014
12	25.10.2009	FB	3–1	FB	−0,026	0,614	−0,023	0,000	0,291	0,003	−0,012	0,569	−0,010	−0,003
13	28.03.2010	GS	1–0	FB	−0,012	−0,413	−0,013	0,005	2,739	0,004	0,008	0,956	0,007	0,001
14	24.10.2010	FB	0–0	B	0,042	1,947	0,043	−0,023	−0,162	−0,022	0,020	0,138	0,021	−0,001
15	18.03.2011	GS	2–1	FB	0,011	−0,240	0,005	−0,030	−0,280	−0,036	−0,006	−0,066	−0,012	0,006
16	07.12.2011	GS	1–3	GS	−0,087	0,327	−0,057	0,002	−0,080	0,032	−0,031	−0,176	−0,002	−0,030
17	17.03.2012	FB	2–2	B	0,024	0,966	0,020	−0,017	−0,114	−0,020	0,000	−0,253	−0,003	0,003

18	22.04.2012	GS	2–1	FB	−0,071	−0,089	−0,064	0,019	2,037	0,026	−0,091	0,815	−0,084	−0,007
19	12.05.2012	FB	0–0	B	−0,020	1,699	−0,003	−0,065	−0,202	−0,048	−0,034	0,423	−0,017	−0,017
20	16.12.2012	GS	1–2	GS	−0,007	0,361	−0,023	−0,035	0,978	−0,050	−0,018	1,828	−0,033	0,015
21	12.05.2013	FB	2–1	FB	−0,018	−0,670	−0,021	−0,005	−0,146	−0,008	−0,014	−0,485	−0,016	0,002
22	10.11.2013	FB	2–0	FB	−0,039	0,403	−0,015	−0,059	0,528	−0,035	−0,033	−0,294	−0,009	−0,024
23	06.04.2014	GS	0–1	GS	−0,009	0,279	−0,007	−0,010	0,668	−0,009	−0,047	−0,452	−0,045	−0,001
24	18.10.2014	GS	1–2	GS	0,005	0,119	−0,005	−0,003	−0,188	−0,014	0,045	0,252	0,035	0,011
25	08.03.2015	FB	1–0	FB	−0,037	−0,268	−0,041	0,007	0,360	0,002	0,000	−0,299	−0,004	0,004

Tab. 2:

					GS			FB			BJK			BIST
	Match Date	H	Score	Win	Return	Vol	Ab Returns	Return	Vol	Ab Returns	Return	Vol	Ab Returns	Returns
1	25.04.2004	BJK	1–3	FB	−0,032	1,125	0,012	0,049	1,002	0,092	−0,023	−0,532	0,020	−0,044
2	30.10.2004	BJK	2–1	BJK	0,034	0,888	0,021	−0,018	−0,230	−0,031	0,004	−0,200	−0,009	0,013
3	17.04.2005	FB	3–4	BJK	−0,038	0,023	−0,016	−0,081	−0,195	−0,060	−0,006	−0,512	0,015	−0,021
4	18.09.2005	BJK	1–2	FB	−0,016	−0,650	−0,014	0,007	0,131	0,009	−0,008	−0,245	−0,006	−0,002
5	26.02.2006	FB	2–2	O	−0,016	−0,664	−0,035	0,005	0,114	−0,014	0,000	−0,382	−0,019	0,019
6	19.11.2006	FB	0–0	O	0,000	−0,351	0,002	0,005	−0,400	0,007	0,015	0,415	0,018	−0,002
7	05.05.2007	BJK	0–1	FB	−0,021	0,523	−0,018	0,042	2,253	0,045	−0,037	−0,087	−0,034	−0,003
8	03.11.2007	FB	2–1	FB	0,000	−0,447	0,014	0,000	0,507	0,014	−0,033	−0,800	−0,019	−0,014
9	29.03.2008	BJK	1–2	FB	−0,019	3,428	−0,007	0,028	1,404	0,040	−0,084	0,606	−0,072	−0,012
10	29.11.2008	FB	2–1	FB	−0,008	−0,092	0,046	−0,033	−0,125	0,021	−0,044	−0,616	0,010	−0,054
11	03.05.2009	BJK	1–2	FB	−0,016	0,692	−0,033	−0,006	−0,384	−0,022	−0,063	−0,514	−0,080	0,016
12	21.11.2009	BJK	3–0	BJK	−0,007	−0,656	−0,020	−0,032	0,090	−0,045	0,036	−0,011	0,023	0,013
13	18.04.2010	FB	1–0	FB	−0,006	−0,379	−0,005	0,162	−0,023	0,163	−0,049	1,024	−0,048	−0,001
14	19.09.2010	FB	1–1	O	0,178	1,787	0,171	0,019	−0,841	0,012	−0,019	−0,649	−0,025	0,007
15	20.02.2011	BJK	2–4	FB	0,006	0,498	0,019	0,082	4,680	0,095	−0,069	−0,494	−0,056	−0,013
16	27.10.2011	BJK	2–2	O	−0,004	−0,394	−0,012	−0,010	−0,098	−0,018	−0,010	0,352	−0,018	0,008
17	05.02.2012	FB	2–0	FB	0,017	−0,006	0,008	−0,009	−0,343	−0,018	−0,006	−0,560	−0,015	0,009

18	29.04.2012	FB	2–1	FB	−0,023	−0,065	−0,014	−0,066	0,292	−0,057	0,008	1,216	0,018	−0,010
19	03.05.2012	BJK	1–0	BJK	0,061	−0,096	0,065	−0,061	−0,325	−0,057	0,008	1,620	0,012	−0,005
20	07.10.2012	FB	3–0	FB	−0,022	0,128	−0,022	0,000	−0,366	−0,001	−0,012	−0,643	−0,013	0,001
21	03.03.2013	BJK	3–2	BJK	−0,012	0,768	−0,021	−0,013	0,563	−0,022	0,009	1,112	−0,001	0,009
22	30.11.2013	FB	3–3	O	−0,014	−0,021	−0,004	−0,021	−0,810	−0,011	−0,009	0,036	0,001	−0,011
23	20.04.2014	BJK	1–1	O	−0,013	0,225	−0,013	−0,025	−0,572	−0,025	0,009	−0,099	0,010	0,000
24	02.11.2014	BJK	0–2	FB	0,000	−0,325	0,007	0,009	1,732	0,015	0,008	−0,320	0,014	−0,007

Tab. 3:

					GS			FB			BJK			BIST
	Match Date	H	Score	Win	Return	Vol	Ab Returns	Return	Vol	Ab Returns	Return	Vol	Ab Returns	Returns
1	04.04.2004	GS	2–1	BJK	−0,008	−0,750	−0,001	−0,016	−0,784	−0,009	−0,009	−0,730	−0,002	−0,008
2	19.09.2004	BJK	0–0	O	0,007	1,178	0,029	−0,050	0,129	−0,028	−0,010	−0,310	0,012	−0,022
3	05.03.2005	GS	0–1	GS	0,059	0,573	0,054	0,008	−0,206	0,003	0,097	0,968	0,092	0,005
4	10.12.2005	GS	2–3	GS	0,000	−0,364	−0,019	0,000	−0,656	−0,019	−0,036	1,145	−0,055	0,019
5	07.05.2006	BJK	1–2	GS	0,008	0,201	−0,003	0,017	0,322	0,006	−0,017	−0,434	−0,028	0,011
6	17.09.2006	GS	0–1	GS	−0,007	0,745	−0,009	0,004	0,102	0,002	−0,007	−0,581	−0,009	0,003
7	03.03.2007	BJK	2–1	BJK	0,006	−0,088	0,027	0,005	−0,370	0,025	−0,015	−0,270	0,005	−0,020
8	29.09.2007	GS	1–2	GS	0,000	2,149	−0,003	0,009	−0,098	0,007	−0,004	−0,560	−0,007	0,003
9	02.03.2008	BJK	1–0	BJK	0,000	−0,022	0,032	0,005	−0,019	0,037	0,051	4,442	0,083	−0,032
10	21.12.2008	GS	2–4	GS	0,008	5,268	0,009	0,006	1,686	0,006	−0,008	1,158	−0,007	0,000
11	24.05.2009	BJK	2–1	BJK	−0,008	−0,719	−0,019	0,029	−0,542	0,017	−0,017	−0,116	−0,028	0,011
12	12.09.2009	GS	0–3	GS	0,032	2,003	0,034	0,025	0,857	0,027	−0,025	0,704	−0,023	−0,002
13	21.02.2010	BJK	1–1	O	−0,016	0,667	−0,003	0,025	0,528	0,038	−0,030	−0,197	−0,016	−0,014
14	28.11.2010	GS	2–1	BJK	−0,030	0,341	0,002	−0,030	0,825	0,001	−0,012	6,592	0,019	−0,031
15	30.04.2011	BJK	2–0	BJK	0,023	0,738	0,019	−0,034	−0,540	−0,039	0,072	2,775	0,068	0,005

16	20.11.2011	BJK	0–0	O	−0,072	0,020	−0,040	−0,052	−0,147	−0,020	−0,056	−0,369	−0,024	−0,032
17	26.02.2012	GS	2–3	GS	0,010	−0,261	0,025	−0,060	−0,720	−0,045	−0,006	3,010	0,010	−0,015
18	16.04.2012	BJK	0–2	GS	0,007	0,663	0,004	−0,028	−0,002	−0,031	−0,025	0,657	−0,028	0,003
19	06.05.2012	GS	2–2	O	−0,060	−0,366	−0,056	0,079	2,777	0,083	0,008	0,061	0,011	−0,003
20	26.08.2012	BJK	3–3	O	−0,013	−0,310	−0,018	0,002	−0,541	−0,002	0,000	0,141	−0,004	0,004
21	27.01.2013	GS	1–2	GS	−0,011	2,210	0,031	−0,028	−0,162	0,014	−0,050	−0,377	−0,007	−0,042
22	22.09.2013	BJK	0–3	GS	0,004	−0,187	0,017	0,007	0,828	0,021	−0,114	0,051	−0,100	−0,014
23	22.02.2014	GS	0–1	GS	−0,004	−0,345	−0,009	0,000	−0,181	−0,005	−0,015	−0,351	−0,020	0,005
24	04.01.2015	BJK	0–2	GS	−0,003	1,266	−0,014	0,010	2,368	−0,001	−0,033	1,322	−0,045	0,012

time period of the match (-1,+1) average abnormal return of the stocks are GS 0,0036898, FB 0,0036122 and BJK -0,0043273.

6 Conclusion

We examined football matches in Turkey 3 big clubs played each other. This specifically named derby matches. It is important for investors because of income of matches. Many fans, many advertisement income, federations payments... There is a huge economy on this matches. On the other side supporters emotions is important factor of this clubs. So, are these supporters act emotional on markets after or before this matches?

In this study we tested the abnormal returns of the football clubs stocks after derby games. And we want to show that with this study, whether stocks that playing against teams are effect match score in addition third teams stock returns are effect. Results showed that after Galatasaray Fenerbahçe match investors 3 team has negative returns. Respectively Galatasaray, Fenerbahçe and Beşiktaş effected negative after this derby game. And after the Fenerbahçe Beşiktaş derby game Galatasaray and Fenerbahçe effected positively and Beşiktaş effected negatively, Latest derby game same results founded. After Beşiktaş Fenerbahçe derby Galatasaray and Fenerbahçe effected positive and Beşiktaş effected negatively. This results show that after derby games football teams stocks abnormal returns has effects by the score and After derbies Beşiktaş stocks are more effects than the other teams stocks.

Bibliography

Ashton, J. K., Gerrard, B., & Hudson, R. (2003). Economic Impact of National Sporting Success: Evidence from the London Stock Exchange. Applied Economics Letters 10, 783–785.

Aygören, H., Uyar, S. ve Sarıtaş, H. (2008). Yatırımcılar Futbol Maçlarından Etkilenir mi? İstanbul.

Baur, D. Mckeating, C. (2009). The Benefits of Financial Markets: A Case Study of European Football Clubs.

Berument, H., Ceylan, N.B., Gözpınar, E. (2006). Performance of Soccer on The Stock Market: Evidence From Turkey, The Social Science Journal 43, pp. 695–699.

Berument, H., Başak Ceylan, N. ve Gözpınar, E. (2006). Performance of Soccer on the Stock Market: Evidence from Turkey. The Social Science Journal. 43, 695–699.

Campbell, J., Lo, A. and MacKinlay, A. (1997). The Econometrics of Financial Markets, 2nd edn, Princeton University Press, Princeton N.J.

Demirhan, Dilek (2013). Stock Market Reaction to National Sporting Success. Pamukkale Journal of Sports Sciences, Vol: 4, No: 3, pp. 104–118.

Menkul Kıymetler Borsası'nda bir Uygulama. H.Ü. İktisadi ve İdari Bilimler Dergisi. 26 (1), 121–137.

Stadtmann, G. (2003). An Empirical Examination of the News Model: The Case of Borussia Dortmund GmbH & Co. KGaA.

Stephen, Brown J., Jerold, Warner B. (1985). Using Daily Stock Returns: The Case of Event Studies. Journal of Financial Economics, Volume 14, Issue 1, March, Pages 3–31

Stephen, Brown J., Jerold, Warner B. (1980). Measuring Security Price Performance. Journal of Financial Economics, Volume 8, Issue 3, September 1980, Pages 205–258.

Uludağ, B.K. & Varan, S., (2013). Futbol Maç Sonuçlarının 4 Büyüklerin Hisse Senedi Getirilerine Etkisi. In 17.Finans Sempozyumu. Muğla.

Ali Konak

Electronic Commerce (E-Commerce)

1 Definition of Electronic Commerce

At present, expressions of e-commerce are very similar to each other, with various definitions being made by different persons and organizations. Sarısakal and Aydın (2003, p. 83) defined e-commerce as sale, purchase, order and delivery by traditional means through an electronic network. Whereas, Turban and King (2003, p. 9) defined e-commerce as the production, advertisement, sale and distribution of services and products through electronic media and telecommunication networks, while Gottschalk (2006, p. 15) defines e-commerce as an important concept referring to the purchase, sale or exchange of products, services and information via computer networks. In e-commerce, promotions and sale of products and services for customers, along with their payments relating to goods and services, are provided in order to solve the problems that customers face with. All processes such as customers support and delivery of the products are carried out via internet (Büyükyıldırım, 2014, p. 4). The similar point in the definitions of e-commerce made by various institutions and the individuals is the production of goods and services, the marketing, distribution and processes related to payments are conducted whether in the form of closed or open network environments (Kalaycı, 2008, p. 141). In this context, in summary, it is possible to express e-commerce, all kinds of goods and services to be sold via internet.

2 Scope of Electronic Commerce

Electronic commerce began being used in the late 1970's, with the development of electronic data interchange (EDI) system for small businesses having high installation costs in the United States (Çetin, 2014, p. 67). Whereas Today e-commerce has greatly extended it is scope. In the context of definition made in relation to e-commerce, it is possible to say that the electronic transactions of commercial effects enter into the scope of e-commerce (Özbay and Devrim, 2000, p. 33). The ordering and delivery of goods and services outline the scope of e-commerce (Arıkan, 2001). Most broadly, the scope of e-commerce includes the trade of goods (movable, immovable) and services (information services, consulting, finance, law, health, education, transport etc), written text converted to digital format, audio, processing and communicating video format, product design, production marketing directly to consumers, shipment, tracking, promotions, advertisements, ordering and information services contracts, banking and funds transfer, custom clearance, joint design development and engineering, public procurement, electronic money (virtual money) release, electronic stock exchange and stock markets, auctions, digital signatures, e-notary, taxation, and tax collection, transfer of intellectual property rights, leasing etc. (Aktan and Arslan 2002, p. 85; Korkmaz, 2004, pp. 7–8). This reflects the operational simplicity of the technology over the activities.

3 Stages of Electronic Commerce

Both in individual and institutional sense, e-commerce is the process taking place after a series of operations which is held among the business parties. This process begins with the exchange of information and documents related to commercial activities carried out over computer networks. Afterwards, ordering electronically, billing, contracting, insurance, shipping and payment processes are performed. In later stages, the processes like gaining digital status for written signature, the adoption of electronic records as documents, customs, legislation and considering the issues such as taxation, which is authorized by the state according to International Regulations are arranged. At the final step, the information and documents are exchanged securely through the internet and the trade of goods and the services have been carried out (Ölçer and Özyılmaz, 2007, p. 77).

In addition to these steps, it is also possible to say that there are three dimensions of electronic commerce (Schuknecht and Perez-Esteve, 1999, p. 2; Koçak, 2008, p. 20). The first stage is advertisement and the information covering stage of e-commerce prior to buying. The second stage is the ordering, goods receipt and payments including acquisitions phase. The third stage is delivering stage (Kayabaşı, 2010, pp. 22–23).In short, the stages can be arranged in order as; the research stage of procedures and consumers or buyers or sellers, the agreement of order and payment stage between the parties and the stage of distribution of the goods to the recipients.

4 Products and Services Appropriate for E-Commerce

Electronic commerce structure and properties are better suited to some sectors in terms of application and the rate of success in these industries is higher. At this point, it is possible to group the commercial products suitable for e-commerce and products which are non-complaint. Pırnar (2005:35–36) has ordered the products appropriate for e-commerce activities and better suited for selling as follows;

1) Commercial products like books, magazines. Videos, CD's
2) Services which don't need purchasing the products (travel services, consulting, insurance)
3) Hunting supplies entering the special interest groups such as sports equipment products.
4) The same number of products purchased at regular intervals such as spare parts and office supplies.
5) Tickets of transportation, entertainment and sports events.

6) Technological products such as computers, cameras, mobile phones and software programs.
7) Products that are rare in markets such as out of print publications and rare stamps.

These products are the reflection of the personal preference and show the ease of accessibility to these products electronically. In addition, Pırnar (2005:36) has also listed the products which are not appropriate for e-commerce and which have less sales ratio on internet as;

1. Products that are difficult to transport such as furniture, white appliances etc.
2. Legally forbidden products such as drugs, explosives etc.
3. The products tested and rehearsed prior to buying such as clothing and shoes

The lack of opportunity for testing the products by customers constitutes the most important obstacle to the failure of these products for becoming a subject to e-commerce.

5 Electronic Trading Tools

Today, e-commerce can be performed by conventional and modern means. Kayıhan and Yıldız (2004, p. 42) listed the means of classic e-commerce as car, phone, fax, television, electronic payment, automated teller machines (ATM), money transfer system (credit cards, pos machines) while the means of modern commerce as internet, intranet and extranet. Due to the popularity of classic e-commerce and the carrying out of e-commerce with the modern means, a detailed description is given for these means.

Internet is the most widely used e-commerce tool today. At this point, it is useful to clarify some applications utilized while the internet is used. WWW (World Wide Web-World Wide Network) which is the best important of these applications provides to the user all kinds of information at the internet. Web pages are also displayed with HTTP (Hasıloğlu, 1999, p. 25). After the internet, intranet is most widely used application in the e-commerce, which is a derivative of the internet. The intranet concept is known as an abbreviation of the phrase IntraNetwork. It is an advanced computer network model within the business field. All individuals can benefit from the internet but intranet can only be used by special individuals who have access to the network facilities and have memberships. Members can access the relevant web content by filling in the membership form and password-controlled (Elibol and Kesici, 2004, p. 314). It reduces the workload of the business and provides ease of communication with the customers.

An another application used in e-commerce is the Extranet. Extranet is a private network where users can share their information and data with their departments, users and other businesses that they work with, via the Internet. It is closed to the third parties. Netscape, Oracle, Java Script and Corba can be mentioned as examples (Budak, 2010, pp. 27–28). It is the order provider in the interdepartmental electronic media communication.

6 Types of Electronic Commerce

It is possible to group electronic commerce considering its parties. Within this context, it is possible to group the types of e-commerce as below:

i. E-commerce from consumer to consumer (C2C)
ii. E-commerce from business to consumer (B2C)
iii. E-commerce among businesses (B2B)
iv. E-commerce from consumer to government (C2G)
v. E-commerce from business to government (B2G).

C2C (Consumer to Consumer): It is a type of commerce developed among consumers. Websites such as "sahibinden.com ve letgo," etc. can be given as example. With accelerating applications developed by companies like E-Bay or QXL, it is called in many countries as Customer Auction Bazaar (Saydan, 2008, p. 387).A company undertaking consumer to consumer e-commerce, has in fact not have any goods and services to sell. The only purpose is the meeting of buyer and seller.

B2C (Business to Consumer): In this type of e-commerce, goods and services go directly to the final consumer. In terms of the growth of the business markets, consumers are profitable in terms of having the chance of getting rid of too many people. This practice involves companies selling products directly to consumers via the internet. Amazon.com is the world biggest B2C site. This e-commerce application from business to consumer, is the second biggest application group in terms of e-commerce. Shopping platforms like Amazon, Ebay and n11.com, Gittigidiyor ve Hepsiburada.com from Turkey, are the bridges between seller and consumer (Gökgül, 2014, p. 49).E-commerce in type of B2C, is a continuous growing type of e-commerce.

B2B (Business to Business): It is called and well-known as e-commerce and is the most preferred type of commerce. This type of commerce which is considered business to business is undertaken by sector portals and their own sites (Sarısakal and Aydın, 2003, p. 84). B2B, can be defined as transactions among businesses directly on Networks. This application provides decreasing of commerce communication costs, increasing of productivity, easiness of monitoring of profit and stocks, being strong in sector, opportunity to obtain new markets and new customers in times of crisis. It has the most value in terms of financial aspects. Compared to e-commerce due to customers, B2B has a wider scope and has larger effects considering businesses. That is why B2B, composes the %80 of the e-commerce activities revenue (Saydan, 2008, p. 387). The reason why B2B has a big market is that, since sale of product has been realized among businesses, wholesalers and retailers, values of transactions ad amounts that have been paid, are realized high.

C2G (Customer to Goverment): It can be defined as an application to allow governments to give faster and interactive responses in the relations of government via electronic networks (Ekici, 2013, p. 70). Like in e-devlet, it is seen in applications to exercising of public services on net. Especially electronic application of driving licenses, passports, marriage, birth and death registries can be given as example.

B2G (Business to Government): At this commercial application type which is defines coming together of businesses and public institutions in electronic environment and involving commercial transactions between the parties;

i. Public procurements may be announced in electronic environment
ii. Bids can allowed in electronic environment
iii. Tax can be paid in electronic environment
iv. Customs transactions can be undertaken in electronic environment
v. Social security transactions can be exercised in electronic environment

Transactions between the enterprise and the government are carried out in electronic environment in this system (Altınışık, 2003, p. 32). In this type of e-commerce, generally a public institution announces its procurements for any needs on internet and realizes trade with the company that delivers the best suitable bid.

7 Payment Methods in Electronic Commerce

There are many different payment methods in e-commerce besides cash payment (payment at door). But since trade has mostly been exercised in virtual environment, payments are also mostly exercised in virtual environment as well. Here are the most commonly used payment methods in electronic commerce:

i. Credit card
ii. Electronic money
iii. Electronic cheques
iv. Virtual credit card
v. Automatic cashier machines
vi. Electronic fund transfer
vii. Smart cards
viii. Mobile payment

Credit card is the most commonly used payment method in e-commerce. Since it has a worldwide valid standard payment infrastructure, caused credit cards to be the most commonly used payment method on internet. After shopping on internet, during the payment which will be done by credit cards, in order to avoid third parties to achieve the information related with credit card and to ensure payment safety, SSL and SET protocols, which are based on the logic of coding of card information, have been used. One other means of payment in electronic commerce is electronic money. Electronic money is a money unit, composed to be used in internet. We can define electronic money as shopping receipts in virtual environment. Electronic cheque is a payment method to allow the companies exercising e-commerce to accept the payments in cheque forms.

A virtual credit card is a credit card used only for internet shopping and the limit of the card is increased before shopping and the remaining limit is reset after shopping is completed. In this regard, the risks associated with the use of the card are minimized. Automatic cashier machines, which used to allow only for withdrawing money opportunity, are in time started to be used to deposit money from the account, to withdraw money from the account, to pay bills, to take information about account, to transfer funds among the accounts, to take cheque books and to apply for credits to certain amounts. Electronic Fund Transfer (EFT) is an e-commerce payment method that allows very fast transfer of monetary funds from one place to another as real money by using modern communication tools and computers instead of cash, cheques, payment orders that have been used in traditional banking (Zengin and Güngördü, 2013, p. 136). E-commerce can also be undertaken by methods such as smart cards and mobile phones. Generally, in online shopping, credit cards and at door payments are the most preferred methods of payment.

8 Advantages of Electronic Trade

E-commerce is both economical and has many positive effects on social life. E-commerce activities make it easier to trade existing business relationships between businesses, direct sales to customers from customers, and exchange transactions between consumers. Besides, e-commerce has the power to influence the commercial environment at national, regional and global level. Furthermore, e-commerce provides important opportunities in terms of improving business opportunities, allows increment of market share and purchasing of new income sources (İnternational Chamber of Commerce [ICC], 1999, pp. 10–11). The most important one of the opportunities that e-commerce provides to businesses is the opportunity to find new markets and new customers. Thanks to internet and e-commerce, consumers are able to follow new products and services and they are able to find products that they need cheaper, in shorter period in globalizing markets (Coşkun, 2004, p. 246). In another words, with e-commerce, in terms of businesses, customers and administrations, costs of the purchased goods and services decrease, the quality of the purchased goods and services increase and finally the speed of accessing to goods and services increase (Turban and King, 2003, p. 9).

Apart from afore-mentioned benefits of e-commerce, e-commerce also provides opportunity to customers to have information about the products in all markets in the globe and allows businesses to access in world markets. As the products with higher qualities in lower prices enter into markets, compatibility increases while costs of all commercial transactions decrease (Strauss and Frost, 2000, p. 15). Furthermore, it allows formation of closer relations among businesses and customers and thus allows companies to present custom designed products for customers. With this context, e-commerce will have a significant contribution to global economy in terms of economic efficiency, competitiveness, profitability and emerging of information society.

9 Disadvantages of Electronic Commerce

E-commerce is a type of business activity that has many advantages as well as a number of disadvantages. Security is at the forefront of these disadvantages.

Potential security issues and concerns about this issue while e-commerce is the most important hurdle affecting the success of e-commerce. Palumbo and Herbig (1998, pp. 253–261) have expressed that the security problems deriving from the use of credit card while especially purchasing goods and services from e-commerce, effects e-commerce negatively. Especially financial institutions being open to such risks, disturbs users technically as well as psychologically and creates unsafety among the potential e-commerce customers. That is why, the most important issue e-commerce has to solve, is the issue of safety (Olcay, 2006, p. 110). Safety perception is the problem to be solved in priority in shopping on internet.

One other disadvantage of e-commerce on the way of success is that consumers are unable to touch and experience the products. On this issue Kotler (2002) mentioned that, besides the fact that consumers were unable to touch, experience and see the real sizes of the problem, the fact that consumers could not have the products immediately also affected the e-commerce in significant amount. Before buying a product, consumers generally want to touch the item, and want to examine its texture, durability or similar characteristics, but this is not possible in online shopping. In e-commerce process, consumers have to purchase the products only based on visual examination without touching, feeling and trying.

One another valid problem in e-commerce, is emerged in the area of taxation. In terms of e-commerce, every country deals with taxation problems within its own legal framework. Developments in communication and information technologies provide great opportunities to taxation agencies on one hand, but on the other hand increase the possibilities of tax evasion and tax fraud (Yükçü and Gönen, 2009, p. 5). Since e-commerce is a global phenomenon, national level solutions being adopted by other companies would contribute to the effective solutions on taxation problems of e-commerce.

10 Effects of Electronic Commerce on International Trade

International trade has gained a great deal of momentum and momentum nowadays. It is possible to say that in such a development process, there are significant influences and contributions of e-commerce. Thanks to e-commerce, the process of economic globalization has been realized. In the most general sense, it is possible to express economic globalization as the integration of the world into a single market (Aydemir and Kaya, 2007, p. 268). By means of economic globalization, the economic intensification observed worldwide, has caused development of capital, products and services. Technological developments have significant contributions to this process and allow making of new commercial connections (Steger, 2009). But technological developments had different effects on countries. While some countries have been positively affected by technological developments and e-commerce activities, some others have been affected negatively. Especially for countries which are facing with capital problems and have current account deficits (especially developing countries), the access of foreign capital, negatively affects such countries' economies (Balkanlı, 2002, p. 15).

Despite these negative effects of e-commerce on economies of developing economies, it is possible to say that, there are some positive effects as well. By the help of new technologies, e-commerce has many effects economically such as decrease in manufacture and marketing costs, increasing of global competition, contribution to economic development (Chaston, 2004, p. 2). One other positive effect of e-commerce is on employment. By means of e-commerce, the new emerged trade type, emerging of new products, expanding of market share, increase of income and manufacture amounts and fall in prices, will contribute to increment of employment. Thus, increase in employment will cause increasing demand on foreign products and naturally increment of international trade as well.

Furthermore, by means of e-commerce, managements can be opened to international markets with very small costs, data processing and communication costs decrease and management of customer demands can be possible (Thomke and Hıppel, 2002, pp. 74–81). Especially by means of e-commerce, removing of borders among states, gives great opportunities to managements in terms of marketing and manufacture. This helps businesses to exercise serial production and thus to minimize the costs and to be able to reach new customer groups. Addition to that, by providing of fast, safe and efficient share of information and knowledge in trade, the management of supply/purchase chain becomes easier (Cherian, 1999). In addition, e-commerce emerged with the contribution of technology in trade, has allowed the goods and services manufactured by the businesses to be sold on national and international markets and has encouraged the businesses to engage in activities on international fields (Gülmez, 2007, p. 339). In case all these components are undertaken with attention in efficient way, e-commerce will contribute to the developments of economies of countries.

11 Concluding Remark

In transformation from industrial society to information society, e-commerce, taking the place of traditional trading methods, cause redefinition of trade and different approaches to the concept of market. Electronic commerce cause acceleration in transition period from traditional trade perception to access to new economy. By means of information society, manufacture undertaken in any part of the world is transferred to another part of the world and thus global interaction occurs. E-commerce while presenting some advantages to consumers and businesses (SME's), at the same time brings some disadvantages along. In order to eliminate the disadvantages deriving from e-commerce, there is the need of international level arrangements and efficient safety applications and especially for the issue of safety, important steps have been taken. Besides, trade in internet environment has some social impacts as well as economic ones. It is possible to say that, today e-commerce has become a phenomenon that increases international trade volume, accelerates trade and contributes to the development of countries.

Bibliography

Aktan, B. and Arslan, A. (2002). Use of internet in business life and an overview to the electronic commercial, *Standard (Economic and Technical Journal)*, 41(490), 84–88.

Altınışık, U. (2003). *Electronic contracts*, Ankara: Seçkin Publishing.

Arıkan, A. S. (2001). *Electronic trade, law ve notary. Symposium of electronic developments and law*, In the symposium book (pp.13–52), Ankara: Publication of Notary Law Research Institute Foundation.

Aydemir, C. and Kaya, M. (2007). The globalızatıon concept and ıts economıcal sıde, *Electronic Journal of Social Sciences*, 6(20), 260–282.

Balkanlı, A. O. (2002). On determining factors of global economy, *Journal of Uludag University Economy And Society*, 21(1), 13–26.

Budak, B. (2010). *E-commerce (trade on ınternet)*, İstanbul: Etap Publishing.

Büyükyıldırım, Ü. (2014). *E-commerce for the beginners (basic application guide for e-commerce investors*, Longplay Digital Services Agency,.

Chaston, L. (2004). *Small business e-commerce management*, London: Palgrave Macmillan,.

Cherian, E. J. (1999). Electronic Commerce Changes Organizational Structures. Working Paper.

Coşkun, N. (2004), Fundamental dynamics in the development of electronic commerce and obstacles in front of its development, *Journal of Cukurova University Social Sciences Institute*, 13(2), 243–257.

Çetin, H. (2014). Academıcıans' behavıours ın onlıne shoppıng and the dırectıng factors to onlıne shoppıng, *Journal of Suleyman Demirel University Economics And Administrative Sciences Faculty*, 19(4), 65–76.

Ekici, K. M. (2013). *E-commerce* (1. Print), Ankara: Savaş Publishing.

Elibol, H. and Kesici, B. (2004). Electronic commerce ın terms of modern businesses, *Journal Of Selcuk University Institution of Social Sciences.* (11), 303–329.

Gottschalk, P. (2006). *E-business strategy, sourcing and governance*, Hershey: Idea Group Publishing.

Gökgül, M. (2014). Electronic commerce in turkey and its advantages and disadvantages to the businesses, consumers. Unpublished Master Thesis, İstanbul: Istanbul Culture University.

Gülmez, M. (2007). Effects of ınternet on ınternational marketing: a conceptual study, *Selcuk Unıversıty Journal of Economics And Administrative Sciences*, (13), 337–367.

Hasıloğlu, S. B. (1999). *Elektronik ticaret ve stratejileri*, İstanbul: Türkmen Kitabevi

ICC (İnternational Chamber of Commerce), 1999, *A global action plan for electronic Commerce* (2nd Edition), Prepared By Business With Recommendations For Governments, https://cdn.iccwbo.org/content/uploads/sites/3/1999/10/A-Global-Action-Plan-for-Electronic-Commerce.pdf (Erişim: 18.05.2018)

Kalaycı, C. (2008), E-commerce and ıts effects on small to medıum sızed enterprıses(smes), *International Journal of Economic and Administrative Studies*, 1(1), 139–150.

Kayabaşı, A. (2010). Analysis of customer complaints and a field research on the logistics in electronic (online) shopping, *Journal of Business Research*, 2(2), 21–42.

Kayıhan, Ş. and Yıldız, H. (2004). *Law and tax dimension of electronic commerce* (1st Edition), Ankara: Seçkin Publishing.

Korkmaz, N. (2004). *E-commerce with questions, e-work*", İstanbul: Publication of Istanbul Trade Room (New Sequence Of Trends In Business Management), Publish No:2004–27.

Kotler, P. (2002). *Experts talking (very private analysis by the world's 10 most leading managing and ınternet experts)*, İstanbul: Capital Publishers.

Koçak, F.F., (2008), A new opportunıty ın marketıng of cosmetıcs: Electronıc commerce, *Journal of Commerce & Tourism Education Faculty*, (2), 15–33

Olcay, D. (2006). *Basics of e-commerce* (1st Edition), İstanbul: Pusula Publications.

Ölçer, F. and Özyılmaz, A. (2007). Elektronic commerce and its implementation in virtual organizations, *Journal of Suleyman Demirel University Economics And Administrative Sciences Faculty*, 12(2), 67–94.Özbay, A. and Devrim, J. (2000). *E-ticaret rehberi*, İstanbul: Hayat Publishing.

Palumbo, F. and Herbig, P. (1998). International marketing tool: the Internet. *Industrial Management & Data Systems*, 98(6), 253–261

Pırnar, İ. (2005). E-trade in Tourism Industry, *The International Journal of Economic and Social Research*, (1), 28–55.

Sarısakal, M.N. and Aydın, M. A. (2003). E-commerce's new face mobile trade, *Journal of Aeronautics and Space Technologies*, 1(2), 83–90.

Saydan, R. (2008). Perceıved rısks and benefıts by consumers ın onlıne purchasıng: A comparative study between online and non-online consumers, *Electronic Journal of Social Sciences*, 7(23), 386–402.

Schuknecht, L. & Pérez-Esteve, R. (1999). A quantitative assessment of electronic commerce, Geneva: World Trade Organization (WTO), Economic Research and Analysis Division, Staff Working Paper ERAD-99-01.

Steger, M. (2009). *Globalization: A very short ıntroduction* (3rd Edition), USA: Oxford University Press.

Strauss, J. and Frost, R. (2000). *E-marketing* (2nd Edition), New Jersey: Prentice-Hall Inc.

Thomke, S. H. and Hıppel, E. V. (2002). Customers as ınnovators: A new way to create value, *Harvard Business Review*, 80(4), 74–81.

Turban, E. and King, D. (2003). Introduction to e-commerce, Prentice Hall.

Yükçü, S. and Gönen, S. (2009). Suggestions For Accounting Applications Of Electronic Commerce İn Turkey, *Journal Of Ataturk University Faculty Of Economics And Administrative Sciences*, 23(2), 1–13.

Zengin, B. and Güngördü, A. (2013). A revıew on possible effects of electronic payment systems, *Gazi University Journal of Economics And Administrative Sciences*, 15(3), 129–150.

İsmail Dülgeroğlu

Green Consumption: Barriers and Drivers in Kırklareli

1 Introduction

The concept of environmentally consciousness or sustainable consumption is a matter that is closely watched by businesses, states and non-profit institutions. In some literature, the concept of "green" is used instead of "environmentally sensitive" or "sustainable" concepts. In this context, green consumption is sustainable and clean in all aspects (Hess, 2012: 23).

Although today, the importance of using green (non-harm to environment and society) products is accepted by everyone and the amount of green consumption is increased, the rate of using green products has not yet reached the desired level. As a matter of fact, green product consumption accounts for 4 % of total consumption (Ritter, Borchardt, Vaccaro, Pereira and Almeida, 2015: 508). Therefore it is needed to understand what the drivers and barriers are for green consumption. So that green consumption can be improved. In this study, it is aimed to measure awareness, availability, inertia and price sensitivity are whether barriers or drivers of green purchasing behaviour in Kırklareli.

2 Literature Review

Green advertising must be able to create a bond between products and the environment, attend as a campaign to promote a green lifestyle. As a result it can improve the corporate image of the company (Hasan and Ali, 2015: 466–67). Hence green advertising can lead to green consumption.

It is not easy for consumers to turn to green products and expect them to purchase green products. There is needed a transformation. There is also a share of settled-up consumption attitudes as this transformation is slow. It is not possible to explain consumer behaviours solely with attitudes, but some of the variables that affect consumer purchasing decision are purchasing power, expected quality of product, educational level of consumer, experience and culture. One of the most important variable that affects consumers' decision to consume a product is the price of the product and many studies have reported that prices of green products are higher than those of non-green ones (Polonsky and Rosenberger III, 2001).

The green marketing has been through three phases (Peattie, 2001 quoted by Moreno, Carreón and Moreno, 2016: 100). These are ecological green marketing, environmental green marketing and sustainable green marketing. In especially sustainable green marketing there is consumer biased view of the concept. The consumer is aware of the environmental impact of his/her consumptions (Moreno, et al., 2016: 100). Green consumerism motivates consumers to establish an environmentally friendly behaviour (Tseng, 2016: 325). In this study awareness refers to consumers' knowledge and recognition of green products. Availability refers to consumers' ability to reach green products. Price sensitivity is consumers' willing to pay lower prices. And also in this study inertia refers to consumers' personal effort to purchase green products.

3 Research Design

Onward part of the study sample, scale, hypothesis, method of the research and findings are included.

3.1 Sample

The universe of this research is Kırklareli. Kırklareli is a border city of Turkey to Bulgaria and Kırklareli is a neighbour city to İstanbul located in Marmara Province. Sampling is used in the research and sampling method is convenience sampling. Data were collected by face-to-face survey method. The number of the questionnaires collected is 664.

3.2 Scales

All the questions except the ones that revealed the demographic characteristics in the survey form were asked with Likert scale. The scales subject to the survey are below:

- Green purchasing behaviour scale was taken Lee's (2008: 580) and Giray, Ergen, and Bozkurt's (2012: 289) study. In Lee's (2008:580) study the green purchasing behaviour scale consists of 4 items. Giray et al. (2012: 289) used the same scale with 3 items and their adaptation is used in this study.
- Awareness, availability, inertia and price sensitivity scales were taken from Gleim, Smith, Andrews and Cronin Jr's (2013: Appendix Section A) article.

The variables/items used in the questionnaire are below with their legend:

- **Green Purchasing Behaviour**
  - o I prefer green products over non-green products when their product qualities are similar. (g1)
  - o I choose to buy products that are environmentally-friendly. (g2)
  - o I buy green products even if they are more expensive than the non-green ones. (g3)
- **Awareness**
  - o I can identify green products. (c1)
  - o I can recognize green products among other products. (c2)
  - o I am aware of green products. (c3)
  - o I do know the difference between green products and standard products. (c4)

- **Availability**
  - I can easily determine where I can purchase green products. (c5)
  - Buying green products is convenient. (c6)
  - Green products are easy to find. (c7)
  - I know where to find green products. (c8)
  - Green products are readily available. (c9)
- **Inertia**
  - Purchasing green products is a bother. (c10)
  - For me, the cost in time, effort, and grief to purchase green products is high. (c11)
  - It's just not worth the hassle to me to purchase green products. (c12)
- **Price Sensitivity**
  - When buying a brand I look for the cheapest brand available. (c13)
  - When it comes to buying things I rely heavily on price. (c14)
  - I tend to buy the lowest priced brand that will fit my needs. (c15)

3.3 Hypothesis of the Research

In the literature of green consumption there were used too many types of factors to measure drivers and barriers of green consumption. After a brief investigation of the literature according to green consumption, it is aimed to measure awareness, availability, inertia and price sensitivity are whether barriers or drivers of green consumption in Kırklareli.

3.4 Analysis Method

The demographic data were analysed by SPSS 20. Analysis was done by structural equation modelling. SmartPLS 2.0 software was used to perform the analysis (Ringle, Christian, Wende, Sven, and Will, Alexander, 2005). This method and software are preferred because the data do not show a normal distribution. SmartPLS 2.0 software performs bootstrapping to stop sampling problems and calculate t-values. The software is not subject to parametric assumptions because it uses the partial least squares method (Hair Jr, Sarstedt, Hoppikns and Kuppelwieser, 2014: 108–109).

3.5 Findings

Tab. 1 below shows the demographic status of subjects participating in the survey.

In addition to Tab. 1 above the age and average income of the participants can be included. The average age of the participants is 32. The average income of the participants is 2020 Turkish Liras.

Tab. 2 below has validity and reliability values. The analysis was performed with 664 sample counts and 5000 bootstrapping counts.

Tab. 1: Demographic descriptive statistics

Variable	Frequency	Percentage
Gender		
Male	353	53,2
Female	311	46,8
Marital Status		
Married	341	51,4
Single	323	48,6
Education		
Elementary	111	16,7
High School	232	34,9
Associate Degree	162	24,4
Bachelor Degree	133	20,0
Postgraduate Degree	26	3,9

Tab. 2: Scale validity and reliability values

	AVE	Composite Reliability	R^2	Cronbach's Alfa
Awareness	0,6979	0,9022	0,0000	0,8552
Availability	0,6004	0,8824	0,0000	0,8354
Inertia	0,6243	0,8313	0,0000	0,7086
Price Sensivity	0,7332	0,8918	0,0000	0,8184
Green Purchasing Behaviour	0,6002	0,8088	0,3308	0,6513

The factor loadings are expected to be greater than 0.70. All factor loads are greater than 0.70 as seen in Fig. 1 except g1 (Hair, et al., 2014: 111).

Composite reliability needs a value greater than 0.70 (Lowry, Gaskin, 2014: 137). All values are greater than 0.70, as shown in Tab. 2. It is expected that the extracted common variance (AVE) values are greater than 0.5 (Hair, et al., 2014: 111). As shown in Tab. 2, AVE values are greater than 0.50.

To ensure discriminant validity, the square root of the AVE values of each implicit variable must be greater than its correlation value (Hair, et al., 2014: 112). The root square of AVE values shown in Tab. 3 below are larger than their correlation values.

In Fig. 1 below, the structure of latent variables of the model is shown with standardized values.

Tab. 3: Discriminant validity table

	AVE				
Availability	**0,7748***				
Awareness	0,5964	**0,8354***			
Green Purchase	0,4532	0,5281	**0,7747***		
Inertia	−0,301	−0,1905	−0,1461	**0,7901***	
Price Sensivity	−0,061	−0,1513	−0,2167	0,2879	**0,8562***

* The square root of AVE values.

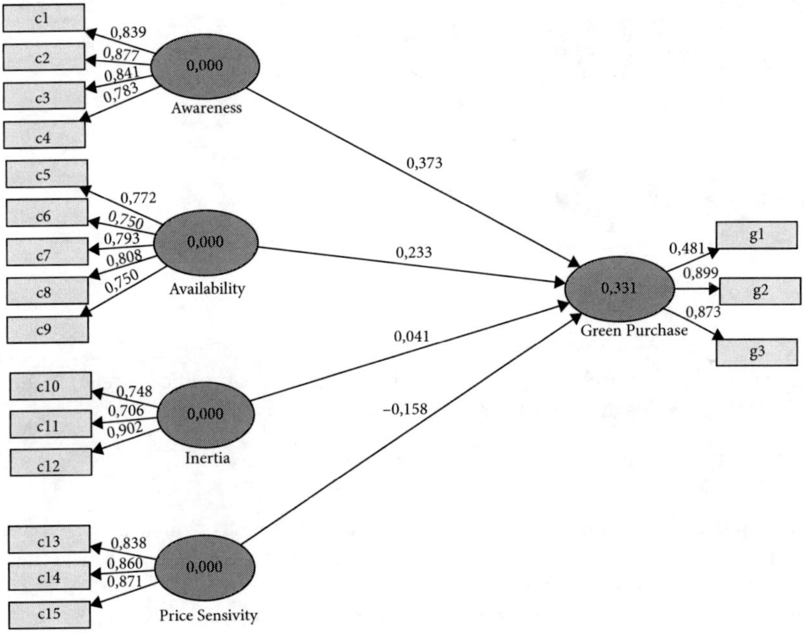

Fig. 1: Standardized values of the model

Awareness has a positive effect on green purchasing behaviour that is 0,373. Also availability has a positive effect on green purchasing behaviour that is 0,233. The challenging finding comes with price sensitivity. Price sensitivity has a negative effect on green purchasing behaviour and has a value of -0,158.

In Fig. 2 below, t-values of the model are shown. In Fig. 2 it is observed that all of t-values is greater than 1.96 except one. Every relationship is not significant.

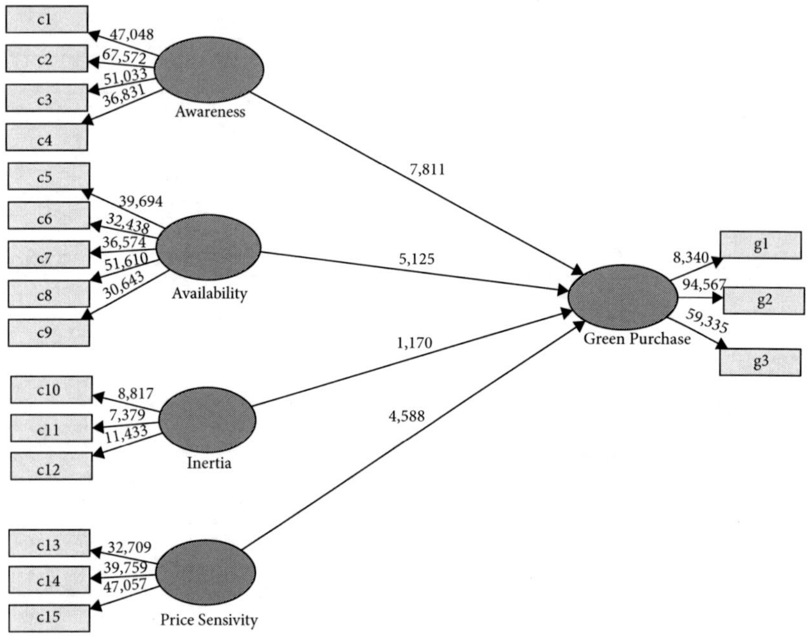

Fig. 2: T-values of the model

Inertia and green purchasing behaviour does not have a significant relationship. Other relationships are significant.

4 Result

Awareness of green consumption and availability of green consumption are found to have positive effects on green purchasing behaviour in Kırklareli. If awareness increases 1 unit then green purchasing behaviour increases 0,373 units. If availability increases 1 unit then green purchasing behaviour increases 0,233 units. Therefore investing in awareness of green consumption and availability of green consumption will improve green purchasing behaviour in Kırklareli and protect environment. Price sensitivity and green purchasing behaviour relationship have a challenging result in Kırklareli. If price sensitivity increases 1 unit then green purchasing behaviour decreases 0,158 units. According to this result pricing has a crucial place in green consumption. The participants of the survey are price sensitive. They don't want to pay more to get green products. As it is written before Kırklareli is a border city of Turkey to Bulgaria and Kırklareli is a neighbour city to İstanbul located in Marmara Province. Consequently Kırklareli can represent Turkey partially. The results of this research can be taken into consideration about what to do for improving green consumption in Turkey as a partial indicator. Hence while augmenting availability and awareness of green consumption, companies must keep prices the same to make green marketing in Kırklareli.

Bibliography

Giray, C., Ergen, A. and Bozkurt, F. (2012). "Yeşil Satın Alma Davranışını Paradigma, İmaj, Sorumluluk Ve Sağlık Üzerinden Açıklamaya Yönelik Bir Araştırma", 17. Ulusal Pazarlama Kongresi Bildiri Kitabı, Elhan Kitap Yayın Dağıtım, pp. 277–296.

Gleim, M. R., Smith, J. S., Andrews, D. and Cronin Jr, J. J. (2013). "Against the green: a multi-method examination of the barriers to green consumption", Journal of retailing, 89(1), pp. 44–61.

Hair Jr., J.F., Sarstedt, M., Hopkins, L. and Kuppelwieser, V.G. (2014). "Partial least squares structural equation modeling (PLS-SEM)", European Business Review, 26 (2), pp. 106–121.

Hasan, Z., and Ali, N. A. (2015). "The impact of green marketing strategy on the firm's performance in Malaysia", Procedia-Social and Behavioral Sciences, 172, pp. 463–470.

Hess, D. J. (2012). Good Green Jobs in a Global Economy: Making and Keeping New Industries in the United States. Cambridge, MA: MIT Press.

Lee, K. (2008)."Opportunities for green marketing: young consumers", Marketing Intelligence & Planning, 26(6), pp. 573 –586.

Lowry, P.B. and Gaskin, J. (2014). "Partial least squares (PLS) structural equation modeling (SEM) for building and testing behavioral causal theory: When to choose it and how to use it", IEEE Transactions on Professional Communication, 57 (2), pp. 123–146.

Moreno, F. M., Carreón, F. Á., and Moreno, S. M. (2016). "The adoption of the green marketing in the millennium generation", International Journal of Marketing Studies, 8(2), pp. 97–104.

Peattie, K. (2001). "Toward sustainability: the third age of green marketing", The Marketing Review, 2(2), pp. 129–146.

Polonsky, M. J. and Rosenberger III, P. J. (2001). "Reevaluating Green Marketing: A Strategical Approach", Business Horizons, 44(5), pp. 21–30.

Ringle, C.M., Wende, S. and Will, A. (2005). SmartPLS 2.0.M3. Hamburg: SmartPLS, http://www.smartpls.de.

Ritter, A. M., Borchardt, M., Vaccaro, G. L.R., Pereira, G. M. and Almeida, F. (2015). "Motivations for promoting the consumption of green products in an emerging country: exploring attitudes of Brazilian consumers", Journal of Cleaner Production, 106, pp. 507–520.

Tseng, C. H. (2016). "The effect of price discounts on green consumerism behavioral intentions", Journal of Consumer Behaviour, 15(4), pp. 325–334.

Derya Öztürk

The Effect of Success Factors of New Product Development on Product Development Performance: An Application on White Goods Sector

1 Introduction

Rapid technological advances, changes in customer preferences, increased competition in the information economy (Onurlubaş et al., 2015:43), transformations in marketing practices, globalization, economic growth, increased international competition and pace of communication have led to the intensification of competition among companies on a global scale. To keep pace with this global transformation, companies should focus on making a difference (Hancıoğlu and Yeşilaydın, 2016:106), and one of the ways they can achieve this is by developing new products. New product development (NPD) is a crucial value creation strategy that helps companies to survive, compete and advance in the global market. This value creation strategy can also be viewed as a product innovation that allows companies to improve the quality of a product or to develop a completely new product and introduce it to the market (Hancıoğlu and Atay, 2017). In general, NPD involves all activities necessary to launch a different and new concept to the market. These activities include the generation of a new product idea, business operation analysis, marketing studies, engineering design activities, preparation of production planning, approval of product design, and implementation of all these plans in a harmonious way (www.ekosinerji.com, 2018). Crawford and Di Benedetto (2008) define new product development as a 5-step process; opportunity identification and selection, concept generation, concept/project evaluation, product development and product launch. Companies can reduce the uncertainty about the success of a new product and minimize the risk by making the right decisions at different stages of the NPD process. The ability of companies to make the right decisions depends on to what extent they take into account success factors of new product development. Many studies investigate success factors of new product development and address various factors, and especially highlight cross functional integration and organization of project teams (Lee et al., 2000; Ernst, 2002). Many studies (Griffin, 1997; Souder et al., 1997; March-Chordà et al., 2002; Cooper et al., 2004; Sherman et al., 2005; Jugend and Silva, 2012) state that cross functional integration has a positive effect on new product outcomes (Mendes and Ganga, 2013:85). Other key factors determining success are having a solid product strategy (Barczak et al., 2009; Cormican et al., 2009) and selecting products effectively (Barczak et al., 2009; Nicholas et al., 2011). Monitoring a well-functioning product development process (Barczak et al., 2009; Cormican et al., 2009), marketing skills (Rabor et al., 2011; Cooper and Brentani, 1991), technology sources (Cooper, 1984), effective communication (Barczak et al., 2009; Nicholas et al., 2011) and inter-departmental team work (Barczak et al., 2009; Cormican et al., 2009; Nicholas et al., 2011) are also important success factors of new product development. Collaborating with customers and including especially those referred to as lead users in the new product development process are also significant (Altun et al., 2013; Gruner et al., 2000).

Companies that combine technological innovations with their experiences and develop new products to meet ever-changing consumer needs achieve competitive advantage over their rivals. This is why product development processes occupy an important place in the agenda of companies. New product development activities are organized around the interdisciplinary approach of the R&D department, and systematic and creative team work from the outset of the process. Because, firms which realize R&D activities investigate innovations and they stay one step ahead in the way of using innovations (Tekin and Nas İlhan, 2017:1190). One of the sectors where R&D activities are extensively used is the white goods sector. Intensive cooperation between companies in the fields of R&D, production, sales, marketing and technology, and large-scale production and marketing of a wide range of products are important and distinctive characteristics of the white goods sector (Koçman, 2007:6). Having started its manufacturing activities as an assembly industry at the beginning of the 1960s, the Turkish white goods industry has come to a point where it develops its own design and technology, and even sells it to the world, and therefore, has had significant achievements in its manufacturing activities today. Thanks to the brands it has introduced so far, the Turkish white goods industry has managed to increase its share in the world markets, especially in the European Union countries (Yaşar, 2010:151). With its production technologies, product designs, increased production and export capacity, the Turkish white goods industry today has a distinguished place in the Turkish manufacturing sector. The aim of this study is to determine the effect of the success factors of new product development on the product development performance of a leading company operating in the white goods sector in the organized industrial zone in the city of Manisa. I believe that this study will guide companies operating in the white goods sector to make effective decisions in their new product development processes.

2 Methodology

2.1 Research Objective and Importance

The aim of this study is to determine the effect of the success factors of new product development on the product development performance of a leading company operating in the white goods sector. The findings from this study will make important contributions to businesses operating in the sector in terms of improving product development performance in the decisions they will take during new product development process.

2.2 Population and Sample

The research population consisted of employees who contribute to the new product development process in the R & D department of a company operating in the white goods sector in Manisa Organized Industrial Zone. The study sample consisted of 100 employees working in that department. All participants were recruited using simple random sampling. The name of the company was kept confidential on request.

2.3 Data Collection

Data were collected through face-to-face interviews using questionnaire forms prepared to measure the research variables. The company was visited in November-December of 2017. They were informed of the purpose of the survey to make sure that participants could answer the questions in a healthy way. The survey consisted of three parts. The first part included questions regarding information on demographics while the second part was a scale developed by Mendes and Ganga (2013) to measure success factors of new product development. This scale consisted of 7 factors; marketing skills, product strategy, technology sources, company skills, project leader skill, functional integration and organization of the project team. The third part of the survey was a product development performance scale including product, process and financial performance measures developed by Perçin (2006). The items in the survey were scored on a 5-point Likert scale; strongly disagree (1), disagree (2), neither agree nor disagree (3), agree (4), strongly agree (5). Percentage,

Tab. 1: Demographics of Participants and New Product Idea Sources

		%			%
Job Positions of Participants	R&D manager	6.0	Gender	Woman	49.0
	R&D engineer	12.0		Man	51.0
	R&D specialist	21.0		**Total**	**100.0**
	R&D design engineer	13.0			
	R&D technician	1.0	Years of Employment	1-3	18.0
	R&D researcher	1.0		4-6	36.0
	Production engineer	5.0		7-9	23.0
	Mold raw material engineer	3.0		≥10	23.0
	Mechanical engineer	7.0		**Total**	**100.0**
	Lab technician	6.0			
	Lab engineer	7.0	Education level	Bachelor's degree	23.0
	EMC engineer	2.0		Graduate degree	77.0
	OMC engineer	3.0		**Total**	**100.0**
	Technical personnel	12.0			
	Program manager	1.0	What is the origin of a new product idea in your company? *	Top management	35.0
	Total	**100.0**		Engineer (R&D)	60.0
				Rivals	45.0
Age	18-25	5.0		Marketing managers	14.0
	26-30	33.0		Customers	28.0
	31-35	24.0		Academia	11.0
	36-40	24.0		Engineer	17.0
	≥41	14.0		Distribution network	6.0
	Total	**100.0**		Integrated producing company	2.0

* *More than one one option marked*

mean, factor analysis, correlation analysis and stepwise regression analysis were used. Data were analyzed using the SPSS, version 24 (IBM Inc., Chicago, IL, USA) at a significance level of 0.05.

3 Findings

Tab. 1 shows the demographics of the employees who contribute directly or indirectly to the product development process of the company operating in the white goods sector in the organized industrial zone in the city of Manisa.

Tab. 1 shows that 21 % of participants are R&D specialists, 13 % R&D design engineers, 12 % R&D engineers and 12 % technical personnel. 49 % of participants are women. The majority (48 %) of participants contributing to the new product development process are between the ages of 31 and 40 years while only 5 % are between the ages of 18 and 25 years. 36 % of participants have been employed for 4 to 6 years while 23 % have been employed for 10 years and more. The majority (77 %) of participants have a master's degree. Having a large number of young and educated employees is a great advantage for companies with great ideals and a future goal to become a technology giant. The results show that new product ideas are usually generated by engineers working in the R&D department (60 %), which can be regarded as a competitive advantage in an environment where competition is intensifying and the number of companies is increasing because today competitive advantage requires continuous introduction of new products to the market and systematic R&D activities. To this end, companies are urged to make continuous innovation and undertake R&D activities. Tab. 2 shows participants' views of success factors of new product development and product development performance.

The validity and reliability of the scales were assessed using an exploratory factor analysis and Cronbach-alpha coefficients, respectively. First, exploratory factor analysis was performed on two scales to assess the structure of the relationship between the variables. Principal component analysis and varimax rotation were used to examine the factor structure, and those with an eigenvalue greater than 1 were chosen to determine the number of factors. In factor analysis, dependent and independent variables were analyzed separately. Tab. 3 shows the results of analysis of the success factors (independent variables) of new product development. The total variance explained was 69.33 % and all factor loadings were above 0.5 (Tab. 3). In factor analysis, factor loadings ≥ 0.5 are considered to be quite good (Kalaycı, 2005). According to the factor analysis, the KMO and Bartlett's Test value was 0.791, indicating the suitability of the factor analysis.

Tab. 4 shows the results of factor analysis of product development performance (dependent variable), indicating that all factor loadings were above 0.5 and the total variance explained was 59.59 %. According to the factor analysis, the KMO and Bartlett's Test value was 0.547, indicating the suitability of the factor analysis.

Afterwards, reliability analysis was performed, and the results are given in Tab. 5. The reliability of a scale depending on the reliability coefficient varies as follows:

Tab. 2: Participants' Views of Success Factors of New Product Development and Product Development Performance (%)

FACTORS		Strongly Disagree	Disagree	Neither Agree nor Disagree	Agree	Strongly Agree
Marketing Skills MS	Assessment of the market potential of the project was properly made.	0.0	6.0	22.0	50.0	22.0
	This kind of product was highly requested by the customers.	1.0	7.0	25.0	50.0	17.0
	User requirements for the product were comprehended and translated.	1.0	8.0	21.0	52.0	18.0
Product Strategy PS	The product provides solutions the same as, but cheaper than its rivals do.	4.0	11.0	21.0	47.0	17.0
	The product exhibits superior technical performance to its rivals	0.0	6.0	25.0	47.0	22.0
	The product was clearly described using competitive strategies	0.0	3.0	16.0	49.0	32.0
Technology Sources TS	Employment of third-party employees to provide skills the company lacks	0.0	7.0	24.0	36.0	33.0
	Implementation of licensing policies	3.0	14.0	16.0	38.0	29.0
	Collaboration and teaming with customers	7.0	12.0	15.0	40.0	26.0
	Collaboration and teaming with suppliers	5.0	11.0	16.0	40.0	28.0
	Collaboration and teaming with other entities	5.0	11.0	17.0	44.0	23.0
	Internal development (technology entirely developed by the company)	4.0	8.0	18.0	45.0	25.0
Company Skills CS	The Technical Assistance team had the technical skills	2.0	6.0	15.0	46.0	31.0
	The Commercial team had the technical skills	1.0	6.0	20.0	49.0	24.0
	The Manufacturing team had the technical skills	1.0	4.0	17.0	47.0	31.0
Project Leader Skill PLS	The project leader had the technical skills	1.0	3.0	11.0	48.0	37.0
	The project leader had the interpersonal skills	1.0	0.0	9.0	40.0	50.0
	The leadership style adopted by the project leader was appropriate to encourage execution, communication and conflict management.	2.0	1.0	6.0	56.0	35.0
	The leadership style enabled team members to participate	1.0	1.0	9.0	57.0	32.0
	The staff development team was encouraged to carry out the project.	0.0	2.0	15.0	48.0	35.0
Functional Integration FI	Different areas/departments were involved in the project to perform the technical development activities (product design).	1.0	1.0	9.0	52.0	37.0
	Production and R&D were properly integrated in the project.	0.0	1.0	12.0	46.0	41.0
	Different areas/departments were involved in the project to undertake the objectives of idea generation and selection	0.0	3.0	8.0	50.0	39.0
	Commercial and R&D were properly integrated in the project.	0.0	0.0	9.0	47.0	44.0
	Different areas/departments were involved in the project to perform the feasibility analysis	0.0	1.0	11.0	48.0	40.0
	Different areas/departments were involved in the project to undertake the testing activities of the product/market	0.0	0.0	14.0	44.0	42.0
	Different areas/departments were involved in the project to perform the prototype development activities	0.0	0.0	14.0	44.0	42.0
Organization of the Project Team OPT	A functional structure was employed to carry out the project activities.	0.0	4.0	13.0	53.0	30.0
	A separate project structure was employed to carry out the project activities.	0.0	4.0	22.0	51.0	23.0
	A matrix structure was employed to carry out the project activities.	1.0	2.0	25.0	45.0	27.0
Product Development Performance PDP	Product reliability, which reflects the success of the new product, is an important indicator for the company.	0.0	1.0	16.0	45.0	38.0
	The engineering time and cost for new product development must be low.	3.0	8.0	17.0	48.0	24.0
	The development of the new product provides the projected profitability growth.	0.0	8.0	21.0	33.0	38.0

Performance (%)

- Not reliable if $0.00 \leq \alpha < 0.40$
- Reliability is low if $0.40 \leq \alpha < 0.60$
- Quite reliable if $0.60 \leq \alpha < 0.80$
- Highly reliable if $0.80 \leq \alpha < 1.00$ (Kalaycı, 2005; Yayla et al., 2009).

Tab. 3: Factor Analysis of New Product Development Success Factors

	Factors						
Scales	**MS**	**PS**	**TS**	**CS**	**PLS**	**FI**	**OPT**
MS1	.833						
MS2	.862						
MS3	.853						
PS1		.860					
PS2		.865					
PS3		.604					
TS1			.616				
TS2			.871				
TS3			.950				
TS4			.934				
TS5			.894				
TS6			.779				
CS1				.808			
CS2				.908			
CS3				.838			
PLS1					.721		
PLS2					.777		
PLS3					.756		
PLS4					.739		
PLS5					.560		
FI1						.577	
FI2						.650	
FI3						.635	
FI4						.573	
FI5						.719	
FI6						.792	
FI7						.684	
OPT1							.781
OPT2							.900
OPT3							.809
Total Variance Explained: 69.33%			Kaiser-Meyer-Olkin Measure of Sampling Adequacy (KMO Test): .791				
Bartlett's Test of Sphericity Approx. Chi-Square: 1891.387				Sig. .000			

MS: Marketing Skills, PS: Product Strategy; TS: Technology Sources, CS: Company Skills, PLS: Project Leader Skill, FI: Functional Integration, OPT: Organization of the Project Team

Tab. 4: Factor Analysis of Product Development Performance

Factors	
Scales	**PDP**
PDP1	.591
PDP2	.812
PDP3	.883

Total Variance Explained: 59.59 % Kaiser-Meyer-Olkin Measure of Sampling Adequacy (KMO Test): .547
Bartlett's Test of Sphericity Approx. Chi-Square: 56.226 Sig. .000

PDP: Product Development Performance

Tab. 5: Reliability Analysis

Variable Name	Number of Items in the Scale	Reliability Coefficient (α)
MS	3	.807
PS	3	.683
TS	6	.921
CS	3	.810
PLS	5	.760
FI	7	.787
OPT	3	.774
PDP	3	.658

Since the confidence coefficient (α) values for the independent variables (success factors of new product development) and dependent variable (product development performance) were ≥ 0.60, these scales were considered to be quite reliable. Regression analysis was conducted to assess the effect of success factors of new product development on product development performance. Regression analysis is a statistical method that is used to establish a cause and effect relationship between two variables, in other words, to explain the change in one by the change in the other. Providing more valid models related to the assessment of the effect of more than one independent variable on a dependent variable, multilinear regression analysis has become one of the most frequently used statistical procedures. Before performing multiple linear regression, it is necessary to check whether data provide the basic assumptions required for analysis (normality, multiple linear connectivity test, etc.) (Eroğlu, 2010:207). A number of tests were performed to check whether the data were suitable for analysis prior to regression analysis. The dataset was checked to see whether it had a multivariate normal distribution or not. Normality test was used to determine whether the data were normally distributed. The normal distribution of the data was based on skewness and kurtosis values (Kline, 2011:60). Skewness and kurtosis values in the range of -2 to +2 suggest that data meet the normality assumption (Hair et al., 2010:71) while those in the range of -3 to +3 suggest that variables show normal distribution (Kalaycı, 2010:209). The results in Tab. 6 show that the data have a normal or approximately normal distribution. Next, multicollinearity was checked using correlation coefficients. As can be seen in Tab. 6, the VIF value is smaller than 5 and the tolerance value is greater than 0.20, indicating that there was no multicollinearity problem. Afterwards, Durbin Watson (D-W) statistics were used to determine autocorrelation between variables. D-W statistics was around 2, indicating that there was no autocorrelation (Akgül and Çevik, 2005:316–317, Çetin et al., 2016:303).

Tab. 6: Descriptive Statistics and Correlation Values

Variable	Skewness	Kurtosis	VIF	Tolerance	X_{mean}	SD.	1	2	3	4	5	6	7	8
1.MS	−.740	.600	2.573	.389	3.80	.722	1							
2.PS	−.359	−.823	2.073	.482	3.86	.690	.677**	1						
3.TS	−.780	−.203	1.949	.513	3.77	.920	.624**	.455**	1					
4.CS	−1.012	1.869	1.693	.591	3.97	.759	.490**	.424**	.534**	1				
5.PLS	−1.080	2.909	1.793	.558	4.22	.541	.506**	.520**	.297**	.489**	1			
6.FI	−.859	1.225	1.292	.774	4.28	.464	.237*	.248*	.113	.168	.338**	1		
7.OPT	−.446	.513	1.226	.816	3.99	.659	.144	.204*	.217*	.105	.012	.325**	1	
8.PDP	−.708	−.007			4.01	.695	.380**	.422**	.399**	.260**	.204*	.301**	**.573****	1

Durbin-Watson (D-W): *1.958*

** $p<0.01$; * $p<0.05$

Tab. 7: Results of Stepwise Regression Analysis of Predictors of Product Development Performance

Model	R	R Square	Adjusted R Square	Std. Error of the Estimate	Durbin-Watson
1	.573[a]	.329	.322	.57270	
2	.652[b]	.425	.414	.53254	
3	.673[c]	.452	.435	.52260	1.979

[a] Predictors: (Constant), OPT
[b] Predictors: (Constant), OPT, PS
[c] Predictors: (Constant), OPT, PS, TS
[d] Dependent Variable: PDP

Tab. 6 shows the means and standard deviations of the new product development success factors and product development performance of the company. In the new product development process, the mean functional integration (X_{mean}: 4.28) and project leader skill (X_{mean}: 4.22) scores is very high while the mean scores of the factors, product development performance, organization of the project team, company skills, product strategy, marketing skills and technology sources are high. The Pearson correlation (r) coefficients in Tab. 6 show that all 7 success factors are statistically significantly and positively correlated with product development performance. There is a positive and moderate correlation between organization of the project team and product development performance. There is a weak correlation between product development performance and all factors except project leader skills. The correlation between product development performance and project leader skills is very weak.

Stepwise regression analysis was used to determine which of the independent variables better explain product development performance (dependent variable). In stepwise regression analysis, the independent variable with the highest correlation with product development performance was added to the model first. Tab. 6 shows that organization of the project team has the highest correlation with product development performance ($r= 0.573$; $p<0.01$). The stepwise regression was performed to determine the extent to which each independent variable explained product development performance. The total variance explained by the independent variables was determined. Tabs. 7 and 8 show the results.

Organization of the project team showed regression equality in the first model (Tabs. 7 and 8). R^2 is the coefficient of determination that indicates what percentage of the total variance is accounted for by all independent variables (factors). In models with multiple independent variables, R^2 is not sufficient, and therefore, it is more appropriate to interpret the data according to the adjusted R^2 value (Akgül and Çevik, 2005:333, Çetin et al., 2016:305). Organization of the project team accounted for 32.2 % of variance of product development performance (Adj.

Tab. 8: B and Beta Correlation Coefficients and Significance Levels of Variables

Model	Predictors	B	Std. Error	Beta	t	Sig.	Tolerance	VIF
1	(Constant)	1.596	.353					
	OPT	.605	.087	.573	6.927	.000	1.000	1.000
2	(Constant)	.634	.406		1.564	.121		
	OPT	.537	.083	.508	6.467	.000	.958	1.043
	PS	.320	.079	.318	4.042	.000	.958	1.043
3	(Constant)	.515	.402		1.283	.203		
	OPT	.511	.082	.484	6.216	.000	.939	1.065
	PS	.240	.086	.238	2.784	.006	.781	1.280
	TS	.141	.065	.186	2.174	.032	.777	1.287

[a] Dependent Variable: PDP

R^2 =0,322). In other words, the organization of the project team is a more powerful predictor of product development performance. The positive beta indicates that there is a linear relationship between the organization of the project team and product development performance, which means that the higher the organization of the project team, the higher the product development performance. In the second regression model, the variable of product strategy was also to the model, which resulted in an increase in the percentage of variance of product development performance explained from 32.2 % to 41.4 % (Adj. $R^2 = 0.414$). This indicates that the variable of product strategy explained about 9.2 % of variance of product development performance. The beta of 0.318 indicates that there is a positive correlation between product strategy and product development performance, which means that the higher the product strategy, the higher the product development performance. In the third regression model, the variable of technology sources was added to the model, which resulted in an increase in the percentage of variance of product development performance explained from 41.4 % to 43.5 % (Adj. R^2 = 0,435). This indicates that the variable of technology sources explained about 2.1 % of variance of product development performance. The beta of 0.186 indicates that there is a statistically significant and positive correlation between technology sources and product development performance (sig. = 0.032, $p < 0.05$) (Tab. 8).

4 Conclusion

This study examined the effects of success factors of product development performance on new product development in a company operating in the white goods sector in the city of Manisa. The results show that there is a statistically significant and positive correlation between success factors of product development performance and new product development and that the factor with the strongest effect on product development performance is the organization of the project team. There is a positive and moderate correlation between the company's organization of the project team and product development performance. In other words, the more importance given to the organization of the project team by the company, the better its product development performance in the new product development process. As new product development projects require the knowledge and collaboration of people from different branches, the realization of project activities requires the use of a variety of specialties. Matrix structure encourages relationships between project units and functional division members. A reasonable project team encourages information sharing, improves skills to solve development problems and facilitates an efficient integration between product and process technologies, and results in better product designs (Urban and Hippel, 1988). Also, new markets, new production vehicles, new sources, new sectors and new products effect the performance of export (Tekin and Hancıoğlu, 2017). Therefore, companies can improve their performance if they approach new product development processes in a systematic way and involve various organizational units in them. The stepwise regression analysis shows that the strongest predictor explaining product development performance is the organization of the project team. Product strategy and technology sources make 9.2 % and 2 % contributions, respectively, to the improvement of the product development performance of the company, the project team of which has a high level of organization. In general, a company should use competitive product strategies to produce and launch new products with superior technical performance and price advantages. In new product development processes, companies sometimes turn to external sources, such as licensing agreements or patent acquisitions, instead of developing their products by making use of their own research activities. Outsourcing allows companies not only to access new technologies but also to avoid the cost of keeping up with technology by benefitting from R&D activities of supplier companies.

Bibliography

Akgül, A. and Çevik, O. (2005). İstatistiksel Analiz Teknikleri SPSS'te İşletme Yönetimi Uygulamaları. 2. Baskı, Ankara: Emek Ofset Ltd. Şti.

Altun, K., Dereli, T. and Baykasoglu, A. (2013). Development of a Framework for Customer Cocreation in NPD through Multi-İssue Negotiation with İssue Trade-Offs, Expert Systems with Applications, 40(3): 873–880.

Barczak, G., Griffin, A. and Kahn, K. B. (2009). Perspectıve: Trends and Drivers of Success in NPD Practices: Results of the 2003 PDMA Best Practices Study, Journal of Product Innovation Management, 26(1): 3–23.

Cooper, R. G. (1984). How New Product Strategies İmpact on Performance, Journal of Product Innovation Management, 1: 5–18.

Cooper, R. G. and Brentani, U. B. (1991). New İndustrial Financial Services: What Distinguishes The Winners, Journal of Product Innovation Management, 8: 75–90.

Cooper, R. G., Scott, E., Kleinschimidt, E. and Elko, J. (2004). Benchmarking Best NPD Practices -I. Research Technology Management, 47: 31–43.

Cormican, K. and O'Sullivan, D. (2009). "Auditing Best Practice for Effective Product Innovation Management", Technovation, 24(10): 819–829

Crawford, M. and Di Benedetto, A. (2008). New Products Management, Ninth Edition, McGraw-Hill International Edition.

Çetin, A., Erenler Tekmen, E. and Şentürk, M. (2016). Mesleki Bağlılık ve Mesleki Öz-yeterlik Algısının Bilgi Paylaşma Davranışına Etkisi, Çankırı Karatekin Üniversitesi İİBF Dergisi, 6(2): 25–51.

Eroğlu, A. (2010). Çok Değişkenli İstatistik Tekniklerin Varsayımları, (Ed.) Ş.Kalaycı, SPSS Uygulamaları Çok Değişkenli İstatistik Teknikleri, Ankara: Asil Yayın Dağıtım.

Ernst, H. (2002). Success Factors of New Product Development: A Review of the Empirical Literature. International Journal of Management Review, 4: 1–40.

Griffin, A. (1997). PDMA Research on New Product Development Practices: Updating Trends and Bechmarking Best Practices. Journal of Product Innovation Management, 14: 429–458.

Gruner, K. E. and Homburg, C. (2000). Does Customer İnteraction Enhance New Product Success?, Journal of Business Research, 49(1): 1–14.

Hair, J. F., Black, W. C., Babin, B. J. and Anderson, R. E. (2010). Multivariate Data Analysis. 7th Edition, New York: Pearson.

Hancıoğlu, Y. and Atay, Ö. (2017). "İnovasyon Sistemleri" İnovasyon Tanımından İnovasyon Politikalarına Geniş Bir Perspektif. Ankara: Detay Yayıncılık.

Hancıoğlu, Y. and Yeşilaydın, G. (2016). Stratejik Yönetimde Yeni Bir Rekabet Yaklaşımı: Stratejik İnovasyon, Uluslararası Yönetim İktisat ve İşletme Dergisi, 12(29): 105–124.

Jugend, D. and Silva, S.L. (2012). Integration in New Product Development: Case Study in a Large Brazilian High-Technology. Company, Journal of Technology Management&Innovation, 7(1): 52–63.

Kalaycı, Ş. (2005). SPSS Uygulamalı Çok Değişkenli İstatistik Teknikleri, Ankara: Asil Yayın Dağıtım.

Kalaycı, Ş. (2010). SPSS Uygulamalı Çok Değişkenli İstatistik Teknikleri, Ankara: Asil Yayın Dağıtım.

Kline, R. B. (2011). "Principles and Practice of Structural Equation Modeling (Third Edition)", New York: The Gouilford Press.

Koçman, Ö. (2007). Avrupa Birliği Sürecinde Türk Beyaz Eşya Sanayinin Uluslararası Pazarlara Açılması. İzmir: Ege Üniversitesi Sosyal Bilimler Enstitüsü Yayınlanmamış Yüksek Lisans Tezi.

Lee, J., Lee, J. and Souder, W. E. (2000). Differences of Organizational Characteristics in New Product Development Crosscultural Comparison of Korea and Us. Technovation, 20: 497508.

March-Chorda, I., Gunasekaran, A. and Begoña, L. (2002). Product Development Process in Spanish Smes: An Empirical Research, Technovation, 22: 301–312.

Mendes, G.H. and Ganga, G. M.D. (2013). Predicting Success in Product Development: The Application of Principal Component Analysis to Categorical Data and Binomial Logistic Regression, Journal of Technology Management & Innovation, 8(3): 83–97.

Nicholas, J., Ledwith, A. and Perks, H. (2011). New Product Development Best Practice in SMEs and Large Organisations: Theory vs Practice, European Journal of Innovation Management, 14(2): 227–251.

Onurlubaş, E., Öztürk, D. and Yılmaz, N. (2015). The Attıtudes of Students towards the Use of Internet Bankıng, The Journal of Academic Social Science, 3(21): 42–56.

Perçin, S. (2006). İmalat İşletmelerinin Yeni Ürün Geliştirme Performansını Etkileyen Faktörler: ISO 1000 Firmalarına Yönelik Bir Araştırma, Atatürk Üniversitesi İİBF Dergisi. 20(1): 357–377.

Rabor, F.M., Reza, Z., Hossein, S. and Behzad, A. (2011). Modeling Factors Affecting Innovation Performance of Firms Using the Integrated Cognitive Mapping Method and Bayesian Networks (A Case Study in the Iranian Insurance Industry), European Journal of Social Sciences, 23(1): 22–36.

Sherman, J. D., Berkowitz, D. and Souder, W. E. (2005). New Product Development Performance and the İnteraction of Cross-Functional İntegration and Knowledge Management, Journal of Product Innovation Management, 22: 399–411.

Souder, W. E., Buisson, D. and Garret, T. (1997). Success through Customer-Driven New Product Development: A Comparison of US and New Zealand Small Entrepreneurial High Technology Firms, Journal of Product Innovation Management, 14: 459–472.

Tekin, E. and Nas İlhan, T. (2017). Firma ve Üst Düzey Yönetici Özelliklerinin Türkiye'de Faaliyette Bulunan KOBİ'lerin İhracat Performansı Üzerindeki Etkisi, Ankara SBF Dergisi, 72(4): 1185–1217.

Tekin, E. and Hancıoğlu, Y. (2017). The Effects of Innovation on Export Performance in Developing Countries, (Eds.) Bilici Nurettin; Akgül Birol and Pehlivanlı Ragıp, Global Issues in Social Sciences: Different Perspectives-Multidisciplinary Approaches, Frankfurt am Main: Peter Lang GmbH, pp. 21–34.

Urban, G.L. and von Hippel, E. (1988). Lead User Analyses for the Development of New Industrial Products, Management Science, 34: 569–582.

Yaşar, O. (2010). Türkiye'de Beyaz Eşya Sanayi, Marmara Coğrafya Dergisi, 21: 150–183.

Yayla, A.Y., Yıldız, A. and Akyüz, B. (2009). İşletmenin Örgütsel Özellikleri ile Ürün Geliştirme Ekiplerinin Başarısı Arasındaki İlişkinin İncelenmesi: Seramik Sektöründe Bir Saha Araştırması, İstanbul Ticaret Üniversitesi – Fen Bilimleri Dergisi, 8(16): 13–30.

Ürün Tasarımı ve Üretim Süreci Seçimi (2018). Erişim adresi http://www.ekosinerji.com/mp-include/uploads/2016/07/run-tasarimi-ve-uretim-sureci-secimi.pdf

A.Cansu Gök-Kisa and Mihriban Cindiloğlu Demirer

An Application of Multi-Criteria Decision Making Method in the Selection of Knowledge Management Strategies

1 Introduction

Knowledge can be regarded as the most crucial strategic resource for capturing and sustaining competitive advantage in organisations (Zack, 1999: 127). In the knowledge economy, a key principle of sustainable competitive advantage and profitability depends on how to generate and share the knowledge (Desouza, 2003: 63).

The concept of knowledge has become an important source of competitive advantage. It started to be used as a strategic input in the competition efforts of the organisations while the concept emerged as an indispensable element in the strategies of the organisations (Kurt and Özcan, 2007: 383). According to Drucker (2009: 219), who foresaw the future importance of knowledge for the first time (Nonaka and Takeuchi, 1995: 7), the essence of management is not to make techniques and procedures, but to make knowledge productive. In this respect, what is important for organisations is how to manage the information that plays a strategic role. At this stage, the question to be answered is what the concept of "knowledge management" is.

The concept of knowledge management (KM) is defined as a set of strategies and processes that aim to create, find, acquire and act on information, by considering previous experience, current and future decision-making activities to enhance a team effectiveness and efficiency (Gümüştekin, 2004: 204; Jennex, 2007: 4). In the increasingly competitive business environment, the companies take into consideration the importance of KM to respond their opponents (Wu and Lee, 2007: 842). KM and relevant strategy concepts are supported as significant and necessary components for organisations to survive and remain competitive (Martensson, 2000: 204). KM systems are developed to support and enhance the organisational processes of knowledge creation, storage, transfer, and application (Alavi and Leidner, 2001: 114). KM enables to transmit knowledge to all departments within an organisation. Also, KM systems integrate various knowledge processes to solve the organisational problems.

KM strategies are a dynamic and living social phenomenon. They are related to technology, knowledge, and, majorly people. Group companies, like KM strategies, attach importance to human, technology, system and dynamic structure. In particular, it can be argued that these companies need to be strategically guided to achieve competitive advantage and sustainability in the long term. It is thought that these enterprises are managed strategically, considering that many group companies have started their businesses from a single business. It is important to know which KM strategy is adopted by the company executives who succeeded in becoming a group company and aiming institutional sustainability. Besides, the group companies have a very important place in terms of city and country economies. Within this framework, this study is designed by asking "What kind of KM strategy do the group companies care about?"

For organisational purposes selecting proper KM strategy is important for implementation of effective KM. To practice successful KM process, companies need to evaluate various complex factors of KM strategies together (Wu, 2008: 828). In relevant literature, several researches have examined various factors for evaluating KM strategies such as, "organizational capabilities", "managerial supports (Davenport et al, 1998), "creativity", "organizational learning" (Johannessen et al, 1999), information technology, "education/training measurement", "organizing knowledge-oriented culture" and "knowledge-based systems" (Ewing and West, 2000; Gold et al, 2001; Lee and Kim, 2001).

In other studies, "culture and people", "organizational structure", "communication", "trust", "incentives"," sharing knowledge", "time", "innovation, cost" (Martensson, 2000; Alavi and Leidner, 2001; Lee and Choi, 2003; Wu and Lee, 2007; Wu, 2008; Perçin, 2010) criteria are taken into consideration. Taking all these factors into account ensures that the KM process is carried out effectively. But in this case, decision makers have to deal with a complex structure. Therefore, the selection of the KM strategies that constitute the subject of the study can be considered as an MCDM (multicriteria decision making) problem. In the study, the use of Analytic Network Process (ANP) from the MCDM methods provides a detailed decision methodology for such complex problems. ANP method allows considering all evaluation criteria, alternatives and the relationships among them involving feedbacks and interdependencies by constructing the problem in a network system (Meade and Sarkis, 1999: 246).

Even though selecting proper KM strategy is one of the key success factors in organisations, there are limited numbers of studies on this subject. In this sense, this study proposes a model for the selection of favourable KM strategy in group companies by evaluating both decision criteria and alternatives. Besides, presented ANP model in this paper provides constructing the problem in a hierarchical network that combines the dimensions (main criteria) and enablers (sub-criteria) for evaluating alternatives of KM strategies. Also, this ANP model allows dealing with interdependencies among all components.

In studies dealing with the selection of the KM strategy as the MCDM problem, Wu and Lee (2007) used the ANP method in a company that is a producer of wireless networking business in Taiwan. Wu (2008) used ANP-DEMATEL method for the semiconductor industry in Taiwan, Perçin (2010) used ANP method for the Turkish manufacturing industry in choosing proper KM strategy, Nadali et al (2011) used the ANP-FIS (fuzzy inference system) for the Iranian bank. As for this paper, it is presented an application for group companies by using ANP method in addition to few applications conducted about KM strategy selection in literature.

Accordingly, in the study firstly knowledge management strategies were examined theoretically and then a decision model was established by theoretical framework and support from decision makers. Then an application is proposed to select KM strategy for group companies operate in a province of Turkey. The remaining of paper is organised as follows. In the second part, KM strategies are explained. In the third part, research methodology of the study Analytic Network Process (ANP) is presented. In the fourth part, the decision model and application is proposed to evaluate KM strategies for group companies. Finally, in the last part of the paper, the conclusion and discussion of the results are submitted.

2 Knowledge Management Strategies

KM brings together several concepts from different areas such as organisational behaviour, strategic management, information technology, and so on. The point to be considered is how to share and create valuable knowledge in line with the organisation's strategic purposes (Liebowitz, 2001:1). In this sense, KM concept is researched strategically and KM strategies are separated into three types with regard to tacit/explicit forms of knowledge.

Two types of information, tacit and explicit, are mentioned in the information management process by Nonaka and Takeuchi (1995: 9). According to Nonaka and Takeuchi (1995: 9), explicit information refers to information that is transmitted electronically or stored in a database and can be easily processed by a computer. Tacit knowledge is the individual's own, that is, it is subjective and has an intuitive nature, and it is difficult to manipulate and communicate it systematically and logically. However, since tacit knowledge is a kind of information communicated and shared within the organisation, it is necessary to translate it into words or numbers that everyone can understand. Knowledge management strategies can be divided into three as a human-oriented strategy, a system-oriented strategy, and a dynamic strategy, depending on whether they have explicit and tacit knowledge (Choi and Lee, 2003; Wu, 2008).

The human-oriented strategy focuses on the opinion that the most valuable knowledge is tacit knowledge existing in peoples' mind. In this strategy, people share knowledge via interpersonal communication and social relationships (Zack, 1999: 125). Building networks are important for transferring the knowledge by meetings and one-to-one conversations (Eving and West, 2000: 227). This information is obtained informally from social networks and here standard procedures can be ignored for better information. The human-oriented strategy has a critical role for the KM strategy. In this way, information that cannot be obtained from the database or the repository can be accessed. In this strategy, communication and trust are critical success factors (Choi and Lee, 2003: 406).

System-oriented information is encoded and coded for repeatability. Businesses that have embraced the system-driven strategy attach importance to reuse of information. In this way, businesses encode information and reduce the complexity of using and obtaining information. Thus, business information is communicated to the customer at a lower cost and faster, and it is possible to react to them. In system-oriented strategy, management skills can be enhanced in the group and standard training programs, and it may abandon the need for further communication and coordination among the members of this organisation (Choi and Lee, 2003: 406). In this strategy, explicit knowledge is classified and stored in databases ready to be accessed by anyone in the organisation. Also, this strategy allows reusing the knowledge that provides a company to complete projects quickly and cheaply (Eving and West, 2000: 227–229).

The dynamic KM strategy integrates the context of system and human-oriented KM strategies and emphasises both explicit and tacit knowledge (Perçin, 2010: 454). They are integral and aggressive. Businesses that do not adopt this strategy do not depend on a particular culture, but they come together to support group work among different individuals in terms of time and space. The aim of businesses that have chosen this dynamic style is to exploit proven knowledge and discover new potentials (Choi and Lee, 2003: 406).

In order to be evaluated within the organisation, it is necessary to take into consideration the alternatives of such KM strategies, some key factors and the components that constitute them are need to take in consideration. A successful KM strategy requires determining organisational key factors and enhancing them to succeed business goals (Wu and Lee, 2007: 842). These factors can be grouped into four main groups as "strategic dimension", "technology and innovation dimension", "cultural and human dimension" and "financial dimension" (Chuang, 2004: 461). In the decision-making model that constructed for the selection of the KM strategy, these dimensions are reported in detail.

3 Research Methodology: Analytic Network Process (ANP)

The ANP methodology is widely studied and successfully applied in various areas in literature (Saaty, 1999; Sarkis, 1998; Meade and Sarkis, 1999; Jharkharia and Shankar, 2007; Cheng and Li, 2005; Bayazıt, 2006; Perçin 2010; Tjader et al, 2014). Analytical Network Process (ANP) is a general form of Analytic Hierarchy Process (AHS) and is a multi-criteria decision-making approach that expresses the criteria affecting the decision-making process, the relationships among the criteria and the directions of these relations in a hierarchical network model (Saaty, 2006: 2). ANP is a method that allows defining complex relationships such as dependence and feedback between criteria and alternatives in solving multi-criteria decision problems (Sarkis, 1998: 167). The ANP approach provides for the determination of the relative importance (eigenvector) for all components of the problem by making pairwise comparisons between the criteria (Lee and Kim, 2000: 370).

The steps of the ANP method can be summarised as in the followings (Saaty, 1999; Meade and Sarkis, 1999; Cheng and Li, 2005; Bayazıt 2006, Lin ve Tsai, 2010).

Step 1. Formulation of the decision model: In the ANP approach, after defining the problem, the decision model is constructed by determining the dependent and independent relationships among all the criteria in a network structure (Cheng and Li, 2005: 459; Lin and Tsai, 2010: 381).

Step 2. Calculation of eigenvectors by making pairwise comparisons: Pairwise comparisons include binary comparisons of the criteria and alternatives with each other based on the relationships in the model (Meade and Sarkis 1999: 247). With the help of pairwise comparison matrices, the eigenvectors for the criterion are calculated. The decision makers use the fundamental scale given in Tab. 1 when making these comparisons.

Step 3. Formation of the supermatrix: The supermatrix form is obtained by combining the eigenvectors obtained from the pairwise comparison matrices and displaying them in a united matrix (Saaty, 1999: 4). If the weights of the sub-criteria in each criterion group are assumed to be w_{11}, w_{12}, ..., w_{ij}, the W supermatrix is shown as in the followings.

$$W = \begin{bmatrix} w_{11} & w_{12} & \cdots & w_{1j} \\ w_{21} & w_{22} & \cdots & w_{2j} \\ \cdots & \cdots & \cdots & \cdots \\ w_{i1} & w_{i2} & \cdots & w_{ij} \end{bmatrix} \quad (1)$$

Step 4. Weighting of the supermatrix: Since the column weights in the supermatrix show the importance levels, the matrix is in a stochastic structure and the column

Tab. 1: The Fundamental Scale

Importance level	**Definition**	**Explanation**
1	Equally important	Both activities are equally contributing to the goal.
3	Moderately important	As a result of experience and evaluations, an activity is slightly more preferred than the other.
5	Strongly important	As a result of experiences and evaluations, an activity is much more preferred than the other.
7	Very strongly important	An activity is strongly preferred over another.
9	Extremely important	An activity is preferred at the highest possible level relative to the others.
2,4,6,8	Intermediate values	When a consensus is needed in making an assessment, a value in the middle of the numerical values is given.

totals should be equal to 1 (Saaty, 1999: 4). Therefore, the weighted supermatrix is obtained by weighting the column sums to be equal to 1.

Step 5. Creating Limit Supermatrix and the determination of the final priorities: The limit supermatrix is created by taking a certain force of the weighted supermatrix to measure the long-lasting effects of the criteria on each other. For this, the weighted supermatrix is multiplied itself until each line is constant at a certain value. For this purpose, the $(2k + 1)$ power of the matrix is calculated and k is a large randomly selected number. The new matrix which was obtained is called the limit supermatrix. After this process, the matrix columns are normalised and the priority for all matrix elements is obtained (Lin and Tsai, 2010: 381).

4 Application: Selecting KM Strategies for Group Companies

The steps of the implementation for determining the most appropriate strategy for the group companies are explained as follows.

Step 1: Establishing the Model and Identifying the Problem: In the study, the ANP decision model was established to determine the most appropriate KM strategy for the group companies. The aim of the model is to determine the relationships between the criteria affecting the selection of the KM strategy and the sub-criteria and define them in a hierarchical network model and select the most appropriate alternative accordingly. In the creation of the model and in the determination of the relationships, the expert decision-making group has been utilised. The expert decision-making group consists of academicians and group company managers operating in Çorum, Turkey. In this context, the four main criteria and 16 sub-criteria have been agreed upon to be evaluated in the light of the information provided in the literature on the views of 5 administrators and 3 academicians.

At the first level of the model, there are four main criteria that make up the 4 different dimensions of the KM strategy choice. At the second level, sub-criteria related to these criteria and at the third level, System Oriented Strategy (SOS), Human Oriented Strategy (HOS) and Dynamic Strategy (DYS) alternatives of 3 KM strategy are located. In the model, there is interdependence between the sub-criteria, that is, there is an intra-group interaction. Therefore, these sub-criteria are dependent on the dimensions. To show the interdependency in the analysis the looped arc is used in ANP model. Fig. 1 shows the decision model for the selection of KM strategy.

The explanations for the main criteria and sub-criteria evaluated within the scope of the study are as follows:

The strategic dimension has been examined in four sub-criteria as "management support, strategic alignment, time and core capabilities". *Management support* has an important place in all the work of the organizations (Wu, 2008: 833). In order for the KM process to be successful, it is critical that top management informs employees and encourage them and support their views (Martensson, 2000: 211; Liebowitz, 2001: 2; Nadali, et al., 2011: 111). *Strategic alignment* refers to the

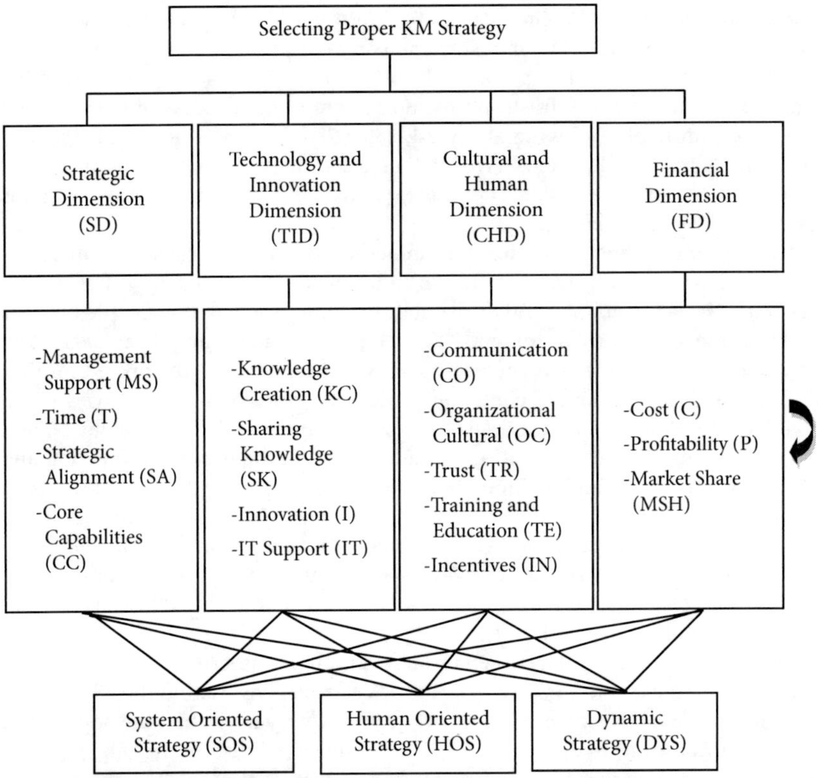

Fig. 1: Decision Model of Selecting KM Strategies for Group Companies.
Source: (Saaty, 2006:3)

harmonisation of KM strategies with the operational processes of organisational strategies (Zack, 1999: 129). *Time* refers to a good use of the time required to obtain, share, and access information (Martensson, 2000: 2012; Nadali, et al., 2011: 111). *Core capabilities* are valuable, rare, not easily imitable, unsubstitutable operational skills used to create knowledge (Gold et al, 2001: 190; Ulgen and Mirze, 2007: 118).

The dimension of technology and innovation is examined in four sub-criteria as "knowledge creation, sharing knowledge, innovation and information technology (IT) support". From the perspective of KM, *knowledge creation* is the process of creating and producing new information (Alavi and Leidner, 2001: 116; Lee and Choi, 2003: 193). *Sharing knowledge* is the transfer of information to those who will benefit from it both inside and outside the organisation (Martensson, 2000: 211, Alavi and Leidner, 2001: 119). *Innovation* is the acceptance and implementation of new product and service ideas in the process of KM (Johannessen et al, 1999: 133;

Martensson, 2000: 209; Perçin, 2010: 458). Innovative knowledge is a knowledge that enables a firm to lead its industry and competitors and to significantly diversify itself from its competitors (Zack, 1999: 132). *IT support* is the provision of the necessary technological infrastructure and system in the process of creation and transfer of information (Ewing and West, 2000: 238; Lee and Choi, 2003: 188, Lee and Kim, 2001: 301). It is also evident that technology plays an increasing role in communication in decision support, expertise and knowledge-based systems (Ewing and West, 2000: 231).

The cultural dimension has been examined in five sub-criteria as "communication, organizational culture, trust, training and education, and incentives". *Communication* is the act of vertical and horizontal communication among people in order to share information (Martensson, 2000: 211; Sabuncuoğlu and Tüz, 2005: 129). *Organizational culture* is that subjects such as values shared in the process of KM, language and behaviour are compatible and serve for common purposes (Gold et al, 2001: 189; Sabuncuoğlu and Tüz, 2005: 331). *Trust* is the belief in talent, benevolence and honesty for the creation of mutual trust in the process of creation and transfer of knowledge among individuals (Lee and Choi, 2003: 191, Eser, 2010: 140). *Training and education* is the level of training given to increase the knowledge of employees in the KM process. (Lee and Kim, 2001: 301; Lee and Choi, 2003: 191). *Incentives* are the existence of a reward and incentive system that promotes the performance of employees in the process of participating in KM. (Martensson, 2000: 212; Lee and Kim, 2001: 301).

The financial dimension has been examined in three sub-criteria as "cost, profitability and market share". *Cost* is to keep the costs incurred within the KM system at the desired level (Nadali et al., 2011: 111). *Profitability* refers that the application of KM contributes to the profitability of the company (Davenport et al, 1997: 12). *Market share* means that the KM process has a positive effect on the share of the business (Chuang, 2004: 462).

Step 2: Determining Importance Weights by Creating Pairwise Comparison Matrices.: In this step, firstly, decision makers were asked to make pairwise comparisons of all the criteria and alternatives in the model by questionnaire. Accordingly, based on the criterion that each criterion in the model is related to the upper level, the significance of the these criterion was determined using the values of the fundamental comparison scale. For example, such questions as "According to technology and innovation dimension, what is the importance level of the strategic dimension in selecting the appropriate KM strategy?" were benefited. Thus, by creating pairwise comparison matrices, eigenvectors representing the importance weights of the criteria were calculated. Tab. 2 shows the pairwise comparison of the main criteria (dimensions) and the weights (eigenvectors) of the criteria calculated in the Super Decision program. According to this, the value of 5.8 in the second column of Tab. 2 shows that the strategic dimension is 5.8 times more important than the technological and innovation dimension. In the same way, the opposite of this is also true. Thus and so, the strategic dimension according to Tab. 2 was identified as the most important main criterion with the highest weighting of0.599.

Tab. 2: Pairwise Comparison Matrix for Dimensions

Dimensions	SD	TID	CHD	FD	E-vector
SD	1	5.8	5.8	3.8	0.599
TID	0.17	1	3.8	0.55	0.138
CHD	0.17	0.26	1	0.24	0.059
FD	0.26	1.8	4.2	1	0.204

Tab. 3: Pairwise Comparison Matrix for Sub-criteria of SD

SD	MS	T	SA	CC	E-vector
MS	1	6.2	2.2	4.2	0.549
T	0.16	1	0.5	1.6	0.123
SA	0.45	2	1	1.8	0.222
CC	0.24	0.6	0.55	1	0.106

Tab. 4: Pairwise Comparison Matrix for Alternatives Based on MS Criterion

MS	SOS	HOS	DYS	E-vector
SOS	1	0.38	3.8	0.286
HOS	2.6	1	5.8	0.624
DYS	0.26	0.17	1	0.090

Subsequently, pairwise comparison matrices for the sub-criteria, which are below the main criteria, were prepared and the importance weights of the sub-criteria were calculated. Here, each main criterion is treated as a control criterion and sub-criteria are compared with each other. For example, decision makers have responded to the question "What is the level of importance of the management support criteria within the strategic dimension according to the time criteria?" In Tab. 3, this comparison matrix and eigenvectors are shown. Accordingly, the most important sub-criterion within SD is the MS criterion having a weight of 0.549.

In a similar way, pairwise comparisons of KM strategy alternatives were made according to sub-criteria and their e-vectors were calculated. As an example, in Tab. 4, the pairwise comparison matrix of the KM strategy alternatives based on the MS criterion is shown. Accordingly, the HOS alternative has the highest significance level of 0.624 weighting in terms of MS criterion.

Finally, in order to reflect interdependencies, it is necessary to make pairwise comparisons between sub-criteria under the same main set of criteria. Tab. 5 shows

Tab. 5: Pairwise Comparison Matrix for Sub-criteria Cluster of SD Under MS Criterion

MS	**T**	**SA**	**CC**	**E-vector**
T	1	1	3	0.450
SA	1	1	1.6	0.365
CC	0.333	0.625	1	0.185

the pairwise comparison matrix of the MS criterion under SD according to the other sub-criteria in the same cluster. Accordingly, the criterion with the highest importance in terms of MS in the SD cluster is T with a weight of 0.450. In this sense, pairwise comparisons of all sub-criteria were made following the same method.

Step 3: Creating Supermatrix: According to all the relations in the model, a supermatrix containing the eigenvectors obtained from all the matrices was created. In this direction, the prepared initial supermatrix is shown in Tab. 6.

Step 4: Creating the Limit Supermatrix and choosing the appropriate alternative: The limit supermatrix calculated to determine the final weights for the criterion is shown in Tab. 7. The weights obtained from the limit supermatrix are used to decide which alternative of the KM strategy should be chosen. According to obtained sub-criteria weights the most important criteria for KM strategy selection are seen as P (profitability), MS (managerial support), SK (sharing knowledge), and C (cost).

The calculation for selecting the appropriate alternative is presented in Tab. 8. Here, P values represent the weights obtained from Tab. 2 with respect to the main criteria, P_j values represent the weights of the sub-criteria obtained from the limit supermatrix, and S_{SOS}, S_{HOS} and S_{DYS} represent the weights of the criteria on the alternatives shown in Tab. 4. In this context, all these weights were multiplied for all three alternatives and total importance weights were obtained.

In Tab. 8, when total importance weights obtained for the KM strategy alternatives are taken into consideration, it is seen that the SOS option has a weight of 0.255, HOS has a weight of 0.425, and DYS has a weight of 0.320. According to these results obtained from the ANP method, HOS (Human-Oriented Strategy) is chosen as the most appropriate KM strategy for the related group companies.

5 Conclusion

In this study one of the multi-criteria decision making (MCDM) methods Analytic Network Process (ANP) is used for selecting proper KM strategy in group companies. Within the scope of the study, it is provided to determine evaluation criteria and decision model of the problem in accordance with literature review and expert opinions. Then, the selection of optimum strategy is applied among three types of KM strategies (human-oriented, system-oriented and dynamic) for group companies which operate in a province of Turkey namely Çorum.

Tab. 6: Supermatrix

	MS	T	SA	CC	KC	SK	I	IT	CO	OC	TR	TE	IN	C	P	MSH
MS	0	0.528	0.694	0.561												
T	0.450	0	0.174	0.163												
SA	0.365	0.301	0	0.277												
CC	0.185	0.171	0.132	0												
KC					0	0.436	0.197	0.358								
SK					0.454	0	0.492	0.214								
I					0.290	0.275	0	0.428								
IT					0.256	0.287	0.311	0								
CO									0	0.206	0.293	0.512	0.356			
OC									0.366	0	0.263	0.205	0.202			
TR									0.214	0.376	0	0.197	0.212			
TE									0.287	0.319	0.302	0	0.230			
IN									0.133	0.099	0.143	0.086	0			
C														0	0.545	0.132
P														0.773	0	0.868
MSH														0.227	0.455	0

Tab. 7: Limit Supermatrix

	MS	T	SA	CC	KC	SK	I	IT	CO	OC	TR	TE	IN	C	P	MSH
MS	0.375	0.375	0.375	0.375												
T	0.235	0.235	0.235	0.235												
SA	0.247	0.247	0.247	0.247												
CC	0.143	0.143	0.143	0.143												
KC					0.251	0.251	0.251	0.251								
SK					0.282	0.282	0.282	0.282								
I					0.245	0.245	0.245	0.245								
IT					0.222	0.222	0.222	0.222								
CO									0.256	0.256	0.256	0.256	0.256			
OC									0.214	0.214	0.214	0.214	0.214			
TR									0.201	0.201	0.201	0.201	0.201			
TE									0.226	0.226	0.226	0.226	0.226			
IN									0.103	0.103	0.103	0.103	0.103			
C														0.281	0.281	0.281
P														0.450	0.450	0.450
MSH														0.269	0.269	0.269

Tab. 8: Calculation of Weights of Alternatives for Selecting the Suitable KM

P		P_j	S_{SOS}	S_{HOS}	S_{DYS}	**SOS**	**HOS**	**DYS**
SD 0.599	MS	0.375	0.286	0.624	0.090	0.064	0.140	0.020
	T	0.235	0.173	0.402	0.425	0.024	0.057	0.060
	SA	0.247	0.240	0.364	0.396	0.036	0.054	0.059
	CC	0.143	0.144	0.592	0.264	0.012	0.051	0.023
TID 0.138	KC	0.251	0.297	0.371	0.332	0.010	0.013	0.011
	SK	0.282	0.401	0.203	0.396	0.016	0.008	0.015
	I	0.245	0.224	0.383	0.393	0.008	0.013	0.013
	IT	0.222	0.428	0.214	0.358	0.013	0.007	0.011
CHD 0.059	CO	0.256	0.145	0.736	0.119	0.002	0.011	0.002
	OC	0.214	0.230	0.608	0.162	0.003	0.008	0.002
	TR	0.201	0.271	0.617	0.112	0.003	0.007	0.001
	TE	0.226	0.160	0.725	0.115	0.002	0.010	0.002
	IN	0.103	0.184	0.576	0.240	0.001	0.004	0.001
FD 0.204	C	0.281	0.343	0.199	0.458	0.020	0.012	0.026
	P	0.450	0.299	0.167	0.534	0.027	0.015	0.049
	MSH	0.269	0.249	0.304	0.447	0.014	0.017	0.025
Total importance weights						**0.255**	**0.425**	**0.320**

It is critically important that the KM strategy adopted by the managers of a company investing in different sectors and employing many employees and becoming a group company. According to the result of the analysis, the human-oriented strategy is more important than the dynamic and system-oriented strategy in related group companies. KM systems, which assume businesses as dynamic and social fact, are related to technology and knowledge, and to large scale human. Because the creative force for an organisation is human capital. Likewise, KM strategies are also an application of collective knowledge and skills of the workforce as a whole, to achieve the goals that the organisation has identified. In this study, it is understood that group companies that thought to make big contributions to city economies need to focus mostly in managerial support and organizational skills for sharing and creating knowledge during the KM process. In this sense, adopting human-oriented strategy by group companies will provide positive results such as organisational commitment, loyalty and high motivation for workers. And these results will supply to people an effective way of knowledge creation and sharing within the organization in accordance with the objectives of company.

In compliance with the results of this study, Swan et al. (2000) proposed that a human-oriented strategy is superior to system-oriented strategy. According to Martensson (2000), the knowledge transformation process is affected by people's experiences, attitudes, and the context in which they work. Also (Mayo, 1998) mentioned that KM process must develop systems where people are able to navigate effectively. This can be made by storing the knowledge in different databases and make it possible for people to access documents speedily and easily. (Ash, 1998) refers that "information has little value and will not become knowledge until it is processed by the human mind" and emphasizes application of the human-oriented strategy.

The limitation of this study was that it was carried out only on group companies in Çorum city centre by taking into account time and financial opportunities. In this context 5 group companies are taken in consideration. From this point of view, in future researches, the proposed decision model can be studied on different group companies in other cities in terms of identifying possible differences. Due to this limitation, it is not possible to generalise the results. As a suggestion, it makes possible to get more generalizable results through repeating the research on larger samples. It can also be expressed as a suggestion obtaining different results and evaluations with comparative examination of the research model on different provinces. With this empirical study, it is aimed to present the applicability of the proposed method and guide managers about the evaluation of KM strategies. Also, obtained results from this study are expected to contribute to the relevant literature and practitioners.

Bibliography

Alavi, M. & Leidner, D. E.(2001), Knowledge Management And Knowledge Management Systems: Conceptual Foundations And Research Issues, *MIS Quarterly*, 25 (1), 107–36.

Ash, J. (1998), Managing Knowledge Gives Power, Communication World, 15 (3), 23–6.

Bayazıt, Ö. (2006), Use of Analytical Network Process in Vendor Selection Decisions, *Benchmarking: An International Journal*, 13 (5), 566–579.

Cheng, E. W. L. & H. Li (2005), Analytic Network Process Applied to Project Selection, *Journal and Construction Engineering and Management*, 131 (4), 459–466.

Choi, B. & Lee, H. (2003), An Empirical Investigation of KM Styles and Their Effect on Corporate Performance, *Information & Management*, 40 (5), 403–417.

Chuang, S.-H. (2004), A Resource-Based Perspective On Knowledge Management Capability And Competitive Advantage: An Empirical Investigation, *Expert Systems with Applications*, 27 (3), 459–65.Davenport, T.H., Delong, D.W. & Beers, M.C. (1998), Successful Knowledge Emanagement Projects, *Sloan Management Review*, 39 (2), 43–5.

Desouza, K. C. (2003), Strategic Contributions of Game Rooms to Knowledge Management: Some Preliminary Insights, *Information & Management*, 41 (1), 63–74.

Drucker, P. F. (2009), Büyük Değişimler Çağında Yönetim, Çev: Zülfü Dicleli, Acar Basım, İstanbul.

Eser, G. (2010), Güven Eğilimi, İçinde: Kurumlarda İyilik de Var, Ed: Güler İslamoğlu, Nobel Yayın Dağıtım, Ankara.

Ewing, T. M. & West, C. D. (2000), Advertising Knowledge Management: Strategies And Implications, *International Journal of Advertising*, 19 (2), 225–243.

Gold, H. A., Malhotra, A. & Segars, A. H. (2001), Knowledge Management: An Organizational Capabilities Perspective, *Journal of Management Information Systems*, 18 (1), 185–214.

Gümüştekin, G. E. (2004), Bilgi Yönetiminin Stratejik Önemi, *Atatürk Üniversitesi İktisadi ve İdari Bilimler Dergisi*, 18 (3–4), 201–212.

Jennex, E, M. (2007), What is Knowledge Management. In: Knowledge Management in Modern Organizations, Ed: Jennex, E, Murray, Idea Group Publishing, USA.

Jharkharia, S. & Shankar, R. (2007), Selection of logistics service provider: an analytic network process (ANP) approach, Omega, 35 (3), 274–89.

Johannessen, J.-A., Olsen, B. & Olaisen, J. (1999), Aspects Of Innovation Theory Based On Knowledge-Management, *International Journal of Information Management*, 19 (2), 121–139.

Kurt, M. & Özcan, K. (2007), Yeni Ekonomi, Bilgi ve Bilgi Temelli Kalkınma: Türkiye Temelinde Bir Değerlendirme. In: İçinde: Türkiye'de İşletmecilikte Yeni Perspektifler, Ed: Mustafa Kurt ve Serkan Bayraktaroğlu, Gazi Kitabevi, Ankara.

Lee, H. ve Choi B. (2003), Knowledge Management Enablers, Processes, and Organizational Performance: An Integrative View and Empirical Examination, *Journal of Management Information Systems*, 20 (1), 179–228.

Lee, J. W. & Kim, S. H. (2000), Using Analytic Network Process and Goal Programming For Interdependent Information System Project Selection, *Computers & Operations Research*, 27, 367–382

Lee, J. H. & Kim, Y. G. (2001), A Stage Model Of Organizational Knowledge Management: A Latent Content Analysis, *Expert Systems with Applications*, 20, 299–311.Liebowitz, J. (2001), Knowledge Management and its Link to Artificial Intelligence, *Expert Systems with Applications*, 20, 1–6.

Lin, C. T. & M. C. Tsai (2010), Location Choice for Direct Foreign Investment in New Hospitals in China by Using ANP and TOPSIS, *Qualitative Quantitative*, 44, 375–390

Mårtensson, M. (2000). Journal Of Knowledge Management Emerald Article: A Critical Review Of Knowledge Management As A Management Tool, *Journal of Knowledge Management*, 4 (3), 204–216.

Mayo, A. (1998), Memory Bankers, People Management, 4 (2), 34–8.

Meade, L. & J. Sarkis (1999), Analyzing Organizational Project Alternatives for Agile Manufacturing Processes: an Analytical Network Approach, *International Journal of Production Research*, 37 (2), 241–261.

Nadali, A.; Nosratabadi, H. E. & Pourdarab, S. (2011), ANP-FIS Method for Determining the Knowledge Management Strategy, *International Journal of Information and Education Technology*, 1 (2), 107–113.

Nonaka, I. & Takeuchi, H. (1995). The Knowledge Creating Company: How Japanese Companies Create The Dynamics Of Innovation, New York: Oxford University Press.

Perçin, S. (2010), Use Of Analytic Network Process In Selecting Knowledge Management Strategies, *Management Research Review*, 33 (5), 452–471.

Saaty, T. L. (1999), Fundamentals of the Analytic Network Process, ISAHP 1999, Kobe, Japan, 1–14

Saaty, T. L. (2006), Decision Making with the Analytic Network Process: Economic, Political, Social and Technological Applications with Benefits, Opportunities, Costs and Risks, USA: Springer.Sabuncuoğlu, Z. & Tüz, M. (2005), Örgütsel Psikoloji, Alfa Aktuel Basım, Bursa.

Sarkis, J. (1998), Evaluating Environmentally Conscious Business Practices, European Journal Of Operational Research 107, 159–174.

Swan, J., Newell, S. & Robertson, M. (2000), Limits Of IT-Driven Knowledge Management For Interactive Innovation Processes: Towards A Community-Based Approach, Proceedings of 33rd HICSS, 1–11.Tjader, Y., May, J. H., Shang, J., Vargas, L. G. & Gao, N. (2014), Firm-Level Out Sourcing Decision Making: A Balanced Scorecard-Based Analytic Network Process Model, *Int. J. Prod. Econ.*, 147, 614–623.

Ülgen, H. & Mirze, S. K. (2007), İşletmelerde Stratejik Yönetim, Arıkan Basım, İstanbul.Wu, Wei-Wen, (2008), Choosing Knowledge Management Strategies by Using a Combined ANP and DEMATEL Approach, *Expert Systems With Applications*, 35, 828–835.

Wu, Wei-Wen & Lee, Yu-Ting (2007), Selecting Knowledge Management Strategies By Using The Analytic Network Process, *Expert Systems with Applications*, 32, 841–847.

Zak, M. H. (1999), Developing a Knowledge Strategy, California Management Review, 41 (3), 125–145.

Aysel Çetindere Filiz, Cengiz Duran and Sema Behdioğlu

Modern Production Approaches

1 Introduction

While production activities took place in workshops built upon craft in the early ages, high volume standard products started to be manufactured in factories with James Watt's invention of the steam engine in 1764. High volume and low cost products have been produced with automobile assembly line, which was first developed by Henry Ford in 1913, facilitating the production of standard products. In factories, it was aimed to produce labor-intensive standard products with the use of traditional systems such as make-to-order, batch production, continuous production. Rapid developments in transportation and information technologies have also led to changes in market conditions, and this has supported the formation of a dynamic competitive environment. In a dynamic competitive environment, businesses have begun to tend to gain competitive advantage by quickly meeting customer demands. Rapid changes in technology over time have increased the diversity of customer needs and new approaches have become a current issue to be used in production processes due to the swift increase in population. In this study, for enterprises to obtain competitive advantage with the applications expressed as modern production approaches, it has been fundamental to make customers satisfied by producing better and more efficient production. At the same time, businesses that have successfully implemented these applications have started to earn more customers in the market as well as improving the satisfaction of current customers by producing faster, higher quality, more flexible and less costly than other businesses. In historical process, it has been the main objective of modern production approaches to increase efficiency by adding value to resources through various changes and transformations depending upon the developments in production systems and technologies, to invigorate the economy, to meet the product/service demands towards customers' expectancies at a level of price that can maximize the profit via the expected quality and the use of optimal resource. In line with this aim, the approaches of six sigma with the aspect of enhancing the quality, reengineering with the aspect of increasing the efficiency of processes, agile manufacturing with the aspect of speed, theory of constraints that aims to maximize the profit with effectively using resources are discussed.

2 Six Sigma (6σ) Approach

The small "sigma" letter in the Greek alphabet -σ- is the symbol used in the statistic to represent the "standard deviation" of a population. Standard deviation is an indication of the amount of "variability" or inconsistency in any object or process group. For example, it is variability that a fast food, which you have bought, is hot and delicious one day, and is tepid another day. Or if all three shirts you have bought are the same size, and one of them is narrower for you, this is also variability. In fact, an infinite number of examples of variability can be given because everything varies in one way or another; variability is a part of life (Pande et al., 2018, p. 60). The biggest obstacle in upgrading the quality levels of companies that offer products or services is the variability in the processes (Öztürk, 2013, p. 450). Six sigma is a project-based approach that provides concrete gains on the basis of continuous improvement targeting 3,4 errors in a million by reducing variability in processes to improve quality. Sigma value is a statistical term that refers to the variability in the process. Six sigma is a strategic management practice that makes significant changes in the structure of the organization. For this reason, the values and culture of the company are also important in the six sigma applications.

A cultural structure, which is open to change, allows enterprises to implement these applications easily. However, when significant changes are made in most businesses, employees may tend to show resistance because they do not know the consequences of these changes and lack the information about what needs to be done. This often occurs even more prominently in organizations that are not allowed to fault or where the fault is not tolerated. For this reason, the attitude of executives and the cultural structure of organization are very important in the success of the six sigma practices. Motorola, General Electric and Allied Signal are the first companies to successfully implement six sigma projects.

In 1986, Motorola's engineer, Bill Smith, found six sigma, which is related to the quality level that corresponds to a 3,4 part error rate in a million, and approved it as a standard. Bill Smith, considered as the father of six sigma, admitted that external error rates would be higher than expected, paying attention to the fact that external failure rates were not well predicted by internal estimates (Öztürk, 2013, p. 451). Arçelik, Bosh, and Aselsan are some of the companies that have achieved significant success by implementing six sigma in Turkey. Six sigma projects consist of five basic stages: define, measure, analyze, improve and control. These steps and the six sigma tools used in each are shown in Tab. 1.

The following conditions must be met for the establishment of a process management system in organizations with six sigma projects (Breyfogle, 2003, p. 22):

- Identification and understanding of process parts and boundaries,
- Identification of *internal/external customers* and other stakeholders involved in the process in order to make effective use of the process as a whole,

Internal customer: One or more employee taking place in the workshop or department that follows the previous process outputs to perform processes. External customer: Customers who are end user or intermediary who buy the products or services of the businesses (Yüksel, 2013, p. 243).

Tab. 1: Six Sigma Implementation Steps. **Reference:** Oakland, 2014, p. 297; Yüksel, 2013, p. 274.

Steps	Remarks	Six Sigma Tools
Define	The scope and objectives of the project to be developed in terms of inputs, outputs and processes that meet customer requirements are defined	Proximity Diagram, Critical Quality Variable, Flow Diagrams, SIPOC (Suppliers, Input, Process, Output, Customer) Diagram, Customer's Voice, Quality Function Deployment, Relations Diagram
Measure	By evaluating the current process performance over input, output and process, process adequacy is measured according to sigma value in long or short term	Control Charts, Signal Charts, Flow Diagrams, Failure Mode and Effects Analysis, Pareto Diagram, Process Adequacy, Sampling, Quality Function Deployment, Histogram
Analyze	Process outputs, products, or services are compared to predetermined standards to analyze the gap between current and desired performance, prioritize problems, and identify the root causes of these problems	Proximity Diagram, Brainstorming, Cause and Effect Diagram, Control Charts, Signal Charts, Experimental Design, Flow Diagrams, Hypothesis Tests, Pareto Diagram, Regression, Sampling, Spreading Diagram
Improve	Improvements are made to prevent repetition of the problems by developing appropriate solutions to these problems to achieve financial and other performance goals	Brainstorming, Control Charts, Signal Diagrams, Experimental Design, Flow Diagrams, Failure Mode and Effects Analysis, Pareto Diagram, Process Adequacy, Sampling, Tree Diagram
Control	This phase involves practices related to the ways providing permanence of improved processes. Standards for processes can be documented by systems such as ISO 9000, and performance standards can be documented by statistical process control techniques	Control Charts, Signal Charts, Flow Diagrams, Sampling, Poka Yoke

- Indicating the maximum benefit that the organization will achieve with effective six sigma practices,
- Formation of measurement systems for the measurement and documentation of the basic processes involved in the implementation are required.

It is an undeniable fact that the quality characteristics of products produced by a certain process using the same machine and method will not be similar to each

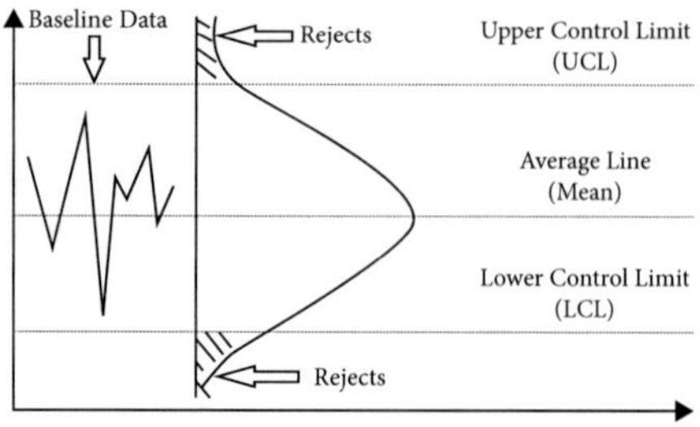

Fig. 1: Control Limits Chart

other. This difference can be defined as variability or change. In all processes, it can be stated that there are six factors causing the change, namely machinery, tools and equipment, materials, methods and environmental conditions used in production. Thus, even if the products are produced in the same system or in the same processes, it is seen that the quality characteristics of the product differ even if just a bit. This also explains the necessity of specifications in the production process (Işığıçok, 2005, p. 14). Therefore, the adequacy of the process needs to be defined.

2.1 Definition of Process Adequacy

If only random variables play a role in a process, then any variable will have a normal distribution. In any process, before starting adequacy analysis, process must be under control and data must have normal distribution (Şahin, 2013, p. 255). Once process has been statistically checked, process adequacy analyses allow the process outputs to determine the degree of meeting the product specifications, and if the outputs fail to meet the process specifications, show the necessity of making corrective actions to increase the process adequacy. Following the removal of special causes from the process, the natural behavior of the process indicates process adequacy. Process adequacy analysis explains how control schemes and other statistical techniques can be used to predict a processes natural ability and determine how to proceed according to product specifications (Yüksel, 2013, p. 297). Upper and lower control limits in Fig. 1 shows the limits of the change. Apart from that, the remaining values are shown as rejects (faulty product/service). By investigating the special causes that cause the formation of rejects, alternative solutions are created.

Processes under control may not always be sufficient to meet specifications. The following three indices are used to determine the adequacy of any process:

- **Adequacy ratio (Cr):** It is the ratio of general variability (6σ) to specification deployment in the process. The adequacy ratio should be 75 % or less.
- **Potential adequacy of the process (Cp):** It is calculated according to the formula (Upper Control Limit(UCL)-Lower Control Limit(LCL)/6σ), and evaluated with regard to following cases:

Cp ≤ 1; the process is insufficient, improvements need to be done.
1 < Cp ≤ 1,33; the process doesn't meet the specifications,
Cp ≥ 1,33; the process meets the specifications.

- **Performance of the process (Cpk):** It is used to express how the process performs according to the target value (process average-average line) and is calculated according to the following formula;

  Cpk = lowest [(UCL-Process Average)/3σ; (Process Average-LCL)/3σ]

  (This value should be 1 or greater than 1 in order to be sufficient to meet the process design specifications).

Cpk is a value that is always equal to or less than Cp. If Cp = Cpk, it is understood that the process averages are in the middle of the control limits. If Cpk < Cp, then the process is away from the predicted center. If the Cpk value equals zero, the process average equals one of the control limits, and if the Cpk value is negative, the process average is out of the control limits. The Cp index indicates only the variability of the process, while the Cpk index indicates both the variability and the status of the process with regard to the center (Yüksel, 2013, p. 299). The contents of sigma levels in production and service sectors are as shown in Tab. 2.

According to Tab. 2, as the value of sigma grows, it appears that the faulty production decreases in the organization. The error rate is 66800 in a million at sigma 3, and it falls to 6210 at sigma 4. In this case it appears that the organization has a performance of 99.379 %.

The duties and responsibilities of the team agents working on the projects must be determined for a successful six sigma implementation. The duties and responsibilities of those agents who will take part in the six sigma project are defined according to the color of belt as it is in far-eastern sports (Gürsakal, 2005, p. 19). While the teams are established, the internal and external members involved in

Tab. 2: Content of Sigma Levels in Production and Service Sectors. **Reference:** Öztürk, 2013, p. 456

Sigma Value of the Process	Error in a Million	Success (%)	Services	Production
0	933000	0		
1	691000	30,9	Weak	
2	309000	69,1	Average	Weak
3	66800	93,32	Good	Average
4	6210	99,379	Very Good	Good
5	233	99,9767	World Class	Very Good
6	3,4	99,99966		World Class

Tab. 3: *Roles and Responsibilities in Six Sigma Organization.* **Reference:** Özveri & Çakır, 2012, p. 19; Breyfogle, 2003, p. 27–28

Champion	Master Black Belt	Black Belt	Green Belt
To determine the six sigma vision	To enable education and certification of black belts	Managing the change	To operate in the functional fields of the project
To be responsible for the deployment and implementation of six sigma	To be a consultant for green belt and black belt in project works	Selecting the most effective tools in project work and training the team in this regard	Ensuring that the six sigma techniques are learned and used during the implementation of the projects
To determine project priorities	To direct agents to the vision of the organization	To improve the project details	They are less educated and work part-time on projects than black belts

the processes are utilized. Examples of external members include customers and suppliers. When setting up the team, if possible, individuals from different nations and cultures should be brought together for a common purpose (Yang & El-Haik, 2003, p. 70). In Tab. 3, the roles and responsibilities that agents should have in order to achieve organizational success with six sigma applications are defined according to the color of the belt.

According to Tab. 3, black belts seem to be primarily responsible for the implementation and results of the six sigma project. They coach the six sigma improvement teams and actually lead the team. Black belts should have a personality that can build flexible relationships with the team, have problem-solving ability, understand customer needs, analyze and optimize processes, and facilitate the implementation and acceptance of organizational change (Gürsakal, 2005, p. 133–134). There are three main factors for the successful implementation of the six sigma. The first one is *customer orientation*. Products and services must match the features desired by the customer. Customer needs and expectations should be well perceived, new products/services should be designed to meet these demands and expectations. Another important issue in six sigma is that *this management technique is based on the data*. Inputs, outputs and activities within the process must be monitored for the production of products and services based on the data. Quality development will not happen at random. With data analysis, resources will be allocated to better projects, both internal and external customers will be more satisfied with outputs. One of the essential things to implement the six sigma approach is that *it is a powerful methodology*. The data alone cannot be used to solve the problem. The use of a methodology including error definitions, measurement, analysis, development and control will increase productivity within the organization (Doğan & Demiral, 2008, p. 347).

3 Reengineering

Reengineering does not mean correcting the existing fundamental structure or making small changes to the system with incremental improvements and making the existing structure better work with several additions. Apart from these, reengineering means to start from the very beginning to all necessary operations to manufacture the product or service in a manner that presents value to the customer, by ignoring all the predefined job procedures and instructions. In other words, reengineering can generally be described as "recommencing to everything". The question to be asked in this process is "If I recreate this company with the information and technology I have, what would it be like?" If reengineering is being applied in a system, it means that the old systems are ignored and the system is starting from the very beginning. With reengineering practice, rather than progressive improvements, ways to do the job better are looked for (Hammer & Champy, 1997, p. 28). Developing companies' competitiveness is possible not because they make their personnel work more, but because they learn to work differently. This means that companies and their staff must forget the principles and techniques that make them successful up to this time. Companies have developed successful principles and techniques with the pressure of "customer-competition-change" elements of the business world. Thus, reengineering has emerged through the transformation of management conceptions in the revolutionary trait. Reengineering tries to get rid of old rules about how to organize and finalize our work. Reengineering cannot be accomplished with rigorous preparation, small and timid steps. Reengineering is the all-or-none formula related to an ambiguous result (Öztürk, 2013, p. 288). Reengineering can be described as a radical redesign of business processes in order to make significant improvements in the most important performance benchmarks of the modern world, such as cost, quality, service and speed (Hammer & Champy, 1997, p. 29). Radically, the design of work processes means getting down to the roots. Getting down to the roots means to design the way of doing business through changing the business processes completely or restarting the work by ignoring the existing business processes rather than improving them in small steps. The process concept in the definition refers to interrelated works that creates value for internal or external customers when they come together (Hammer & Stanton, 1995, p. 3).

3.1 Implementation Phases of Reengineering

The implementation steps of reengineering are shown in Tab. 4.

The analysis of organizational internal and external environment needs to be done very well in order for reengineering to succeed; who are the internal and external environment of the organization, what are they, how is its structure, what specifications does it have, why such a change is needed, what must be the direction of the change, what is the ultimate goal, how should the relevant time planning and strategic plan be, who will actively work on this project, etc. Such a

Tab. 4: Implementation Steps of Reengineering. **Reference:** Love & Gunasekaran, 1997, p. 187

1.Step	Identify issues for processes to be reengineered	An effective communication network with employees should be established after the need for change is determined
2.Step	Establishing process goals	The objectives for reengineering should be determined and explained to all employees. The goals may be to reduce costs and time, increase customer satisfaction levels, and increase quality. The stated objectives can be used to measure the level of development
3.Step	Determine the processes on which reengineering will be implemented	All basic processes in the organization should be determined at the beginning. However, in all these processes, reengineering can not be applied at the same time. Before choosing the processes on which reengineering will be implemented, the current performance of each process is assessed by asking questions such as: Which processes are causing the most problems? What are the possible processes for implementing reengineering? What costs are involved? What is the responsibility of the workforce? Is the process obsolete or technologically too far behind? Responses to questions can be weighted according to the needs of the organization and employees
4.Step	To measure and interpret existing processes	The current process must be fully understood and diagnosed. For this, firstly performance parameters which will be obtained from the organization's quality systems are required
5.Step	Identification and evaluation of facilitators	The necessary facilitators such as information technology (IT), organizational structure, human resources and total quality management activities should be identified and assessed. In addition, additional requirements should be identified, such as the boundaries of facilitators and training programs for new skills
6.Step	Designing and creating a new process	The existing process may need to be removed to implement reengineering. In order to create and design a new process, the principles of reengineering should be applied by using various tools and techniques such as simulation
7.Step	Testing the new process	Newly designed processes must be tested before they are applied. Estimated comparisons can be made. The use of simulation to test new processes is critical
8.Step	To actualize the process on which reengineering has applied to	Management should be continuously involved and support reengineering practices. Collaboration should be provided among all employees in the organization. Employees should be given prizes in the direction of their efforts, and environments where they will gain new skills to create business groups should be created. Improvements, advancements and requirements should be determined by comparing old processes with the processes on which reengineering has applied to

large-scale organizational environment analysis requires knowledge management (Pira & Kocabaş, 2003, p. 93). The application of reengineering to business processes represents a significant change. Because, there will be some changes about the subjects such as organizational structure, management systems, evaluation of employees' responsibilities and performances, use of information technology (Aksu, 2000, p. 38).

4 Agile Manufacturing

In today's market conditions, competition has moved to a global dimension, markets have increased in variability, products and services have become shorter in use, and customers need to satisfy their personal and special needs. The uncertainty of product life cycles, the speed of development of technology, the increasing demand for personal products has created a dynamic and uncertain environment. Such an environment has also begun to trigger change in production systems. For this reason, it is necessary to evaluate the changes in terms of production that the enterprises have to do in an environment where the uncertainties and changes are intense. While the enterprises were based on the mass production system in which the products were produced in large groups in the traditional production style, they have begun to improve their "personalized" production systems, in which customer demands are prominent, in order to cope with the increasing competition as a result of increasingly differentiated customer demands in the 21st century. One of them is the "Agile Manufacturing" paradigm, which was revealed by a group of US government-sponsored researchers in the 1990s. The concept of agile manufacturing first emerged in 1991 at Lehigh University as a result of the US government-sponsored research effort. After the "*21st Century Manufacturer Company Strategies*" report, which was published by the Iacocca Institute, the agile manufacturing concept has been started to use widely. *According to the definition of Iacocca Institute (1991); agile manufacturing is a production system with superior capabilities (internal capabilities, software and hardware technologies, human resources, management, information) aimed at meeting the rapidly changing needs of the market. With this system, enterprises can fully respond to customer requests by increasing product types quickly in the direction of changing customer demands and changing production line very quickly in this way (flexibility).* Agility in the development of the agile manufacturing system as shown in Fig. 2.

The most important aspects of agile manufacturing include customer prosperity, people and information, co-operation within and between firms, and fitting a company for change (Maskell, 2001, p. 6). Many businesses are reluctant to share their knowledge with other businesses, even if they are not directly competitors, for fear of losing their competitive edge. However, due to changes in the competitive environment, businesses alone lack the resources they have to implement each step of the value creation process. For this reason, enterprises need to build strong and dependable power associations with other enterprises (Kasap & Peker, 2009, p. 65). This co-operation is needed within the firm. Often traditional companies

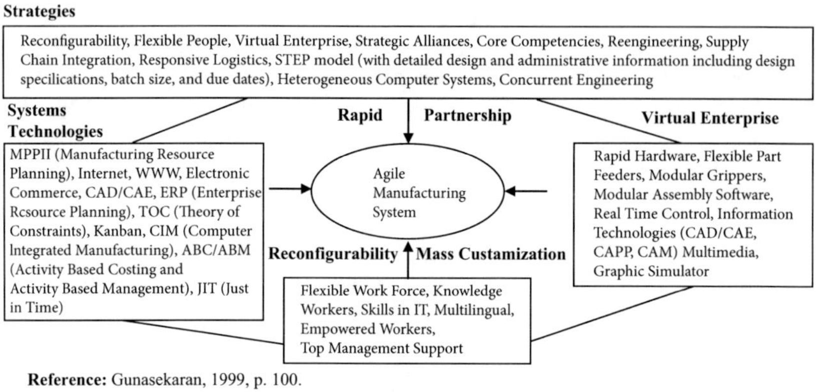

Fig. 2: Development of an Agile Manufacturing System. **Reference:** Gunasekaran, 1999, p. 100

have very little flexibility and co-operation from one department to another. This must be solved and the various departments or areas of the company must work together for the enrichment of the customers, irrespective of the department's short-term benefit (Maskell, 2001, p. 8–9).

Agility requires a company to be able to respond to unpredictable changes in the market or customer requirements. It requires a capability beyond flexibility, where responses are made to known changes with predetermined procedures. Agility is context specific where the capabilities depend on the competitive situation so no standard model can be used for all firms to follow (Vokurka & Fliedner, 1998, p. 170). The principles of agile manufacturing are linked with company strategy that is based on added value to satisfy the customer in highly customized products and high quality. These require flexible processes, speed of response from suppliers, reduced life cycle of processes, business co-operation within the supply chain, use of high tech and highly qualified human resources. The agile manufacturing takes it as important key principles to internal and external co-operation and the domain of changes and uncertainties (Leite & Braz, 2016, p. 563).

5 Theory of Constraints (TOC)

Theory of Constraints (TOC) has focused on maximizing the profit of the organization and effective usage of resources. For this reason, in order to maximize profits, the factors affecting the effective use of resources are considered as constraints and a systematic management approach is adopted to eliminate these constraints. TOC was developed by Eliyahu M. Goldratt in 1984. This theory outlines a conscious process to define constraints and manage them well. When the process is referred to, it focuses not only on the effectiveness of individual processes but also on the bottlenecks that deal with the system as a whole by considering all processes with the system approach. According to the TOC, *machines and in-process materials represent the cash inventory in the system because they have the potential to be sold and be converted into money.* Producing a product and service that an organization cannot sell will not increase the capacity or output level. Accordingly, removing the constraint from the system by using bottleneck sources to maximize the capacity or output of the system is a way of managing the system in the best way (Krajewski et al., 2012, p. 264–265).

5.1 Basic Principles of the Theory of Constraints

In the TOC, system approach can be thought of as a chain extending from the market to the organization, from there to the suppliers. For example, the capacity of the organization will increase when studies on the efficiency of the organization's internal processes are carried out. If the capacity increases more than usual and insufficient demand occurs, the presence of a large number of stocks in the enterprise will lead to a constraint. This constraint is related to the sales and marketing process (Breyfogle, 2003, p. 886).The eight guiding principles of theory are listed below (Yüksel, 2013, p. 211–212):

1. *Flows* should be balanced rather than capacities throughout the workshop. The aim is not to balance the use of capacities, equipment and human resources, but to ensure a quick and smooth flow of material through the production system. The use of non-bottleneck resources is determined by other constraints of the system, such as bottlenecks. Non-bottleneck sources do not limit the amount of output a production system can generate. For this reason, these resources should be managed to support the operations of other sources (bottlenecks) that limit the amount of output. If a non-bottleneck source is operated at a higher output ratio than a bottleneck source, there will be no improvement in the entire production system. An hour saved in a bottleneck is an additional hour in the entire production system. However, an hourly savings in a non-bottleneck source adds just one more hour to idle time.

   Flow: Traditionally, the speed at which the system produces products. According to the theory of constraints, it is revenue that the system obtains through sales. According to the theory of constraints, unless a piece is sold, it is not flow, but stock.

2. "Use" of a workstation; is different from *"activation"*. The use of a workstation (production when material is not needed) does not mean the same as activation. Activation of a non-bottleneck source does not improve the flow or provide better performance in financial measures.

   Activation: It means production which does not contribute to the flow.

3. One hour of loss in a bottleneck means one hour of loss at the whole workshop. Since the bottleneck limits the amount of output that the whole system

can create, this means loss in the total system during the time when it does not produce output.

4. Since non-bottleneck sources do not limit the output of the production system, gaining time from these sources will not increase the total output. Therefore, bottleneck sources need to be focused.
5. Bottlenecks manage the flow and semi-finished goods.
6. The *transfer party* does not have to be the same size as the *process party.* The parts can be transported in small parties between business centers according to the process parties. Long transfer times will occur if there are large transfer party sizes. Because the first part at the party will have to wait for other parts, in order to be processed in the other machine. *Transfer party: The amount of parts produced before the pieces pass to another stage in the process. Process party: It is the amount of production before the change is made to produce something else in the business center.*
7. The process party size should be variable, not constant. At all stages of production, it is not necessary that the process parties are the same size, but the size of the party at each stage should be determined by the economic level of that phase.
8. A workshop plan should be established by examining all workshop constraints. According to the TOC, simultaneous evaluation of all constraints is supported in the development of plans. Also TOC argues that procurement periods are the result of the plans and therefore cannot be determined in advance.

5.2 Evaluation of the Theory of Constraints in the Context of Continuous Improvements

The application of the TOC according to the continuous improvement approach involves a five-stage process. It is stated that these steps are as follows (Ünal et al., 2005, p. 434): *Determination of the constraints in the system, deciding how to fix the constraints in the system, effective management of the constraint in the second step in the system, removal of constraints in the system and returning to the first step once the constraint expressed in the fourth step is eliminated.*

5.2.1 Determination of the Constraints in the System

When it is assumed that there is always at least one constraint on all organizations, it is necessary to determine this constraint or constraints within the existing system in the first step. Constraints within the organization may be internal capacity constraints and political constraints as well as external demand constraints. There may be only one of these constraints in the system but it should not be ignored that there may be more. In addition to this, it is necessary to investigate and determine the effect of the constraint on the targets of the organization other than just determining the constraint in this step (Büyükyılmaz & Gürkan, 2009, p. 185–186).

5.2.2 Deciding How to Fix the Constraints in the System

In the first step, the constraint defined in the first step must be managed effectively in order to increase the performance of the organization. If there is more than one constraint in the organization or system, it is necessary to determine which one will be given priority, and to develop strategies for removing or reducing the effect that this constraint has created. This constraint may also be within the organization, such as capacity constraints. In this case, the capacity of the organization is related to the capacity of the people and machines in the place or section where the constraint is located. In the production process, the effect of capacity constraint will be eliminated or reduced by shortening machine preparation times, activating process flow charts, reducing waiting time in the process, and controlling the process more effectively. In this way, the organization will make faster production and benefit from people and machinery in the most appropriate way (Kaygusuz, 2005, p. 139).

5.2.3 Management of the Corrected Constraints in the System

In order to increase the performance of the system under the assumption that the performance of a system is determined by the constraints in that system, the performance of the existing constraint needs to be increased first. If this is not done, the increase of other resources will lead to waste of these resources in the system. This result will cause the current situation to worsen further. Consequently, it can be stated that increasing the performance of the system is directly proportional to increasing the performance of the constraint. Only the improvement in the performance of the constraint will improve the performance of the entire system (Büyükyılmaz & Gürkan, 2009, p. 186).

5.2.4 Removal of Constraints in the System

The fourth step, after identifying the constraints and determining the way to be followed to eliminate or reduce them, concerns the decision given by the management about which constraints to remove. If there is a capacity constraint, management should look for ways to increase capacity. If there is a demand constraint, actions to increase demand have to be performed such as creating demand by making promotional advertisements for use of the product or service. An increase in the profit will be provided by removing the existing constraints in the system. At this step, we need look at what the organization expects from the future. However, it should not be forgotten that removing a constraint does not show that there are no other constraint or constraints in the system (Kaygusuz, 2005, p. 140). Removing the constraints means defining how the system's performance will be improved according to its objectives. If the constraint is a business center, additional preventive maintenance can be applied to lift the constraint from the center, or additional machines can be purchased to increase the capacity (Yüksel, 2013, p. 211).

5.2.5 Returning to the First Step Once the Constraint is Eliminated

New constraints will be formed in the system after the constraints are removed. In this case, after each constraint is removed, the performance of the system will try to be improved by returning to the first step, finding new constraint or constraints, and removing these constraints. This cycle must last forever in order to ensure continuous improvement. In the model described here, there is a preparatory step prior to application of the first, second and third steps. It can be said that these three steps are related to the organizational policy. The fourth step, which is the implementation step, requires the organization's resource demand or its investments. This five-step model provides more success in systems where there are usually physical constraints. With the use of this model, the physical constraints diminish and leave the place to political constraints towards the market or regarding the management, such as inadequate demand. Thus, Goldratt stated that physical constraints are generally solved with money, and very few of these constraints lead to major problems in the organization (Büyükyılmaz & Gürkan, 2009: 187).

6 Conclusion

The competitive environment of today's global marketplace continues to undergo change. Markets are more international, dynamic, and customer driven. Customers are more sophisticated and are demanding more variety, better quality, and greater service in terms of reliability and response time. Product life cycles continue to shorten and product proliferation is expanding. Technological developments are occurring at an ever-increasing pace, resulting in both product innovations and manufacturing process improvements. (Vokurka & Fliedner, 1998, p. 166). This has led to new approaches in production systems. In this context, automobile assembly line developed by Henry Ford at the beginning of the 20th century has become a revolutionary point in mass production when the development process of production systems is evaluated. As a result of this development, until the 1980s, low-cost-oriented mass production was dominant in production processes. When it comes to 1980's, a quality oriented production concept that customer needs are taken into consideration has begun to be adopted. In the 1990s, it was understood that product quality was not only dependent on the employees involved in the production process, but also on design, procurement, distribution and marketing. From the 1990s onwards, instead of mass production, the conception of production focused on customer needs began to be adopted. In the mass production systems, while the tools and machines were being used labor intensively for a single determined purpose, the share of people in the automation increased production started to decrease with the use of internet and information technologies in production with the 2000s. The traditional production concept, where the workforce is intense and the mass production is adopted, has left its place to modern production understanding in which automation is dominant and quality oriented production is aimed at customer needs. Within this understanding, six sigma, reengineering, just in time production, agile manufacturing and theory of constraints are studied in the study.

In modern production systems, it is generally aimed to produce more variety of products in the direction of changing customer demands by using multipurpose production equipments. In the case of changes, uncertainties and unexpected developments in the environment, agile manufacturing approaches step in to meet customer needs immediately. With this approach, changes in the environment are dealt with not only by taking into consideration processes by establishing relations with suppliers but also by seeking ways to adapt with strategy, system, technology and human dimension at the same time. Businesses will be preferred and successful in the market to the extent they meet their customer needs at certain quality levels. One of the approaches utilized in this sense is six sigma. Benefits of enterprises from six sigma projects are evaluated according to sigma levels. This approach focuses on; preventive actions, improving the processes, redesigning these if necessary, reducing the error rate to 3,4 unit per million (at 6 sigma level), and the profit to be gained from sales. In today's market conditions, cost increases originating from the low quality adversely affect profitability levels of businesses and reduce competition power. Because of the large number of businesses in the internet and the market, consumers can easily reach a desired product. It is seen that reengineering practices, which are modern production approaches, are more risky than other approaches. Because the information that exists in these applications is rejected. Reconstruction of business processes without existing knowledge can be very risky. Therefore, the risk of failure in reengineering studies is quite high. In addition to these, organizations that have succeeded with reengineering applications can become significant organizations in the sector or world scale. Businesses always have to maintain their operations according to certain factors in an economic structure, regardless of which approach they adopt. These factors are expressed as constraints according to the theory of constraints. Theory of constraints sees businesses as a whole system and states that the performance to be achieved depends on these constraints. Accordingly, the theory acknowledges that every system has at least one constraint, and that these constraints can create opportunities for businesses to develop but also can create bottlenecks. For this reason, all constraints must be managed effectively in order for the production systems to achieve their goals.

Reference

Aksu, A. A. (2000). Değişim mühendisliği uygulamalarında karşılaşılan dirençler ve yapılan hatalar. *Dokuz Eylül Üniversitesi İktisadi ve idari Bilimler Fakültesi Dergisi, 15*(2), 37–48.

Breyfogle, F. W. (2003). *Implementing six sigma: Smarter solutions using statistical methods.* New York: John Wiley&Sons.

Büyükyılmaz, O. & Gürkan, S. (2009). Süreçlerde en zayıf halkanın bulunması: Kısıtlar Teorisi. *Zonguldak Karaelmas Sosyal Bilimler Dergisi, 5*(9), 177–195.

Doğan, S. & Demiral, Ö. (2008). Yalın yöntemler ve altı sigmayı içeren bütünleşik bir yaklaşım: Yalın altı sigma. *Atatürk Üniversitesi İktisadi ve İdari Bilimler Dergisi*, *22*(1), 343–366.

Gunasekaran, A. (1999). Agile manufacturing: A framework for research and development. *International Journal of Production Economics*, *62*(1–2), 87–105.

Gürsakal, N. (2005). *Altı sigma: Müşteri odaklı yönetim*. Ankara: Nobel Yayın Dağıtım.

Hammer, M. & Stanton, A. S. (1995). *Değişim mühendisliği devrimi: Ne yapmalı, ne yapmamalı?* (Çev: Sinem Gül). İstanbul: Sabah Kitapları, 1995.

Hammer, M. & Champy, J. (1997). *Değişim mühendisliği: İş idaresinde devrim için bir manifesto*. (Çev: Sinem Gül). İstanbul: Sabah Kitapları, 1993.

Işığıçok, E. (2005). *Altı sigma kara kuşaklar için hipotez testleri yol haritası*. Bursa: Ezgi Kitapevi.

Kasap Coşkun, G. & Peker, D. (2009). Çevik üretim: Otomotiv ana sanayinde faaliyet gösteren bir işletmenin çevikliğinin ortaya konmasına yönelik bir araştırma: Agile manufacturing. *Elektronik Sosyal Bilimler Dergisi*, *8*(27), 57–78.

Kaygusuz, S. Y. (2005). Kısıtlar Teorisi: Varsayımlar, süreçler ve bir uygulama. *Ankara Üniversitesi Sosyal Bilimler Fakültesi Dergisi*, *60*(4), 133–156.

Krajewski, L. J., Ritzman L. P. & Malhotra, M. K. (2012). *Üretim yönetimi süreçler ve tedarik zinciri*. (Çeviri Editörü: Semra Birgün). İstanbul: Nobel Yayınları, 2009.

Leite, M. & Braz, V. (2016). Agile manufacturing practices for new product development: Industrial case studies. *Journal of Manufacturing Technology Management*, *27*(4), 560–576.

Love, P. E. D. & Gunasekaran, A. (1997). Process reengineering: A review of enablers. *International Journal of Production Economics*, *50*(2–3), 183–197.

Maskell, B. (2001). The age of agile manufacturing. *Supply Chain Management: An International Journal*, *6*(1), 5–11.

Oakland, J. S. (2014). *Total quality management and operational excellence: Text with cases*. New York: Routledge.

Pande, P. S., Neuman, R. P. & Cavanagh, R. R. (2018). *Six sigma yolu: GE, Motorola ve zirvedeki diğer firmaların performanslarını yükseltme yöntemleri*. (Çev: Nafiz Güder & Güneş Tokcan). İstanbul: Klan Yayınları, 2000.

Pira, A. & Kocabaş, F. (2003). Örgütsel iletişim açısından değişim mühendisliği. *Kocaeli Üniversitesi Sosyal Bilimler Enstitüsü Dergisi*, *5*(1), 87–102.

Şahin, O. (2013). İstatistiksel proses kontrolünde proses yeterlilik analizi ve tekstil endüstrisinde uygulama. *Atatürk Üniversitesi İktisadi ve İdari Bilimler Dergisi*, *27*(2), 253–271.

Öztürk, A. (2013). *Kalite yönetimi ve planlaması*. Bursa: Ekin Yayınevi.

Özveri, O. & Çakır, E. (2012). Yalın altı sigma ve bir uygulama. *Afyon Kocatepe Üniversitesi İktisadi ve İdari Bilimler Fakültesi, 14*(2), 17–36.

Ünal, E. N., Tanış, V. N. & Küçüksavaş, N. (2005). Kısıtlar Teorisi ve bir üretim işletmesinde uygulama. *Çukurova Üniversitesi Sosyal Bilimler Enstitüsü Dergisi, 14*(2), 433–448.

Vokurka, R. J. & Fliedner, G. (1998). The journey toward agility. *Industrial Management & Data Systems, 98*(4), 165–171.

Yang, K. & El-Haik, B. S. (2003). *Design for six sigma: A roadmap for product development.* London: Mc Graw Hill.

Yüksel, H. (2013). *Üretim/İşlemler yönetimi temel kavramlar.* Ankara: Nobel Yayıncılık.

Aykut Acar

Total Quality Management in Public Administration: A Return from Weber, Fayol and Taylor or Not?

1 Introduction

In our age, despite all the opposite opinions, the effects of globalization are felt intensely in almost every field. It is difficult to keep pace with the developments in this era where constant changes and competition exist. Organizations must be continually innovative, competitive, exchanging, creative and learning organizations to be successful (Aykaç & Özer, 2006, p. 172). Essentially, this process is rooted in the 1930s, the Total Quality Management (TQM) concept that was first applied in the United States (USA), then Japan and some European states in the 1950s. At the roots of TQM is the idea of Scientific Management. Essential elements of scientific management such as *"time and motion studies"* have provided important data for TQM (Aykaç & Özer, 2006, pp. 173–174).

In the early 1990s, modernization and reform became a growing need in the non-functional bureaucratic mechanism. Improvement in the public sector was a goal in order to meet the needs of society in a globalized competitive environment. Achieving efficiency in the public sector is almost in the top positions of the political agenda in all industrialized countries. With the adoption of the Lisbon agenda in 2000, the European Union member states have taken on a difficult task to make the region the most competitive economic region in the world. Based on information, sustainable growth and better business opportunities, higher social sensitivity and a simplified regulatory environment were targeted. In fact, the goal with the Lisbon Treaty was simply to modernize public administration (Karyotakis & Moustakis, 2014, p. 31).

The management consciousness was born and developed in two separate disciplines that are separate and completely separate from each other in the private and public sectors. The management philosophy was born with the ideas of American engineer Frederick W. Taylor and Henry Ford, who is also an engineer and industrialist. In short, the philosophy of management, called Taylorism and Fordism in short, was generally accepted from the beginning of the century to almost the second half of the century. On the scientific level, the first person to examine Public Administration was the German social scientist Max Weber. At the time of Weber's work in public administration, another scientist named Henry Fayol was also working on this field.

2 Weberian Bureaucratic Management and Fayolism

Max Weber (1864–1920) worked on how to manage a large organization he called bureaucracy. According to Weber, the following principles were important for bureaucracy and state administration (Aktan, 2003):

- Clear authority and accountability in the organization,
- Pre-identification and planning of tasks and tasks,
- Continuous control and inspection,
- Creation and storage of written rules in the organization,
- Bringing managers in place by election rather than election,
- Establishing a hierarchical organizational structure within command and command chain,
- Employees are accepted to work after an official exam and a specific training seminar.

Henry Fayol, considered to be one of the first representatives of public administration science, except Weber, in his "Management Principles" published in 1892, emphasized the importance of centralism, authority and hierarchy in the state administration like Max Weber. The following principles were adopted in the management understanding of Fayol, known as Fayolism (Aktan, 2003):

- Management structure based on division of labor and specialization,
- Management has authority and responsibility,
- The dominance of discipline in management,
- Employees should act in accordance with orders and instructions from a person,
- Movement of the units in the direction of a single target and plan,
- Keeping the organization's interests on everything,
- Decisions taken at the organization from the center,
- Continuity of employment of the workforce; the fact that they do not get involved often,
- Prioritizing the creativity of employees,
- Employees should be treated in accordance with the principles of justice and equality,
- Placement of a desire to work together in the spirit of cooperation in the organization.

Max Weber and Henry Fayol's views on bureaucracy and state governance were generally accepted in many countries. Over time, central administration, hierarchy, "equal pay for equal work", rule, seniority and registry based ascension, routine inspections and inspections became widespread in the framework of these two understandings (Aktan, 2003).

The technological, economic, social and political developments that have taken place since the second half of the 20th century have dragged the whole world into a process of change and development not seen in history. These changes and developments have led to the need for renewal, which will ensure compliance with the new conditions of the public sector (Muter & Gökbunar, 2003). Thus, the traditional understanding of public administration has collapsed over time. Increasing public administration problems have increased the need for a new management approach (Aktan, 2003). Because the quality and efficiency of the management for national wealth is very important. In this context, the pressures to make public services more sensitive and cost-effective are increasing. The environment we live in is extremely flexible and adaptable quickly; providing quality products and services; calculating the cost; working with conviction and incentive, not with command-command chain; It also requires institutions that have the ability to have authority, control line to their staff (Gökbunar & Kayalı, 2003).

Traditionally, the use of private sector management techniques has gradually begun to enter public administration, even though public and private sectors are totally separate and different from each other, depending on the criteria of efficiency, clear management performance, clearly defined performance criteria, competition within the public sector. These innovations force the restructuring of the public sector (Muter & Gökbunar, 2003).

3 "New" Management Approach: Total Quality Management

Taylorism and Fordism have gradually lost importance in the field of business management due to the studies made since 1950's. A new philosophy of management called TQM was born with the contributions of American and Japanese scientists. Quality management authors W. Edwards Deming, Joseph Juran and Philip Crosby have built the roof of the concept of *"Total Quality Management"*, and Arman V. Feigenbaum, Kaoru Ishikawa have contributed to the development of quality by working in Kaoru Ishikawa. Quality is undoubtedly developed by Masaki Imai with Kaizen (continuous improvement) philosophy and has become the key to the strength of the Japanese economy in the world economy (Andrle, 1994, pp. 3–4; Uzun Kocamış, 2016, p. 2). TQM was essentially a management approach developed for the private sector (Aktan, 2003). Because the most important thing for businesses is to keep competitive power. It is very important to be able to see the future in a continuously changing competitive environment, to be able to innovate accordingly and to keep its creativity at the highest level. The changing plan will be in the best places in the shortest possible time, and the most important ones are those that can hold the information. It is observed that in the environment of variable competition, the importance of TQM is more comprehended and TQM orientation is accelerating (Gürsözlü, 2003).

Quality refers to compliance with standards in a narrow sense and in a broader sense a product and service's ability to meet needs and satisfy customer demands. Quality is a precaution, it creates its solutions before problems arise, it adds to the structure of products and services the search for superiority and excellence through design; quality is achieved with efficient, competent and educated personnel; quality is flexibility, getting changeable to meet requests, willingness to be in this issue; quality is activity, work is to do it quickly and accurately; to adhere to a program of quality, to do things in a timely manner (Dirik & Özdemir, 2004).

As it can be seen, quality has introduced concepts of prevention, education and most important change (harmony) within the framework, while maintaining the principle of conformity to the standards in the classic definition. All three of these new factors are permanent. It has been found that the activities for continuous improvement of quality have been found to be an effective way to achieve the stated goals. TQM has started to be pronounced in the world and successfully implemented in the private sector for a long time, TQM has started to enter into public administration systems.

Initiatives to implement TQM in public administration first came to the US in the United States. In the federal state, the Federal Quality Institute, which is directly affiliated, was established. Work in the TQM area has been widespread in all public institutions, especially with the support of President Clinton and his assistant, Gore (Al Gore Report, which Gore has written, emphasizes that the size or the smallness of the public sector is a problem at the secondary level and how the public administration should work on the main problem). The findings are divided into four main groups, which are: Reducing stationery, giving priority to customers, empowering employees to get results, and returning casually (Önder, 1997, pp. 117–135).

As its name suggests, TQM is a management philosophy that aims to increase quality in the organization. TQM is the continual improvement of all existing activities of an organization and ensures that all employees involved in these activities participate fully and actively in the continuous improvement efforts and that the maximum benefit is achieved by satisfying the employees, beneficiaries of the service or producers and society as a whole (Ergezer, 2004). In TQM understanding, it is argued that achievement and high performance can be achieved in the organization by improving management, human and process quality, not just the quality of the product and service offered. It is emphasized that the quality of products and services can be achieved by the efforts of the leader and top management and the well-trained "quality" human power in the organization. It is argued that the organization is a whole in this new management concept and that all the elements of this whole (managers, employees, structure, system, process, machinery, tools, environment, etc.) should be "good quality" (Aktan, 2003).

Completely different new principles defended the fundamental values and principles of TQM in public administration in the traditional sense. Total quality philosophy in the first place is a customer-focused management approach. However, we know that people who benefit from goods and services in traditional public management sense are not "customers" but "citizens". Citizens have the right to determine the administration (or rather, the political power that will take place on the bureaucracy) to provide goods and services only by voting. The elected political party decides which goods and services will be offered in line with their own decisions, appreciation and preferences, not in accordance with the wishes of the voters who voted for them. Therefore, it can be easily understood that customer sensitivity in private management does not need to be shown in public administration.

In traditional public administration, centralized management understanding and tradition dominated authority, orders and instructions. However, the TQM concept advocates a decentralized management structure that envisages the transfer of duties and powers to sub-units and employees to a large extent. Another dimension of TQM is "total participation management". In this management approach, importance is given to cooperation and communication between managers and employees at every level. Total participation management is also called "synergistic management".

Understanding of TQM is based on the understanding that mistakes and mistakes should be removed from the beginning with the measures to be taken. In this management philosophy, the principle of "zero error" sets out an ideal and moreover a goal. TQM is already emphasizing problem solving. Traditional approach to public administration is not "preventative" but "therapeutic" approach. As faults and mistakes arise, solutions are being sought.

Another important aspect of TQM is the importance given to "information and analysis". With this new management approach, it is aimed to improve the quality continuously by collecting data and making statistical analyzes. The TQM technique called "benchmarking" focuses on providing information, collecting data and adapting it to the organization from other successful organizations. This is not "copycat" or "imitation" but is defined as getting the best practices in successful organizations and applying them to themselves.

4 Human Resources Management Instead of (Public) Personnel Administration

Unlike traditional public management approach, "human resources management" (HRM) is of great importance in TQM. The new principles apply to issues such as hiring staff, raising employees, raising wages and wage policy in total quality philosophy. This new management approach aims to create a management structure based on merit. However, in public administration, favoritism is often widespread, although one of the principles of the personnel regime is merit. The rules regarding the public withdrawal are also quite strict. On the other hand, TQM advocates "flexibility" in working life. While the rise in traditional public management understanding is based on seniority and position or title, the criteria for entry into employment in TQM conception are clear and just, job promotion and wage policy are based on the characteristics and performance of managers and employees (Aktan, 2003). [In the public bureaucracy, the bureaucrats are based on the seniority system, which means that the staffing system is based on years of waiting, and when they reach insufficient levels in their old age when they are close to retirement, they come to the posts of senior management (Gökbunar & Kayalı, 2003), which Laurence Peter describes with the famous Peter principle that: *"People in a hierarchy tend to rise to their level of incompetence"* (Peter & Hull, 1994)].

HRM is primarily a matter that develops and widespread within the private sector. In this respect, it should be argued whether it is suitable for public administration having different purposes and principles (Öztürk, 1999, pp. 123–131). There is also no consensus on the definition of this concept. HRM is the result of a combination of theory and practice, seeking to integrate more self-management practices and personnel management in businesses. In this sense, HRM desires to transfer HRM from traditional management approach and tries to establish connection with personnel management. The main features of HRM and their differences with traditional personnel management are summarized below (Öztürk, 1997, pp. 123–131):

- Management mentality; Long-term and strategic predictability in HRM, and short-term in Personnel Administration (PA).
- Concept of organization; Individuals in the HRM (shared values, individuals whose dependence on organizational goals and general identities are brought together), pluralism in the PA (collective solidarity within groups and clearly defined rules and structures in circumstances).
- In terms of organizational structure and functioning; Natural flexibility in HRM, bureaucratic rule in PA and limited role are dominant.
- Trends towards work; Higher confidence, cooperation, solidarity and auto control in the HRM, low confidence in the PA, imposition and control to reduce costs.
- Authority and responsibility of the staff; Horizontal hierarchy in the HRM, horizontal management and distributed authority, vertical management and centralization in the PA.
- Importance given to the family; Quality in HRM, quantity in PA.

5 Application of TQM in the Public Sector

In the past TQM was applied in the private sector, but now public sector and public services. This is why organizations operating in global competitive environment customer-focused organizations need to offer quality products and services in order to compete. TQM is a philosophy that aims to improve the quality of products and services with the means to obtain more with less (Ajmal, Tuomi, Helo & Sandhu, 2016, pp. 34–35). TQM can be defined as the development of an organization culture that identifies and supports the continuous acquisition of customer satisfaction from a holistic perspective. TQM is a way of managing an organization in its entirety to improve its efficiency, flexibility and competitive power. The most common principles of TQM: leadership and management, strategic planning, customer orientation, focus on employees, focus on suppliers, focus on material resources, process management and performance results (Ajmal, Tuomi, Helo & Sandhu, 2016, pp. 36–37). However, implementation of TQM in public institutions it is often associated with the rise of the New Public Administration (NPM). With NPM TQM faced many criticisms. The underlying argument of these criticisms was that the NPM and TQM would undermine public service actions because they defended entrepreneurial approaches to providing public services. In addition to discussing the appropriateness of TQM for public institutions, there is a constant debate about the negative aspects of TQM. One of the most serious objections made to TQM is that it produces mechanical solutions and increases bureaucracy (Vinni, 2007, p. 103).

It is possible that TQM can be implemented in our public administration system. However, certain characteristics of the Turkish public administration make it difficult to implement this practice in an absolute way, at least in the short run. First and foremost, there are many factors that actively or passively prevent the exchange and restructuring of the public. Public administrators, especially those who take a stand against the wind of change, are among these factors. So "status quoism" is a common behavior. In this respect, it is said that managers have great responsibilities in adapting and successfully applying all TQM techniques to the public sector. Otherwise, it will be difficult or even impossible to institutionalize this new management philosophy in the public sector.

Our country had serious problems in public administration. In the beginning, it can be said that traditional public administration (Weberian bureaucratic administration model and Fayolism) is dominant in almost all public institutions. Our public administration has been continuing the tradition of strict centralist and ward management for a long time. Bureaucracy and paperwork, indifference and indifference to service to citizens, leaving jobs to crawl [Northcote Parkinson proposed the famous Parkinson's Law by *"Work expands so as to fill the time available for its completion"* (Parkinson, 1996)], low employment and low labor productivity, wasting and waste are the main problems that are widespread in many public institutions. Moreover, the lack of transparency in management, lack of communication and participation in management, and other similar problems reflect different dimensions of "quality weakness" in the state administration, such as poor quality and disqualified staff employment, weak manpower planning, lack of employee motivation and rewarding, widespread fiduciary involvement in transfers and transfers. Unfortunately, the words "Health from Allah, salary from the State" and "Move head, take salary" clearly reveal the problems of bureaucracy and state administration. Political degeneration, which has become increasingly widespread in recent years, has put the issue of "immorality" in public administration at the beginning of the day. Bribery, corruption, nepotism, favoritism services, benefice (without service officialism) took place frequently in Turkey's agenda.

Because of the poor quality of education, the tragedies living in state hospitals, the problems in the justice system, the problems of local governments, the problems of social security institutions and the public administration in the focus, it has always brought about the debate that this structure should change in the past. At the heart of these debates is the expression of the redefinition and restructuring of the state. Particularly in the process of restructuring the state, it is foreseen that some of the functions and duties of the state are transferred to the private sector (privatization), the authorities of the central state are transferred to local governments to the extent possible (localization) and some functions are transferred to the third sector (voluntary).

As for the criticism about the public personnel system, personnel system, personnel rules, practices, techniques and processes, and it shows a rapidly growing and changing dynamic structure. The main problems in this structure are (Önder, 1997, pp. 117–135):

- A very broad classification has been adopted.
- There are no clear criteria as to how to ascend up to the upper echelons, but elevation also deviates from its purpose.
- On-site employment is not provided due to lack of staff identification and analysis.
- The fees are low and the fee system is complex.
- The performance appraisal criteria are not well developed and the appraisal of the staff is left to the discretion of the managers only.
- Deviated from the purpose of in-service training and training, is used as a penalty or a prize.
- Task descriptions are missing, out of purpose, or none at all.
- In the execution of certain duties, unity of service and integrity principle is a problem.
- Some tasks cannot be done because there is no organizational arrangement.
- Some tasks with secondary presets can replace the actual tasks.

Here is the concept that comes to mind at this point TQM. The necessity of disseminating TQM in all public institutions in the process of state restructuring is expressed at every opportunity. In order to be able to apply this successfully in our country, it must be planned, systematic, stable and patient. First of all, it is important to approach the subject in a planned and systematic way. Since TQM has elements such as information and analysis, strategic planning management, dialogue and decision making based on consensus, it is necessary to start using TQM techniques. This process may develop as follows:

- Information process about TQM
- Institutional structuring (organization) process related to TQM
- Implementation of TQM process
- Continuous development process (kaizen)

Here, it is important to inform top management in public administration about TQM. It is not possible to achieve success without top management's support and contribution (Aktan, 2003). Commitment to the concept of TQM is spreading from top to bottom after first being adopted by top management. At this stage, search conferences and training seminars are being held at various levels of the bureaucracy to ensure that managers are not informed. The second phase involves the process of establishing an upper body to plan, coordinate and monitor TQM implementation in public administration. It is said that it is necessary to establish an institution similar to the above-mentioned America. The application stage means that the TQM philosophy is passed on to all public administration.

Finally, it is imperative that the philosophy of continuous development be adopted and implemented in public administration. The philosophy of continuous development expressed by the Japanese as kaizen predicts that the lessons and experiences gained from the implementation of TQM will be analyzed and the qualifications will be further improved (Aktan, 2003).

Looking at the general philosophy of TQM it is possible to see (Gökbunar & Kayalı, 2003):

- Not controlling, directing and helping employees.
- Data are used to give decisions.
- Concentrate on doing the right things instead of finding the problems.
- Team activity occurs instead of individual activities.
- It helps to develop an environment based on confidence and trust instead of doubt and complaint.

Quality control circles (QCCs) in TQM are important tools. QCCs are small groups formed by a certain number of volunteers who are in the same professional activity or who work in the same unit. These groups are thought to be important for the participation and motivation of the individuals. The main goal in QCCs is to improve communication between workers at all levels of the production line and the management, solve business problems and contribute to development activities.

Today, there is debate about the possible application of TQM in Turkish public administration, but with great change. It is argued that transforming the desire for change in the public to reality can be possible through "change management". It is hardly realistic to say that all the problems in public administration will be radically solved by applying TQM, regardless of how the method is followed. Today, attention is also drawn to some of the drawbacks that TQM can reveal, for example (Dirik & Özdemir, 2004):

- In TQM, efforts to increase productivity due to the adoption of flexible employment policies in place of previous rigid employment policies have been removed from the workplace,
- Influence of union-institutional relations on important and fundamental changes in the organization of organizations,
- Even if they do not get out of the way, more work and responsibility should be paid to employees without going to any adjustments in fees, and one of the most problematic points in TQM and public sector marriage is the difference in customer concept.

6 Conclusion

Public administration has to serve a very wide "client" group (public) with a wide variety, even opposing demands. Under these circumstances, there are questions about whether TQM's customers are happy and satisfied with their principle of usefulness.

Despite the doubt that quality management is incompatible with some scholars, TQM is still debatable in today's public administration. Customer orientation, problem solving, problem prevention, long-term strategic planning, team work and employee involvement, case based decision making, continuous improvement, horizontal and decentralized organizational structures, and stakeholders are emerging concepts of this process.

TQM reached the public sector with the spread of NPM ideas in the 1980s. For example, it is proposed that "the NPM, which is based on rational choice and public preference and contains the elements of TQM, aims to provide more effective mechanisms to provide goods and services and improve government performance levels". There is a significant overlap between TQM and NPM. TQM is seen as a better approach for public institutions than Weberianism, just as TQM proved to be a better approach for private institution s than Taylorism (Vinni, 2007, p. 110). Quality management in a public institution requires a comprehensive organizational culture. Leadership and employee involvement at all levels is important. Leaders must be willing to empower their subordinates and employees and accept additional responsibility to meet and exceed the expectations of their citizens. Whatever public goods and services, it is necessary to meet the expectations (Stringham, 2004, p. 203).

Bibliography

Ajmal, M. M., Tuomi, V., Helo, P. T. & Sandhu, M. A. (January-March 2016), TQM Practices in Public Sector, *International Journal of Information Systems in the Service Sector: Case of Finnish Healthcare Organizations*, 8(1), 34–44.

Aktan, C. C. (2003), "Toplam Kalite Yönetimi Kamudaki Kalitesizliğe Çözüm Olabilir mi?", Retrieved from: [www.canaktan.org / yonetim / toplam-kalite / kamuda-toplam-kalite / devlette-kalite.htm], Date: 09.06.2003.

Andrle, S. J. (October 1994), Total Quality Management in Public Transportation, *Research Results Digest*, (3), 1–39.

Aykaç, B. & Özer, M. A. (2006), Toplam Kalite Yönetiminin Kamu Kuruluşlarında Uygulanması: Sorunlar Ve Yeni Arayışlar, *Gazi Üniversitesi İktisadi ve İdari Bilimler Fakültesi Dergisi*, 8(3), 171–202.

Dirik D. & Özdemir, İ. (2004), "Kalite Trendini Yakalamak-Devlet Yönetiminde Toplam Kalite", Retrieved from: [www.insankaynaklari.tv / paylas / paylasimlar1.asp], Date: 20.05.2004.

Ergezer, Ş. (2004), "Toplam Kalite Yönetimi ve Yöneticilik", Retrieved from: [www. siteky.com/...], Date: 20.05.2004.

Gökbunar, R. & Kayalı, C. (2003), "Kamu Yönetiminde Toplam Kalite Uygulamasının Olanakları", Retrieved from: [www.canaktan.org/...], Date: 09.06.2003.

Gürsözlü, S. (2003), "Toplam Kalite Yönetimine Bakış", Retrieved from: [www. siteky.com / frameset / tky / tkymak.htm], Date: 09.06.2003.

Karyotakis, K. M. & Moustakis, V. S. (2014), Reinvention Of The Public Sector: Total Quality Management And Change Management, *Singidunum Journal Of Applied Sciences*, 11(2), 30–44.

Muter, N. B. & Gökbunar, R. (2003), "Müşteri ve Hizmet Yönlü Bir Kamu Sektörüne Doğru", Retrieved from: [www.canaktan.org/...], Date: 09.06.2003.

Önder, M. (September 1997), "Toplam Kalite Yönetimi: Kamu Sektöründe Uygulanması ve Karşılaşılan Sorunlar", *Türk İdare Dergisi*, (416), 117–136.

Öztürk, N. K. (September 1999), "Kamu Yönetiminde İnsan Kaynakları Yönetimi", *Türk İdare Dergisi*, (424), 123–131.

Parkinson, C. N. (1996), Parkinson Kanunu (Trans. Şaban Sitembölükbaşı), Ankara: Vadi Yayınları.

Peter, L. J. & Hull R. (1994), Peter İlkesi (Trans. Melih Ölçer), Ankara: Bilgi Yayınevi.

Stringham, S. H. (2004), Does Quality Management Work In The Public Sector?, *Public Administration and Management: An Interactive Journal*, 9(3), 182–211.

Uzun Kocamış, T. (2016), Toplam Kalite Yönetimi (TKY) ve İç Denetimin TKY'deki Rolü, *İstanbul Üniversitesi Sosyal Bilimler Dergisi*, (1), 1–21.

Vinni, R. (2007), Total Quality Management and Paradigms of Public Administration, *International Public Management Review*, 8(1), 103–131.

Selami Erdoğan

Socio-Politic Analysis of Constitutional Movements in Turkish History

1 Introduction

The Turkish Political History reveals that it does not have a stable and sound constitution. Many of the constitutions that have not been prepared by considering social demands. The constitutions, which ignored social demands or social participation, prevented democracy from consolidating.

The Constitutions are social contracts that people living in the community have agreed upon in order to live in peace. The constitution determines the limits of the state's power and the fundamental rights and freedoms of its citizens. When preparing such a basic document, the preparation method is very important as well as the content. Different classifications have been made regarding the methods of preparing the constitutions. Among them, hierarchical method (top-down), organic method and contract method. The last one (contract method) is the most appropriate and the most healthy method. The side of the agreement (the people and the state) must be done through reconciliation. In this case, the contract can be robust and long lasting. Referring to Turkey's constitutional history (except for 1921), constitutions are made unilaterally without considering the element of compromise. However, After World War II, many countries have made a constitution by way of contract (Italy 1948, Spain 1976, etc.).

Since the constitutions in these countries have a solid basis for legitimacy, the constitutions are very healthy and up to date. In fact, the concepts of democracy, human rights and participation before World War II are not as precious as they are today. However, after the 1950s these concepts gained value and began to be taken into consideration during the constitutional drafting process. In contrast, Turkey went towards the opposite direction because both anti-democratic constitution-making process have been experienced in preparing the 1961 and 1982 constitutions. Both constitutions were made during military coups and by excluding the real representatives of the people. Constituent assemblies that made constitutions were not legitimate assemblies elected by the people. In this respect, the formation of the parliament, which prepares the constitution, is also very important. While these constitutions were already being drafted, the most important criterion for the preparers (elites) should have elected to establish an inspection mechanism on the power to work. It did not matter if the constitutions were drafted by legitimate methods and that referendums were held with legitimate methods.

2 Why Were Constitutions Needed? The Constitutionalism

Today, many states around the world have a written constitution. However, in some very few countries there is no written constitution (England, Israel etc). Certainly, constitutions were born as a result of needs. Since mankind has existed, it has been seen that the power of those possessing power has used this power arbitrarily many times. For this reason, we see that constitutional movements have begun in order to protect fundamental rights and freedoms as well as to prevent an absolutely unlimited ruling power, namely to restrict the state. Even though in the case of thinkers (such as Jean Bodin) who in the early ages gave absolute and unlimited power to the state, this concept changed in the end of the 1700s, which corresponds to the modern turn. It has become a prevailing opinion that the power state that states possesses must be used by citizens to protect their safety and to establish justice (Lijpart, 1986: 25).

In fact, it seems that the constitutional movements around the world have come to fruition at a time not too far away. The oldest known constitution is the American constitution of 1787. İt is followed by the French Constitution of 1791. In later years, we can see that the European countries and the Ottoman State (1876) progressed in this way (Gözler, 2011: 20). This process, which we can call modern constitutionalism, is an advanced phenomenon based on liberal freedoms. It is worth mentioning that John Locke and Montesquieu were important contributors to the emergence and formation of the idea of constitutionalism. Both thinkers have pointed to the importance of the "separation of powers" principle, which is considered to be the most basic stance of constitutionalism. In his work "Two Treaties On Government", which Locke wrote in 1690, he emphasized that the legislative and executive forces should be gathered in separate hands. According to him, the legislation that sets the general code of conduct for the protection of freedoms and the executor who carries out their implementation must be in separate hands (Özbudun, 2015: 25). Locke was a thinker who stroke the British constitutional stamp. According to him, people who are not fully assured of freedom in the case of nature constitute civil-political administration by contracting with each other, in this case it is the duty of the authorities to make laws on their own initiative, so that the state protects the individual and his/her assets. The political authority, which also uses the obligatory means of the State, adheres to the rules set by it. The power of the political authority is not limitless, but when it interferes with areas outside its own authority, a legitimacy problem arises in terms of political authority (Locke, 1998: 4).

On the other hand, Montesquieu, the most strongly identified thinker with the theory of the separation of powers, gave a close definition to the contemporary meaning of the theory of separation of powers in his 1748 "Spirit of Laws". Montesquieu regards the separation of powers as the most important principle in terms of the establishment of freedoms. Montesquieu emphasizes the principle of separation of powers in the Constitution of 1776 and the Declaration of French Human and Citizen Rights of 1789 (Özbudun, 2015: 15).

In the course of this process, this principle has been adopted in many countries of the world and has become one of the most fundamental elements of constitutional movements. However, it has acquired a written constitution of more than half of the world's states after 1974 (Sartori, 1997: 253). In this respect, the written constitution for many countries is a fairly new concept (Sartori, 1997: 253). For this reason, the written constitution for many countries is a fairly new concept. The notion of the constitution, at the same time, has become a very closely related concept with the subject of human rights and democracy, which has become very popular in the 20th century. Important documents related to human rights. We have witnessed the emergence of in the 20th century. In this context, documents such as the Universal Declaration of Human Rights of 1948 and the European Convention on Human Rights established in 1950 started to become effective through constitutions prepared after World War II. Constitutions, – liberal character constitutions – are texts that also protect the rights of minorities. In this context, there are advocates that have formed a dichotomy with democracies, which is the power of majority of the people. On the other hand, some authors suggest that these concepts (democracy and constitution) function today complement each other. Because of the desire of a majority of democracy lacking constitutionalism; constitutionalism devoid of democracy leads to the domination of privileged minorities (Özbudun, 2015: 25). 20th Century is the democracies century and some of the countries are adopting a way of making a new constitution while transitioning to a democratic regime.

On the other hand, in the context of constitutionalist movements, the question of constitutions, as well as the content of constitutions, can be made by whom and within what boundaries. Political science has also occupied one of the most controversial issues in the literature.

3 In Which Way and by Whom Should Be Prepared a Constitution?

One of the main problems faced in the process of making a constitution is the question of who can prepare the constitution and how far its boundaries are. In this context, we are confronted with two basic concepts in the constitutional literature. The former is the concept of "primary constituent power" and the other is the concept of "secondary constituent power".

The primary constituent power is roughly defined as the power that makes the new constitution unrelated to any legal rule. The secondary constituent power, which has a more limited power, is used to express the power that changes the constitution by staying within the boundaries drawn by the primary constituent power (Atar, 2000: 164, Özer, 2013: 221).

It is assumed that the primary constituent power usually emerges in extraordinary circumstances, such as revolution, government coup, war, and has an unlimited power in preparing the constitution (Gözler, 2011: 21). On the other hand, it is stated that despite the fact that the ruling constituent power is a legal (legitimate) power, it does not have the right to make constitution from scratch and faces significant restrictions. This situation is very controversial and contradictory. As a matter of fact, Ergun Özbudun, an important constitutional scientist, points out that the real constituent power is the people or their elected representatives (Özbudun, 2014: 35). In fact, it is not consistent with the fact that the forces that have no legitimacy and emerged during extraordinary periods are accepted as the fundamental founding power.

What is important in terms of the process of making a constitution is that the body preparing the constitution is determined by elections, the constitutional period is open to the participation of the people, and the constitution is adopted after putting it in the vote. In addition, all freedoms, including expression and propaganda, which ensure that voters will is freely formed during the period of this popular vote, must be guaranteed (Yazıcı, 2011: 11). In the process of making constitutions, the methods of making constitutions as well as the content of constitutions arise as a matter of debate. It is difficult to say that constitutional scientists and political scientists have a compromise on methods. Nevertheless, it seems possible to say that the three main methods emerged during the constitutional preparation process are generally accepted. These are hierarchical method, organic method and contract method (Atar, 2000: 155).

Hierarchical Method: In the hierarchical method, the constitution is made in the form of accepting a constitution by a parliament that is not a board or a representative. This approach is a product of Jacobin style. Constitutions in which a committee of experts or an advisory body has been established enter this class. Constitutional texts, for which a constituent assembly that is not based on elections, have prepared a hierarchical example (İba, 2014: 37).

Constitutions adopted in modern authoritarian and dictatorial regimes, or in some countries in the process of transition to democracy, are usually made by this method. The administrators of these regimes have resorted in some ways to show that the constitution is not hierarchical. For example, they have appointed constituent assemblies that are not representative (non-elected) and have prepared the constitution. Today, many African countries and some Latin American countries in transition to democracy, Turkey and Eastern European countries have made constitutions using this method (Atar, 2000: 157). When the constitutional construction methods are compared, the most anti-democratic method is the hierarchical method.

Organic Method: The more democratic form of "organic method" is the method adopted by the current constitutional institutions of the constitution according to the rules in power. In the Parliament, a ruling party with a majority of constitutional amendments can be mentioned in organic terms when it comes to making a constitution on its own. Because at this point the constitution of parliament chosen by the people is the issue of constitution. However, this method excludes important segments of the society (İba, 2014: 38). In this way, in a chosen parliament, the ruling party can make or change the constitution without considering the parties, opposition parties and ideas. This understanding is neither a hierarchical method nor a contract method which we will discuss below (Atar, 2000: 162).

Contract method: In the Pact method, constitution making is carried out in the form of a "social contract" based on the principles of "participation and compromise" by political forces (groups and parties) representing the society or by a constituent assembly in an elected council. This may not always be possible (Atar, 2000: 162), as it is at the core of the contractual procedure, which may also be called constitutional construction, from the bottom up. Magna Carta Libertatum in 1215 in England and Sened-i İttifak (Document of Alliance) in local government in 1808 in the Ottoman Empire are examples of the contract method. The Italian Constitution of 1948, which was prepared especially after the Second World War and came up to date, is quite striking in the examples of constitutional examples that conform to the contract management.

4 Making Methods of the Turkish Constitutions

It is the way of preparing the content, which makes it possible to describe a constitution as "democratic" in the contemporary world. A constitution that does not rely on social negotiation and reconciliation, even if its content is democratic, will experience a constant legitimacy problem (Duran, 2015: 1). In this context, the constitution making process and method is also an element that influences the life span of democracies. We can see that the social legitimacy and participation which enables both the democracy and the constitution to survive for a long time is not taken into account in the History of Turkish Constitutionalism (Özbudun, 1993: 50), which will greatly increase the chance of democratic consolidation of consensus and partnership constitutional style. When we look at Turkey, can see a good historical experience about constitutionalism. It is approximately 150 years since the first Constitution was prepared in 1876.

4.1 The Constitution of 1876

1876 Kanun-i Esasi (Constitution) despite being the first constitution in Turkish political life, it still has the quality of a document created with the initiative of the Sultan (Hakyemez, 2013: 213). In fact, the small but effective group of reformist bureaucrats (Young Ottomans, Jeunes Turcs) and the Sultan II. Abdülhamid prepared by a special commission. This commission of 28 members consists of 3 non-Muslim Ottoman citizens. However, it should be noted that there is no constituent assembly representing the people (Karatepe, 1993: 86). The people who work here are those appointed by the Sultan himself.

In fact, since the written constitution was not experienced in the Ottoman period, no one had knowledge about the method to be followed in the preparation of a new constitution. Mithat Pasha and other Jeunes Turcs wanted a constitution to represent the nation. However, the Sultan II. Abdülhamit finished the discussions on this subject saying "I represent the nation" (Karatepe, 1993: 86). Thus, the constitution was to be missed by a parliament elected by the people. This constitution was a unilateral declaration of the will of the Sultan, a constitution prepared in a hierarchical way.

At that time, it was not possible to talk about a consensus among those who prepared the constitution. Foreign historians described Mithat Pasha and his friends as "liberals". The opposite point was the "conservatives" represented by Ahmet Cevdet Pasha. In the mid-1876s, liberal (constitutional) and conservative political circles seemed to polarize the Ottoman bureaucracy. They have argued that those who do not want the constitutional rule and the constitutional regime, that is, the political regime, are contrary to the law. At the same time, they wrote that the constitutional institutions were Russian imitators (Tunaya, 2009: 56). It is also important that a constitution can be written and put into effect even though such difficult obstacles are encountered. It can be said, this constitution was prepared by the method of hierarchy. For this reason, it cannot be seen as democratic constitution.

4.2 The Constitution of 1921

The 1921 Constitution, which defines the principles of the state, is the first constitution of the newly established state. This first constitution, which is an extraordinary term constitution, was prepared at an extraordinary period by the de facto ruling power of the independence movement in Anatolia. This constitution is more democratic than other Ottoman and Turkish constitutions (Ergin, 2013: 40), although it is a product of extraordinary circumstances and not very comprehensive. It is perhaps the only democratic example in terms of its preparation and acceptance characteristics (Tanör, 2017: 250). The 1921 constitution, even if it came with a two-way election, was prepared by a parliament with parliamentary representatives representing their own, with a relatively pluralistic and opposition component (Parla, 2002: 71). Indeed, this constitution was adopted by a constituent assembly representing Turkey in the sociological sense of the present society. The first period, which constituted this constitution, consisted of those who had religious influence in political, social, bureaucrats, religions, merchants, self-employed persons, clergy and farmers. In this context, the Parliament which adopted the 1921 Constitution had actual groupings with no political party groups in the present sense. There was a group opposite to Mustafa Kemal who was called as the second group in the parliament. Consequently, this constitution was born as a consequence of serious negotiations. In this respect, the 1921 constitution can be regarded as a constitution that conforms to the contract method.

The 1921 Constitution was a short constitution, very short-lived. However, Turkey's political constitutional law that the lower and upper range of great transformation in three years' time and have been living under the 1921 constitution. This constitution has been enriched with a practice that is not worth comparing with its short life span. Following the success of the War of Independence under this constitutional regime, radical reforms such as abolishing the Ottoman dynasty, announcing the republic, and removing the Caliphate were carried out during the constitutional period (Tanör, 2017: 269). The 1921 constitution was based on a system of powers (parliamentary government), a solid form of the rule of superiority. On the other hand, even if the 1921 Constitution was made, the law of 1876 (the Constitution) remained in force.

4.3 The Constitution of 1924

In Turkey in mid-1923 and early elections, which opponent group to Ataturk (II. Group) stayed outside the parliament majority. This constitution is the first constitution to be made after the declaration of the republic. In fact, this constitution was held by the representatives of the Grand National Assembly and elected. However, this constitution has been drafted and adopted by a single parliament and a parliament where it dominates (monotheism). The election of this council may wake up at first the impression that the constitution is prepared in a democratic way. However, in the process of electing the parliament that prepares the 1924 Constitution, none of these process democratic principles are available. The elections were held in a place where the one-party method was dominant, by applying a two-step method among the candidates shown by the CHP. For this reason, the election process lacks the dimension of competitiveness. In other words, when parliamentary composition was determined, not the will of the people but the influence of the electors became effective. Since the CHP had liquidated opposition elements before the 1923 elections, the candidates nominated by the party were largely homogenous (Yazıcı, 2009: 16). The 1924 parliament is not a constituent assembly. It is an ordinary legislative. Also, 1874 French Constitution and 1921 Polish Constitution affected to this Constitution 1924 (Abdülhakimoğulları, 2013: 227). Although, the choice of the people who made it was made with antidemocratic methods, this constitution was made at a time when the authoritarian regime of the CHP was not yet in consciousness. However, during the preparation of the constitution, this constitution was adopted by free debate in the TGNA. Again, there is no provision in this constitution to call the authoritarian nature of the regime which is about to be established. The authoritarian regime of the CHP was created not through the 1924 Constitution but against it. Turkey did not need to amend the constitution passes to democracy in 1950. It is clear that the 1924 Constitution, which did not create a problem for democracy transition, created serious problems in terms of democracy consolidation. Above all, this constitution was drafted according to the understanding of majoritarian democracy. There were no constitutional democracy mechanisms to balance the majority power and protect minority rights (Özbudun, 1993: 53--54).

It is not possible to say that the second term TBMM, in which this constitution was prepared, was chosen by democratic methods. From this point of view, it is not possible to put the method of a constitution prepared by the people who were not democratically elected into the democratic method class. For this reason, the 1924 constitution cannot be considered as an "organic method" or "contract method" in terms of its preparation. Although the negotiations have been made seriously during the preparing of the Constitution, it is better to use the "hierarchical method" as the making method of this constitution.

4.4 The Constitution of 1961

First of all, it should be noted that the constitution of 1961 is the product of a military coup d'état (Abdülhakimoğulları, 2013: 228), a group of 38 people with low-level military rankings and a group called themselves the National Unity Committee (NUC) The military committee, who made the coup d'état in the 1960, played an important role in the preparing of this Constitution. While preparing it, a special constituent assembly which had not been seen in previous Turkish Constitutions was appointed to prepare just the constitution.

This constituent assembly, which had been appointed to prepare the new constitution, consisted of two wings. The members of the first one were already members of the NUC who had already carried out the military coup. The second wing consisted of civilians. This wing was called "the assembly of representatives". In fact, even if the concept of "representatives" was a democratic connotation, it did not deserve this name because of its anti-democratic formation. These civilians, who served in the representatives' council, came there by co-optation, not election. The Assembly included representatives of the two opposition parties, the CHP (Republican People's Party) and the Republican and Peasant People's National Party (CKMP). It also consisted of representatives of some non-governmental organizations. Nevertheless, there were no representatives of the ousted Democratic Party representing nearly half of the Turkish voters at that time (Özbudun, 2014: 82). Thus, this constituent assembly, which had no electoral and democratic legitimacy, prepared and presented the Constitution to the people. The text of this new constitution prepared by the Constituent Assembly was presented to the public on 9 July 1961. It was a risky situation to act as an opposition during the propaganda period for this constitution. At least there was a psychological pressure environment that the soldiers created. Moreover, it was not possible to say that this popular vote took place in a free environment, since the current political parties did not have the right to publicly propagate the constitution. Even under these conditions, the coup d'état had to settle for a lower vote than they had hoped. This constitution was approved by 61 % of the votes (Erdoğan, 2012: 112).

When the 1961 Constitution is evaluated both in terms of content and construction conditions it appears that it has been prepared without allowing the participation of a large majority of Turkish society. Turkey's largest party, the former Democratic Party completely excluded due to their voters, they use negative vote in the plebiscite for the 1961 Constitution (Özbudun, Gençkaya, 2010: 27). On the other hand, with this constitution, mechanisms have been introduced to control the movement of the electors. The constitution of 1961 did not win sufficient sociological legitimacy in terms of the conditions of construction. This constitution was not made by elected representatives (Abdülhakimoğulları, 2013: 222–229).

As a result, the NUC, which removed the Menderes Government from the administration by election with an illegal method, directed the constitution making process and this constitution was drafted under their supervision. From this point of view, the 1961 Constitution has taken its place in history as one of the most problematic constitutions by the method of preparation. This constitution was a problem because the constituent assembly was formed by appointment rather than election. In addition, it is also anti-democratic due to the fact that the appointed persons represent only certain segments. Because of the features such as the lack of necessary freedom environment in the constitutional voting process of the Constitution, it is undoubtedly considered as a "hierarchical method" within the existing constitution preparation methods.

4.5 The Constitution of 1982

1980 in Turkey generals who seized power on September 12, themselves the National Security Council (5 units generals) were called. This coup d'état was different from 1960 Coup. Because 1960 was done by senior officers. NSC this junta forbade all political activities. Parliament was abolished, political parties closed. The junta began their work to prepare a new constitution to restructure the social and political structure, just as it was in 1960.

The putschists wanted to do this restructuring through a constituent assembly established by the NSC. The structure was double-parliamentary as it was in the constituent assembly of 1960–1961. this constituent assembly was a wing of the NSC. In other words, the first wing of the constituent assembly was the NSC, and the second wing consisted of the council with the name of the Advisory Council. All Members of the Advisory Council were appointed by the NSC. Moreover, in order to be able to take part in the council, one had to have no connection with any political party. This advisory council was a parliament created entirely by state elites (Özbudun, Gençkaya, 2010: 29). It was an organization founded on the initiative of coup generals. Indeed, it was a form of consultation that was not consulted appropriately on behalf of the Advisory Council, but only for consultation.

The council had 160 members. 40 members were elected directly by the National Security Council, and 120 members were elected by the National Security Council among the three-fold candidates to be shown in the governors of each province. The National Security Council worked as an upper chamber (parliament). In this respect, the model created by the founding power of 1961 was moved to an extreme point in 1982 (Parla, 2002: 80). Within the Constituent Assembly, the NSC had the right to say the last word. In other words, the NSC was the absolute authority to change or reject the draft Constitution prepared by the Advisory Council. The draft prepared by the Constituent Assembly was presented to the public on 7 November 1982. In fact, there was a constitutional commission preparing this draft. This Commission consisted of persons selected from within the Consultative Assembly. Chief of the Commission was Professor Dr. Orhan Aldıkaçtı. The NSC made changes from time to time on the items written by the commission. Finally, a draft was drafted by the commission and inspected and approved by the NSC. The referendum process began when this draft was adopted by the Constituent Assembly.

It was also forbidden to criticize this constitution in the referendum process. This was in fact evoking authoritarian rule. The 1961 constitution and the referendum were held in a relatively free environment. However, during the referendum on the 1982 constitution, the president and the chairman of the NSC Org. Apart from Kenan Evren's one-sided campaign, no opposing views were allowed. At the same time, a NSC decision, which was issued at the time, banned the expression of opinions aimed at influencing voters' votes. It was even forbidden to criticize the speeches Kenan Evren made for the purpose of promoting the constitution (Özbudun, Gençkaya, 2010: 29).

There are many factors that indicate that the construction period of the 1982 Constitution does not coincide with the definition of the civil and democratic constitution. The first of these factors is that the constituent assembly, which prepares the constitution, is not elected. Secondly, civil and political rights are suspended. Thirdly, it is the exclusion of the will of the people in the process of constitutional construction. In addition, the freedom of expression, propaganda, press and meetings were suppressed in the process of submission of the constitution to the people. Many such freedoms were restricted to prevent this debate from being freely discussed in public (Yazıcı, 2011: 22). This constitution was adopted with a rate of 91.5 % yes, which was a very high percentage of votes in an environment where all kinds of democratic rights were abolished. In fact, it is a more accurate qualification to refer to it as plebiscite, which is a practice specific to the authoritarian regimes, rather than a referendum.

To conclude, legitimacy of the 1982 constitution was the most quickly faded one among that of the other constitutions of Turkey. The main reason for this is that there is no democratic representation in its structure (Parla, 2002: 8). While considering all what was happened in the constitution-making process, the 1982 constitution is the most anti-democratic and enforcing one in Turkey's history. In this respect, the 1982 constitution undoubtedly belongs to the hierarchical constitutional class.

5 Conclusion

Considering the constitution to the way in Turkey, it is observed that many of them is not based on a democratic ground. The participation of the public was ignored during these preparatory processes. This has made the legitimacy of these constitutions controversial. Since they did not sit on a democratic platform, these constitutions were at the same time one of the causes of political instability. Many new constitutions in the countries were prepared in normal times. And they also prepared by elected parliaments unlike Turkey. In most of the democratic countries the founders or ordinary assemblies, elected by the people, have prepared their constitutions. When we look at the Republic of Turkey, three constitutions were prepared (1924–1961–1982), but none of them has been made by democratically and elected assembly Likewise, the 1876 Constitution was appointed by a special commission appointed by the Sultan instead of the elected parliament. Only the 1921 Constitution is different from other constitutions because it is prepared by the representatives coming by legitimate means. The basic philosophy of Turkish Constitutions (1961 and 1982), especially after the coups, is based on a custodial understanding.

Turkey Constitutions is usually the product of an authoritarian and militarist understanding. Obviously, they serve a purpose, such as supervising elected politicians. They have failed to solve social and political problems. Turkey constitution is not serve solution of the problems of the political system, it has been the cause to emerge of problems. In times, when these constitutions without democratic legitimacy were in force, military coups were not prevented. Because, these constitutions were lacking in the mechanisms to strengthen and protect democracy. The last two constitutions have been subjected to intense criticism from the moment they entered into force. For example, criticism of the 1982 constitution came to light just after the 1983 general elections. Since the early 1990s, some non-governmental organizations have begun drafting new constitutional drafts (1992 TÜSİAD). Since then, these studies have gained even more momentum. Even though the Turkish Grand National Assembly (2011–2013 experience of the Constitutional Reconciliation Commission) entered a constitutional drafting study in 2011, the result was not reached at all. However, when the criticism comes so early, the content of the constitution, as well as the legitimacy problems of the construction process, have an important place.

That there was a problematic constitution of the 1982 Constitution that almost everyone in Turkey has similar ideas. There is also public consensus that this should be changed through a social contract. However, it is very difficult to prepare a constitution with absolute agreement. For this reason, it should be preferred to make a constitution in the form of the broadest possible agreement. If Turkey makes a democratic constitution as a result of negotiations by the elected representatives will be able to eliminate some of the problems largely as political instability. On this count, Turkey will be able to use his energy to solve his more macro problems.

Bibliography

Abdülhakimoğulları, E. (2013). Yapım Süreçleri Açısından Anayasalarımız ve Yeni Anayasa İçin Öneriler. Yeni Türkiye Dergisi (50), 233–240.

Atar, Y. (2000). Demokrasilerde Anayasa Yapımı. Konya: Mimoza Yayınları.

Erdoğan, M. (2012). Türkiyede Anayasalar ve Siyaset (8 b.). Ankara: Liberte Yayınları.

Ergin, S. (2013). Yeni Anayasa Eşiğinde Türkiye. Yeni Türkiye Dergisi (50), 38–50.

Gözler, K. (2011). Anayasa Hukukuna Giriş (18 b.). Bursa: Ekin Kitabevi.

Hakyemez, Y. Ş. (2013). Türkiye'nin Anayasa Sorunu ve Yeni Anayasanın Hazırlanmasına İlişkin Notlar. Yeni Türkiye Dergisi(50), 213–220.

İba, Ş. (2014). Yeni Anayasa Arayışları ve Kırmızı Çizgiler (I b.). Ankara: Nobel Yayınları.

Karatepe, Ş. (1993). Darbeler Anayasalar ve Modernleşme. İstanbul: İz Yayıncılık.

Lıjpart, A. (1986). Çağdaş Demokrasiler. (E. ONULDURAN, & E. ÖZBUDUN, Çev.) Ankara: Türk Demokrasi Vakfı ve Siyasi İlimler Derneği.

Locke, J. (1998). Hoşgörü Üstüne Bir Mektup (II b.). (M. YÜRÜŞEN, Çev.) Ankara: Liberte Yayınları.

Özbudun, E. (2014). Türkiye'de Demokratikleşme Süreci, Anayasa Yapımı ve Anayasa Yargısı (I b.). İstanbul: İstanbul Bilgi Üniversitesi Yayınları.

Özbudun, E. (2015). Anayasacılık ve Demokrasi (I b.). İstanbul: İstanbul Bilgi Üniversitesi Yayınları.Özbudun, E., & Gençkaya, Ö. F. (2010). Türkiye'de Demokratikleşme ve Anayasa Yapımı Politikası. İstanbul: Doğan Kitap.

Özer, A. (2013). Anayasanın Yapılması ve Kabul Edilmesi. Yeni Türkiye Dergisi (50), 220–223.

Parla, T. (2002). Türkiye'nin Siyasal Rejimi (1980–1989) (3 b.). Ankara: İletişim Yayınları.

Sartorı, G. (1997). Karşılaştırmalı Anayasa Mühendisliği. (E. ÖZBUDUN, Çev.) Ankara: Yetkin Yayınevi.

Tanör, B. (2017). Osmanlı-Türk Anayasal Gelişmeleri (28 b.). İstanbul: Yapı Kredi Yayınları.

Tunaya, T. Z. (2009). Türkiye'de Siyasal Gelişmeler (1876–1938). İstanbul: İstanbul Bilgi Üniversitesi Yayınları.

Uzun, C. D. (2015). Yeni Anayasa Yapımında Yöntem Arayışı. SETA Perspektif, 1–5.

Yazıcı, S. (2011). Yeni Bir Anayasa Hazırlığı ve Türkiye. İstanbul: İstanbul Bilgi Üniversitesi Yayınları.